July 15 – 17, 2019
Aberdeen, Scotland, UK

**Association for
Computing Machinery**

Advancing Computing as a Science & Profession

ITiCSE '19

Proceedings of the 2019 ACM Conference on
Innovation and Technology in Computer
Science Education

Conference Chairs:
Bruce Scharlau (University of Aberdeen, UK)
Roger McDermott (Robert Gordon University, UK)

Programme Chairs:
Arnold Pears (KTH Royal Institute of Technology, Sweden)
Mihaela Sabin (University of New Hampshire, USA)

Sponsored by:
ACM SIGCSE

**Association for
Computing Machinery**

Advancing Computing as a Science & Profession

**The Association for Computing Machinery
2 Penn Plaza, Suite 701
New York, New York 10121-0701**

ISBN: 978-1-4503-6253-5 (Digital)

ISBN: 978-1-4503-4062-2 (Print)

Additional copies may be ordered prepaid from:

ACM Order Department
PO Box 30777
New York, NY 10087-0777, USA

Phone: 1-800-342-6626 (USA and Canada)
+1-212-626-0500 (Global)
Fax: +1-212-944-1318
E-mail: acmhelp@acm.org
Hours of Operation: 8:30 am – 4:30 pm ET

Foreword

On behalf of the organizing committee, we are delighted to welcome you to the 2019 ACM International Symposium on Physical Design (ISPD), held in San Francisco, California. Continuing the great tradition established by its twenty-seven predecessors, which includes a series of five ACM/SIGDA Physical Design Workshops held intermittently in 1987-1996 and twenty-two editions of ISPD in the current form since 1997. The 2019 ISPD provides a premier forum to present leading-edge research results, exchange ideas, and promote research on critical areas related to the physical design of VLSI and other related systems.

The regular papers in the ISPD 2019 program were selected after a rigorous, month-long, double-blind review process and a face-to-face meeting by the Technical Program Committee (TPC) members. The papers selected exhibit latest advancements in a variety of topics in physical design, including emerging challenges for current and future process technologies, FPGA architectures, placement, detailed routing, floorplanning and interconnect planning, partitioning techniques, manufacturability and yield optimization, timing and crosstalk issues, analysis and management of power dissipation, hardware security, placement and routing approaches of networks on chips, gate sizing and clock skew scheduling, electromigration, and application of machine-learning based techniques to physical design.

The ISPD 2019 program is complemented by three keynote addresses, thirteen invited talks, a FPGA special session on advances in adaptable heterogeneous computing and acceleration, a cyber physical systems session, the detailed routing contest session results, the ISPD lifetime award tribute session, and a special panel discussion session on machine learning in physical design, all of which are delivered by distinguished researchers from both industry and academia.

Mr. Shankar Krishnamoorthy, Senior Vice President of Digital Implementation at Synopsys, will deliver the Monday morning keynote address entitled "Fusion: The Dawn of the Hyperconvergence Era in EDA." Mr. Krishnamoorthy's keynote will explore how the concepts of hyperconvergence (integration of disparate areas of compute, storage, and networking on a unified architecture) can be applied to the EDA design tool chain flow to deliver further disruptive improvements in IC power, performance, and area.

Dr. Ken Plaks, DARPA Program Manager for Obfuscated Manufacturing for GPS, will deliver the Tuesday morning keynote address entitled "A Perspective on Security and Trust Requirements for the Future." In his keynote, Dr. Plaks will address a key aspect of hardware security: Design obfuscation. He will share his in-depth insights on (1) what type of metrics are required to measure effectiveness of obfuscation techniques, (2) what types of design implementation tools needed, and (3) how to ensure implemented obfuscation solutions that are scalable and performance preserving.

Professor Edward Lee will deliver the ISPD Lifetime Achievement Award keynote address entitled "Freedom from Choice and the Power of Models" in honor of Professor Sangiovanni. He will share an insightful perspective on modeling paradigms, how their construction is influenced by practical real-life constraints, and how their functions vary and manifest differently in the engineering and scientific disciplines.

Given the breadth of Professor Alberto Sangiovanni-Vincentelli's research work, two commemorative sessions on Tuesday afternoon will pay tribute to his decades-long contributions in the areas of physical design, VLSI applications and cyber physical systems. These sessions will feature talks from research colleagues who are luminaries in their respective fields. Their talks will span topics from the early start of Spice, advanced research areas in logic synthesis, EDA to automotive design automation, a perspective on design automation of cyber physical systems, secure and trustworthy cyber physical systems, and platform-based design. These will be culminated with a talk by Professor Sangiovanni entitled "My 50-Year Journey from Punched Cards to Swarm Systems."

There will be other invited talks interspersed with the presentations of the regular papers. The topics of the invited papers range from advanced FPGA architectures for heterogenous and adaptive computing, large-scale graph analytics FPGA acceleration, electromigration-aware interconnect design, deep learning applications and infrastructure enablement in physical design, electromigration-aware physical design, recent advances in analog layout synthesis, among others.

Since 2005, the ISPD has organized highly competitive contests to promote and advance research in placement, global routing, clock network synthesis, discrete gate sizing, and detailed routing-driven placement. The contest this year, organized by Cadence, focuses on detailed routing. Continuing the tradition of all the past contests, a new large-scale real-world benchmark suite for detailed routing has been specified using LEF/DEF and will be released in the ISPD website (http://www.ispd.cc). The 2019 ISPD contest augments the 2018 ISPD initial detailed routing contest by adding more realistic design rule settings faced by physical design practitioners in the industry. Detailed routing can be divided into two steps. First, an initial detailed routing step is used to generate a detailed routing solution while handling the major design rules. Then a detailed routing refinement is performed to fix the remaining design rule violations. This contest focuses on the initial detailed routing step. It is expected to lead and motivate more research and contributions on the detailed routing of large integrated circuits.

This year we are hosting a special panel session entitled "Machine Learning in Physical Design: Opportunities, Infrastructure, and Deployment." It will feature machine learning practitioners from industry and academia. The goal of the panel is to highlight current application domains, explore required infrastructure for offline training and online inference especially when the existing tool base code is not python-based, and how to prescribe relevant ML benchmarks (e.g. through contests) to academia when device/design data is proprietary and considered IP.

Different from prior years, all accepted paper authors will present posters of their work in a poster session. This will give plenty of opportunities for discussion, in addition to the Q&A part after each talk. Furthermore, we extend an invitation to the ISPD detailed routing contestants to present their works in this session as well.

Finally, would like to take this chance to express our gratitude to the authors, the presenters, the keynote/invited speakers for contributing to the high-quality program, and the session chairs for moderating the sessions. We would like to thank our Technical Program Committee members and external reviewers, who provided insightful constructive comments and detailed reviews to the authors. We greatly appreciate the exceptional set of invited talks put together by the Steering Committee, which is chaired by Chris Chu. We also thank the Steering Committee for selecting the best paper. Special thanks go to the Publications Chair Jens Lienig and the Publicity Chair Laleh Behjat for their diligence and tremendous services. We would like to acknowledge the team organizing the contest led by Gracieli Posser and Wen-Hao Liu. We are also grateful to our sponsors. The symposium is sponsored by the ACM SIGDA (Special Interest Group on Design Automation) with technical co-sponsorship from the IEEE Circuits and Systems Society and the IEEE Council on Electronic Design Automation. Generous financial contributions have also been provided by (in alphabetical order): Cadence, Intel Corporation, Mentor Graphics, Synopsys, TSMC, and Xilinx. Special thanks to Erfan Aghaeekiasaraee for his tireless management of the ISPD website, Paulina Andrews for always being jovially there with her administrative support, Sade Rodriguez and John Otero from the ACM for their logistics behind-the-scenes diligent help and assistance, and Emily Nichols from the Sir Francis Drake Hotel for helping us with venue logistics. And last but not least, we thank Lisa Tolles, Cindy Edwards, Adrienne Griscti, and Mikaela Brunstetter from Sheridan Communications for their expertise and enormous patience during the production of these proceedings.

The organizing committee hopes that you will enjoy the 2019 ISPD and San Francisco's beautiful April spring! We look forward to seeing you again in future editions of the ISPD.

Ismail Bustany
ISPD 2019 General Chair

William Swartz
Technical Program Chair

Table of Contents

Keynote
Session Chair: Ismail Bustany *(Xilinx, Inc.)*

Session: New Advances in Placement
Session Chair: Stephen Yang *(Xilinx, Inc.)*

FPGA Special Session: Advances in Adaptable Heterogeneous Computing and Acceleration for Big Data
Session Chair: Mahesh Iyer *(Intel Corporation)*

Session: Routing in All Forms
Session Chair: Patrick Madden *(SUNY Binghamton)*

Keynote
Session Chair: Noel Menezes *(Intel Corporation)*

Session: Patterning and Machine Learning
Session Chair: Evangeline Young *(The Chinese University of Hong Kong)*

Session: Cyber-Physical Systems
Session Chair: Patrick Groeneveld *(Cadence Design Systems)*

Session: Lifetime Achievement Award Tribute to Professor Alberto Sangiovanni-Vicentelli
Session Chair: Pierluigi Nuzzo *(University of Southern California)*

Lifetime Achievement Award Dinner Banquet Keynote

Session: Physical Design - Where are we going?
Session Chair: C.K. Cheng *(University of California, San Diego)*

Session: Detailed Routing Contest Results
Session Chair: David Chinnery *(Mentor Graphics)*

Special Panel on ML in Physical Design: Opportunities, Infrastructure, and Deployment
Session Chair: Ismail Bustany *(Xilinx, Inc.)*

- Panelists: Laleh Behjat, *(University of Calgary)*; Ivan Kissiov, *(Mentor Graphics)*; Harold Levy, *(Synopsys, Inc)*; Ashish Sirasao, *(Xilinx, Inc.)*; Haoxing Ren, *(Nvidia Corporation)*; Venkat Thanvantri, *(Cadence Design Systems)*

ISPD 2019 Organization

General Chair: Ismail Bustany *(Xilinx Inc.)*

Program Chair: William Swartz *(TimberWolf Systems Inc. & University of Texas at Dallas)*

Past Chair: Chris Chu *(Iowa State University)*

Steering Committee Chair: Chris Chu *(Iowa State University)*

Steering Committee: Yao-Wen Chang *(National Taiwan University)*
Patrick Groeneveld *(Cadence Design Systems)*
Jiang Hu *(Texas A&M University)*
Andrew Kahng *(University of California at San Diego)*
Noel Menezes *(Intel Corp.)*
David Pan *(University of Texas at Austin)*
Prashant Saxena *(Synopsys Inc.)*
Evangeline Young *(The Chinese University of Hong Kong)*

Technical Program Committee: Nima Karimpour Darav *(Microsemi, a Microchip Company)*
Sheqin Dong *(Tsinghua University)*
Rickard Ewetz *(University of Central Florida)*
Amin Farshidi *(Cadence Design Systems)*
Mahesh Iyer *(Intel Corp.)*
Marcelo Johann *(Federal University of Rio Grande do Sul)*
Wen-Hao Liu *(Cadence Design Systems)*
Joseph Shinnerl *(Mentor Graphics, a Siemens Business)*
Ulf Schlichtmann *(Technical University of Munich)*
Vishal Suthar *(Xilinx Inc.)*
Yasuhiro Takashima *(University of Kitakyushu)*
Hua Xiang *(IBM Corp.)*
Gary Yeap *(Synopsys Inc.)*
Bei Yu *(The Chinese University at Hong Kong)*

Publications Chair: Jens Lienig *(Dresden University of Technology)*

Publicity Chair: Laleh Behjat *(University of Calgary)*

Contest Chair: Gracieli Posser *(Cadence Design Systems)*

Webmaster: Erfan Aghaeekiasaraee *(University of Calgary)*

Additional reviewers:

Gregg Baeckler
Sarvesh Bhardwaj
H.T. Chang
Jack Changfan
Gengjie Chen
Tinghuan Chen
Marko Chew
David Chinnery
Aravind Dasu
Shounak Dhar
Sergei Dolgov
Lin Du
Jeff Dyck
Grigor Gasparyan
Tiago J. Reimann
Vasudeva Kamath
Parivallal Kannan
Bapi Kar
Ivan Kissiov
Abhijeet Kolpekwar
Alex Korshak
Pat LaCour
Michael Leonard
Derong Liu
Yuzhe Ma
Thai Mai
Dmitry Malafei

Dimitris Mangiras
Pavlos Matthaiakis
Eric McCaughrin
Sergei Mikhaylov
Dmitry Mironov
Nilanjan Mukherjee
Nikita Nikitin
Fred Obermeier
Kaushik Patra
Satish Pillai
Artur Pogiel
Vlademir Rerikh
Ankur Sharma
Valery Shchehlik
Love Singhal
Satish Sivaswamy
Tom Spyrou
Andres Torres
Ilhami Torunoglu
Alex Volkov
Haoyu Yang
Stephen Yang
Rong Yue
Vladimir Yutsis
Vassilis Zebilis
Lu Zhang
Nan Zhuang
Wei Zou

Special Thanks:
- Professor Pierluigi Nuzzo (USC) for organizing both the Cyber Physical Systems and the ISPD Lifetime Achievement Award Sessions.
- Lisa Tolles and Cindy Edwards (Sheridan Communications) for their expertise and enormous patience during the production of these proceedings.
- Sade Rodriguez and John Otero (ACM) for their diligent help and logistics support.
- Paulina Andrews (Xilinx Inc.) for her administrative support.

ISPD 2019 Sponsors & Corporate Supporters

Sponsor:

Technical Co-Sponsors:

Corporate Supporters:

Fusion: The Dawn of the Hyperconvergence Era in EDA

Shankar Krishnamoorthy

Senior Vice President, Digital Implementation

Synopsys, Inc.

ABSTRACT

Hyperconvergence is a software-centric architecture which has disrupted the datacenter industry in a dramatic way by bringing the disparate areas of compute, storage and networking into a single system. A hyperconverged system allows the integrated technologies to be managed as a single system through a common tool set. By overcoming the barriers to change and progress created by traditional silos, the hyperconverged infrastructures have been delivering major benefits in terms of power consumption, performance and total cost of ownership.

This talk will explore how the concepts of hyperconvergence can be translated and applied to the Electronic Design Automation industry and in particular IC implementation to deliver unique benefits to the users. The fusion of technologies and convergence of flows can enable unprecedented improvements in chip performance, power consumption, die-area, total throughput and cost of results for high-end digital designs. Bringing disparate areas like logic synthesis, IC layout, test and sign-off analysis into a single unified hyperconverged architecture promises to elevate IC design results and productivity to the next level.

KEYWORDS

EDA, IC implementation, hyperconvergence, fusion, quality of results, QoR, time to results, PPA, TTR, cost of results, CoR, digital design

SPEAKER BIO

Shankar is Senior Vice President of Digital Implementation at Synopsys. His organization is responsible for the Synopsys digital design platform including synthesis, place-and-route, test automation and formal verification solutions. Shankar has more than 25 years of experience leading world-class teams that have delivered the industry's premier IC physical design and logic synthesis solutions. Prior to Synopsys, he was at Mentor Graphics where he was general manager of the IC Design Solutions Division, responsible for their analog and digital design implementation platforms. He joined Mentor with the 2007 acquisition of Sierra Design Automation where he was Founder and CTO. Prior to Sierra Design, Shankar led Synopsys' Physical Synthesis and Logic Synthesis R&D organizations. He began his career at Synopsys in 1992 working on logic synthesis technology.

Shankar received his M.S. in Computer Science from the University of Texas, Austin in 1992 and his B. Tech in Computer Science from the Indian Institute of Technology, Bombay in 1990.

How Deep Learning Can Drive Physical Synthesis Towards More Predictable Legalization

Renan Netto[1], Sheiny Fabre[1], Tiago Augusto Fontana[1], Vinicius Livramento[2], Laércio Pilla[3],
José Luís Güntzel[1]

[1]Embedded Computing Lab, PPGCC, Federal University of Santa Catarina, Brazil

[2]ASML, Netherlands

[3]LRI, Univ. Paris-Sud — CNRS, France

{renan.netto,sheiny.fabre,tiago.fontana}@posgrad.ufsc.br

ABSTRACT

Machine learning has been used to improve the predictability of different physical design problems, such as timing, clock tree synthesis and routing, but not for legalization. Predicting the outcome of legalization can be helpful to guide incremental placement and circuit partitioning, speeding up those algorithms. In this work we extract histograms of features and snapshots of the circuit from several regions in a way that the model can be trained independently from region size. Then, we evaluate how traditional and convolutional deep learning models use this set of features to predict the quality of a legalization algorithm without having to executing it. When evaluating the models with holdout cross validation, the best model achieves an accuracy of 80% and an F-score of at least 0.7. Finally, we used the best model to prune partitions with large displacement in a circuit partitioning strategy. Experimental results in circuits (with up to millions of cells) showed that the pruning strategy improved the maximum displacement of the legalized solution by 5% to 94%. In addition, using the machine learning model avoided from 22% to 99% of the calls to the legalization algorithm, which speeds up the pruning process by up to 3×.

KEYWORDS

Physical synthesis, placement, legalization, machine learning

ACM Reference Format:

Renan Netto, Sheiny Fabre, Tiago Augusto Fontana, Vinicius Livramento, Laércio Pilla, José Luís Güntzel. 2019. How Deep Learning Can Drive Physical Synthesis Towards More Predictable Legalization. In 2019 International Symposium on Physical Design (ISPD'19), April 14–17, 2019, San Francisco, CA, USA. ACM, New York, NY, USA, 8 pages. https://doi.org/10.1145/3299902.3309754

1 INTRODUCTION

The high flexibility provided by machine learning (ML) models allows their use to predict the outcome of physical design algorithms. They have been employed so far to help choose between different clock tree synthesis algorithms [11], to fix miscorrelations between different timing engines [7], and to identify detailed routing violations during the placement stage [2, 17, 19]. The benefits of ML models come from their ability to improve the quality of physical design algorithms by predicting information that would otherwise be too costly to evaluate during execution.

Machine learning techniques have yet to be employed to help predict the outcome of legalization algorithms. As technology nodes advance, new challenges affect modern legalization algorithms. Some of these challenges include pin accessibility, usage of multi-row cell libraries, complex design rules, physical floorplan complexity, as well as tight performance and power constraints. In addition, modern legalization algorithms have to keep a low circuit displacement to avoid degrading the solution of upstream steps.

The prediction of the outcome of legalization algorithms by ML techniques has multiple applications: (1) choosing, among multiple legalization algorithms, the one that will result in the lowest displacement for a given legalization region, similar to what has been done for clock tree synthesis [11]; (2) guiding an incremental placement technique. The ML models could predict which cell movements result in the greatest improvement on different metrics, without requiring the execution of the legalization algorithm itself; (3) guiding a circuit partitioning strategy. Circuit partitioning can be used to decompose the circuit in smaller disjoint parts, which can reduce the execution time of legalization algorithms by more than one order of magnitude. However, it can also degrade some quality metrics since it reduces the solution space available to the legalization algorithm.

In this work we explore mainly option (3) by integrating the proposed machine learning model into a circuit partitioning strategy to avoid partitions that result in large displacement. Furthermore, we partially explore option (2), because the proposed model can be used to predict when some optimizations will largely degrade the solution obtained by upstream steps. We do so by training different ML models to detect when the maximum displacement of a given partition exceeds a specified threshold. Then, we select the model with the best results to be integrated in the partitioning strategy, acting as a pruning mechanism. The main contributions of this paper are:

- We propose a feature extraction strategy for training machine learning models using the information of circuit partitions as input. This set of features is independent of the partition size.

- To the best of our knowledge, this is the first work to use machine learning models to help a legalization algorithm. We evaluate different ML models in order to select the best one for this problem (which achieved an accuracy of 80% and an F-score ≥ 0.7).
- We employed the best ML model as a pruning mechanism for a circuit partitioning strategy. Results using circuits from both ICCAD 2017 and ICCAD 2015 CAD Contests show that the pruning strategy reduced the maximum displacement of those circuits by up to 94%, and the use of ML accelerated the pruning by up to 3×.

The remaining sections are organized as follows. Section 2 displays the related work on ML models used for physical design, and multi-row legalization. Sections 3 and 4 present the proposed ML methodology and its integration into a legalization algorithm. Finally, Section 5 shows the experimental results and Section 6 provides concluding remarks.

2 RELATED WORK

Machine learning techniques have been used to solve different physical design problems. The work from [11] trains a regression model to predict the outcome of different clock tree synthesis engines. The authors extract features from architectural, floorplanning and design parameters. In order to handle a large number of linearly correlated parameters, they separate the features in two models, which are trained separately and combined using linear regression. Another application is predicting the outcome of golden signoff timing engines [7], where the authors propose a regression model to correct miscorrelations between two commercial signoff tools. For that, they extract multiple features concerning capacitance, resistance and delay of cells and wires.

Recently, machine learning techniques have been used to predict the violation of routability constraints in a placed netlist. For example, the work from [19] extracts features regarding pin distribution, routing blockage, global routes and local nets in order to predict the number of DRC violations in a placed area. The work from [2] improves this idea by predicting the actual locations of the DRC violations, using a different set of features. Finally, the work from [17] focuses on predicting only the existence of detailed routing short violations, so that this information can be used in a detailed placement flow, for example. Although different works make use of machine learning techniques, none of them aim to predict the quality of legalization algorithms, which is the focus of this work. Since legalization is performed not only after the global placement, but also after other placement optimization techniques, improving the legalization solution consequently improves the quality of those optimizations.

Several recent works have been proposed to legalize circuits from advanced technology nodes, which contain multi-row cells. For example, the works from [4] and [18] propose algorithms that legalize cells one at a time. Their algorithms enumerate a set of valid insertion points for each cell and place each in the location that minimizes circuit displacement. While the algorithm from [4] uses a greedy heuristic, the algorithm from [18] adapts the Abacus legalization algorithm [16] that uses dynamic programming.

Instead of handling each cell at a time, the works from [10] and [3] propose algorithms that simultaneously legalize multiple cells. The authors of [10] propose an Integer Linear Programming (ILP) model to solve the multi-row legalization problem. Due to the high complexity of the ILP model, they divide the circuit into bins, solving the problem for multiple bins in parallel. Such strategy leads to better results, but at the cost of longer run times. The authors of [3], by their turn, relax some constraints of the problem in order to model it as a Linear Complementarity Problem. This way, they can still achieve better results than the previous works, but with a more reasonable run time. Finally, the work of [15] improves over [4] and considers additional metrics for legalization problem, such as routability constraints.

A machine learning model that predicts the outcome of such legalization algorithms can be used to guide incremental optimization techniques or partitioning strategies. For example, the work of [6] proposes a circuit partitioning strategy to speed up legalization by executing the legalization algorithm in smaller regions of the circuit. This way, the authors sped up the legalization, but at the cost of maximum displacement degradation, since the partitioning reduces the solution space of the legalization algorithm. Therefore, in this work we also integrate the proposed machine learning model to this partitioning strategy, so that the model guides this process to avoid partitions with large displacement.

3 MACHINE LEARNING METHODOLOGY

We model the legalization outcome prediction as a binary classification problem. Given a legalization algorithm $\mathcal{L}$, a partition of cells p_i, and a displacement threshold Δ, the output of the ML model is a binary variable $y \in \{0, 1\}$, indicating whether $\mathcal{L}$ legalizes the cells of p_i without any cell displacement exceeding Δ^1.

In this work, instead of using $\mathcal{L}$ and Δ as inputs of the ML model, we train models for a specific combination of $\mathcal{L}$ and Δ. As consequence, the model receives as input the rectangular region (given by $R(p_i)$) and cells of a partition (given by $C(p_i)$), and must predict if the legalization algorithm $\mathcal{L}$ used to train the model is able to legalize this partition under a maximum displacement threshold of Δ. In order to do so, we must provide a large number of samples to train the ML model, so that it can identify which patterns lead to a partition with a large displacement.

3.1 Training data generation

Algorithm 1 shows how we generate the data for training and validation of the ML model. Given a set of cells $C = \{c_1, c_2, ..., c_{n-1}, c_n\}$, a legalization algorithm $\mathcal{L}$ and the rectangular area of the circuit $R = (X_{left}, X_{right}, Y_{top}, Y_{bottom})$, the algorithm aims to generate data from partitions of different sizes. The first step consists in defining the number of samples that will be generated for each partition size (line 1). By generating the same number of samples for each size (1024 in this work), we avoid having the ML model become biased to a specific partition size. In addition, increasing the number of samples acts as a data augmentation strategy, which

---

[1]The displacement of a cell c_i is given by the Manhattan distance between its legalized location $l(c_i) = (x(c_i), y(c_i))$ and its location before legalization $l'(c_i) = (x'(c_i), y'(c_i))$.

Algorithm 1: GENERATE_DATA($C, \mathcal{L}, R$)

```
1  n_samples ← 1024;
2  max_height ← 9; F ← ∅;
3  for height ← 1 to max_height do
4  |    n_iterations ← n_samples / 2^height;
5  |    for num_it ← 1 to n_iterations do
6  |    |    MOVE_CELLS(C, R);
7  |    |    P ← CIRCUIT_PARTITIONING(C, height);
8  |    |    foreach p_i ∈ P do
9  |    |    |    Λ, result ← L(C(p_i), R(p_i));
10 |    |    |    F ← F ∪ GET_FEATURES(C(p_i), R(p_i), Λ, result, Δ);
11 |    |    end
12 |    end
13 end
14 SAVE_DATA(F);
```

Algorithm 2: MOVE_CELLS(C, R)

```
1  foreach c_i ∈ C do
2  |    r_x ← RANDOM(−10000, 10000);
3  |    r_y ← RANDOM(−10000, 10000);
4  |    x(c_i) ← x'(c_i) + r_x;
5  |    y(c_i) ← y'(c_i) + r_y;
6  |    x(c_i) ← min(X_right − w(c_i), max(X_left, x(c_i)));
7  |    y(c_i) ← min(Y_top − h(c_i), max(Y_bottom, y(c_i)));
8  end
```

generates more samples from the same circuit and helps avoiding overfitting.

In order to generate the circuit partitions, we used the strategy from [6], which partitions the circuit using a k-d tree data structure, where each leaf node represents a partition. The strategy receives as input a desired height for the k-d tree and generates 2^{height} partitions. Therefore, Algorithm 1 iterates over different values for the tree height (line 3), and the necessary number of iterations to generate the desired number of samples is calculated in line 4. We limit the maximum height of the k-d tree to 9 because, as the height increases, the partitions become smaller. A height higher than 9 would result in partitions with less than a few hundred of cells, which would be too small.

For each iteration, a new circuit partitioning is generated (line 7). To ensure that the partitions are different from each other, we apply a vector of random movements to the cells in C (line 6). The MOVE_CELLS function in Algorithm 2 is responsible for applying this movement. For each cell, two random variables $r_x, r_y \in \mathbb{Z}$ are generated representing the cell movement on x and y coordinates, respectively. We generate them using a uniform integer distribution in the range [-10000, 10000] to ensure that the movement is large enough to generate significantly different placements[2]. After moving the cells, we make sure that they lie within the circuit boundaries R (lines 6–7). Observe that the MOVE_CELLS function is called before partitioning the circuit, so the amount of movement is not dependent of the partition size.

After generating the set of partitions P, Algorithm 1 legalizes each partition (lines 8-11). Observe that it legalizes only the cells in $C(p_i)$ inside the partition and the legalization area is limited to the partition area $R(p_i)$. In addition, the legalization function from line 9 does not actually move the cells, it only finds legal locations for the cells and returns those locations (denoted by Λ). It also returns a boolean variable indicating if the legalization was successful or not (denoted by $result$), as the legalization may fail for a given partition. Observe that the proposed ML methodology is independent from a specific legalization algorithm, as long as the algorithm may be executed for a subset of the circuit cells and for a subregion of the circuit area. For this reason, we do not present the pseudocode of the legalization algorithm, but we used an adaptation of the Abacus legalization algorithm from [16] to handle multi-row cells.

3.2 Feature selection

Given the legalization result and legal locations, the next step is obtaining the features for this partition. In the end, when all features are collected, the data is saved in an output file in line 14. In this work we evaluate traditional and convolutional neural network models, so we need features for both of them. For convolutional models, the input is simply a snapshot image of the partition. We used different colors to distinguish between movable and fixed cells. Movable cells are represented by shades of the same color. This way, the model can identify overlaps since they are represented by the combined colors of multiple cells. On the other hand, for the traditional models we need to select an appropriate set of features. Partitions become hard to legalize with low displacement when they have a high density of cells, or when they have many cell overlaps. Therefore, we selected the features presented in Table 1 for our ML methodology.

Table 1: Features used by the ML model.

Feature	Meaning
D	Density of the partition area
A_h	Area occupied by cells of each height
H_a	Normalized histogram of area occupied by cells on each partition subrow
H_o	Normalized histogram of area occupied by overlaps on each partition subrow

The first two features aim to represent global information of the partition density. Since partitions with multi-row cells are harder to legalize, we measure not only the cell density, but also the area occupied by cells of each height. However, just the global information is not enough to identify partitions that are hard to legalize, since some circuit rows may be more crowded than others. The third feature aims to represent this information by means of an histogram of the area occupied by cells on each partition subrow. A subrow is a row segment that does not overlap with any macroblocks and/or fixed cells. Finally, a subrow may be overcrowded but with few cell overlaps, which makes it easier to legalize. Therefore, the last feature measures the area occupied by overlaps on each subrow, so that the ML model can correlate this information to the result.

Figure 1 shows by means of an example how the histograms for the last two features are generated for a given partition. Figure 1(a) illustrates a partition with 20 movable cells (blue rectangles), one fixed cell (gray rectangle) and 10 subrows (σ_1 to σ_{10}). Figures 1(b) and (c) show the area and overlap histograms for this partition. For illustration purposes, the histograms contain 5 bins, but we

---

[2]The smallest circuit used in the experiments has an area of 342000×342000, so this movement corresponds to at most 3% of the circuit dimensions.

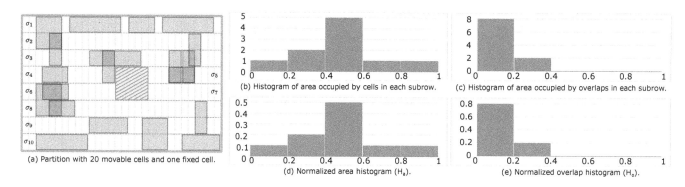

Figure 1: Circuit features extracted for a hypothetical partition.

Algorithm 3: GET_FEATURES($C(p_i)$, $R(p_i)$, Λ, *result*, Δ)

```
1  A_f ← 0; A_m ← 0; A_r ← w(p_i) × h(p_i); A_h ← [];
2  δmax ← -∞;
3  foreach c_i ∈ C(p_i) do
4      if fixed(c_i) then
5          box ← intersection(c_i, R(p_i));
6          A_f ← A_f + w(box) × h(box);
7      else
8          A_m ← A_m + w(c_i) × h(c_i);
9          A_h[h(c_i)] ← A_h[h(c_i)] + (w(c_i)×h(c_i))/A_r;
10     end
11     δ(c_i) ← |l(c_i) - λ(c_i)|;
12     δmax ← max(δmax, δ(c_i));
13 end
14 Δ ← A_m/(A_r-A_f);
15 y ← δmax ≤ Δ;
16 A ← []; O ← []; Σ ← partition subrows;
17 foreach σ_i ∈ Σ do
18     C(σ_i) ← cells intersecting σ_i;
19     a(σ_i) ← 0; o(σ_i) ← 0;
20     foreach c_i ∈ C(σ_i) do
21         a(σ_i) ← a(σ_i) + w(c_i);
22     end
23     C' ← cells intersecting in C(σ_i);
24     foreach c_j ∈ C' do
25         o(σ_i) ← o(σ_i) + w(c_j);
26     end
27     A[σ_i] ← a(σ_i)/w(σ_i); O[σ_i] ← o(σ_i)/w(σ_i);
28 end
29 H_a ← normalized histogram with values of A;
30 H_o ← normalized histogram with values of O;
31 return (y, Δ, A_h, H_a, H_o);
```

Algorithm 3 shows the details of how these features are collected from a given partition. The loop from lines 3–13 calculates the values for the first two features (density and area occupied by cells of each height), so it starts by initializing the necessary variables to do so. Those variables are: the area occupied by fixed cells (A_f), the area occupied by movable cells (A_m), the area of the partition itself (A_r) and a list with the areas occupied by cells of each height (A_h). Observe that the area occupied by fixed cells is not considered in A_h, since those cells are not moved by the legalization algorithm. However, their area is important to measure the partition density, which is given by the area occupied by movable cells A_m divided by the free area in the partition (A_r - A_f) in line 14. In addition, for each height, A_h is normalized by the partition area. The first loop also measures the maximum displacement of the legalized cells in lines 11–12. This information is used to determine the class of this partition in line 15.

The loop from lines 17–29, on the other hand, is responsible for obtaining the data for the histograms H_a and H_o. This is done by iterating through all subrows $\sigma_i \in \Sigma$ of the partition and, for each one, measuring the width occupied by the cells intersecting the area of σ_i, storing this information in variable $a(\sigma_i)$. In addition, for the subset of cells $C' \in C(\sigma_i)$ that have some overlap with other cells in said subrow, we compute how much overlap there is using variable $o(\sigma_i)$. Finally, both $a(\sigma_i)$ and $o(\sigma_i)$ are normalized by the subrow width $w(\sigma_i)$ in line 27. This normalization ensures that the ML model is not biased by large subrows that have larger absolute values of $a(\sigma_i)$ and $o(\sigma_i)$. The last part of the algorithm creates the normalized histograms H_a and H_o in lines 30–31.

4 PHYSICAL DESIGN INTEGRATION

After training and validating the ML model proposed in Section 3, we integrated it in the circuit partitioning strategy of [6] as a use case to evaluate the ML model. As mentioned in Section 3, their work partitions the circuit using a k-d tree data structure, in a way that the leaf nodes represent the partitions, which are legalized separately. If a partition can not be legalized, it is merged with its sibling node, and the legalization proceeds to their parent node. In the end, the whole circuit legalization can be sped up, since the partitioning strategy reduces the input size of the legalization algorithm. However, doing so may degrade the solution quality, especially maximum displacement. Therefore, we modified their partitioning strategy to merge sibling nodes not only when the

actually used histograms with 20 bins for better precision. Each bin indicates the number of rows whose area of cells (or overlap of cells) is within a given range. We can see that the histogram in Figure 1(b) concentrates on the middle region, with most subrows having from 40% to 60% of their area occupied by cells. On the other hand, the histogram in Figure 1(c) concentrates on the 0% to 20% bin, with only two subrows having more than 20% of their area occupied by overlaps. However, using absolute values for the y axis of those histograms may bias the ML model to large partitions, since they would have a larger number of subrows. In order to avoid this issue, we normalize the y axis with relation to the number of subrows in the partition, resulting in the histograms H_a and H_o in Figures 1(d) and (e). Observe that they have the same structure of the previous histograms, with the only difference being the normalized vertical axis.

Algorithm 4: PARTITIONED_LEGALIZATION $(\mathcal{P}, \mathcal{L}, \Delta)$

```
1  foreach p_i in P do
2  |   P ← P \ {p_i};
3  |   if parent(p_i) ∉ P then
4  |   |   Λ, result ← L(C(p_i), R(p_i));
5  |   |   δ_max ← -∞;
6  |   |   foreach c_i ∈ C(p_i) do
7  |   |   |   δ(c_i) ← |l(c_i) - λ(c_i)|;
8  |   |   |   δ_max ← max(δ_max, δ(c_i));
9  |   |   end
10 |   |   if δ_max > Δ ∨ ¬result then
11 |   |   |   P ← P ∪ {parent(p_i)};
12 |   |   else
13 |   |   |   foreach c_i ∈ C(p_i) do
14 |   |   |   |   l(c_i) ← λ(c_i);
15 |   |   |   end
16 |   |   end
17 |   end
18 end
```

Algorithm 5: ML_PARTITIONED_LEGALIZATION $(\mathcal{P}, \mathcal{L}, \Delta, \mathcal{M})$

```
1  foreach p_i in P do
2  |   P ← P \ {p_i};
3  |   if parent(p_i) ∉ P then
4  |   |   if M(C(p_i), R(p_i)) then
5  |   |   |   P ← P ∪ {parent(p_i)};
6  |   |   else
7  |   |   |   Λ, result ← L(C(p_i), R(p_i));
8  |   |   |   if ¬result then
9  |   |   |   |   P ← P ∪ {parent(p_i)};
10 |   |   |   else
11 |   |   |   |   foreach c_i ∈ C(p_i) do
12 |   |   |   |   |   l(c_i) ← λ(c_i);
13 |   |   |   |   end
14 |   |   |   end
15 |   |   end
16 |   end
17 end
```

legalization fails, but when it results in a large displacement as well. This way, we can prune partitions that would otherwise degrade the solution quality.

There are two ways of doing this pruning strategy: (1) running the legalization algorithm and measuring the displacement of the obtained solution; (2) using the ML model to predict the outcome of the legalization without running the legalization algorithm. We compare these two solutions in order to evaluate the efficiency and impact of the ML model.

Algorithm 4 shows how we implemented the first pruning strategy. The algorithm receives as input the partitions to be legalized ($\mathcal{P}$), the legalization algorithm ($\mathcal{L}$) and the maximum displacement threshold (Δ). Then, it iterates through all partitions trying to legalize them. For each partition p_i, it runs the legalization algorithm (line 4) and measures the obtained maximum displacement δ_{max} (lines 5–9). If δ_{max} exceeds the threshold Δ or if the legalization fails, the partition is ignored and its parent node is added to $\mathcal{P}$ to be legalized instead (lines 10–11). Otherwise, its cells are placed in their legal locations (lines 13–15). Observe that, by adding the parent node of p_i in $\mathcal{P}$, it is possible to avoid the legalization of the sibling of p_i as well with the verification of line 3. If the parent of p_i is already in $\mathcal{P}$, this means the sibling of p_i resulted in a large displacement or could not be legalized, so p_i should be ignored as well.

Running the legalization algorithm to prune partitions with large displacement results in several unnecessary calls to the legalization algorithm, which may take too much time. Therefore, the second pruning strategy relies on the ML model to predict when a partition should be ignored, as detailed in Algorithm 5. Observe that now the algorithm receives as input the machine learning model $\mathcal{M}$ as well, which is used in line 4 to predict when the partition can be pruned. Then, it runs the legalization algorithm $\mathcal{L}$ only if it was not pruned (line 7), and checks only if the partition was legalized (lines 8–10). If the partition was successfully legalized, it places the cells in the legal locations. In the end, the whole circuit is legalized, but requiring fewer calls to the legalization algorithm $\mathcal{L}$ than in Algorithm 4.

5 EXPERIMENTAL RESULTS

5.1 Experimental setup

This work uses the benchmarks from ICCAD 2015 and ICCAD 2017 CAD Contest [5, 13]. Table 2 presents the names and number of cells of each circuit. We divided the circuits in three groups: ***training***, ***validation*** and ***test***. The *training* and *validation* sets were obtained by randomly separating the circuits from the ICCAD 2017 CAD Contest into those groups using the holdout method for cross validation. They were used to evaluate different ML models and to select the best model for the integration described in Section 4. This way, the ML model is trained and validated using circuits with multi-row cells, which are more challenging to legalize. On the other hand, the *test* set is used along with the *validation* one for a second experiment, which evaluates the quality of the selected ML

Table 2: Benchmarks used in the experiments.

Benchmark	# Cells of different heights				Benchmark set	Group
	1	2	3	4		
pci_bridge32_a_md1	26K	1.7K	597	448	ICCAD17	validation
pci_bridge32_a_md2	25K	2K	1.1K	994	ICCAD17	validation
pci_bridge32_b_md1	26K	1.7K	585	439	ICCAD17	validation
pci_bridge32_b_md2	28K	292	292	292	ICCAD17	validation
pci_bridge32_b_md3	27K	292	585	585	ICCAD17	training
fft_2_md2	28K	2.1K	705	529	ICCAD17	training
fft_a_md2	27K	2K	672	504	ICCAD17	training
fft_a_md3	28K	672	672	672	ICCAD17	training
des_perf_a_md1	103K	4.6K	0	0	ICCAD17	training
des_perf_a_md2	105K	1K	1086	1K	ICCAD17	training
des_perf_1	112K	0	0	0	ICCAD17	training
des_perf_b_md1	106K	5.8K	0	0	ICCAD17	training
des_perf_b_md2	101K	6.7K	2.2K	1.6K	ICCAD17	training
edit_dist_1_md1	118K	7.9K	2.6K	1.9K	ICCAD17	training
edit_dist_a_md2	115K	7.7K	2.5K	1.9K	ICCAD17	training
edit_dist_a_md3	119K	2.5K	2.5K	2.5K	ICCAD17	training
superblue18	768M	0	0	0	ICCAD15	test
superblue4	795M	0	0	0	ICCAD15	test
superblue16	981M	0	0	0	ICCAD15	test
superblue5	1086M	0	0	0	ICCAD15	test
superblue1	1209M	0	0	0	ICCAD15	test
superblue3	1213M	0	0	0	ICCAD15	test
superblue10	1876M	0	0	0	ICCAD15	test
superblue7	1931M	0	0	0	ICCAD15	test

model when integrated in a circuit partitioning strategy. The *test* set is composed by the ICCAD 2015 CAD Contest benchmarks, which were not used when selecting the best ML model. Although those circuits do not contain multi-row cells, they are much larger than the others. Therefore, they provide a way to evaluate the speedup achieved by the ML model on large designs.

We performed all experiments in a Linux workstation with an Intel® Xeon® E5430 processor with 4 cores @ 2.66 GHz and 16GB DDR2 667MHz RAM. In order to identify the best ML model for our problem we evaluated three options: an artificial neural network (**ANN**) with a single hidden layer with 10 neurons, a decision tree (**DT**) and a deep convolutional neural network (**CNN**), using the resnet34 CNN architecture [8]. The first two models were prototyped using the Knime platform [14], while the CNN was prototyped using the fast.ai library [9]. After selecting the best ML model, it was retrained with the same parameters using the Keras framework [12], so that we could integrate the model in the C++ code of the circuit partitioning strategy. All experiments are available under public domain, so that they can be reproduced [1].

5.2 Evaluation of machine learning models

Table 3 shows the results of the ML models on the *validation* set for three different maximum displacement thresholds (Δ): 5, 10, and 15 rows. We evaluated the models by their accuracy, precision, recall and F-score[3]. We selected the best results obtained for each model. Since the number of samples of each class (true positive, false positive, etc.) is not necessarily balanced, it is important to evaluate not only the accuracy of the model, but also the precision and recall. A low precision means a model assumes that some partitions would result in a large displacement when that is not the case, resulting in worse execution times as it takes longer to legalize the larger parent partition. On the other hand, a low recall means that the model will not prune some partitions that should have been pruned. This will result in quality degradation, since Algorithm 5 will accept the legalization even though it should not.

When the maximum displacement threshold is 5 rows, ANN and CNN are very similar in accuracy, with CNN achieving a better F-score. The DT model, on the other hand, seems to be the worst of the three models, with lower accuracy, precision, and recall. When we increased the maximum displacement threshold to 10 rows, there is a slight increase on the accuracy of the DT and ANN models, and no difference for the CNN model. However, there was a reduction on the precision for all models, due to the more unbalanced data for this displacement threshold. The recall was only affected on DT, which again makes it the worst of the three models. Finally, when the maximum displacement threshold is 15 rows, the data is even more unbalanced, with less positive instances. In this case, there was an F-score reduction on both ANN and CNN models. The impact was greater on the CNN, whose F-score dropped from 0.83 (with threshold of 5 rows) to 0.68 (with threshold of 15 rows).

These results led us to the following conclusions: (1) DT has a worse F-score for all maximum displacement thresholds, which makes it a poor model for the analyzed problem; (2) increasing the maximum displacement threshold degrades the quality of all models, due to more unbalanced data. Thus, an evaluation with

even higher thresholds would require the generation of data with more positive instances.

5.3 Integration with circuit partitioning

Based on the evaluation of the ML models, we selected the ANN model to be integrated in the circuit partitioning strategy. Although the CNN achieved a higher accuracy and F-score for the maximum displacement threshold of 5 rows, we selected ANN over CNN for the following reasons: (1) the ANN model achieved a higher accuracy and F-score for the highest displacement threshold (15 rows), which suggests that this model is more robust to unbalanced data; (2) the CNN model is more complex, and therefore it takes longer to classify partitions using it. In order for this increased run time to be compensated, the CNN model must have a much higher accuracy than ANN, which is not the case for the evaluated models; (3) further experiments showed that the CNN model has lower accuracy on smaller partitions than on larger partitions. Since smaller partitions are the majority in the partitioning strategy, it is better to have a higher accuracy for them.

Table 4 shows the results of applying the pruning strategy presented in Section 4 on the *validation* and *test* circuits with relation to average displacement, maximum displacement and half-perimeter wirelength (HPWL)[4]. Observe that none of the circuits presented in this table were used for the model training. For each metric we present the ratio of the result when using the pruning strategy by the original result from [6]. This way, a ratio lower than 1 for a given metric means that its value was reduced (and improved) when using the pruning strategy. For each metric, the table shows the results of two versions of the pruning strategy: LEG (Algorithm 4), and ANN (Algorithm 5 using the ANN model). In addition, the table is divided in the same maximum displacement thresholds as Table 3 (5, 10 and 15 rows).

First of all, observe that for LEG, the results remain the same for all metrics even when increasing the threshold from 5 to 15 rows. The ratios were on average 0.96, 0.32 and 0.99 for average displacement, maximum displacement and HPWL, respectively. This means that increasing the maximum displacement threshold does not make a significant difference for those circuits. The improvement was especially high for the maximum displacement, since this is the metric being verified by the pruning strategy. In addition, there was a significant reduction on the average displacement of circuits *pci_bridge32_a_md*2, *pci_bridge32_b_md*1, *pci_bridge32_b_md*2, *pci_bridge32_a_md*1, *superblue*18 and *superblue*4, which are the smallest circuits used on this experiment. This happened because, for larger circuits, legalizing the parent nodes in the partitioning strategy may increase the average displacement, since they have a larger area and, therefore, allow more cell movement. However, the increase on average displacement is largely compensated by the reduction on maximum displacement.

When using the ANN model with a maximum displacement threshold of 5 or 10 rows, the results were the same as LEG for almost all circuits, which means the accuracy of the ML model was enough to avoid degrading the solution quality. However, when

---

[3]F-score is calculated by the harmonic mean of precision and recall.

[4]Although circuit *des_perf_b_md*1 belongs to the *validation* set, it was not used in this experiment because the legalization algorithm was not capable of legalizing this circuit.

Table 3: Results of different ML models for different maximum displacement thresholds.

ML model	Max disp threshold of 5 rows				Max disp threshold of 10 rows				Max disp threshold of 15 rows			
	accuracy	precision	recall	F-score	accuracy	precision	recall	F-score	accuracy	precision	recall	F-score
ANN	81%	86%	72%	0.78	85%	78%	73%	0.75	84%	69%	72%	0.70
DT	76%	83%	63%	0.71	82%	76%	58%	0.66	83%	71%	63%	0.67
CNN	82%	84%	83%	0.83	82%	72%	83%	0.77	80%	70%	66%	0.68

Table 4: Results when integrating the ANN model to the partitioning strategy

Design	Max disp threshold of 5 row						Max disp threshold of 10 row						Max disp threshold of 15 row					
	Avg disp		Max disp		HPWL		Avg disp		Max disp		HPWL		Avg disp		Max disp		HPWL	
	LEG	ANN	LEG	ANN	LEG	ANN	LEG	ANN	LEG	ANN	LEG	ANN	LEG	ANN	LEG	ANN	LEG	ANN
pci_bridge32_a_md2	0.92	0.92	0.77	0.77	0.95	0.95	0.92	0.92	0.77	0.77	0.95	0.95	0.92	0.92	0.77	0.77	0.95	0.95
pci_bridge32_b_md1	0.69	0.69	0.30	0.30	0.99	0.96	0.69	0.69	0.30	0.30	0.99	0.96	0.69	1.01	0.30	0.91	0.99	1.00
pci_bridge32_b_md2	0.90	0.91	0.33	0.33	0.98	0.98	0.90	0.91	0.33	0.33	0.98	0.98	0.90	0.87	0.33	0.45	0.98	0.98
pci_bridge32_a_md1	0.89	0.89	0.95	0.95	0.98	0.98	0.89	0.89	0.95	0.95	0.98	0.98	0.89	0.89	0.95	0.95	0.98	0.98
superblue10	1.01	1.01	0.21	0.21	1.00	1.00	1.01	1.01	0.21	0.21	1.00	1.00	1.01	1.01	0.21	0.21	1.00	1.00
superblue18	0.96	0.96	0.11	0.11	1.00	1.00	0.96	0.92	0.11	0.11	1.00	1.00	0.96	0.92	0.11	0.24	1.00	1.00
superblue4	0.87	0.87	0.17	0.17	1.00	1.00	0.87	0.87	0.17	0.17	1.00	1.00	0.87	0.85	0.17	0.17	1.00	0.99
superblue7	1.04	1.04	0.13	0.13	1.00	1.00	1.04	1.04	0.13	0.13	1.00	1.00	1.04	1.04	0.13	0.13	1.00	1.00
superblue1	1.08	1.08	0.06	0.06	1.00	1.00	1.08	1.08	0.06	0.06	1.00	1.00	1.08	1.08	0.06	0.06	1.00	1.00
superblue16	1.06	1.06	0.52	0.52	1.00	1.00	1.06	1.06	0.52	0.52	1.00	1.00	1.06	1.06	0.52	0.52	1.00	1.00
superblue3	1.01	1.01	0.18	0.18	1.00	1.00	1.01	1.01	0.18	0.18	1.00	1.00	1.01	0.94	0.18	0.28	1.00	1.00
superblue5	1.05	1.05	0.12	0.12	1.00	1.00	1.05	1.05	0.12	0.12	1.00	1.00	1.05	0.96	0.12	0.34	1.00	1.00
Average	**0.96**	**0.96**	**0.32**	**0.32**	**0.99**	**0.99**	**0.96**	**0.96**	**0.32**	**0.32**	**0.99**	**0.99**	**0.96**	**0.96**	**0.32**	**0.42**	**0.99**	**0.99**
Median	**0.98**	**0.98**	**0.19**	**0.19**	**1.00**	**1.00**	**0.98**	**0.96**	**0.19**	**0.19**	**1.00**	**1.00**	**0.98**	**0.95**	**0.19**	**0.31**	**1.00**	**1.00**

increasing the maximum displacement threshold to 15 rows, the lower precision of the ANN model results in degradation of the max displacement metric, whose average ratio becomes 0.42. However, this value is still much lower than the results from [6].

Besides analyzing the solution quality, it is important to also analyze how many calls to the legalization algorithm were avoided by using ANN, and what was the impact on the execution time. Figure 2 shows the ratio of the number of calls to the legalization algorithm performed by ANN compared to LEG. For all cases, the ANN model reduced the number of legalization calls, with a greater reduction in the larger circuits. This happens because the larger number of cells in these circuits increases the probability of a cell resulting in a large displacement, requiring more partition merges. In addition, this reduction is greater with a threshold of 5 rows because it requires more merges, which increases the number of legalization calls for LEG. However, even in the worst case, ANN required 22% less calls to the legalization algorithm (*pci_bridge32_a_md*1, 15 rows), but up to 99% in the best case (*superblue*7, 5 rows). This reduction on number of legalization calls resulted in the speedup presented in Figure 3. This figure shows the speedup only for ICCAD 2015 CAD Contest benchmarks, since the speedup is negligible for the other circuits due to their small size. The speedup was calculated as the ratio of the execution time of LEG by the execution time of ANN, so a speedup greater than 1 means ANN is faster.

The results in Figure 3 show that ANN is faster for all cases, except for *superblue*16 with the maximum displacement threshold of 15 rows, achieving speedups from 0.86 to 3. In addition, for

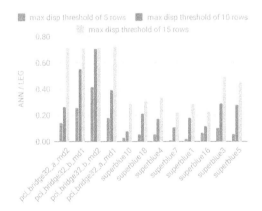

Figure 2: Comparison between the number of calls to the legalization algorithm done by LEG and ANN.

most cases, the speedup is higher when the maximum displacement threshold is lower because, as observed in Figure 2, in those cases the reduction in the number of legalization calls is greater. However, there are some exceptions, such as *superblue*18 for thresholds of 10 and 15 rows, as well as *superblue*3 and *superblue*5 for thresholds of 15 rows. These cases are also situations where the solution quality has changed when increasing the maximum displacement threshold (Table 4). In these cases, ANN failed to identify some partitions

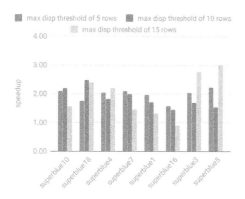

Figure 3: Comparison between LEG and ANN's execution times (speedup = ratio LEG/ANN).

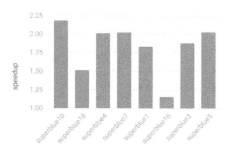

Figure 4: Comparison of the execution times between LEG with threshold of 15 rows and ANN with threshold of 5 rows (speedup = ratio LEG/ANN).

with large displacement, which reduces the execution time but can degrade the solution quality.

Finally, although ANN degrades the quality of the pruning for some circuits when using larger displacement thresholds, we observed that the pruning quality is the same for all thresholds when using LEG. Therefore, for the evaluated circuits, increasing the maximum displacement threshold does not improve the solution quality, but only reduces the execution time. Figure 4 shows the speedup achieved by the ANN results for the threshold of 5 rows (which achieved the best solution quality for ANN) compared to the results of LEG for the threshold of 15 rows (which has the smallest execution times for LEG). In this figure, it is possible to see that the best ANN solution is still faster than the best LEG solution by at least 1.14 and up to 2.3, which shows that ANN can effectively speed up the pruning strategy without compromising the solution quality. The speedup of at least 2 in some cases means that, for some circuits, it is possible to evaluate two different maximum displacement thresholds using ANN in the time that only one could be evaluated with LEG.

6 CONCLUSIONS

In this work we evaluated how ML models can be used to improve the predictability of legalization algorithms. We evaluated three models, including one deep convolutional neural network. The best model was integrated into a circuit partitioning strategy, to act as a pruning mechanism to identify partitions that will result in

large displacement after legalization. This pruning strategy greatly reduces the maximum displacement of the legalized solution, and the ML model accelerates this process by avoiding up to 99% of the calls to the legalization algorithm.

As future work, we intend to investigate the possibility of using ML models not only to predict when a partition will violate a given displacement threshold, but to estimate the resulting displacement itself. This can be used to guide incremental placement algorithms, by using the ML model to evaluate the quality of different optimizations (or different legalization algorithms), without requiring to call the legalization algorithm.

7 ACKNOWLEDGMENTS

This study was financed in part by the Coordenação de Aperfeiçoamento de Pessoal de Nível Superior - Brasil (CAPES) - Finance Code 001 and by the Brazilian Council for Scientific and Technological Development (CNPq) through Project Universal (457174/2014-5) and PQ grants 310341/ 2015-9.

REFERENCES
[1] Ophidian: an open source library for physical design research and teaching. https://gitlab.com/renan.o.netto/ophidian-research.
[2] W.-T. J. Chan, P.-H. Ho, A. B. Kahng, and P. Saxena. Routability optimization for industrial designs at sub-14nm process nodes using machine learning. In *Proceedings of the 2017 ACM on International Symposium on Physical Design*, pages 15–21. ACM, 2017.
[3] J. Chen, Z. Zhu, W. Zhu, and Y.-W. Chang. Toward optimal legalization for mixed-cell-height circuit designs. In *DAC*, page 52. ACM, 2017.
[4] W.-K. Chow, C.-W. Pui, and E. F. Young. Legalization algorithm for multiple-row height standard cell design. In *DAC*, pages 1–6. IEEE, 2016.
[5] N. K. Darav, I. Bustany, A. Kennings, and R. Mamidi. Iccad-2017 cad contest in multi-deck standard cell legalization and benchmarks. In *ICCAD*, 2017.
[6] S. Fabre, J. L. Güntzel, L. L. Pilla, R. Netto, T. Fontana, and V. Livramento. Enhancing multi-threaded legalization through kd tree circuit partitioning. In *Symposium on Integrated Circuits and Systems Design*, 2018.
[7] S.-S. Han, A. B. Kahng, S. Nath, and A. S. Vydyanathan. A deep learning methodology to proliferate golden signoff timing. In *Proceedings of the conference on Design, Automation & Test in Europe*, page 260. European Design and Automation Association, 2014.
[8] K. He, X. Zhang, S. Ren, and J. Sun. Deep residual learning for image recognition. In *Proceedings of the IEEE conference on computer vision and pattern recognition*, pages 770–778, 2016.
[9] J. Howard and R. Thomas. fast.ai - Making neural networks uncool again. http://www.fast.ai/, 2018. [Online; accessed 28-September-2018].
[10] C.-Y. Hung, P.-Y. Chou, and W.-K. Mak. Mixed-cell-height standard cell placement legalization. In *GLSVLSI*, pages 149–154. ACM, 2017.
[11] A. B. Kahng, B. Lin, and S. Nath. High-dimensional metamodeling for prediction of clock tree synthesis outcomes. In *System Level Interconnect Prediction (SLIP)*, *2013 ACM/IEEE International Workshop on*, pages 1–7. IEEE, 2013.
[12] Keras. Keras: The Python Deep Learning library. https://keras.io/, 2018. [Online; accessed 28-September-2018].
[13] M. Kim, J. Hu, J. Li, and N. Viswanathan. ICCAD-2015 CAD contest in incremental timing-driven placement and benchmark suite. 2015.
[14] Knime. Knime - open for innovation. https://www.knime.com/, 2018. [Online; accessed 28-September-2018].
[15] H. Li, W.-K. Chow, G. Chen, E. F. Young, and B. Yu. Routability-driven and fence-aware legalization for mixed-cell-height circuits. In *Proceedings of the 55th Annual Design Automation Conference*, page 150. ACM, 2018.
[16] P. Spindler, U. Schlichtmann, and F. M. Johannes. Abacus: fast legalization of standard cell circuits with minimal movement. In *ISPD*, pages 47–53. ACM, 2008.
[17] A. F. Tabrizi, L. Rakai, N. K. Darav, I. Bustany, L. Behjat, S. Xu, and A. Kennings. A machine learning framework to identify detailed routing short violations from a placed netlist. In *2018 55th ACM/ESDA/IEEE Design Automation Conference (DAC)*, pages 1–6. IEEE, 2018.
[18] C.-H. Wang, Y.-Y. Wu, J. Chen, Y.-W. Chang, S.-Y. Kuo, W. Zhu, and G. Fan. An effective legalization algorithm for mixed-cell-height standard cells. In *ASP-DAC*, pages 450–455. IEEE, 2017.
[19] Q. Zhou, X. Wang, Z. Qi, Z. Chen, Q. Zhou, and Y. Cai. An accurate detailed routing routability prediction model in placement. In *Quality Electronic Design (ASQED), 2015 6th Asia Symposium on*, pages 119–122. IEEE, 2015.

Graceful Register Clustering by Effective Mean Shift Algorithm for Power and Timing Balancing*

Ya-Chu Chang
Institute of Electronics
National Chiao Tung University
Hsinchu 30010, Taiwan
qwha019@yahoo.com.tw

Tung-Wei Lin
Department of Electrical Engineering
National Taiwan University
Taipei 10617, Taiwan
b04502032@ntu.edu.tw

Iris Hui-Ru Jiang
Graduate Institute of Electronics Engineering
National Taiwan University
Taipei 10617, Taiwan
huiru.jiang@gmail.com

Gi-Joon Nam
Thomas J. Watson Research Center
IBM Research
Yorktown Heights, NY 10598, USA
gnam@us.ibm.com

ABSTRACT

As the wide adoption of FinFET technology in mass production, dynamic power becomes the bottleneck to achieving low power. Therefore, clock power reduction is crucial in modern IC design. Register clustering can effectively save clock power because of significantly reducing the number of clock sinks and register pin capacitance, clock routed wirelength, and the number of clock buffers. In this paper, we propose effective mean shift to naturally form clusters according to register distribution without placement disruption. Effective mean shift fulfills the requirements to be a good register clustering algorithm because it needs no prespecified number of clusters, is insensitive to initializations, is robust to outliers, is tolerant of various register distributions, is efficient and scalable, and balances clock power reduction against timing degradation. Experimental results show that our approach outperforms state-of-the-art work on power and timing balancing, as well as efficiency and scalability.

KEYWORDS

Register clustering; Clock power; Timing; Clustering; Mean shift

ACM Reference format:
Ya-Chu Chang, Tung-Wei Lin, Iris Hui-Ru Jiang, and Gi-Joon Nam. 2019. Graceful Register Clustering by Effective Mean Shift Algorithm for Power and Timing Balancing. In *Proceedings of 2019 International Symposium on Physical Design (ISPD '19)*. ACM, New York, NY, USA, 8 pages. https://doi.org/10.1145/3299902.3309753

*This work was supported in part by Synopsys, TSMC, and MOST of Taiwan under Grant MOST 106-2628-E-002-019-MY3.

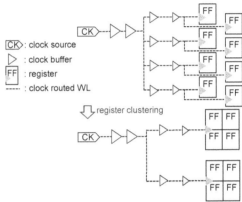

Figure 1. Register clustering reduces the switching capacitance in a clock network in all aspects.

1 INTRODUCTION

The wide adoption of FinFET technology at advanced nodes results in a dramatic drop in leakage power; therefore, dynamic power is now the bottleneck to achieving low power in modern IC design [1][2][3]. Clock power has been considered the dominant contributor to dynamic power because of its high toggle rate and large capacitive loading.

In addition to voltage scaling and clock gating, register clustering is an effective technique to save clock power. Register clustering, which gathers registers[1] into clusters, reduces the switching capacitance in a clock network in the following aspects (see Fig. 1): 1) The clock sink capacitance (in terms of register capacitance) is lowered because the number of clock sinks is greatly reduced. Furthermore, by sharing clocking circuitry within the cell, a multi-bit register has a smaller pin capacitance at the clock sinks than separate single-bit registers. 2) The clock network capacitance (in terms of clock routed

---

[1]A register generally means a sequential element, i.e., a flip-flop or a latch.

wirelength and clock buffers) is lessened because the depth of clock tree becomes shallow.

Recently, studies have extensively investigated register clustering, e.g., [5][6][7][8][9][10][11][12][13]. Depending on the available bit numbers, there exist two register cluster designs presented in literature: 1) Rigid cell [6][7][8][9][10][11][12][13], i.e., discrete bits. 2) Flexible template (structured latch template) [4][5], i.e., each template covers a range of bits instead of a specific number.

Most of existing works perform either in-placement or post-placement register clustering, and their solutions fall into two main categories: clique partitioning and K-means clustering. The clique partitioning approach first constructs a compatibility graph (recording the clustering compatibility between any two registers based on their timing feasible regions) and then extracts maximal cliques to form multi-bit registers without timing degradation [6][7][8][9][10][13]. The most up-to-date results were reported by Seitanidis *et al.* in [13], who enumerated all valid multi-bit registers from these cliques and then formulated an integer linear program (ILP) to generate as few feasible multi-bit registers as possible.

On the other hand, the K-means approach relaxes timing constraints to maximum displacement constraints, trying to minimize the impact on timing. K-means, however, is sensitive to initializations and outliers (distant from other registers) [14]; it starts with a prespecified number of clusters and initial cluster centers (seeds), iteratively assigns registers to nearest clusters, and finally converges to a local minimum of within-cluster total displacement [5][11][12]. Very recently, for minimizing the number of generated clusters, Wu *et al.* in [11] proposed weighted K-means, introducing a cluster size balancing weight into displacement cost. Because they intended to form large clusters (nearly maximum allowable bits of a register cell) and possibly moved outliers away, significant timing degradation cannot be avoided. Moreover, adding weights cannot guarantee elimination of oversized clusters; thus, additional processes were performed to fix over-displacement on outliers and control size overflows. Later, Kahng *et al.* in [12] adopted capacitated K-means and ILP to form feasible sized clusters. Nevertheless, due to high complexities, clique enumeration and ILP may not be applicable for large multi-bit register cells or large-scale designs.

Consider a timing-optimized placement as the input. Creating large clusters or dragging outliers far away inevitably causes large disruption to placement thus incurring significant timing degradation. The more timing degradations, the more timing ECO efforts. Besides, once registers are clustered (even few), we can save clock power. Based on these investigations, a good register clustering algorithm is desired 1) to require no prespecified number of clusters, 2) to be insensitive to initializations, 3) to be robust to outliers, 4) to be tolerant of various register distributions, 5) to be efficient and scalable, and 6) to balance power and timing.

Therefore, in this paper, we propose *effective mean shift* to perform *graceful register clustering* for reducing clock power while minimizing timing degradation (see Fig. 2). Effective mean

shift augments classic mean shift with special treatments for register clustering to attain these goals.

Conceptually, clusters are expected to reside in dense regions of registers. Our idea is to direct registers towards their nearest densest spots to form clusters naturally.

In our effective mean shift algorithm, the register distribution is first mapped to a density surface; dense regions form hills. Each register climbs up (shifts) to the nearest peak in a specified search window. For register clustering, the search window (bandwidth) reflects timing criticality and local density/sparsity. Furthermore, we propose to consider effective neighbors via k-nearest neighbors (KNN) during iterative shift vector computation for efficiency and stability. Subsequently, we reassign registers and relocate clusters to further improve displacement (for timing) and refine cluster count (for power).

Effective mean shift fulfills the aforementioned requirements for being a good register clustering algorithm.

1) It requires no prespecified number of clusters. It exploits the density of registers to generate a reasonable number of clusters naturally.

2) It is insensitive to initializations. Actually, no initial seeds are needed.

3) It is robust to outliers. Our effective neighbor consideration and bandwidth setting prevent outliers in sparse regions from over-displacement.

4) It is tolerant of various register distributions. According to local density and sparsity, our clustering can tolerate uneven register distribution.

5) It is efficient and scalable. Our KNN and bandwidth setting expedites shift vector computation for each register, and our algorithm is highly parallelizable.

6) It balances power reduction against timing degradation because of graceful register clustering.

Our approach is evaluated by 2015 CAD Contest in incremental timing-driven placement benchmark suite [20], containing 768K~1932K cells with 101K~262K registers. Our approach is compared with physical design flows without performing register clustering and with the weighted K-means clustering [11]. Compared with the flow without register clustering, our method has achieved 75% reduction on clock routed wirelength, 46% decrease on clock buffer usage, and 26% savings on clock sink power with less than 2% timing degradation (in terms of total negative slack). The weighted K-means flow suffers from 11% timing degradation but with 1~2% more savings than ours on clock power. Our respective

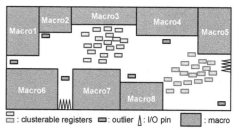

: clusterable registers ☐ : outlier ⋀ : I/O pin ▨ : macro

Figure 2. Graceful register clustering.

maximum register displacement and total register displacement is 19% and 43% of weighted K-means. For efficiency and scalability, our method achieves 39X (single-threaded) and 215X (multi-threaded) speedups compared with weighted K-means.

The remainder of this paper is organized as follows. Section 2 introduces preliminaries about the classic mean shift algorithm and describes the register clustering design methodology adopted in this paper. Section 3 details register clustering based on our effective mean shift algorithm. Section 4 shows experimental results. Finally, Section 5 concludes this work.

2 PRELIMINARIES

2.1 Classic Mean Shift Algorithm

Classic mean shift was introduced by Fukunaga and Hostetler [15], generalized by Cheng [16], and applied to cluster analysis in various fields, e.g., Computer Vision [17].

First, it views the data points are samples from a probability density function. Placing a kernel on each data point (Gaussian kernel is widely used [16][17]) and adding all of the individual kernels up generates a density surface (see Fig. 3). Considering a kernel k of bandwidth h, the kernel density estimator for a d-dimensional data point x is

$$f(x) = \frac{1}{nh^d} \sum_{i=1}^{n} k\left(\frac{x-x_i}{h}\right). \qquad (1)$$

If dense regions are present, then they correspond to local maxima of the density surface, and clusters associated with these local maxima can be identified. Classic mean shift iteratively shifts each data point uphill until it reaches the nearest peak of density surface within the bandwidth h.

The algorithm starts with making a copy of the original data points and freezing the original ones. The copied points are iteratively shifted against the original frozen points. The shift m of each point is computed by performing gradient ascent on the density function until it converges to a stationary point.

$$m(x) = \frac{\sum_{i=1}^{n} x_i g\left(\left\|\frac{x-x_i}{h}\right\|^2\right)}{\sum_{i=1}^{n} g\left(\left\|\frac{x-x_i}{h}\right\|^2\right)} - x, \qquad (2)$$

where Gaussian kernel function $k(x) = \kappa(\|x\|^2)$, $\|x\|^2$ means squared Euclidean distance, and gradient $g(x) = -\kappa'(x)$. $m(x)$ points towards the direction of maximum increase in density. Finally, all points associated with the same stationary point

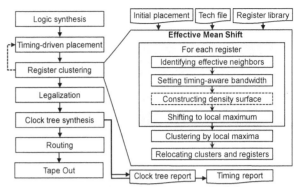

Figure 4. Register clustering methodology.

belong to the same cluster.

The main disadvantage of classic mean shift is its inefficiency; its time complexity is of $O(Tn^2)$, where T is the number of iterations, and n is the number of data points.

Classic mean shift shares the same kernel bandwidth h for all data points. Depending on the kernel bandwidth parameter used, the resultant density function and end clustering will vary. The bandwidth value is chosen based on domain-specific knowledge.

2.2 Problem Formulation and Methodology

In register clustering, data points represent registers in a given placement (i.e., a two-dimensional plane, $d = 2$). The induced register displacement can be approximated as the Manhattan distance between each register and the cluster center.

The inputs of the register clustering problem are a timing-optimized placement, multi-bit register library, and a user-defined maximum allowable displacement. Then, for saving clock power without placement/timing disruption, our goal is to minimize the total sum of register displacement as well as the number of clusters, while satisfying the cluster size constraint and maximum displacement constraints. The cluster size constraint is a given constant value according to the register library, while the maximum displacement for each register is set according to its timing criticality and the given maximum allowable displacement.

It can be seen that the classic mean shift algorithm cannot be directly applied due to the extra constraints and the efficiency requirement. We shall detail how we handle them by our effective mean shift in Section 3.

Fig. 4 shows the register clustering methodology adopted in this paper. Register clustering can be performed either post-placement or in-placement (if incremental placement is allowed).

3 EFFECTIVE MEAN SHIFT ALGORITHM

3.1 Overview

In this section, we propose effective mean shift to perform graceful register clustering for reducing clock power while minimizing timing degradation. We augment classic mean shift with special treatments for register clustering.

Effective mean shift naturally forms clusters according to register distribution without placement disruption. First, the

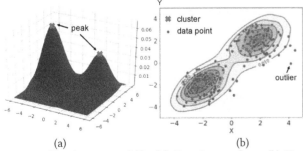

| (a) | (b) |

Figure 3. Classic mean shift. (a) Density surface. (b) Data distribution with density contour.

Table 1. Comparison of Classic, Adaptive, Effective Mean Shift.

Classic Mean Shift	Adaptive Mean Shift (Variable Bandwidth)	Effective Mean Shift
Density estimator		
$\frac{1}{nh^d}\sum_{i=1}^{n}k\left(\frac{x-x_i}{h_i}\right)$	$\frac{1}{n}\sum_{i=1}^{n}\frac{1}{h_i^{d}}k\left(\frac{x-x_i}{h_i}\right)$	$\frac{1}{n}\sum_{i\in KNN'(x)}\frac{1}{h_i^{d}}k\left(\frac{x-x_i}{h_i}\right)$
Shift point		
$\dfrac{\sum_{i=1}^{n}x_i g\left(\left\|\frac{x-x_i}{h}\right\|^2\right)}{\sum_{i=1}^{n}g\left(\left\|\frac{x-x_i}{h}\right\|^2\right)}$	$\dfrac{\sum_{i=1}^{n}\frac{x_i}{h_i^{d+2}}g\left(\left\|\frac{x-x_i}{h_i}\right\|^2\right)}{\sum_{i=1}^{n}\frac{1}{h_i^{d+2}}g\left(\left\|\frac{x-x_i}{h_i}\right\|^2\right)}$	$\dfrac{\sum_{i\in KNN'(x)}\frac{x_i}{h_i^{d+2}}g\left(\left\|\frac{x-x_i}{h_i}\right\|^2\right)}{\sum_{i\in KNN'(x)}\frac{1}{h_i^{d+2}}g\left(\left\|\frac{x-x_i}{h_i}\right\|^2\right)}$

1. $k(x)=\kappa(\|x\|^2)$, Gaussian kernel   2. $g(x)=-\kappa'(x)$ 3. $d=2$

register distribution is mapped to a density surface; dense regions form hills. Each register climbs up (shifts) to the nearest peak in a specified search window.

The search window (bandwidth) of each register varies and reflects its timing criticality and local density/sparsity. Furthermore, for efficiency and stability, we propose to consider effective neighbors via k-nearest neighbors (KNN) during iterative shift vector computation. Subsequently, we reassign registers and relocate clusters to further improve displacement (for timing) and refine cluster count (for power). Table 1 summarizes classic, adaptive, and effective mean shift.

3.2 Variable Bandwidth Selection

The kernel bandwidth parameter affects the resultant density function and clustering. As an extreme case, we use extremely tall skinny kernels (i.e., an extremely small bandwidth). The resultant density surface has a peak at each point, and thus each point forms its own cluster. In contrast, if we use an extremely short fat kernels (i.e., an extremely large bandwidth). The resultant wide smooth density surface has only one peak where all points climb up, forming one cluster. Kernels in between these two extremes lead to nicer clustering results.

Classic mean shift uses a fixed kernel bandwidth for all points. Nevertheless, the kernel bandwidth confines the search window of each point. Thus, for register clustering, each register is desired to have a variable bandwidth to reflect its timing criticality and local distribution. Then, the density function can be defined based on [18]:

$$f(x)=\frac{1}{n}\sum_{i=1}^{n}\frac{1}{h_i^{d}}k\left(\frac{x-x_i}{h_i}\right). \tag{3}$$

The shift vector becomes:

$$m(x)=\frac{\sum_{i=1}^{n}\frac{x_i}{h_i^{d+2}}g\left(\left\|\frac{x-x_i}{h_i}\right\|^2\right)}{\sum_{i=1}^{n}\frac{1}{h_i^{d+2}}g\left(\left\|\frac{x-x_i}{h_i}\right\|^2\right)}-x. \tag{4}$$

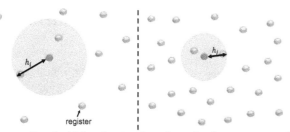

Figure 5. Bandwidth selection based on the distance to M-th nearest neighbor ($M=2$).

For a register lying in dense regions, we select a small bandwidth, thus identifying the local maximum quickly in a narrow neighborhood and avoiding a large cluster size. Hence, considering local distribution, bandwidth is first set to as the distance to its M-th nearest neighbor (see Fig. 5). Furthermore, considering the timing criticality and maximum allowable displacement, the bandwidth of register i is

$$h_i=\min\left(h_{\max},\alpha\|x_i-x_{i,M}\|\right), \tag{5}$$

where $h_{\max}$ denotes the maximum allowable displacement, $\|x_i-x_{i,M}\|$ means the Euclidean distance between register i and its M-th nearest neighbor ($x_{i,0}=x_i$), and α is a timing criticality coefficient; $\alpha\rightarrow0$ for the most critical register (i.e., a very tall and skinny kernel).

3.3 Identifying Effective Neighbors

Classic mean shift considers all original data points during shift vector computation (n is usually large in practice, 101K~262K in our experiments).

However, the points that correspond to the tails of the underlying density function receive small weights in Equations (3) and (4), and thus they are almost automatically discarded. Moreover, we do not expect registers to travel far away (for minimizing disturbance to timing and placement), and try to avoid oversized clusters. Thus, we can ignore distant registers.

For achieving this goal, we identify effective neighbors via KNN, $K\ll n$. In addition, registers belonging to KNN of a register but beyond the maximum allowable displacement are also excluded (see Fig. 6). Hence, for a register at x_j, we consider the following set of registers during the computation:

$$i\in KNN(x_j)-\left\{x_{j,m}\big|\|x_j-x_{j,m}\|>h_{\max},m\le K\right\}$$
$$=KNN'(x_j). \tag{6}$$

The density function can be rewritten as:

$$f(x)=\frac{1}{n}\sum_{i\in KNN'(x)}\frac{1}{h_i^{d}}k\left(\frac{x-x_i}{h_i}\right). \tag{7}$$

The shift vector becomes:

$$m(x)=\frac{\sum_{i\in KNN'(x)}\frac{x_i}{h_i^{d+2}}g\left(\left\|\frac{x-x_i}{h_i}\right\|^2\right)}{\sum_{i\in KNN'(x)}\frac{1}{h_i^{d+2}}g\left(\left\|\frac{x-x_i}{h_i}\right\|^2\right)}-x. \tag{8}$$

Although the idea of effective neighbors greatly improves the efficiency of shift vector computation, when the number of iterations to convergence is large, iteratively updating effective neighbors may still be computation intensive.

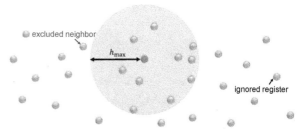

Figure 6. Effective neighbors identified by KNN ($K=12$).

Table 2. Analysis of Distinct Neighbors (K=140).

Circuit	# of Iterations	# of Total Distinct Neighbors	# of Distinct Neighbors per Iteration
Superblue16	213	158.25	0.74
Superblue18	315	158.09	0.50
Superblue10	533	156.13	0.29

Hence, we analyze members of effective neighbors. Compared with the initial set of effective neighbors, distinct neighbors that appear throughout the entire clustering process are few. For the sample circuits, we randomly monitor 100 registers and update their effective neighbors via KNN as $K = 140$ at every iteration. Table 2 lists the statistics on average total distinct neighbors. Since neighbors barely change, effective neighbors can be identified only once (at the beginning).

3.4 Shifting to Local Density Maxima

After identifying effective neighbors and selecting a proper bandwidth for each register, we construct the density surface. We make a copy of the original register coordinates and freezing the original ones. The copied coordinates $\{y_j^t\}$ (t denotes the iteration index) are iteratively shifted against the original frozen points $\{x_j\}$. Hence, each register undergoes the following steps to seek the local density maximum.

1. Set the initial coordinates, $y_j^0 = x_j, j = 1..n$.
2. Identify effective neighbors, $KNN'(y_j^0)$; set bandwidth h_j.
3. Compute the mean shift vector $m(y_j^t)$ by Equation (8).
4. Shift each register,

$$y_j^{t+1} = y_j^t + m(y_j^t) = \frac{\sum_{i \in KNN'(y_j^0)} \frac{x_i}{h_i^{d+2}} g\left(\left\| \frac{y_j^t - x_i}{h_i} \right\|^2 \right)}{\sum_{i \in KNN'(y_j^0)} \frac{1}{h_i^{d+2}} g\left(\left\| \frac{y_j^t - x_i}{h_i} \right\|^2 \right)}.$$

5. Iterate steps 3 and 4 until convergence, $\left| y_j^{t+1} - y_j^t \right| < \delta$.

3.5 Clustering by Local Density Maxima

Classic mean shift clusters points associated with the same stationary point together. Effective mean shift considers only effective neighbors and thus induces an approximation error as computing local density maxima.

For compensating the approximation error, we further merge registers with stationary points within a threshold distance ε into a cluster (ε is very small in our experiments). As shown in Fig. 7, the greater ε, the larger cluster.

3.6 Relocation for Timing and Displacement

The previous steps in effective mean shift can be viewed as seeking the locations of clusters. We further reassign registers and relocate clusters for improving timing and displacement.

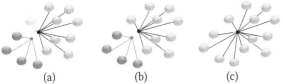

Figure 7. Compensating the approximation error of effective neighbors. (a) Small ε. (b) Medium ε. (c) Large ε.

First, register reassignment can be reduced to the stable matching problem. Gale and Shapley propose a stable matching algorithm [19] to map from a given set of men to the other set of women such that there exists no pair of man and woman who prefer each other to their paired partners. Due to male-optimality, in register reassignment, each register is modeled as a man, while a cluster location is modeled as a woman; the capacity of a cluster location equals the maximum allowable cluster size. The preference is ranked in non-decreasing order of displacement. Notably, the distance used during effective mean shift is measured by Euclidean distance, the displacement defined in register reassignment is the Manhattan distance from the initial location of a register to the investigated cluster location.

Second, after register reassignment, we relocate each cluster to the median coordinate of its register members for minimizing displacement and reducing timing degradation.

3.7 Complexity Analysis

Effective mean shift counts only effective neighbors by KNN and selects a proper bandwidth for each register, thus expediting the search of local density maxima.

Consider n registers, K effective neighbors for each register, T iterations to convergence, and C clusters generated. Shifting to local density maxima can be done in $O(TKn)$ time, while register reassignment and cluster relocation can be done in $O(Cn)$ time. Hence, effective mean shift is of complexity $O(TKn + Cn)$, where $K \ll n$ and $C \ll n$.

3.8 Parallelization

As shown in Fig. 4, the computation for each register is independent and thus highly parallelizable.

Fig. 8 illustrates parallel effective mean shift. First, identifying effective neighbors by KNN and setting variable bandwidth for each register can be computed in parallel. Second, shifting to local density maximum is iteratively calculated in parallel, too.

4 EXPERIMENTAL RESULTS

4.1 Experimental Setting

Our effective mean shift algorithm was implemented in the C++ programming language and compiled by G++ 4.8.5; the program

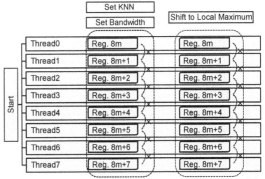

Figure 8. Parallel effective mean shift (8 threads).

Table 3. Benchmark Statistics.

Circuit	# of Cells	# of Registers
superblue16	981,559	142,543
superblue18	768,068	101,758
superblue4	796,645	167,731
superblue5	1,086,888	110,941
superblue3	1,213,253	163,107
superblue1	1,209,716	137,560
superblue7	1,931,639	262,176
superblue10	1,876,130	231,747

Table 4. Pseudo Power of Multi-bit Register Library.

# of Bits	Normalized Pseudo Power per Bit
1	1.000
2~3	0.860
4~7	0.790
8~15	0.755
16~31	0.738
32~63	0.729
64~80	0.724

was executed on a Linux workstation with an Intel Xeon 2.6 GHz CPU and 256 GB memory. Experiments were conducted on ICCAD-2015 CAD contest in incremental timing-driven placement benchmark suite [20] as listed in Table 3, containing 768K~1932K cells with 101K~262K registers in each design. (The circuit size for [20] is far greater than that in [12] (0.5K~17K registers) and [13] (29k~50K registers).)

Our algorithm was evaluated by post-placement register clustering of the experimental flow shown in Fig. 4. We started with a timing-optimized placement and obtained the coordinates of all registers as data points in effective mean shift algorithm. After register clustering, we performed legalization and clock tree synthesis by the state-of-the-art commercial tool [21]. We analyzed the solution quality based on clock tree and timing reports. Because the cell library in [20] does not include multi-bit registers, we adopted a flexible template register library similar to the setting used in prior work [4][6][7][8][9][10] as listed in Table 4, where pseudo power is computed in a conservative way.

4.2 Comparison of Register Clustering Results

In the first experiment, we compared our results with non-clustered designs and state-of-the-art weighted K-means approach [11]. We reimplemented [11] in our flow. The maximum allowable cluster size is 80 (same setting as [11]). The maximum allowable displacement is 400 nm. For effective mean shift, $K = 140$ for KNN, convergence threshold $\delta = 0.0001$ units, cluster merging threshold $\varepsilon = 5000$ units. (In the benchmark suite, 2000 unit length = 1 nm.)

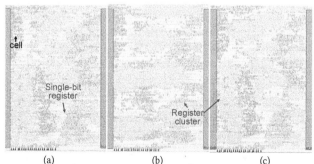

Figure 9. Partial layouts (superblue16). (a) Non-clustered. (b) Weighted K-means. (c) Effective mean shift.

Table 5 compares our register clustering approach with weighted K-means ('WK') on cluster size distribution, displacement (in unit length), and runtime (in second). 'Para.' and 'Seq.' indicates the runtime of the parallel (8 threads are used in our experiment) and sequential version of effective mean shift, respectively. Weighted K-means has 2.33X average displacement of ours. We achieve 215X and 39X speedups for parallel and sequential version, respectively. Fig. 9 shows the partial layouts corresponding to the same region in superblue16 generated by non-clustering (initial timing-optimized placement), weighted K-means, and effective mean shift, where blue boxes indicate registers, and grey boxes indicate other cells. It can be seen that weighted K-means tends to generate large clusters and induce large displacement for outliers, thus incurring significant placement disruption. In contrast, effective mean shift delivers graceful register clustering. Fig. 10 shows full layouts of superblue4, where red spots indicate registers.

In addition, Fig. 10(d) shows the clustering result if the preference is computed based on the wirelength optimum site for each register instead of its initial location during register relocation (Section 3.6). The wirelength optimum site of each register is the median coordinate of its all fanin and fanout gates. Based on optimum sites, numerous registers migrate towards the regions with many obstacles, thus possibly causing severe congestions and incurring large timing degradation.

Table 6 compares the power and timing results after clock tree synthesis for non-clustered designs ('NC'), weighted K-means ('WK'), and our effective mean shift ('Ours'). 'WNS' denotes worst negative slack, 'TNS' total negative slack, 'Clock Routed WL' routed clock wirelength, '#Buffers' the number of clock buffers. 'Clock Sink Power Ratio' is computed based on Table 4. Compared with the flow without register clustering, our method achieves 75.42% reduction on clock routed wirelength, 45.97% decrease on clock buffer usage, and 25.52% savings on clock sink power, maintains the same level of WNS and induces only 1.95% timing degradation on total negative slack. TNS reflects subsequent timing ECO efforts. The weighted K-means flow suffers from 10.88% timing degradation but with 1~2% more savings than ours on clock power.

Table 5. Comparison on Cluster Size, Displacement, and Runtime with Weighted K-Means [11].

Circuit	Method	Cluster Size		Displacement	Runtime (s)	
		Min	Max	Average	Para.	Seq.
superblue16	WK	34	80	56000.54	2370	
	Ours	1	55	22353.75	35	186
superblue18	WK	35	80	60843.50	6080	
	Ours	1	70	25792.54	25	138
superblue4	WK	34	80	48129.71	8470	
	Ours	1	56	19446.86	51	311
superblue5	WK	32	80	69453.46	3590	
	Ours	1	78	29747.90	28	131
superblue3	WK	28	80	54968.00	9098	
	Ours	1	79	25696.45	45	244
superblue1	WK	42	80	64158.15	5295	
	Ours	1	62	24456.03	40	200
superblue7	WK	39	80	54761.63	37692	
	Ours	1	79	26048.28	91	513
superblue10	WK	26	80	57643.75	27474	
	Ours	1	79	27914.53	75	412
Ratio	WK/Ours			2.33	215.03	39.42

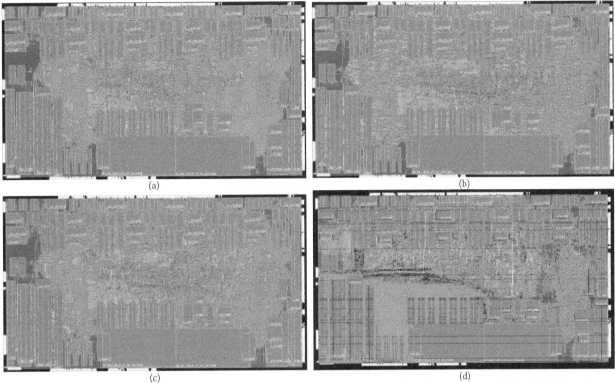

Figure 10. Full layouts (superblue4). (a) Non-clustered (b) Weighted K-means. (c) Effective mean shift. (d) Relocation using optimum sites.

4.3 Power and Timing Tradeoff

In the second experiment, we showed the power and timing tradeoff by adjusting the bandwidth to the distance to different M-th neighbors. Fig. 11 shows the corresponding results of superblue16, where timing is measured by TNS degradation, and power is measured by total clock sink power ratio. The top-left point indicates the register clustering result of weighted K-means [11]. For effective mean shift, $M = 0$ refers to the nearest neighbor (every register itself), i.e., bandwidth = 0, corresponding to non-clustered results. It can be seen that $M = 3$ brings the best power and timing tradeoff.

4.4 Parallelization

In the third experiment, we compared the parallel version (multi-threaded) with the sequential version (single threaded) of effective mean shift. Fig. 12 demonstrates the speedups achieved by effective mean shift on superblue18. It can be seen that effective mean shift has superior efficiency and scalability.

5 CONCLUSIONS

In this paper, we propose effective mean shift to naturally form clusters according to register distribution without placement disruption. Effective mean shift fulfills the requirements to be a good register clustering algorithm because it does not need a prespecified number of clusters, is insensitive to initializations, is

M	0	1	2	3	4	5
Max cluster size	1	30	35	55	78	98

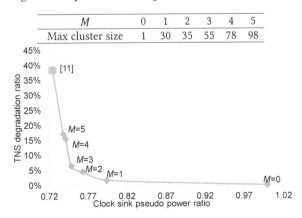

Figure 11. Clock sink power vs. TNS degradation (superblue16).

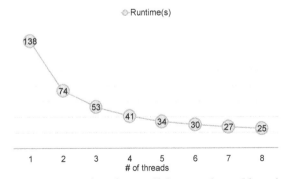

Figure 12. Speedups by parallelization (superblue18).

Table 6. Comparison on Timing and Power with Weighted K-Means (WK) [11] and Non-Clustered Design (NC).

Circuit	Method	Timing			Power				
		WNS	TNS (ns)	TNS Degradation Ratio	Clock Routed WL (um)	Ratio	#Buffers	Ratio	Clock Sink Power Ratio
superblue16	NC	-6.2	-1532.0	0.00%	934,654	100.00%	3,414	100.00%	100.00%
	WK	-6.6	-2120.9	-38.44%	196,543	21.03%	1,872	54.83%	72.47%
	Ours	-6.2	-1629.8	-6.38%	214,560	22.96%	1,873	54.86%	74.86%
superblue18	NC	-9.1	-5148.3	0.00%	629,463	100.00%	2,449	100.00%	100.00%
	WK	-9.4	-5834.8	-13.33%	143,471	22.79%	1,314	53.65%	72.47%
	Ours	-9.1	-5250.0	-1.98%	144,009	22.88%	1,228	50.14%	74.32%
superblue4	NC	-9.7	-15669.9	0.00%	1,017,709	100.00%	4,303	100.00%	100.00%
	WK	-10.1	-16738.6	-6.82%	214,560	21.08%	2,124	49.36%	72.47%
	Ours	-9.9	-15830.8	-1.03%	234,966	23.09%	2,072	48.15%	74.91%
superblue5	NC	-30.2	-19866.8	0.00%	928,619	100.00%	3,626	100.00%	100.00%
	WK	-32.3	-20607.3	-3.73%	273,496	29.45%	2,251	62.08%	72.51%
	Ours	-30.3	-19898.6	-0.16%	291,267	31.37%	2,355	64.95%	74.16%
superblue3	NC	-18.9	-7892.9	0.00%	1,047,502	100.00%	4,251	100.00%	100.00%
	WK	-19.7	-8584.5	-8.76%	266,706	25.46%	2,054	48.32%	72.48%
	Ours	-18.9	-8106.1	-2.70%	262,588	25.07%	2,133	50.18%	74.14%
superblue1	NC	-10.2	-6778.5	0.00%	1,047,502	100.00%	3,759	100.00%	100.00%
	WK	-10.5	-7825.5	-15.45%	262,261	25.04%	2,052	54.59%	72.47%
	Ours	-10.2	-7334.7	-8.21%	255,708	24.41%	2,104	55.97%	74.87%
superblue7	NC	-19.4	-12531.2	0.00%	1,702,650	100.00%	6,482	100.00%	100.00%
	WK	-20.9	-13591.3	-8.46%	362,256	21.28%	3,427	52.87%	72.48%
	Ours	-19.2	-12757.0	-1.80%	379,577	22.29%	3,341	51.54%	74.31%
superblue10	NC	-48.7	-151000.0	0.00%	1,660,396	100.00%	6,189	100.00%	100.00%
	WK	-42.7	-139000.0	7.95%	379,246	22.84%	3,210	51.87%	72.48%
	Ours	-42.3	-141000.0	6.62%	408,500	24.60%	3,495	56.47%	74.25%
Average	NC			0.00%		100.00%		100.00%	100.00%
	WK			-10.88%		23.62%		53.45%	72.48%
	Ours			-1.95%		24.58%		54.03%	74.48%

robust to outliers, is tolerant of various register distributions, is efficient and scalable, and balances clock power reduction against timing degradation. Experimental results show that our approach outperforms state-of-the-art work on power and timing balancing; we deliver similar clock power reduction with minor timing degradation. For efficiency and scalability, our method achieves 39X (sequential version) and 215X (parallel version) speedups. Future work includes the extension of effective mean shift to global placement.

REFERENCES

[1] A. Ranjan. 2015. Micro-architectural exploration for low power design. (November 2015). Semiconductor Engineering. Retrieved from https://semiengineering.com/micro-architectural-exploration-for-low-power-design/

[2] K. Brock. 2016. Six ways to exploit the advantages of finFETs. (November 2016.). Tech Design Forum. Retrieved from http://www.techdesignforums.com/practice/technique/six-ways-to-exploit-the-advantages-of-finfets/

[3] L. Rizzatti. 2015. Dynamic power estimation hits limits of SoC designs. (May 2015). Retrieved from https://www.eetimes.com/author.asp?section_id=36&doc_id=1326542

[4] S. I. Ward, N. Viswanathan, N. Y. Zhou, C. C. N. Sze, Z. Li, C. J. Alpert, and D. Z. Pan. 2013. Clock power minimization using structured latch templates and decision tree induction. In *Proc. Int'l Conf. on Computer-Aided Design (ICCAD '13)*. IEEE, Piscataway, NJ, USA, 599-606.

[5] D. A. Papa, C. J. Alpert, C. C. N. Sze, Z. Li, N. Viswanathan, G.-J. Nam, I. L. Markov. 2011. Physical synthesis with clock-network optimization for large systems on chips. *IEEE Micro* 31, 4 (July 2011), 51–62.

[6] M. P.-H. Lin, C. C. Hsu and Y.-T. Chang. 2011. Post-placement power optimization with multi-bit flip-flops. *IEEE Trans. on CAD of Integrated Circuits and Systems (TCAD)* 30, 12 (December 2011), 1870–1882.

[7] I. H.-R. Jiang, C.-L. Chang, and Y.-M. Yang. 2012. INTEGRA: Fast multibit flip-flop clustering for clock power saving. *IEEE Trans. on CAD of Integrated Circuits and Systems (TCAD)* 31, 2 (February 2012), 192–204. Also see in *Proc. Int'l Symp. on Physical Design (ISPD '11)*. ACM, New York, NY, 115–121.

[8] S.-H. Wang, Y.-Y. Liang, T.-Y. Kuo, and W.-K. Mak. 2012. Power-driven flip-flop merging and relocation. *IEEE Trans. on CAD of Integrated Circuits and Systems (TCAD)* 31, 2 (February 2012), 180–191. Also see in *Proc. Int'l Symp. on Physical Design (ISPD '11)*. ACM, New York, NY, 107–114.

[9] S. S.-Y. Liu, W.-T. Lo, C.-J. Lee, and H.-M. Chen. 2013. Agglomerative-based flip-flop merging and relocation for signal wirelength and clock tree optimization. *ACM Trans. Design Automation Electronic Systems (TODAES)* 18, 3, Article 40 (July 2013), 20 pages.

[10] C.-C. Tsai, Y. Shi, G. Luo, and I. H.-R. Jiang. 2013. FF-Bond: Multi-bit flip-flop bonding at placement. In *Proc. Int'l Symp. on Physical Design (ISPD '13)*. ACM, New York, NY, 147–153.

[11] G. Wu, Y. Xu, D. Wu, M. Ragupathy, Y.-Y. Mo, and C. Chu. 2016. Flip-flop clustering by weighted k-means algorithm. 2016. In *Proc. Design Automation Conf. (DAC '16)*. ACM, New York, NY, Article 82, 6 pages.

[12] A. B. Kahng, J. Li, and L. Wang. 2016. Improved flop tray-based design implementation for power reduction. In *Proc. Int'l Conf. on Computer-Aided Design (ICCAD '16)*. ACM, New York, NY, Article 20, 8 pages.

[13] I. Seitanidis, G. Dimitrakopoulos, P. M. Mattheakis, L. Masse-Navette, D. Chinnery. 2018. Timing-driven and placement-aware multi-bit register composition. *IEEE Trans. on CAD of Integrated Circuits and Systems (TCAD)*, early access. Also see in *Proc. Design Automation Conf. (DAC '17)*. ACM, New York, NY, Article 56, 6 pages.

[14] S. P. Lloyd. 1982. Least square quantization in PCM. *IEEE Trans. Information Theory* 28, 2 (March 1982), 129–137.

[15] K. Fukunaga and L.D. Hostetler. 1975. The estimation of the gradient of a density function, with applications in pattern recognition. *IEEE Trans. Information Theory* 21 (January 1975), 32–40.

[16] Y. Cheng. 1995. Mean shift, mode seeking, and clustering. *IEEE Trans. Pattern Analysis Machine Intelligence (TPAMI)* 17, 8 (August 1995), 790–799.

[17] D. Comaniciu and P. Meer. 2002. Mean shift: A robust approach toward feature space analysis. *IEEE Trans. Pattern Analysis Machine Intelligence (TPAMI)* 24, 5 (May 2002), 603–619.

[18] D. Comaniciu, V. Ramesh, and P. Meer. 2001. The variable bandwidth mean shift and data-driven scale selection. In *Proc. Int'l Conf. on Computer Vision (ICCV '01)*. IEEE, Piscataway, NJ, USA, 438-445.

[19] D. Gale and L. S. Shapley. 1962. College admissions and the stability of marriage. *American Mathematical Monthly* 69 (1962), 9–14.

[20] M.-C. Kim, J. Hu, J. Li, and N. Viswanathan. 2015. ICCAD-2015 CAD contest in incremental timing-driven placement and benchmark suite. In *Proc. Int'l Conf. on Computer-Aided Design (ICCAD '15)*. IEEE, Piscataway, NJ, USA, 921–926.

[21] Innovus, Cadence, Inc.

Device Layer-Aware Analytical Placement for Analog Circuits

Biying Xu
University of Texas at Austin
biying@utexas.edu

Shaolan Li
University of Texas at Austin
slliandy@gmail.com

Chak-Wa Pui
The Chinese University of Hong Kong
cwpui@cse.cuhk.edu.hk

Derong Liu
Cadence Design Systems, Inc.
derong@cadence.com

Linxiao Shen
University of Texas at Austin
lynn.shenlx@utexas.edu

Yibo Lin
University of Texas at Austin
yibolin@utexas.edu

Nan Sun
University of Texas at Austin
nansun@mail.utexas.edu

David Z. Pan
University of Texas at Austin
dpan@ece.utexas.edu

ABSTRACT

The layouts of analog/mixed-signal (AMS) integrated circuits (ICs) are dramatically different from their digital counterparts. AMS circuit layouts usually include a variety of devices, including transistors, capacitors, resistors, and inductors. A complicated AMS IC system with hierarchical structure may also consist of pre-laid out subcircuits. Different types of devices can occupy different manufacturing layers. Therefore, during the layout stage, the devices require co-optimization to achieve high circuit performance. Leveraging the fact that some devices can be built by mutually exclusive layers, they can be carefully designed to overlap each other to effectively reduce the total area and wirelength without degrading the circuit performance. In this paper, we propose an analytical framework to tackle the device layer-aware analog placement problem. Experimental results show that on average the proposed techniques can reduce the total area and half-perimeter wirelength by 9% and 23%, respectively. To verify the routability of the placement results, we also develop an analog global router, which demonstrates that the device layer-aware placement can achieve 18% shorter wirelength during global routing.

ACM Reference Format:
Biying Xu, Shaolan Li, Chak-Wa Pui, Derong Liu, Linxiao Shen, Yibo Lin, Nan Sun, and David Z. Pan. 2019. Device Layer-Aware Analytical Placement for Analog Circuits. In *ISPD '19: 2019 International Symposium on Physical Design, April 14–17, 2019, San Francisco, CA, USA.* ACM, New York, NY, USA, 8 pages. https://doi.org/10.1145/3299902.3309751

1 INTRODUCTION

Analog/mixed-signal (AMS) circuits often contain various types of devices, including transistors, resistors, capacitors, and inductors. In a complicated AMS IC system with hierarchical design, there may

also exist pre-laid out subcircuits as placement devices (e.g., a pre-laid out comparator in an analog-to-digital data converter system). Different types of devices are built by different manufacturing layers: transistors and resistors can reside only on the substrate and polysilicon layers; high-quality capacitors like metal-oxide-metal capacitors can be directly formed by inter-digitized metal fingers [1]; pre-laid out subcircuits containing different types of devices and the interconnections may occupy substrate, polysilicon, and metal layers. To reduce production cost and routing complexity, it has been a common and desirable practice to create overlapping layouts for the devices occupying mutually exclusive manufacturing layers in the high-performance custom analog designs. For instance, implementation examples of overlapping decoupling capacitors on top of transistors and resistors are reported in [2, 3] to address the area and wirelength overhead.

From the above description, we can see that under most circumstances, it is beneficial to allow the overlap between devices with mutually exclusive layers during analog layout optimization. However, there are some devices that should not overlap other devices even if they occupy mutually exclusive layers, e.g., the devices that are critical and sensitive to coupling. Only those that are insensitive to coupling and reside on mutually exclusive layers should be allowed to overlap each other without degrading the circuit performance. To validate that such overlapping will not induce circuit performance degradation, without losing generality, we provide two widely used analog circuits and their layout examples, with and without overlapping between the insensitive devices on different manufacturing layers in the following.

The capacitive-coupled operational transconductance amplifier (CC-OTA) is a prevalent building block in data converters and sensor interfaces, which is shown in Figure 1a. By overlapping the capacitors with the transistors and resistors as in Figure 1b, the area and wirelength are reduced by 30% and 4%, respectively. Table 1 compares the post-layout-simulated phase margin (stability metric), unity gain bandwidth (speed metric) and loop gain (accuracy metric) between the two layout cases, which shows that the impact on the circuit performance is negligible.

The current-controlled ring oscillator (CCO), which is commonly seen in phase-locked loops (PLLs), is shown in Figure 2. By strategically sharing the vertical space between the loading capacitors (C_L) and other devices, the compactness of the design is notably

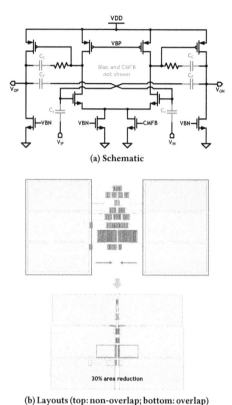

(a) Schematic

(b) Layouts (top: non-overlap; bottom: overlap)

Figure 1: CC-OTA circuit schematic and layout examples.

Table 1: Post-layout simulation results of the CC-OTA circuit.

Layout	Phase Margin (deg.)	Unity Gain Bandwidth (MHz)	Loop Gain (dB)
non-overlap	71.9	103.7	36.3
overlap	71.5	105.4	36.3

Table 2: Post-layout simulation results of the CCO circuit.

Layout	f_{CCO} (kHz)	k_{CCO} (THz/A)
non-overlap	609	0.89
overlap	610	0.9

improved, leading to 30% area reduction and 20% wirelength decrease. As shown in Table 2, the CCO center frequency (f_{CCO}) and tuning gain (k_{CCO}) remain almost unchanged, indicating that the dynamics of the upper system (e.g., the PLL bandwidth and tuning range) will not be affected.

From the above examples, we know that during layout optimization, overlapping the devices that are insensitive to coupling and reside on mutually exclusive layers can result in area and wirelength benefits without degrading the circuit performance. However, existing analog placement algorithms are still limited to consider complex scenarios and characteristics unique to analog designs. Although there exists previous work considering different cell layers in digital placement [4], none of the prior work on analog

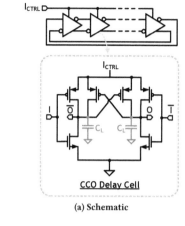

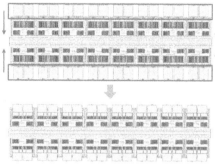

(a) Schematic

(b) Layouts (top: non-overlap; bottom: overlap)

Figure 2: CCO circuit schematic and layout examples.

placement [5–11] considered the possibility of device bounding box overlapping. This flexibility brought by the device layer-aware layout scheme leads to a dramatically different placement methodology for AMS circuits, which can contribute to better layout quality. Moreover, previous works [12–14] have shown that analytical placement methods in ASICs can also achieve high quality results in both FPGA and analog circuit designs. In this paper, we will address the device layer-aware analog placement problem by using an analytical approach. The main contributions are summarized as follows:

- To the best of our knowledge, this is the first work on analog placement to consider overlapping between the devices that are insensitive to coupling and built on mutually exclusive layers, which offers high flexibility for layout optimization.
- A holistic analytical framework is presented to solve the device layer-aware analog placement problem.
- An analog global router is developed to verify the routability of our device layer-aware placement results.

The rest of this paper is organized as follows: Section 2 gives the definition of the device layer-aware analog placement problem. Section 3 details the algorithms and techniques to solve the problem. Section 4 shows comprehensive sets of experimental results. Finally, Section 5 concludes the paper.

2 PROBLEM DEFINITION

The conventional analog placement problem usually tries to minimize the objectives including the total area and the total half-perimeter wirelength (HPWL). Besides the non-overlapping constraint between each pair of devices, it also needs to satisfy many other constraints, including matching, proximity group, and symmetry constraints [5–11, 15]. The conventional analog circuit placement problem can be stated as follows:

Problem 1 (Analog Placement). Given a netlist and the layout constraints (e.g., symmetry constraints), the analog placement problem is to find a legal placement of the devices satisfying all the given constraints, such that the objectives are optimized, including total area and wirelength.

Compared to conventional analog placement, device layer-aware analog placement allows overlap between certain pairs of devices. Without loss of generality, we categorize the devices in analog circuits into three types:

- *Type I device*: the device built without metal or via layers, and not sensitive to coupling.
- *Type II device*: the device built only with metal and via layers, and not sensitive to coupling.
- *Type III device*: the device occupying not only the metal and via layers but also substrate and polysilicon layers, or the device that is critical and sensitive to coupling.

From the above definitions, we know that Type I devices are allowed to overlap with Type II devices, while Type III devices should not overlap with any other devices. Overlaps between devices of the same type are also considered illegal. The device layer-aware analog circuit placement problem can be stated as follows:

Problem 2 (Device Layer-Aware Analog Placement). The device layer-aware analog placement problem is the analog placement problem where devices built by mutually exclusive manufacturing layers and insensitive to coupling are allowed to overlap each other from the designer specification.

3 DEVICE LAYER-AWARE PLACEMENT

This section presents our method to solve the device layer-aware placement for analog circuits. Figure 3 shows the overall flow of our device layer-aware analytical analog placement engine. Given the analog circuit netlist, the placement constraints (e.g., symmetry constraints), the placement boundary, and the device types from the design specification (i.e., circuit designer will manually specify whether a device is Type I, II, or III, as input to our engine), we first generate the global placement result by optimizing a non-linear objective function using conjugate gradient (CG) method. The next step runs the symmetry-aware and device layer-aware legalization to generate a legal placement solution which honors the result from global placement. Finally, a linear programming (LP) based detailed placement is used to further optimize the wirelength.

3.1 Global Placement

Our global placement for analog circuits is based on a non-linear global placement framework [14, 16, 17], which simultaneously considers the following: (1) wirelength, (2) device layer-aware overlapping, (3) placement boundary, and (4) symmetry constraints from

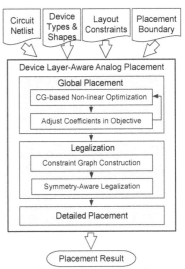

Figure 3: The overall flow of our device layer-aware analytical analog placement engine.

the design specification. To be specific, it minimizes the objective shown in Equation (1) using unconstrained non-linear conjugate gradient algorithm.

$$Objective = f_{WL} + a \cdot f_{OL} + b \cdot f_{BND} + c \cdot (f^x_{SYM} + f^y_{SYM}), \quad (1)$$

where f_{WL} is the wirelength of the placement, f_{OL} is the illegal overlap penalty (overlaps between devices on conflicting manufacturing layers are regarded as illegal), f_{BND} and f_{SYM} are the penalties of violating boundary and symmetry constraints, respectively. Our non-linear optimization-based global placement runs iteratively, until the penalties are below the specified thresholds, or the predefined maximum number of iterations is reached. By gradually adjusting the coefficient values of different penalty functions in each iteration, we can get a placement result honoring symmetry and boundary constraints with short wirelength and small illegal overlapping. Log-sum-exponential (LSE) [18] models $\gamma \log \sum_i \exp(x_i/\gamma)$ and $-\gamma \log \sum_i \exp(-x_i/\gamma)$ are used to smooth the $\max_i(x_i)$ and $\min_i(x_i)$ functions in the objective, respectively, where γ is a very small value. Details of each objective function will be explained as follows.

Wirelength is defined as the total HPWL shown in Equation (2).

$$f_{WL} = \sum_{n_k} (\max_{i \in n_k}(x_i) - \min_{i \in n_k}(x_i) + \max_{i \in n_k}(y_i) - \min_{i \in n_k}(y_i)), \quad (2)$$

where device i contains the pins of net n_k and x_i (y_i) is the x (y) coordinate of the center of device i. This definition assumes that the pins are in the center of the device.

In this work, only the overlaps between devices with conflicting manufacturing layers will contribute to the overlap penalty in the objective. Overlaps in global placement are modeled as an area overlap function similar to [19], which is shown in Equation (3).

$$f_{OL} = \sum_{(i,j) \in L} O^x_{i,j} \cdot O^y_{i,j},$$
$$O^x_{i,j} = \max(\min(x_i + w_i - x_j, x_j + w_j - x_i, w_i, w_j), 0), \quad (3)$$
$$O^y_{i,j} = \max(\min(y_i + h_i - y_j, y_j + h_j - y_i, h_i, h_j), 0),$$

where L is the set of device pairs whose overlapping are illegal, $O_{i,j}^x$ ($O_{i,j}^y$) is the x (y) directional overlap length, x_i (y_i) and w_i (h_i) are the x (y) coordinate of the lower-left corner and width (height) of device i, respectively.

Besides wirelength and overlapping, symmetry constraints are also considered. Symmetry constraint requires: (1) each symmetric pair of devices within the same symmetric group to be symmetric to each other with respect to the same symmetric axis; (2) the self-symmetric devices to be self-symmetric with respect to the same axis as the symmetric pairs. Hence, the penalty for the violation of symmetry constraint on horizontal direction (with a vertical symmetric axis) is shown in Equation (4), and the vertical one can be calculated similarly.

$$f_{SYM}^x = \sum_{g_k \in G} (\sum_{(i,j) \in g_k^p} ((x_i + x_j - 2 \cdot x_k^c)^2 + (y_i - y_j)^2) + \sum_{i \in g_k^s} (x_i - x_k^c)^2),$$

(4)

where G is the set of symmetric groups, g_k^p and g_k^s are the set of symmetric pairs and the set of self-symmetric devices in a symmetric group g_k, respectively, x_i (y_i) is the x (y) coordinate of the center of device i, and x_k^c is the coordinate of the symmetric axis of the symmetric group g_k.

For a given analog design, boundary constraint is usually imposed to control certain circuit area and aspect ratio. In our global placement, given a whitespace ratio and aspect ratio, we can get a desirable placement bounding box for the design. The penalty for the violation of the boundary constraint is shown in Equation (5).

$$f_{BND} = \sum_{i \in D} (\max(x_L - x_i, 0) + \max(x_i + w_i - x_H, 0) + \max(y_L - y_i, 0) + \max(y_i + h_i - y_H, 0))$$

(5)

where D is the set of devices, x_i (y_i) and w_i (h_i) are the x (y) coordinate of the lower-left corner and width (height) of device i, respectively, and x_L (y_L) and x_H (y_H) are the x (y) coordinates of the lower and higher boundaries of the given placement bounding box.

3.2 Legalization

After global placement, a placement result with good wirelength, a small number of violations of overlaps, boundary constraint, and symmetry constraint is obtained. To get a placement without any illegal overlapping and violations of symmetry constraints, we first construct the constraint graphs with minimum edges. Then, given the constraint graphs, we legalize the global placement result using LP-based compaction.

3.2.1 Constraint Graph Construction.
Constraint graphs are directed acyclic graphs which impose positional constraints on the devices, including horizontal and vertical constraint graphs. Each node represents a device and an edge between two nodes imposes a positional constraint on the corresponding devices. For example, in the horizontal constraint graph, if there is an edge e_{ij} from node i to node j, device i should be on the left of device j. An example placement and its corresponding constraint graphs are shown in Figure 4. In Figure 4b, the horizontal and vertical constraint graphs are merged into a single graph, where the solid edges represent the edges in the horizontal constraint graph, and the dashed ones are

vertical constraint edges. The nodes s_h and s_v are the virtual source nodes in the horizontal and vertical constraint graphs, respectively, which indicate the leftmost and bottommost coordinates of the placement.

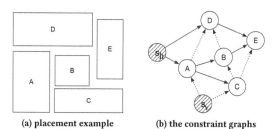

(a) placement example   **(b) the constraint graphs**
Figure 4: Example placement and constraint graphs.

To represent a legal placement, each pair of devices must have positional relationships in either vertical or horizontal constraint graphs, except between Type I and Type II devices. However, with more edges than necessary, extra constraints may lead to a larger placement area or longer run-time. Therefore, we construct the constraint graphs such that the number of edges is minimized and it can guarantee the placement result to be legal.

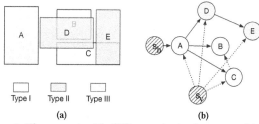

(a)   **(b)**
Figure 5: Placement with different device layers and its constraint graphs.

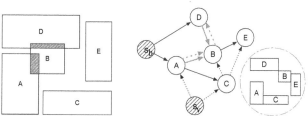

(a) global placement result   **(b) resulting constraint graphs and legalized placement snapshot**
Figure 6: An example of the global placement result, and the constraint graphs resulted from directly applying the plane sweep algorithm as in [20].

First, our irredundant constraint graph construction algorithm is based on the plane sweep algorithm presented in [20]. However, this algorithm does not consider different device layers. To address device layer-awareness, we modify the plane sweep algorithm to be executed in two passes to avoid imposing non-overlapping constraints for the devices on mutually exclusive layers. In the first pass, the inputs are the bounding boxes of the Type I and III devices after global placement, while in the second pass, the inputs are those of the Type II and III devices. Therefore, no constraint edge will be added between Type I and Type II devices. Nevertheless, it will maintain the other necessary constraint edges. A placement example with different device layers and the resulting constraint graphs after running our two-pass procedure are shown in Figure 5, where devices B and C are Type I devices, D and E are Type II devices, and A is a Type III device. In the first pass, edges among devices $\{A, B, C\}$ are added to the constraint graph, while in the second pass the edges among $\{A, D, E\}$ are added.

On the other side, the plane sweep algorithm also encounters problems when the global placement result has illegal overlaps between devices. Figure 6 shows such an example. Directly applying the algorithm to the example global placement result as in Figure 6a will generate the constraint graphs shown in Figure 6b. There are constraint edges in both horizontal and vertical constraint graphs for the device pairs $\{A, B\}$ and $\{B, D\}$, which are highlighted in red. Imposing these positional relationships will over-constrain the legalization and result in a sub-optimal area, as illustrated by the legalized placement snapshot in Figure 6b. To get a more compact placement after legalization, we will remove the extra constraint edges between each pair of devices with illegal overlap by determining their relative position greedily. We choose to spread them in the direction that induces less displacement and decide their relative position. We will only keep the constraint edge corresponding to the chosen positional relationship, while other edges between them will be removed. Continuing our example, Figure 7a shows the resulted constraint graphs after resolving the illegal overlaps, where only the horizontal edge between devices $\{A, B\}$, and the vertical edge between $\{B, D\}$ are kept, which are highlighted in red.

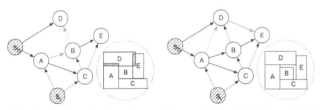

(a) after resolving illegal overlaps   (b) new edges added for the missing postional relationships

Figure 7: The resulting constraints graphs generated by our algorithm after resolving illegal overlaps, and after missing postional relationship detection.

However, there may be missing positional relationships from the graphs we obtain in the previous step. For example, removing the vertical constraint edge between devices A and B causes the missing relationship between A and D in Figure 7a. In other words, the positional relationships between these two devices are undefined in both horizontal and vertical directions, which may result in illegal overlaps after compaction, as illustrated by the snapshot in Figure 7a. To add back those missing edges, we first need to identify them. In order to detect the missing positional relationships, a depth-first-search (DFS) based algorithm is used, which is shown

---

Algorithm 1 Missing Positional Relationships Detection

Input: n devices and their vertical and horizontal constraint graphs G_v, G_h
Output: Find all the missing relationships of the devices
1: let M_h, M_v be two $(n + 1) \times (n + 1)$ Boolean matrices;
2: let s_h, s_v be the source of G_h, G_v respectively;
3: $DFS(G_h, s_h, M_h)$
4: $DFS(G_v, s_v, M_v)$
5: **for** i = 0 to $n - 1$ **do**
6:     **for** j = i + 1 to $n - 1$ **do**
7:         **if** $\neg(M_h[i][j] \vee M_h[j][i]) \wedge \neg()M_v[i][j] \vee M_v[j][i])$ **then**
8:             no positional relationship between devices i, j;
9:         **end if**
10:     **end for**
11: **end for**

12: **function** $DFS(G, v, M)$
13:     label v as discovered;
14:     $M[v][v] = 1$;
15:     **for** all edges from v to w in G.adjacentEdges(v) **do**
16:         **if** vertex w is not labeled as discovered **then**
17:             $DFS(G, w, M)$
18:         **end if**
19:         **if** $M[v]$ is not all 1 **then**
20:             **for** i = 0 to $n - 1$ **do**
21:                 $M[v][i] = M[v][i] \vee M[w][i]$
22:             **end for**
23:         **end if**
24:     **end for**
25: **end function**

in Algorithm 1. First, we use two matrices M_h, M_v to store the relationship between the devices (including the virtual source nodes s_h, s_v with the last indices in the graphs). $M_h[i][j] = 1$ means there is horizontal positional relationship between devices i and j while $M_h[i][j] = 0$ means there is no horizontal positional relationship, and M_v is defined similarly. Then a DFS-based algorithm is used to fill M_h, M_v. After that, we can detect the devices without horizontal (vertical) positional relationship from M_h (M_v). If both horizontal and vertical positional relationships are missing, the pair of devices will be identified as missing positional relationships in the current constraint graphs. For each pair of devices that are not allowed to overlap whose positional relationship is missing, we will add one edge to either the vertical or horizontal constraint graph. To be specific, if the vertical spacing is larger than horizontal spacing between the two devices, we will add an edge to the vertical constraint graph, and vice versa. For example, given the graphs in Figure 7a, our DFS-based algorithm will detect the missing relationships between devices A and D, as well as between D and E. As a result, new edges will be added between them, which are indicated in red in Figure 7b. This will ensure that no illegal overlap exists after compaction, as shown in the snapshot in Figure 7b.

Finally, we will perform transitive edge removal (transitive reduction) on both constraint graphs to remove the redundant edges. To be specific, for each vertex u, we will perform DFS from each vertex v which is the direct descendant of u. Then, for each vertex

v' reachable by v, if edge $e_{uv'}$ exists, it will be removed. The time complexity for this process is $O(|E| \cdot (|E| + |V|))$, where $|E|$ and $|V|$ are the number of edges and nodes in the graph, respectively. After this, the constraint graphs will have the minimum number of edges and can guarantee a legal placement, which is shown in Theorem 1. Due to page limit, the proof is omitted.

Theorem 1. *After our constraint graph construction, the constraint graphs have the minimum number of edges and can guarantee a legal placement.*

3.2.2 Symmetry-Aware Legalization. After constructing the constraint graphs, we can get a legal compact placement solution using LP in accordance with the constraint graphs. The LP problem can be decomposed into two sub-problems without losing optimality, one for solving the x coordinates to minimize the total width, and another for solving the y coordinates to get the optimal total height. Take the placement with symmetry constraints on the horizontal direction (with vertical symmetric axis) as an example. The x and y coordinates sub-problems can be formulated as in Equations (6) and (7), respectively.

$$
\begin{aligned}
\text{Minimize} \quad & W \\
\text{Subject to} \quad & 0 \le x_i \le W - w_i, \forall i \in D, \\
& x_i + w_i \le x_j, \forall e_{i,j} \in G_h, \\
& x_i + x_j + w_j = 2 \cdot x_k^c, \forall (i,j) \in g_k^p, \\
& 2 \cdot x_i + w_i = 2 \cdot x_k^c, \forall i \in g_k^s,
\end{aligned} \quad \forall g_k \in G, \tag{6}
$$

$$
\begin{aligned}
\text{Minimize} \quad & H \\
\text{Subject to} \quad & 0 \le y_i \le H - h_i, \forall i \in D, \\
& y_i + h_i \le y_j, \forall e_{i,j} \in G_v, \\
& y_i = y_j, \forall (i,j) \in g_k^p, \forall g_k \in G,
\end{aligned} \tag{7}
$$

where W (H) is the total width (height) of the placement, G_h (G_v) is the horizontal (vertical) constraint graph, D is the set of devices, x_i (y_i) is the x (y) coordinate of the lower-left corner of device i, w_i (h_i) is the width (height) of device i, G is the set of symmetric groups, g_k^p and g_k^s are the set of symmetric pairs and the set of self-symmetric devices in a symmetric group g_k respectively, and x_k^c is the coordinate of the symmetric axis of the group g_k. There are two sets of constraints which are topology order (non-overlap) and symmetry constraints. The topology order constraints are from the constraint graphs obtained by the previous section, while the symmetry constraints are directly from the design specification. The y coordinates sub-problem differs from the x coordinates sub-problem in that the x coordinates of a symmetric pair need to be symmetric with respect to an axis (i.e., $x_i + x_j + w_j = 2 \cdot x_k^c$), while their y coordinates need to be the same (i.e., $y_i = y_j$). The LP problems for the symmetry constraints on the vertical direction (with horizontal symmetric axis) can be formulated in a similar way.

3.3 Detailed Placement

After legalization, we can get a legal compact placement solution. In the detailed placement stage, we will use LP to further optimize the wirelength for the given legal placement. The formulations are similar to Equations (6) and (7) in the legalization step, except

that the placement boundaries are fixed to the optimal total width and height obtained from legalization to ensure that the placement remains compact, and the optimization objective becomes minimizing wirelength, which is shown in Equation (8), where W^* and H^* are the optimal total width and height obtained from legalization.

$$
\begin{aligned}
\text{Minimize} \quad & Wirelength \\
\text{Subject to} \quad & 0 \le x_i \le W^* - w_i, \forall i \in D, \\
& x_i + w_i \le x_j, \forall e_{i,j} \in G_h, \\
& 0 \le y_i \le H^* - h_i, \forall i \in D, \\
& y_i + h_i \le y_j, \forall e_{i,j} \in G_v, \\
& x_i + x_j + w_j = 2 \cdot x_k^c, \forall (i,j) \in g_k^p, \\
& 2 \cdot x_i + w_i = 2 \cdot x_k^c, \forall i \in g_k^s, \\
& y_i = y_j, \forall (i,j) \in g_k^p,
\end{aligned} \quad \forall g_k \in G, \tag{8}
$$

4 EXPERIMENTAL RESULTS

All algorithms are implemented in C++ and all experiments are performed on a Linux machine with 3.4GHz Intel(R) core and 32GB memory. WNLIB [21] is used as the unconstrained non-linear optimization solver for the global placement. All benchmark circuits used are from experienced analog circuit designers, reflecting the real analog design complexities. Benchmark 1 is an operational amplifier (opamp), which can be widely used to implement gain, filtering, buffering, and voltage regulation. Benchmark 2 is a g_m-C integrator, which can be found in low-power continuous-time filters. Benchmark 3 is a continuous-time delta-sigma modulator (CTDSM). CTDSMs are oversampling ADCs that leverage noise-shaping. As specified by the circuit designer, all capacitors in the circuit benchmarks are allowed to overlap the transistors and resistors without degrading the circuit performance. The devices in benchmark 1 and 2 include Type I and Type II devices. Benchmark 3 contains not only Type I and Type II devices, but also Type III devices. The benchmark circuit information is summarized in Table 3. In the rest of this section, Section 4.1 compares the placement results with and without device layer-awareness, Section 4.2 shows the routability of the placement, and Section 4.3 demonstrates the effectiveness of the analytical framework by comparing with the baseline algorithm.

Table 3: Benchmark circuits information.

Index	Design	#Devices	#Type I	#Type II	#Type III	#Nets
1	opamp	46	42	4	0	29
2	g_m-C integrator	15	13	2	0	9
3	CTDSM	21	6	2	13	27

4.1 Effects of Device Layer-Awareness

Table 4 compares the placement results with and without device layer-awareness in our analytical analog placement framework, where "NLP" means the placement results without device layer-awareness, and "Device layer-aware NLP" means the placement results with device layer-awareness. We can see that area and HPWL benefits are consistently achieved (on average 9% and 23% reduction, respectively) when we co-optimize the devices occupying different layers during placement. The run-time is comparable with and without device layer-awareness. Figure 8 shows the placement results with and without device layer-awareness for the opamp circuit, where the Type I and II devices are indicated in pink and blue, respectively. The figure visualizes and demonstrates that our device layer-aware placement is effective in improving the layout quality.

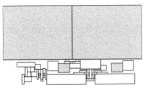
(a) without device layer-awareness

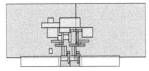
(b) with device layer-awareness

Figure 8: Placement results of the opamp circuit.

4.2 Routability Verification

4.2.1 Analog Global Routing. Since the Type II and Type III devices occupy metal and via layers, they will create routing blockages and lead to fewer available routing resources. From this perspective, routing congestion and the resulting wirelength might be a concern. To validate the routability of the proposed device layer-aware layout scheme, a maze routing based analog global router is developed.

Maze routing is a classic and efficient routing strategy widely used in routers [22–24]. Although it is time consuming compared to other routing methods, the result quality is good due to its optimality for two-pin net. Since there exists a limited number of nets in a constrained area for typical analog circuits, it is preferable to utilize maze routing for designing wire connections. To save the search space, we introduce a detour ratio defining how much detour is allowed. If a legal solution cannot be acquired within the bounding regions defined by the ratio, it will be relaxed to a larger value to cover more routing resources. By constraining the region to be explored, the run-time of our global routing can be controlled efficiently. Meanwhile, to handle the specific characteristics brought by analog circuits, we extend the traditional maze routing by introducing the adjustments as follows.

It is known that the symmetric nets in analog circuits should conform to the stringent topological symmetry constraints. Thus we prefer to route the symmetric nets with higher priorities than the others in our sequential global routing algorithm. Also, as the topologies for two symmetric nets have to satisfy the symmetric constraints, we will treat the symmetric nets as one routing object, similar to [25, 26]. Hence, we consider the blockages confronted by both nets to generate the feasible route.

4.2.2 Congestion Analysis. In our global routing settings, the grid size and routing capacity inside each grid are determined by the metal pitch defined in Process Design Kit (PDK). The number of metal layers used for routing is set to 6, according to the common practice of manual analog layout. This is because our benchmark circuits usually serve as buildings blocks for a larger system, and the higher metal layers can be used for interconnection across different building blocks. The Type II devices in our benchmarks occupy

metal layers 3 to 6, while the Type III devices occupy the substrate, polysilicon, and metal layers 1 to 3. The grids occupied by these devices will be marked as routing blockages on corresponding layers. After running global routing, the results are listed in Table 6, which verify the routability of our device layer-aware analog placement solutions. An average of 18% wirelength improvement is observed, compared with the global routing results on the non-overlapping placement solutions. The run-time of the global routing is very fast (i.e., less than 0.5 seconds), and it is not listed in the table.

4.3 Effectiveness of the Analytical Framework

We further compare our analytical analog placement framework with the Mixed-Integer Linear Programming (MILP) based analog placement engine in [11]. Since none of the previous work considered the overlaps between devices on mutually exclusive manufacturing layers during the placement stage, the comparisons are done in the setting without device layer-awareness. Table 5 shows the comparisons between the results of our analytical framework (NLP) and the baseline algorithm (MILP). In the table, all the metrics are normalized with respect to the results set NLP. The set of results MILP-Q is generated by running the MILP-based placement until it reaches comparable quality as the results set NLP. Another set of results MILP-R is generated by specifying the same (or similar) run-time as the results set NLP, or when the MILP-based algorithm begins to find a solution. Comparing the results sets MILP-Q and NLP, our analytical framework generates comparable (or better) results with the run-time speedup of above 18x. On the other hand, comparing the results sets MILP-R and NLP, we can see that our analytical framework is able to achieve better total placement area and HPWL given the similar run-time (18% area reduction and 13% HPWL improvement on average). Therefore, we can conclude that even when we disable the capability of device layers-awareness, our results are still better than the baseline MILP-based algorithm. Note that for the circuits with a small number of placement devices (e.g., g_m-C integrator and CTDSM circuits), the MILP-based algorithm is effective in achieving good quality in reasonable run-time. However, for medium or large size circuits (e.g., opamp), our analytical framework is much more efficient than [11] to achieve good quality in a short run-time, demonstrating the scalability of our algorithm.

5 CONCLUSION

In this paper, we have presented a device layer-aware analog placement. Different from the prior work where non-overlapping constraints were imposed on every pair of devices, we strategically overlap the devices which reside on mutually exclusive manufacturing layers and are insensitive to coupling, so that the total area and wirelength can be effectively reduced without degrading the circuit performance. We propose an analytical framework to tackle the device layer-aware analog placement problem. We also develop an analog global router to verify the routability of the device layer-aware analog placement solutions. Experimental results show that the proposed techniques can improve the total area and HPWL by 9% and 23%, respectively, and can also achieve an average of 18% reduction on the wirelength after global routing.

Table 4: Results of our analytical analog placement framework (NLP).

Design	NLP						Device layer-aware NLP					
	area (μm^2)		HPWL (μm)		run-time (s)		area (μm^2)		HPWL (μm)		run-time (s)	
	actual	norm.	actual	norm.	actual	norm.	actual	norm.	actual	norm.	actual	norm.
opamp	2973	1	753	1	17.1	1	2370	0.80	498	0.66	10.9	0.64
g_m-C integrator	182	1	73	1	1.2	1	175	0.96	60	0.83	1.2	1.00
CTDSM	57455	1	3129	1	6.5	1	56060	0.98	2580	0.82	6.5	1.00
average		1		1		1		0.91		0.77		0.88

Table 5: Results of MILP-based placement with quality matching (MILP-Q), and run-time matching (MILP-R) our framework without device layer-awareness (NLP).

Design	NLP						MILP-Q						MILP-R					
	area (μm^2)		HPWL (μm)		run-time (s)		area (μm^2)		HPWL (μm)		run-time (s)		area (μm^2)		HPWL (μm)		run-time (s)	
	actual	norm.	actual	norm.	actual	norm.	actual	norm.	actual	norm.	actual	norm.	actual	norm.	actual	norm.	actual	norm.
opamp	2973	1	753	1	17.1	1	3295	1.11	714	0.95	607.2	35.57	4181	1.41	927	1.23	20.2	1.19
g_m-C integrator	182	1	73	1	1.2	1	187	1.03	69	0.95	20.7	17.21	184	1.01	77	1.06	5.7	4.73
CTDSM	57455	1	3129	1	6.5	1	57960	1.01	3611	1.15	20.5	3.16	64472	1.12	3443	1.10	10.5	1.62
average		1		1		1		1.05		1.02		18.65		1.18		1.13		2.51

Table 6: Global routing (GR) results for the proposed analytical placement framework (NLP).

wirelength (μm)	NLP + GR		Device layer-aware NLP + GR	
	actual	norm.	actual	norm.
opamp	839	1	617	0.74
g_m-C integrator	89	1	79	0.89
CTDSM	3591	1	3034	0.84
average		1		0.82

ACKNOWLEDGMENT

This work is supported in part by the NSF under Grant No. 1527320, No. 1704758, and the DARPA ERI IDEA program.

REFERENCES

[1] R. Aparicio and A. Hajimiri, "A noise-shifting differential colpitts vco," *IEEE Journal Solid-State Circuits*, vol. 37, no. 12, pp. 1728–1736, 2002.

[2] R. Kapusta, J. Shen, S. Decker, H. Li, E. Ibaragi, and H. Zhu, "A 14b 80 ms/s sar adc with 73.6 db sndr in 65 nm cmos," *IEEE Journal Solid-State Circuits*, vol. 48, no. 12, pp. 3059–3066, 2013.

[3] L. Kull, T. Toifl, M. Schmatz, P. A. Francese, C. Menolfi, M. Brandli, M. Kossel, T. Morf, T. M. Andersen, and Y. Leblebici, "A 3.1 mw 8b 1.2 gs/s single-channel asynchronous sar adc with alternate comparators for enhanced speed in 32 nm digital soi cmos," *IEEE Journal Solid-State Circuits*, vol. 48, no. 12, pp. 3049–3058, 2013.

[4] Y. Lin, B. Yu, B. Xu, and D. Z. Pan, "Triple patterning aware detailed placement toward zero cross-row middle-of-line conflict," *IEEE TCAD*, vol. 36, no. 7, pp. 1140–1152, 2017.

[5] M. Strasser, M. Eick, H. Gräb, U. Schlichtmann, and F. M. Johannes, "Deterministic analog circuit placement using hierarchically bounded enumeration and enhanced shape functions," in *Proc. ICCAD*, 2008, pp. 306–313.

[6] P.-H. Lin, Y.-W. Chang, and S.-C. Lin, "Analog placement based on symmetry-island formulation," *IEEE TCAD*, vol. 28, no. 6, pp. 791–804, 2009.

[7] P.-Y. Chou, H.-C. Ou, and Y.-W. Chang, "Heterogeneous b*-trees for analog placement with symmetry and regularity considerations," in *Proc. ICCAD*, 2011, pp. 512–516.

[8] Q. Ma, L. Xiao, Y.-C. Tam, and E. F. Young, "Simultaneous handling of symmetry, common centroid, and general placement constraints," *IEEE TCAD*, vol. 30, no. 1, pp. 85–95, 2011.

[9] H.-C. Ou, H.-C. C. Chien, and Y.-W. Chang, "Simultaneous analog placement and routing with current flow and current density considerations," in *Proc. DAC*, 2013, p. 5.

[10] P.-H. Wu, M. P.-H. Lin, T.-C. Chen, C.-F. Yeh, T.-Y. Ho, and B.-D. Liu, "Exploring feasibilities of symmetry islands and monotonic current paths in slicing trees for analog placement," *IEEE TCAD*, vol. 33, no. 6, pp. 879–892, 2014.

[11] B. Xu, S. Li, X. Xu, N. Sun, and D. Z. Pan, "Hierarchical and analytical placement techniques for high-performance analog circuits," in *Proc. ISPD*, 2017, pp. 55–62.

[12] G. Chen, C.-W. Pui, W.-K. Chow, K.-C. Lam, J. Kuang, E. F. Young, and B. Yu, "Ripplefpga: Routability-driven simultaneous packing and placement for modern fpgas," *IEEE TCAD*, vol. 37, no. 10, pp. 2022–2035, 2018.

[13] C.-W. Pui, G. Chen, Y. Ma, E. F. Young, and B. Yu, "Clock-aware ultrascale fpga placement with machine learning routability prediction," in *Proc. ICCAD*, 2017, pp. 929–936.

[14] H.-C. Ou, K.-H. Tseng, J.-Y. Liu, I.-P. Wu, and Y.-W. Chang, "Layout-dependent effects-aware analytical analog placement," *IEEE TCAD*, vol. 35, no. 8, pp. 1243–1254, 2016.

[15] B. Xu, B. Basaran, M. Su, and D. Z. Pan, "Analog placement constraint extraction and exploration with the application to layout retargeting," in *Proc. ISPD*, 2018, pp. 98–105.

[16] T.-C. Chen, Z.-W. Jiang, T.-C. Hsu, H.-C. Chen, and Y.-W. Chang, "Ntuplace3: An analytical placer for large-scale mixed-size designs with preplaced blocks and density constraints," *IEEE TCAD*, vol. 27, no. 7, pp. 1228–1240, 2008.

[17] H.-C. Ou, K.-H. Tseng, J.-Y. Liu, I. Wu, Y.-W. Chang *et al.*, "Layout-dependent-effects-aware analytical analog placement," in *Proc. DAC*, 2015, p. 189.

[18] W. Naylor, "Non-linear optimization system and method for wire length and delay optimization for an automatic electric circuit placer," *US Patent No. 6301693*, 2001.

[19] S. Kuwabara, Y. Kohira, and Y. Takashima, "An effective overlap removable objective for analytical placement," *IEICE transactions on fundamentals of electronics, communications and computer sciences*, vol. 96, no. 6, pp. 1348–1356, 2013.

[20] J. Doenhardt and T. Lengauer, "Algorithmic aspects of one-dimensional layout compaction," *IEEE TCAD*, vol. 6, no. 5, pp. 863–878, 1987.

[21] W. Naylor and B. Chapman, "Wnlib," http://www.willnaylor.com/wnlib.html.

[22] G. Chen, C.-W. Pui, H. Li, J. Chen, B. Jiang, and E. F. Young, "Detailed routing by sparse grid graph and minimum-area-captured path search," in *Proc. ASPDAC*, 2019.

[23] F.-Y. Chang, R.-S. Tsay, W.-K. Mak, and S.-H. Chen, "Mana: A shortest path maze algorithm under separation and minimum length nanometer rules," *IEEE Transactions on Computer-Aided Design of Integrated Circuits and Systems*, vol. 32, no. 10, pp. 1557–1568, 2013.

[24] W.-H. Liu, W.-C. Kao, Y.-L. Li, and K.-Y. Chao, "Nctu-gr 2.0: Multithreaded collision-aware global routing with bounded-length maze routing," *IEEE Transactions on computer-aided design of integrated circuits and systems*, vol. 32, no. 5, pp. 709–722, 2013.

[25] D. Liu, V. Livramento, S. Chowdhury, D. Ding, H. Vo, A. Sharma, and D. Z. Pan, "Streak: synergistic topology generation and route synthesis for on-chip performance-critical signal groups," in *Proc. DAC*, 2017, pp. 1–6.

[26] D. Liu, B. Yu, V. Livramento, S. Chowdhury, D. Ding, H. Vo, A. Sharma, and D. Z. Pan, "Synergistic topology generation and route synthesis for on-chip performance-critical signal groups," *IEEE TCAD*, 2018.

Analytical Mixed-Cell-Height Legalization Considering Average and Maximum Movement Minimization*

Xingquan Li
School of Mathematics and Statistics,
Minnan Normal University
Zhangzhou, 363000, China
xqli@mnnu.edu.cn

Jianli Chen
Center for Discrete Mathematics and Theoretical Computer
Science, Fuzhou University
Fuzhou, 350108, China
jlchen@fzu.edu.cn

Wenxing Zhu
Center for Discrete Mathematics and Theoretical Computer
Science, Fuzhou University
Fuzhou, China
wxzhu@fzu.edu.cn

Yao-Wen Chang
Graduate Institute of Electronics Engineering,
Department of Electrical Engineering,
National Taiwan University
Taipei, 106, Taiwan
ywchang@ntu.edu.tw

ABSTRACT

Modern circuit designs often contain standard cells of different row heights to meet various design requirements. Due to the higher interference among heterogeneous cell structures, the legalization problem for mixed-cell-height standard cells becomes more challenging. In this paper, we present an analytical legalization algorithm for mixed-cell-height standard cells to simultaneously minimize the average and the maximum cell movements. We formulate it as a mixed integer quadratic programming problem (MIQP), which allows cell spreading concurrently in both the horizontal and vertical directions. By relaxing its discrete constraints to linear ones, we convert the MIQP into a quadratic programming problem (QP). To solve the QP efficiently, we further reformulate it as a linear complementarity problem (LCP), and solve the LCP by a modulus-based matrix splitting iteration method (MMSIM). To guarantee the convergence of the MMSIM and the equivalence between the QP and the LCP, we use a series of operations to ensure that its induced objective matrix is symmetric positive definite and its constraint matrix is of full row rank. Experimental results demonstrate the effectiveness of our algorithm in reducing both the average and the maximum cell movements for mixed-cell-height legalization.

CCS CONCEPTS

• **Computer systems organization** → **VLSI circuit design automation**; Physical design; • **Placement** → Legalization;

KEYWORDS

Mixed-cell-height, legalization, VLSI placement, quadratic programming, linear complementarity problem

*This work was supported by Empyrean and the National Natural Science Foundation of China under Grants 11501115, 61672005 and 11331003, and by AnaGlobe, TSMC, MOST of Taiwan under Grant No's MOST 105-2221-E-002-190-MY3, MOST 106-2911-I-002-511, and MOST 107-2221-E-002-161-MY3.

ISPD '19, April 14–17, 2019, San Francisco, CA, USA
© 2019 Association for Computing Machinery.
ACM ISBN 978-1-4503-6253-5/19/04...$15.00
https://doi.org/10.1145/3299902.3309750

ACM Reference Format:
Xingquan Li, Jianli Chen, Wenxing Zhu, and Yao-Wen Chang. 2019. Analytical Mixed-Cell-Height Legalization Considering Average and Maximum Movement Minimization. In *2019 International Symposium on Physical Design (ISPD '19), April 14–17, 2019, San Francisco, CA, USA*. ACM, New York, NY, USA, 8 pages. https://doi.org/10.1145/3299902.3309750

1 INTRODUCTION

Modern circuit designs often contain (tens of) millions of standard cells located at placement sites on rows. To meet various design requirements such as low power and high performance, multi-deck cells occupying multi-rows (e.g., flip-flops) are often used in advanced technologies [2, 11]. Such multi-row height standard cells bring up challenging issues for placement, especially the mixed-cell-height legalization, due to their heterogenous cell structures and additional power-rail constraints, as pointed out in [7, 17].

In traditional single-row height standard-cell legalization, cell overlapping is independent among rows. In contrast, with multi-row height cells, shifting a cell in one row may cause cell overlaps in another row. The heterogenous cell structures could incur substantial global cell interferences among all cells in a circuit. Due to the global cell interference, existing single-row height standard-cell legalizers [4, 6, 8, 10, 13] cannot directly be extended to handle mixed-cell-height standard cells effectively. As a result, a mixed-cell-height legalization method needs to consider the heterogenous cell structures, with more global cell interferences and larger solution spaces. Moreover, the alignment of power (VDD) or ground (VSS) lines must be considered in mixed-cell-height standard-cell legalization. For single-row height standard-cell legalization, such VDD/VSS alignment can easily be handled by vertical cell flipping, for example, the single-row height cell c_1 in Figure 1. However, the vertical cell flipping is invalid for an even-row height cell (e.g., the double-row cell c_2 in Figure 1). During legalization, therefore, each even-row height cell must be aligned to its correct row which meets the VDD/VSS constraint.

In addition, to preserve the quality of a given global placement, an ideal legalization method should minimize not only the average cell movement but also the maximum one [9]; see Figure 2 for an illustration. In Figure 2(a), if we focus only on minimizing the average movement, we may obtain a legalization result as in Figure 2(b); in contrast, if we minimize the average and maximum cell movements simultaneously, we can obtain a better legalization result as

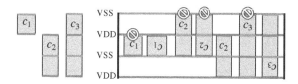

Figure 1: Example of the VDD/VSS alignment constraints.

in Figure 2(c). Both of the results in Figures 2(b) and 2(c) have the same average cell movement, but the maximum cell movement of the result in Figure 2(b) is twice of that in Figure 2(c). In this paper, we aim to minimize the average and maximum cell movements simultaneously for mixed-cell-height legalization.

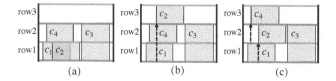

Figure 2: Comparisons on legalization with average cell movement and that with simultaneous average and maximum cell movement.

Recent state-of-the-art works considered the mixed-cell-height standard-cell legalization problem [5, 7, 12, 16, 17]. Wu et al. [17] first investigated the standard-cell legalization with both of single- and double-row height cells. In [7], a multi-row local legalization algorithm was proposed to place cells in a local region. Wang et al. [16] extended Abacus to handle the legalization problem with mixed-cell-height standard cells. Hung et al. [12] proposed a flow-based method to spread cells and placed cells based on an integer linear program (ILP). With a modulus-based matrix splitting iteration method (MMSIM), Chen et al. [5] developed a near optimal legalization method to address mixed-cell-height standard-cell legalization. To guarantee the MMSIM convergence, the authors pointed out that the objective matrix should be symmetric positive definite, and the constraint matrix should be of full row rank. Nevertheless, these legalization methods focus only on minimizing the average cell movement, and do not consider the maximum cell movement.

To minimize the maximum cell movement for single-row height standard-cell legalization, Darav et al. [8] proposed a flow-based legalization method by finding augmentation paths among bins. If the flow of a candidate augmentation path is larger than a preset value (named *maximum cell movement*), it would be pruned. Apparently, their method considers the maximum cell movement as a hard constraint rather than an objective. Further, in order to resolve cell overlapping, cells are moved from a dense bin to a sparse one along paths [8]. In single-row height standard-cell legalization, cell overlapping is independent among rows. With multi-row height cells, in contrast, shifting a cell in one row may cause cell overlaps in another row. What is worse, shifting a multi-row height cell in a bin to anther one may make cells illegal due to a complex domino effect. Furthermore, in order to meet the VDD/VSS alignment constraints, it is much harder for the flow-based method to control cells movement. As a result, it is not easy to extend the flow-based method in [8] to handle the mixed-cell-height cell legalization problem.

In this paper, we present an analytical mixed-cell-height standard-cell legalization algorithm to simultaneously minimize the average

and the maximum cell movements. The major contributions of our work are summarized as follows:

- By analyzing and remodeling the objective function and constraints, we formulate the mixed-cell-height standard-cell legalization problem as a mixed integer quadratic program (MIQP), which considers not only the average cell movement, but also the maximum cell movement, the sub-maximum movement, and the third maximum movement, etc.
- By relaxing its discrete constraints to linear ones, we convert the MIQP into a quadratic programming problem (QP). Unlike the work in [5] which minimizes only the average cell movement in the horizontal direction, we consider cells spreading continuously in both the horizontal and vertical directions.
- To solve the QP efficiently, we further reformulate it as a linear complementarity problem (LCP), and solve the LCP by a modulus-based matrix splitting iteration method (MMSIM). We apply a series of operations to guarantee the convergence of the MMSIM and prove the equivalence between the QP and the LCP.
- We propose a linear programming (LP) based method to further minimize the maximum cell movement in the horizontal direction.
- Experimental results show that our legalization model and algorithm are effective for minimizing both the average and the maximum cell movements. Compared with the state-of-the-art work [5] based on the same set of benchmarks used in [5], for example, our algorithm reduces the average and maximum cell movements by 16% and 64%, respectively.

The rest of this paper is organized as follows. Section 2 gives the problem statement. Section 3 shows our legalization model, which allows cell movements in both the horizontal and vertical directions simultaneously. Section 4 details our legalization algorithms. Experimental results are given in Section 5, and finally conclusions are made in Section 6.

2 PROBLEM STATEMENT

The problem given are a global placement result with n' mixed-cell-height standard cells $C = \{c_1, c_2 \cdots, c_{n'}\}$ with the initial bottom-left coordinate (x_i^0, y_i^0) for each cell, and the height and width of a cell c_i denoted as h_i and w_i, respectively. Each cell has a boundary power-rail type, VSS or VDD. The chip is a rectangular sheet from $(0, 0)$ to (W, H), where W and H are the chip width and height, and R_h and S_w denote the row height and placement site width, respectively. In this paper, the mixed-cell-height standard-cell legalization problem aims at placing each cell to its best position, such that the average and maximum cell movements are minimized and the following constraints are satisfied:

(1) cells should be aligned with correct VDD/VSS rails;
(2) cells should be non-overlapping;
(3) cells should be inside the chip;
(4) cells should be located at placement sites on rows.

Let (x_i, y_i) be the bottom-left coordinate of cell c_i, $i = 1, 2, \cdots, n'$. The problem of mixed-cell-height standard-cell legalization with simultaneous average and maximum movements minimization can be formulated as:

$$\min_{x,y} \frac{1}{n'} \sum_{c_i \in C} (|x_i - x_i^0| + |y_i - y_i^0|) + \omega \cdot \max_{c_i \in C} (|x_i - x_i^0| + |y_i - y_i^0|) \quad (1)$$

$$\text{s.t.} \quad y_i = k_i' R_h, \ \forall c_i \in C,$$

$$k_i' \in \begin{cases} \{0, 1, 2, \ldots\} \text{ if } c_i \text{ is of an odd-row height;} \\ \{0, 2, 4, \ldots\} \text{ (VDD boundaries) or} \\ \{1, 3, 5, \ldots\} \text{ (VSS), otherwise;} \end{cases} \quad (1a)$$

$$x_i + w_i \leq x_j, \ \forall c_i, c_j \in C,$$

$$\text{if } c_i \text{ and } c_j \text{ are in the same row, and } x_i \leq x_j; \quad (1b)$$

$$0 \leq x_i, x_i + w_i \leq W, \ 0 \leq y_i, y_i + h_i \leq H, \ \forall c_i \in C; \quad (1c)$$

$$x_i = l_i S_w, l_i \in \{0, 1, 2, \ldots\}, \ \forall c_i \in C, \quad (1d)$$

where ω is a user-defined weighting parameter for the average and the maximum cell movements.

3 PROBLEM REFORMULATIONS

In this section, we first formulate the mixed-cell-height legalization problem as a mixed integer quadratic programming problem (MIQP), then we convert the MIQP to a quadratic programming problem (QP), and further we reformulate the QP as a linear complementarity problem (LCP).

3.1 Mixed Integer Quadratic Programming (MIQP)

The objective function of Problem (1) is the weighted sum of the average cell movement and the maximum cell movement. We transform the objective as follows:

$$\min_{x,y} \sum_{c_i \in C} \frac{\alpha_i}{2} ((x_i - x_i^0)^2 + (y_i - y_i^0)^2), \quad (2)$$

where α_i can be seen as a weight on the movement of cell c_i. In fact, Objective (2) includes minimizing the maximum cell movement if α_i is assigned a proper value, $i = 1, 2, \cdots, n'$.

Naturally, it would be better that a legalizer can not only reduce the maximum cell movement, but also the sub-maximum movement, the third maximum movement, etc. For example, if a cell c_i overlaps with a macro, in order to resolve the overlap, c_i must be moved out of the macro, then a large cell movement, even the maximum one, is likely generated. If the generated maximum cell movement is much more than the other cell movements, then minimizing the maximum cell movement is meaningless to all the remaining cells. Hence, we handle the above scenario by re-assigning weight α_i to the movement of each cell c_i. An intuitive weight setting rule is that, if the movement of c_i is larger than the movement of c_j, then α_i should be larger than α_j to reduce the movement of c_i. In this paper, α_i is set as follows:

$$\alpha_i = \left(\frac{(x_i - x_i^0)^2 + (y_i - y_i^0)^2}{\frac{1}{n'} \sum_{c_j \in C} (|x_j - x_j^0| + |y_j - y_j^0|)} \right)^{\kappa}, \quad (3)$$

where $\kappa \geq -1$ and is relative to the value of ω in Problem (1). The parameter κ is used to make a trade-off between the average cell movement and the maximum cell movement. If $\kappa \gg 1$, it focuses on minimizing the maximum cell movement; if $\kappa = -1$, it focuses on minimizing the average cell movement. In Equation (3), x_i and y_i

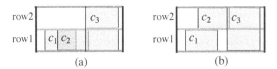

Figure 3: Cells are aligned to the nearest correct rows.

are set as the latest iteration results (coordinates) of cell c_i in our algorithm (to be described in Subsection 4).

We give the handling of constraints and detailed analysis here. First, for Constraint (1a), cells should be aligned with correct rows to meet the VDD/VSS constraints. In order to obtain a high-quality legalization solution with the least vertical movement, a trivial yet effective operation is moving each cell to the nearest VDD/VSS rail. Ideally, after aligning to the nearest correct row, the y-coordinate of each cell c_i is updated to y_i' from y_i^0. If the distribution of cells in a row is locally sparse, then the overlaps among these cells in this row can be desirably solved; in contrast, if the distribution of cells in a row is locally dense, then the locations of some cells in this row may not be desirable. They should be assigned to other rows for which Constraint (4) still should be satisfied:

$$y_i \in \{y_i' - k_i^l R_h, y_i' + k_i^u R_h\}, \ \forall c_i \in C. \quad (4)$$

In the above equation, k_i^l and k_i^u represent the maximum straight down and straight up movements of a cell c_i, respectively. If c_i is of an odd-row height, then $k_i^l \in \{0, 1, 2, \ldots, \lfloor \frac{y_i'}{R_h} \rfloor\}$ and $k_i^u \in \{0, 1, 2, \ldots, \lfloor \frac{H - y_i'}{R_h} \rfloor\}$; if c_i is of an even-row height, then $k_i^l \in \{0, 2, 4, \ldots, \lfloor \frac{y_i'}{R_h} \rfloor\}$ and $k_i^u \in \{0, 2, 4, \ldots, \lfloor \frac{H - y_i'}{R_h} \rfloor\}$. For example, in Figure 3, after aligning to the nearest correct row, the distribution of cells in Row 1 is too dense to resolve the overlaps. As a result, the cell c_2 should be aligned to Row 2.

Second, for Constraint (1b), all cells in the same row are sorted by their initial bottom-left x^0, i.e., $x_i^0 \leq x_j^0$, if cell c_i is on the left of cell c_j according to the global placement result. Furthermore, if cells c_i and c_j are in different rows, then the position constraint between x_i and x_j is free. Hence, Constraint (1b) can be reformulated as follows:

$$x_i + w_i \leq x_j + M(1 - z_{ij}), \ z_{ij} \in \{0, 1\}, \text{ if } x_i^0 \leq x_j^0, \quad (5)$$

where M is a large enough number, say, chip width W. If cells c_i and c_j are adjacent in the same row, then $z_{ij} = 1$; otherwise, $z_{ij} = 0$.

Third, for Constraint (1c), for each cell c_i, $0 \leq y_i, y_i + h_i \leq H$, is satisfied under Constraint (1a). Thus, it can be removed. In addition, since we minimize Objective (2), the horizontal moving of each cell would not be far away from its original position, and there would be few cells out of the boundary. We skip the right boundary constraint temporarily, and then Constraint (1c) is changed as follows:

$$x_i \geq 0, \ \forall c_i \in C. \quad (6)$$

Fourth, in Constraint (1d), if all the cells are placed at their best positions in rows, then we only need to shift each cell to its nearest placement site. We will detail Constraint (1d) in Section 4.

Overall, Objective (2) and Constraints (4), (5), and (6) form a mixed integer quadratic programming problem (MIQP).

3.2 Quadratic programming (QP)

For the MIQP in Subsection 3.1, variable y_i in Constraint (4) and variable z_{ij} in Constraint (5) are integral. In addition, in order to obtain a better result, all cells in a circuit should be considered together instead of row-by-row. Consequently, it is hard to solve the MIQP for large-scale circuits. In this subsection, we relax Constraints (4) and (5) to linear constraints. Accordingly, the MIQP is relaxed to a quadratic programming problem.

In the work [3], Bai proposed a modulus-based matrix splitting iteration method (MMSIM), which is very efficient for solving linear complementarity problems. In addition, Chen et al. [5] applied the MMSIM to the QP legalization problem. In order to use the effective and efficient MMSIM, as in [5], we split all multi-row height cells into single-row ones for the MMSIM solver. Then the mixed-cell-height standard cells $C = \{c_1, c_2 \cdots, c_{n'}\}$ are split as single-row sub-cells $SC = \{sc_1, sc_2 \cdots, sc_n\}$. These single-row height sub-cells should satisfy:

$$
\begin{aligned}
x_{i1} &= x_{i2} = \cdots = x_{ir_i}, \\
y_{i1} + (r_i - 1)R_h &= y_{i2} + (r_i - 2)R_h = \cdots = y_{ir_i}.
\end{aligned} \quad (7)
$$

where sub-cells $sc_{i1}, sc_{i2}, \ldots, sc_{ir_i}$ are split from an r_i-row height cell, $r_i = h_i/R_h$.

After cell splitting, Objective (2) is transformed to

$$
\min_{x,y} \sum_{sc_i \in SC} \frac{\alpha_i}{2r_i}((x_i - x_i^0)^2 + (y_i - y_i^0)^2). \quad (8)
$$

Since an r_i-row height cell is split into r_i single-row height sub-cells and the movement of the r_i-row cell is counted r_i times, we divide the objective function by r_i for each cell in Objective (8).

Next, we relax Constraints (4) and (5) to linear constraints. Actually, for each sub-cell sc_i, after aligning it to its nearest correct row, i.e., $y_i = y_i'$, the movement of sub-cell sc_i in the vertical direction is minimized. Since sub-cells may be re-assigned to other rows to achieve a better legalization solution, we relax the range y_i of sub-cell sc_i from an integer to a real number. That is

$$
y_i \in [y_i' - k_i^l R_h, y_i' + k_i^u R_h], \forall sc_i \in SC, \quad (9)
$$

where $k_i^l \in \{0, 1, 2, \ldots, \lfloor \frac{y_i'}{R_h} \rfloor\}$ and $k_i^u \in \{0, 1, 2, \ldots, \lfloor \frac{H-y_i'}{R_h} \rfloor\}$.

Since the moving range $y_i \in [y_i' - k_i^l R_h, y_i' + k_i^u R_h]$ of sub-cell sc_i is excessive, we can speed up the process by restricting the moving orientation o_i to be vertical (upward or downward) for each sub-cell sc_i. Then, Constraint (9) of sc_i is limited as followed:

$$
y_i \in \begin{cases} [y_i' - k_i^l R_h, y_i'], & \text{if } o_i \text{ is downward;} \\ [y_i', y_i' + k_i^u R_h], & \text{if } o_i \text{ is upward,} \end{cases} \quad (10)
$$

where k_i^l and k_i^u are used to control the range of y_i. Correspondingly, the vertical moving interval VMI_i of sub-cell sc_i is $[y_i' - k_i^l R_h, y_i' + R_h]$ or $[y_i', y_i' + k_i^u R_h]$. The setting of sub-cell orientation is detailed in Algorithm 1 (Section 4). For example, as shown in Figure 4(a), if the orientations of sub-cells sc_1, sc_2, sc_3, sc_4 and sc_5 are upward, downward, upward, upward, and upward, respectively, and $k_1^u = k_2^l = k_5^u = 1$ and $k_3^u = k_4^u = 2$, then the vertical moving interval of each sub-cell is marked by a doubly headed arrow line shown in Figure 4(a), and the corresponding range of y_i for sub-cell sc_i is marked by a square bracket in Figure 4(b).

Next, the mixed integer constraint (5) would be relaxed to a linear constraint. According to Constraint (5), if $x_i^0 \le x_j^0$, and sc_i and sc_j are adjacent, then $x_i + w_i \le x_j + M(1 - z_{ij})$, where $z_{ij} \in \{0, 1\}$ denotes whether two adjacent sub-cells sc_i and sc_j are in the same row. Since all the sub-cells have the same height (i.e., $h_i = R_h$), $z_{ij}R_h$ reflects the overlapping length of sub-cells sc_i and sc_j in the

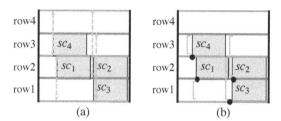

Figure 4: (a) Vertical moving intervals of sub-cells. (b) The moving ranges of bottom-left y-coordinate of sub-cells.

vertical direction. If $z_{ij} = 1$, i.e., $|y_i - y_j| = 0$, then the vertical overlapping length is R_h; if $z_{ij} = 0$, i.e., $|y_i - y_j| \ge R_h$, then the vertical overlapping length is 0. The vertical overlapping length of sub-cells sc_i and sc_j with $z_{ij}R_h = \max\{R_h - |y_i - y_j|, 0\}$. Then, for two adjacent sub-cells sc_i and sc_j, we have

$$
z_{ij} = \max \left\{ 1 - \frac{|y_i - y_j|}{R_h}, 0 \right\}, \text{ and} \quad (11)
$$

$$
x_i + w_i \le x_j + M \cdot \min \left\{ \frac{|y_i - y_j|}{R_h}, 1 \right\}, \text{ if } x_i^0 \le x_j^0. \quad (12)
$$

By Equation (11), the integer variable z_{ij} is relaxed to a continuous variable. In addition, since the VMI_i of each sub-cell sc_i can be pre-calculated, if $VMI_i \cap VMI_j = \emptyset$, then we do not need to consider Constraint (12). For example, for sub-cells sc_2 and sc_5 in Figure 4(a), $VMI_2 \cap VMI_5 = \emptyset$. Otherwise, if $VMI_i \cap VMI_j \ne \emptyset$ for sub-cells sc_i and sc_j, then we would check wether sc_i and sc_j are adjacent.

Observing Constraint (12), it can be seen that this constraint is still hard to handle due to the absolute value function and the minimum one. It should further be transformed to a linear constraint by eliminating the absolute and the minimum value functions.

For two adjacent sub-cells sc_i and sc_j, where $VMI_i \cap VMI_j \ne \emptyset$, there exist four possible cases: (1) sc_i and sc_j are in the same row and have the same orientation, as shown in Figure 5(a); (2) sc_i and sc_j are in the same row and have different orientations, as in Figure 5(b); (3) sc_i and sc_j are in different rows and have the same orientation, as in Figure 5(c); (4) sc_i and sc_j are in different rows and have different orientations, as in Figure 5(d);

For Cases (2) and (3), the relationship between y_i and y_j is known. If $y_i \le y_j$, then $|y_i - y_j| = y_j - y_i$; if $y_i > y_j$, then $|y_i - y_j| = y_i - y_j$. However, for Cases (1) and (4), we do not know which is larger between y_i and y_j. For the two cases, we use the initial y-coordinates to determine the value of $|y_i - y_j|$. That is, if $y_i^0 \le y_j^0$, then $|y_i - y_j| = y_j - y_i$; otherwise, $|y_i - y_j| = y_i - y_j$. We introduce the notation $\ominus$ to denote the operator between y_i and y_j, and let

$$
y_i \ominus y_j = \begin{cases} y_i - y_j, & \text{if } y_i \ge y_j \text{ for Cases (2) and (3),} \\ & \text{and if } y_i^0 \ge y_j^0 \text{ for Cases (1) and (4);} \\ y_j - y_i, & \text{if } y_i < y_j \text{ for Cases (2) and (3),} \\ & \text{and if } y_i^0 < y_j^0 \text{ for Cases (1) and (4).} \end{cases} \quad (13)
$$

Furthermore, since the maximum value of $\frac{y_i \ominus y_j}{R_h}$ is $k_i + k_j$ (where $k_i = k_i^l$ if o_i is downward; otherwise $k_i = k_i^u$), we have $\min\{\frac{y_i \ominus y_j}{(k_i + k_j)R_h}, 1\} = \frac{y_i \ominus y_j}{(k_i + k_j)R_h}$. After these transformations, for two adjacent sub-cells sc_i and sc_j, Constraint (12) is reduced to

$$
x_i + w_i \le x_j + M \cdot \frac{y_i \ominus y_j}{(k_i + k_j)R_h}, \text{ if } x_i^0 \le x_j^0. \quad (14)
$$

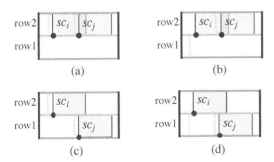

Figure 5: Four possible structures for two adjacent sub-cells i and j with $VMI_i \cap VMI_j \neq \emptyset$.

Finally, in Constraint (14), M is large and $\frac{y_i \ominus y_j}{(k_i+k_j)R_h}$ is a real number instead of an integer. If $y_i \ominus y_j > 0$, then $M\frac{y_i \ominus y_j}{(k_i+k_j)R_h}$ may be too large due to M, and then Constraint (14) may be invalid for resolving the horizontal overlap between sub-cells sc_i and sc_j. In addition, with Objective (2), x_i should not be far away from x_i^0. Hence, we set M as

$$M = \beta_{ij} \cdot (w_i + w_j), \tag{15}$$

where β_{ij} is a user-defined parameter, which is used to control the value of M.

Thus far, the mixed-cell-height standard-cell legalization problem is reformulated into a quadratic programming problem (QP):

$$\min_{x,y} \quad \sum_{sc_i \in SC} \frac{\alpha_i}{2r_i}((x_i - x_i^0)^2 + (y_i - y_i^0)^2) \tag{16}$$

$$\text{s.t.} \quad x_i + w_i \leq x_j + \frac{\beta_{ij} \cdot (w_i + w_j)}{(k_i + k_j)R_h} \cdot (y_i \ominus y_j),$$

$$\forall sc_i, sc_j \in SC, \text{if } VMI_i \cap VMI_j \neq \emptyset,$$

$$sc_i, sc_j \text{ are adjacent, and } x_i^0 \leq x_j^0; \tag{16a}$$

$$y_i \in \begin{cases} [y_i' - k_i^l R_h, y_i'], & \text{if } o_i \text{ is downward,} \\ [y_i', y_i' + k_i^u R_h], & \text{if } o_i \text{ is upward,} \end{cases}$$

$$x_i \geq 0, \forall sc_i \in SC; \tag{16b}$$

$$y_{i1} + (r_i - 1)R_h = y_{i2} + (r_i - 2)R_h = \cdots = y_{ir_i},$$

$$x_{i1} = x_{i2} = \cdots = x_{ir_i}, \ sc_{i1}, \cdots sc_{ir_i} \text{ are from}$$

$$\text{the same cell.} \tag{16c}$$

3.3 Linear Complementarity Problem (LCP)

Since it is usually time-consuming to solve a large-scale quadratic programming problem with many inequality constraints, we convert the QP (Problem (16)) equivalently into an LCP, and solve the LCP by the modulus-based matrix splitting iteration method (MMSIM) [5]. To guarantee the convergence of MMSIM, it requires that the objective matrix is symmetric positive definite and the constraint matrix is of full row rank.

Let $x = (x_1, x_2, \cdots, x_n)^T$, $y = (y_1, y_2, \cdots, y_n)^T$, and $\mu = (\mu_i)_{2n} = \begin{bmatrix} x \\ y \end{bmatrix}$. Problem (16) can be rewritten as follows:

$$\min_{\mu} \quad \frac{1}{2}\mu^T Q\mu + p^T\mu \tag{17}$$

$$\text{s.t.} \quad A\mu \geq b; \tag{17a}$$

$$d \leq y \leq d^u; \tag{17b}$$

$$x \geq 0; \tag{17c}$$

$$E\mu = f, \tag{17d}$$

where Q is a diagonal matrix with its elements $q_{i,i} = q_{n+i,n+i} = \frac{\alpha_i}{r_i}$, $i = 1, 2, \cdots, n$; p is a vector with $p_i = -\frac{\alpha_i x_i^0}{r_i}$, $i = 1, 2, \cdots, n$; $p_i = -\frac{\alpha_i y_i^0}{r_{i-n}}$, $i = n+1, n+2, \cdots, 2n$; and A is the overlap constraint matrix with only four nonzero elements $1, -1, \frac{\beta_{ij}(w_i+w_j)}{(k_i+k_j)R_h}$, and $-\frac{\beta_{ij}(w_i+w_j)}{(k_i+k_j)R_h}$ in each row.

In order to obtain the uniform boundary constraint $\overline{\mu} \geq 0$, let $\overline{y} = y - d$, and $\overline{\mu} = (\overline{\mu}_i)_{2n} = \begin{bmatrix} x \\ \overline{y} \end{bmatrix}$. We have

$$\min_{\overline{\mu}} \quad \frac{1}{2}\overline{\mu}^T Q\overline{\mu} + \overline{p}^T\overline{\mu} \tag{18}$$

$$\text{s.t.} \quad A\overline{\mu} \geq \overline{b}; \tag{18a}$$

$$-I\overline{y} \geq d - d^u; \tag{18b}$$

$$\overline{\mu} \geq 0; \tag{18c}$$

$$E\overline{\mu} = \overline{f}, \tag{18d}$$

where I is an identity matrix, and vectors $\overline{p}, \overline{b}, \overline{f}$ are transformed from p, b, f, respectively.

To guarantee that the constraint matrix is of full row rank, we increase the number of variables by duplicating $\overline{y}$ to $\underline{y}$ with $\underline{y} = \overline{y}$. Then Constraint (18b) is replaced by $-I\underline{y} \geq d - d^u$, and $\underline{y} - \overline{y} = 0$.

Let $E' \begin{bmatrix} \overline{y} \\ \underline{y} \end{bmatrix} = 0$ denote $\underline{y} - \overline{y} = 0$. In this way, Constraints (18a) and $-I\underline{y} \geq d - d^u$ compose a new system of inequality constraints, and Constraints (18d) and $\underline{y} - \overline{y} = 0$ form another new system of equality constraints.

Let $\widetilde{\mu} = \begin{bmatrix} x \\ \overline{y} \\ \underline{y} \end{bmatrix}$, $\widetilde{Q} = \begin{bmatrix} Q & 0 \\ 0 & 0 \end{bmatrix}$, $\widetilde{p} = \begin{bmatrix} \overline{p} \\ 0 \end{bmatrix}$, $\widetilde{A} = \begin{bmatrix} A & 0 \\ 0 & -I \end{bmatrix}$, $\widetilde{b} = \begin{bmatrix} \overline{b} \\ d - d^u \end{bmatrix}$, $\widetilde{E} = \begin{bmatrix} E \\ E' \end{bmatrix}$, $\widetilde{f} = \begin{bmatrix} f \\ 0 \end{bmatrix}$. Then we describe the standard form of the quadratic programming problem as follows:

$$\min_{\widetilde{\mu}} \quad \frac{1}{2}\widetilde{\mu}^T \widetilde{Q}\widetilde{\mu} + \widetilde{p}^T\widetilde{\mu} \tag{19}$$

$$\text{s.t.} \quad \widetilde{A}\widetilde{\mu} \geq \widetilde{b}; \tag{19a}$$

$$\widetilde{E}\widetilde{\mu} = \widetilde{f}; \tag{19b}$$

$$\widetilde{\mu} \geq 0. \tag{19c}$$

For Problem (19), we relax Constraint (19b) by putting it into the objective with a penalty parameter $\lambda > 0$. And a new QP is formulated as follows:

$$\min_{\widetilde{\mu}} \quad \frac{1}{2}\widetilde{\mu}^T (\widetilde{Q} + \lambda\widetilde{E}^T\widetilde{E})\widetilde{\mu} + (\widetilde{p}^T - \lambda\widetilde{f}^T\widetilde{E})\widetilde{\mu} \tag{20}$$

$$\text{s.t.} \quad \widetilde{A}\widetilde{\mu} \geq \widetilde{b}; \tag{20a}$$

$$\widetilde{\mu} \geq 0. \tag{20b}$$

For Problem (20), we have following two propositions:

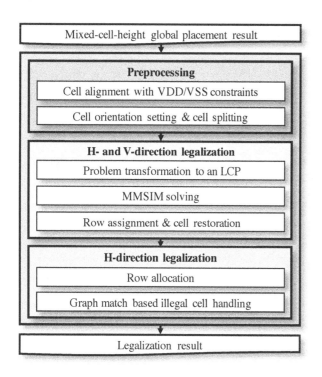

Figure 6: Our legalization framework.

Algorithm 1 Sub-cell Orientation Setting

Input: a circuit with all sub-cells aligned to the correct rows;
Output: orientations o of all sub-cells in the vertical direction.

1: **for** $i = 0 : R_N$
2:     calculate the average density ad_i^u of densities of rows $i + 1$ to NR,
3:     and the average density ad_i^d of densities of rows 0 to $i - 1$;
4:     $r^u = \max\{0, \min\{1, 0.5 + ad_i^u - ad_i^d\}\}$;
5:     $W^u = w_{i,0}, o_{i,0} = 1, W^d = w_{i,1}, o_{i,1} = 0$;
6:     **for** $j = 1 : R_i$
7:         **if** $\frac{W^u}{W^d} \le \frac{r^u}{1-r^u}$, **then** $W^u = W^u + w_{i,j}, o_{i,j} = 1$;
8:         **else** $W^d = W^d + w_{i,j}, o_{i,j} = 0$;
9:         **if** $(1 - o_{i,j-1})o_{i,j} > 0$ and $y_{i,j-1}^0 > y_{i,j}^0$, **then**
10:           $o_{i,j-1} = 1, o_{i,j} = 0$;
11:         **if** $o_{i,j-1}(1 - o_{i,j}) > 0$ and $y_{i,j-1}^0 < y_{i,j}^0$, **then**
12:           $o_{i,j-1} = 0, o_{i,j} = 1$;
13: **Return** o.

is incorporated in Algorithm 1. In Algorithm 1, R_N is the number of rows in a circuit, and R_i is the number of sub-cells in row i. $o_{i,j}$ is the orientation of the j-th sub-cell $sc_{i,j}$ in row i. If $o_{i,j} = 1$, the orientation of sub-cell $sc_{i,j}$ is upward; it is downward, otherwise. $w_{i,j}$ and $y_{i,j}^0$ are the width and initial y-coordinate of sub-cell $sc_{i,j}$, respectively. In Lines 2–4, the ratio of the number of upward cells r^u to that of downward cells $1 - r^u$ are calculated. Lines 7–12 determine the orientation $o_{i,j}$ of the j-th sub-cell in Row R_i.

In the horizontal- and vertical-direction legalization step, we first split cells into sub-cells. Then as described in Section 3, we model the mixed-cell-height standard-cell legalization problem as an $LCP(B, t)$ problem, which simultaneously considers cell moving in both of the horizontal and vertical directions. Then, we apply the MMSIM [5] to solve the $LCP(B, t)$ in Problem (21). If matrix B is positive definite, the convergence of the MMSIM for $LCP(B, t)$ holds [3]. However, the matrix B could be a positive semi-definite asymmetric matrix. As a result, the convergence of the MMSIM for solving $LCP(B, t)$ cannot be guaranteed. In this work, $LCP(B, t)$ in Problem (21) is resolved by an asymptotic modulus-based approach. The matrix B in $LCP(B, t)$ (Problem 21) is approximated by a positive definite matrix $B(\varepsilon) = B + \varepsilon I$, where I is an identify matrix and ε is a small constant. Consequently, the convergence of the MMSIM for solving $LCP(B(\varepsilon), t)$ can be guaranteed.

Our MMSIM-based algorithm is summarized in Algorithm 2. In Algorithm 2, Lines 1–9 give the MMSIM iterations, and each sub-cell is aligned to a correct row in Lines 10–16. In Line 5, we choose the splitting matrices $M(\varepsilon)$ and N with $B(\varepsilon) = M(\varepsilon) - N$ as follows:

$$M = \begin{bmatrix} \frac{1}{\beta^*}(\widetilde{Q} + \lambda \widetilde{E}^T \widetilde{E}) & 0 \\ \widetilde{A} & \frac{1}{\theta^*}D \end{bmatrix}, M(\varepsilon) = M + \varepsilon I,$$

(22)

$$N = \begin{bmatrix} (\frac{1}{\beta^*} - 1)(\widetilde{Q} + \lambda \widetilde{E}^T \widetilde{E}) & -\widetilde{A}^T \\ 0 & \frac{1}{\theta^*}D \end{bmatrix},$$

where $D = tridiag(\widetilde{A}(\widetilde{Q} + \lambda \widetilde{E}^T \widetilde{E} + \varepsilon I_n)^{-1}\widetilde{A}^T)$, in which $(\widetilde{Q} + \lambda \widetilde{E}^T \widetilde{E} + \varepsilon I_n)^{-1}$ can efficiently be calculated similarly as in [5], and β^*, θ^* are two positive constants as in [5]. After the execution of Algorithm 2, all multi-row height cells are restored, and we have the following theorem:

THEOREM 2. *The iteration sequence $\{z^{(l)}\}_{k=0}^{+\infty} \subset \mathbb{R}_+^n$ generated by Algorithm 2 converges to the unique solution $z^* \in \mathbb{R}_+^n$ of $LCP(B(\varepsilon), t)$ for any initial vector $s^{(0)} \in \mathbb{R}^n$.*

PROPOSITION 1. *In Problem (20), $\widetilde{Q} + \lambda \widetilde{E}^T \widetilde{E}$ is a symmetric positive definite matrix.*

PROPOSITION 2. *In Problem (20), if $k_i^l = k_i^u = 1$ for all sub-cells, then matrix $\widetilde{A}$ is of full row rank.*

In this paper, k_i^l and k_i^u are set as 1 for each sub-cell. By Propositions (1) and (2), $\widetilde{\mu}$ is the global minimal solution of Problem (20) if and only if there exist vectors $r, u, v \ge 0$ such that the quadruple $(\widetilde{\mu}, r, u, v)$ satisfies the following KKT conditions [15]:

$$LCP(B, t) : w = Bz + t \ge 0, z \ge 0, \text{ and } z^T w = 0, \quad (21)$$

where $w = \begin{bmatrix} u \\ v \end{bmatrix}$, $B = \begin{bmatrix} \widetilde{Q} + \lambda \widetilde{E}^T \widetilde{E} & -\widetilde{A}^T \\ \widetilde{A} & 0 \end{bmatrix}$, $t = \begin{bmatrix} (\widetilde{p} - \lambda \widetilde{f}^T \widetilde{E}) \\ -\widetilde{b} \end{bmatrix}$, and

$z = \begin{bmatrix} \widetilde{\mu} \\ r \end{bmatrix}$. Problem (21) is a linear complementarity problem. According to Theorem 1 of [5], we obtain the following theorem:

THEOREM 1. *The solution of $LCP(B, t)$ (21) gives the optimal solution of QP (20), and vice versa.*

4 OUR LEGALIZATION FRAMEWORK

In this paper, we simultaneously minimize the average and maximum movements by a bi-directional (both horizontal- and vertical-direction) legalization method for mixed-cell-height standard cells. Our framework is summarized in Figure 6, which consists of three major steps: 1) preprocessing, 2) horizontal- and vertical-direction legalization, and 3) horizontal-direction legalization.

In the preprocessing step, all cells are first aligned to their nearest correct rows while meeting the VDD/VSS alignment constraints by shifting cells in the vertical direction. In addition, each cell is split into single-row height sub-cells. To determine the vertical moving interval VMI_i of y_i for each sub-cell, an orientation setting scheme

Algorithm 2 Horizontal- and Vertical-Direction Legalization

Input: matrices: $M(\varepsilon)$, N, $B(\varepsilon)$; vectors: t, $s^{(0)}$, $z^{(0)}$; parameters: γ, δ, σ, κ;

Output: horizontal- and vertical-direction legalization result.

1: $l = 0$;
2: **do**
3: $\quad x_i^{(l)} = z_i^{(l)}$, $y_i^{(l)} = z_{n+i}^{(l)} + d_i$, $i = 1, 2, \cdots, n$;
4: $\quad \alpha_i = \left(\frac{(x_i^{(l)} - x_i^0)^2 + (y_i^{(l)} - y_i^0)^2}{\frac{1}{n} \sum_{j=1}^{n} (|x_j^{(l)} - x_j^0| + |y_j^{(l)} - y_j^0|)} \right)^{\kappa}$;
5: $\quad$ solve $(M(\varepsilon) + I)s^{(l+1)} = Ns^{(l)} + (I - B(\varepsilon))|s^{(l)}| - \gamma t$;
6: $\quad z^{(l+1)} = \frac{1}{\gamma} (|s^{(l+1)}| + s^{(l+1)})$;
7: $\quad l$++;
8: **until** $|z^{(l)} - z^{(l-1)}| < \delta$
9: obtain the coordinate (x, y) for each sub-cell by $z^{(l)}$;
10: $i = 0$;
11: **do**
12: $\quad$ **if** $\frac{|y_i - y_i'|}{R_h} < \sigma$, **then** $y_i = y_i'$;
13: $\quad$ **if** $\frac{y_i - (y_i' - kR_h)}{R_h} < 1 - \sigma$, **then** $y_i = y_i' - kR_h$;
14: $\quad$ **if** $\frac{(y_i' + kR_h) - y_i}{R_h} < 1 - \sigma$, **then** $y_i = y_i' + kR_h$;
15: $\quad i$++;
16: **until** $i \geq n$
17: **Return** x, y.

Table 1: Experimental results.

Benchmarks	#Cell	#Single	#M	Den.(%)
des_perf_1	112644	112644	0	90.59
des_perf_a_md1	108288	103589	4	55.05
des_perf_a_md2	108288	105030	4	55.86
des_perf_b_md1	112679	106702	0	54.98
des_perf_b_md2	112679	101908	0	64.69
edit_dist_1_md1	130661	118005	0	67.47
edit_dist_a_md2	127414	115066	6	59.42
edit_dist_a_md3	127414	119616	6	56.92
fft_2_md2	32281	28930	0	83.12
fft_a_md2	30625	27431	6	32.41
fft_a_md3	30625	28609	6	31.24
pci_bridge32_a_md1	29533	26680	4	49.57
pci_bridge32_a_md2	29533	25239	4	57.69
pci_bridge32_b_md1	28914	26134	6	26.47
pci_bridge32_b_md2	28914	28038	6	18.20
pci_bridge32_b_md3	28914	27452	6	22.13

After the horizontal- and vertical-direction legalization, there could still exist overlaps due to the row assignment by rounding. In addition, each cell must be aligned to a placement site. In the horizontal-direction legalization step, we first align each cell to its nearest placement site. After that, if cell c_i does not overlap with any other cell, the location of c_i will be fixed; Meanwhile, a cell is marked as an illegal cell if this cell is overlapped with any other cell or out of the right boundary. For every illegal cell, we search all possible empty spaces. Then, a bipartite graph to model the illegal cells and empty spaces is constructed, and the Kuhn-Munkres algorithm [14] is applied to find a best matching for illegal cells and empty spaces, which runs in $O(n_{ill}^3)$ time, where n_{ill} is the number of illegal cells. After the above operations, all cells are placed in the chip region legally.

5 EXPERIMENTAL RESULTS

We implemented our analytical mixed-cell-height legalization algorithm in the C++ programming language. To evaluate the effectiveness of our proposed algorithm, we compared with the method in DAC'17 [5]. The benchmarks are modified from the ICCAD-2017 CAD Contest on Multi-Deck Standard-Cell Legalization [9] by omitting the fence-region constraints and the soft constraints. In our algorithm, the parameter λ in Problem (20) affects the mismatch distances of the sub-cells of a multi-row-height cell. Since the MMSIM is convergent, there will be theoretically no mismatch distance for each multi-row-height cell if the value of λ is large enough. Therefore, the parameter λ was set as 500. According to the works [3, 5], in Algorithm 2, β^* and θ^* in the splitting matrices M and N were both set as 0.5, and γ, σ, and κ were set as 1, 0.4, and 1, respectively, where the convergence of the MMSIM can be guaranteed. With the binaries provided by the authors of [5], all the experiments were run on the same PC with a 2.7GHz CPU and 16GB memory.

Table 1 lists the statistics of the benchmarks and the legalization results. In this table, for all benchmarks, "#Cell" gives the numbers of total standard cells, "#Single" the numbers of total single-row height

standard cells, "#M" the numbers of total macro cells, "Den.(%)" the cell densities of circuits, "ΔHPWL(%)" the HPWL increases from the corresponding global placement results, "Avg. Move. (sites)" the average cell movements measured in the number of placement site width, "Max. Move. (sites)" the maximum cell movements measured in the number of placement site width, and "CPU(s)" the runtimes of all compared algorithms.

The experimental results are reported in Table 2. In the table, "DAC'17", "MIQP" and "LCP" represent the results of the algorithm in [5], the results obtained by solving our mixed integer quadratic programming (MIQP), and the results obtained by solving our linear complementarity problem (LCP), respectively. CPLEX [1] was chosen as our MIQP solver. Compared with the work "DAC'17", our LCP based algorithm achieves 32% shorter ΔHPWL, 14% smaller average cell movement, and 61% smaller maximum cell movement. The reason is that the work [5] resolves overlaps only in the horizontal direction, and if some overlaps among cells cannot be resolved in a row, they are marked and moved into empty positions of a layout in the illegal cell handling step. In contrast, our algorithm allows cells moving in both of the horizontal and vertical directions, and if some overlaps among cells cannot be resolved in a row, these cells are automatically moved into other adjacent rows. This horizontal- and vertical-direction legalization model can reduce not only the average cell movement, but also the maximum cell movement. Since the number of variables in our model is larger than that in [5], our average runtime is longer than that of DAC'17, yet still reasonably. Compared with the results in Columns "LCP", the MIQP based legalization algorithm achieves 2% shorter ΔHPWL, 2% smaller average cell movement. However, our LCP based algorithm can achieve an average speedup of 158× over the MIQP based algorithm.

This comparison further validates the efficiency and effectiveness of our LCP based analytical legalization algorithm.

Figures 7(a) and 7(b) show the respective final layout and a partial layout of the benchmark "fft_2_md2" generated by our LCP based legalization algorithm.

Table 2: Experimental results.

Benchmarks	ΔHPWL(%)			Avg. Move. (sites)			Max. Move. (sites)			CPU(s)		
	DAC'17	MIQP	LCP	DAC'17	MIQP	LCP	DAC'17	MIQP	LCP	DAC'17	MIQP	LCP
des_perf_1	16.21	6.19	6.66	10.86	6.65	6.97	200.82	48.67	48.95	11.23	1672.24	11.75
des_perf_a_md1	3.27	2.47	2.48	6.71	5.93	5.94	607.30	607.30	607.30	2.30	917.02	2.79
des_perf_a_md2	3.35	2.52	2.51	6.77	5.90	5.93	403.86	403.86	403.86	2.19	839.70	6.82
des_perf_b_md1	1.75	1.50	1.52	5.17	4.75	4.77	79.34	51.14	38.45	2.01	905.74	3.64
des_perf_b_md2	2.05	1.68	1.72	5.74	5.22	5.25	198.74	54.75	39.76	2.31	991.30	3.12
edit_dist_1_md1	1.47	1.41	1.39	6.22	5.73	5.79	109.34	107.64	95.45	3.49	1300.40	5.19
edit_dist_a_md2	1.17	1.01	1.01	6.02	5.51	5.51	164.00	164.00	164.00	2.59	1313.57	2.24
edit_dist_a_md3	2.69	1.39	1.48	9.11	6.77	7.08	233.00	233.00	233.00	5.91	1357.08	15.68
fft_2_md2	11.21	8.52	8.78	8.84	7.44	7.54	102.94	62.69	73.60	0.70	69.52	2.89
fft_a_md2	0.98	0.95	0.95	5.03	4.86	4.86	345.50	345.50	345.50	0.69	57.03	0.60
fft_a_md3	1.08	1.07	1.08	4.73	4.54	4.55	109.62	109.62	109.62	0.63	55.56	0.40
pci_bridge32_a_md1	3.61	3.16	3.38	6.01	5.53	5.64	72.48	63.76	63.76	0.61	44.38	2.29
pci_bridge32_a_md2	8.33	4.26	4.38	9.43	7.01	7.14	186.08	121.35	121.35	0.53	54.57	3.34
pci_bridge32_b_md1	2.55	2.23	2.26	6.35	5.94	6.01	322.71	332.71	332.71	0.52	44.03	0.70
pci_bridge32_b_md2	2.80	2.54	2.53	5.92	5.52	5.53	640.12	430.04	430.04	0.50	42.11	0.66
pci_bridge32_b_md3	3.63	3.17	3.17	6.74	6.10	6.10	398.57	398.57	398.57	0.51	43.26	1.58
N.Average	1.32	0.98	1.00	1.14	0.98	1.00	1.61	1.02	1.00	0.67	158.25	1.00

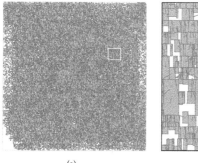

(a)   (b)

Figure 7: (a) Legalization result of the benchmark "fft_2_md2" from our algorithm. Cells are in blue, and movement in red. (b) The partial layout of the region marked in (a).

6 CONCLUSIONS

In this paper, we have considered both the average and the maximum cell movements for the mixed-cell-height standard-cell legalization problem. By analyzing and remodeling the objective function and constraints, we formulated the mixed-cell-height standard-cell legalization problem as an MIQP, which considers not only the average cell movement, but also the maximum movement, the sub-maximum movement, the third maximum movement, etc. Then, the MIQP was relaxed to a QP, which allows cells spreading in both of the horizontal and vertical directions. By substituting and duplicating variables, the QP was further converted to an equivalent LCP. Then the MMSIM was used to solve the LCP efficiently. Experimental results have shown that our analytical legalization method is effective in reducing wirelength and the average and maximum cell movements.

REFERENCES

[1] CPLEX. (2018 May) [Online]. Available: http://www-01.ibm.com.
[2] S. H. Baek, H. Y. Kim, Y. K. Lee, D. Y. Jin, S. C. Park, and J. D. Cho. Ultra high density standard cell library using multi-height cell structure. In *Proceedings of SPIE 7268*, pages 72680C–72680C, 2008.
[3] Z. Z. Bai. Modulus-based matrix splitting iteration methods for linear complementarity problems. *Numerical Linear Algebra with Applications*, 17(6):917–933, December 2010.
[4] U. Brenner. Bonnplace legalization: Minimizing movement by iterative augmentation. *IEEE Transactions on Computer-Aided Design of Integrated Circuits and Systems*, 32(8):1215–1227, 2013.
[5] J. Chen, Z. Zhu, W. Zhu, and Y.-W. Chang. Toward optimal legalization for mixed-cell-height circuit designs. In *Proceedings of ACM/IEEE Design Automation Conference*, 2017.
[6] M. Cho, H. Ren, H. Xiang, and R. Puri. History-based VLSI legalization using network flow. In *Proceedings of ACM/IEEE Design Automation Conference*, pages 286–291, 2010.
[7] W.-K. Chow, C.-W. Pui, and E. F. Y. Young. Legalization algorithm for multiple-row height standard cell design. In *Proceedings of ACM/IEEE Design Automation Conference*, 2016.
[8] N. K. Darav, I. S. Bustany, A. Kennings, and L. Behjat. A fast, robust network flow-based standard-cell legalization method for minimizing maximum movement. In *Proceedings of ACM International Symposium on Physical Design*, 2017.
[9] N. K. Darav, I. S. Bustany, A. Kennings, and R. Mamidi. ICCAD-2017 CAD Contest in multi-deck standard cell legalization and benchmarks suite. In *Proceedings of IEEE/ACM International Conference on Computer-Aided Design*, 2017.
[10] N. K. Darav, A. Kennings, A. F. Tabrizi, D. Westwick, and L. Behjat. Eh?placer: A high-performance modern technology-driven placer. *ACM Transactions on Design Automation of Electronic Systems*, 21(3):37:1–37:27, April 2016.
[11] S. Dobre, A. B. Kahng, and J. Li. Mixed cell-height implementation for improved design quality in advanced nodes. In *Proceedings of IEEE/ACM International Conference on Computer-Aided Design*, pages 854–860, 2015.
[12] C.-Y. Hung, P.-Y. Chou, and W.-K. Mak. Mixed-cell-height standard cell placement legalization. In *Proceedings of Great Lakes Symposium on VLSI*, 2017.
[13] A. B. Kahng, I. L. Markov, and S. Reda. On legalization of row-based placements. In *Proceedings of Great Lakes Symposium on VLSI*, pages 214–219, 2004.
[14] J. Munkres. Algorithms for the assignment and transportation problems. *Journal of the Society for Industrial and Applied Mathematics*, 5(1):32–38, March 1957.
[15] J. Nocedal and S. J. Wright. *Numerical optimization*. New York: Springer, 2006.
[16] C.-H. Wang, Y.-Y. Wu, J. Chen, Y.-W. Chang, S.-Y. Kuo, W. Zhu, and G. Fan. An effective legalization algorithm for mixed-cell-height standard cells. In *Proceedings of IEEE/ACM Asia and South Pacific Design Automation Conference*, 2017.
[17] G. Wu and C. Chu. Detailed placement algorithm for VLSI design with double-row height standard cells. *IEEE Transactions on Computer-Aided Design of Integrated Circuits and Systems*, 35(9):1569–1573, 2015.

FPGA-based Computing in the Era of AI and Big Data

Eriko Nurvitadhi
FPGA Research Lab, Intel Labs
Intel Corporation
Hillsboro, OR, USA
eriko.nurvitadhi@intel.com

ABSTRACT

The continued rapid growth of data, along with advances in Artificial Intelligence (AI) to extract knowledge from such data, is reshaping the computing ecosystem landscape. With AI becoming an essential part of almost every end-user application, our current computing platforms are facing several challenges. The data-intensive nature of current AI models requires minimizing data movement. Furthermore, interactive intelligent datacenter-scale services require scalable and real-time solutions to provide a compelling user experience. Finally, algorithmic innovations in AI demand a flexible and programmable computing platform that can keep up with this rapidly changing field (e.g., [1][2][3]).

We believe that these trends and their accompanying challenges present tremendous opportunities for FPGAs. FPGAs are a natural substrate to provide a programmable, near-data, real-time, and scalable platform for AI analytics. FPGAs are already embedded in several places where data flows throughout the computing ecosystem (e.g., "smart" network/storage, near image/audio sensors). Intel FPGAs are System-in-Package (SiP), scalable with 2.5D chiplets [4]. They are also scalable at datacenter-scale as reconfigurable cloud [5], enabling real-time AI services [6]. Using overlays [5][6][7], FPGAs can be programmed through software without needing long-running RTL synthesis. With further innovations, and leveraging their existing strengths, FPGAs can leap forward to realize their true potentials in AI analytics.

In this talk, we first discuss the current trends in AI and big data. We then present trends in FPGA and opportunities for FPGAs in the era of AI and big data. Finally, we highlight selected research efforts [8][9] to seize some of these opportunities: (1) 2.5D SiP integration of FPGA and AI chiplets to improve the performance and efficiency of AI workloads, and (2) AI overlay for FPGA to facilitate software-level programmability and compilation-speed.

CCS CONCEPTS

Hardware~Reconfigurable logic and FPGAs,
Computing methodologies~Artificial intelligence

KEYWORDS

FPGA; Artificial Intelligence; Big Data;

BIOGRAPHY

Dr. Eriko Nurvitadhi is a senior research scientist and manager of the FPGA Research Lab at Intel Labs. He works on hardware accelerator architectures (e.g., FPGAs, ASICs) for AI and data analytics, with over 30 academic publications and 20 patent filed/issued in this area. His research has contributed to Intel's FPGA and ASIC solutions for AI. He co-founded Intel academic programs on FPGAs (HARP, ISRA). He received his PhD in Electrical and Computer Engineering from Carnegie Mellon University.

REFERENCES

[1] E. Nurvitadhi, G. Venkatesh, J. Sim, et. al., "Can FPGAs Beat GPUs in Accelerating Next-Generation Deep Neural Networks?" International Symposium on Field-Programmable Gate Arrays (ISFPGA), 2017.

[2] E. Nurvitadhi, J. Sim, D. Sheffield, et. al., "Accelerating recurrent neural networks in analytics servers: Comparison of FPGA, CPU, GPU, and ASIC," Field Programmable Logic and Applications (FPL), 2016.

[3] E. Nurvitadhi, D. Sheffield, J. Sim, et. al., "Accelerating Binarized Neural Networks: Comparison of FPGA, CPU, GPU, and ASIC," International Conference on Field-Programmable Technology (FPT), 2016.

[4] S. Shumarayev, "Heterogeneous Modular Platform," Hot Chips, 2017.

[5] A. Putnam, A Caulfield, E. Chung, et. al., "A Reconfigurable Fabric for Accelerating Large-Scale Datacenter Services," International Symposium on Computer Architecuture (ISCA), 2014.

[6] E. Chung, J. Fowers, K. Ovtcharov, et. al., "Accelerating Persistent Neural Networks at Datacenter Scale," Hot Chips, 2017.

[7] J. Ouyang S. Lin, W. Qi, "SDA: Software-defined accelerator for large-scale DNN systems," Hot Chips, 2014.

[8] E. Nurvitadhi, J. J. Cook, A. Mishra, et. al., "In-Package Domain-Specific ASICs for Intel® Stratix® 10 FPGAs: A Case Study of Accelerating Deep Learning Using TensorTile ASIC TensorRAM," Field Programmable Logic and Applications (FPL), 2018.

[9] E. Nurvitadhi, D. Kwon, A. Jafari, et. al., "Evaluating and Enhancing Intel® Stratix® 10 FPGAs for Persistent Real-Time AI," International Symposium on Field-Programmable Gate Arrays (ISFPGA), 2019.

ISPD '19, April 14–17, 2019, San Francisco, CA, USA
© 2019 Association for Computing Machinery.
ACM ISBN 978-1-4503-6253-5/19/04...$15.00
https://doi.org/10.1145/3299902.3311063

Advances in Adaptable Computing

Amit Gupta
Xilinx Inc.
San Jose, California, USA
gupta@xilinx.com

ABSTRACT

Recent technical challenges have forced the industry to explore options beyond the conventional "one size fits all" CPU scalar processing solution. Very large vector processing (DSP, GPU) solves some problems, but it runs into traditional scaling challenges due to inflexible, inefficient memory bandwidth usage. Traditional FPGA solutions provide programmable memory hierarchy, but the traditional hardware development flow has been a barrier to broad,

high-volume adoption in application spaces like the Data Center market. Recent technical challenges in the semiconductor process prevent scaling of the traditional "one size fits all" CPU scalar compute engine. Changes in semiconductor process frequency scaling with the end of Dennard scaling have forced the standard computing elements to become increasingly multicore [Ref 1]. As a result, the semiconductor industry is exploring alternate domain-specific architectures, including ones previously relegated to specific extreme performance segments such as vector-based processing (DSPs, GPUs) and fully parallel programmable hardware (FPGAs). The question becomes: Which architecture is best for which task?

•**Scalar processing elements** (e.g., CPUs) are very efficient at complex algorithms with diverse decision trees and a broad set of libraries but are limited in performance scaling.

•**Vector processing elements** (e.g., DSPs, GPUs) are more efficient at a narrower set of parallelizable compute functions, but they experience latency and efficiency penalties because of inflexible memory hierarchy.

•**Programmable logic** (e.g., FPGAs) can be precisely customized to a particular compute function, which makes them best at latency-critical real-time applications (e.g., automotive driver-assist, ADAS) and irregular data structures (e.g., genomic sequencing), but algorithmic changes have traditionally taken hours to compile versus minutes.

ISPD '19, April 14–17, 2019, San Francisco, CA, USA.
© 2019 Copyright is held by the owner/author(s).
ACM ISBN 978-1-4503-6253-5/19/04.
DOI: https://doi.org/10.1145/3299902.3311064

The solution combines all three paradigms with a new tool flow that offers a variety of different abstractions from framework to C to RTL-level coding into an adaptive compute acceleration platform (ACAP). This new category of devices, Xilinx's Versal™ ACAPs, allows users to customize their own domain-specific architecture (DSA) from these three programmable paradigms.

Xilinx is introducing a revolutionary new heterogeneous compute architecture, the adaptive compute acceleration platform (ACAP), which delivers the best of all three worlds—world-class vector and scalar processing elements tightly coupled to next-generation programmable logic (PL), all tied together with a high-bandwidth network-on-chip (NoC), which provides memory-mapped access to all three processing element types. This tightly coupled hybrid architecture allows more dramatic customization and performance increase than any one implementation alone. See Figure 1.

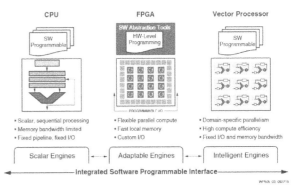

Figure 1: Heterogeneous integration of three programmable engines.

Such a dramatic increase in performance necessitates a similarly dramatic improvement in tools focusing on ease of use. ACAPs are specifically designed to work out of the box with no RTL flow required. ACAPs are natively software programmable, enabling C-based and framework-based design flows. The devices have an integrated shell that comprises a cache-coherent host interface (PCIe® or CCIX technology) with integrated DMA, a NoC, and integrated memory controllers, eliminating the requirement for RTL work.

The new ACAP architecture also yields a dramatic improvement in ease of use. It provides a fully integrated, memory-mapped platform for programming through a unified toolchain. The Xilinx

toolchain supports multiple entry methods for every type of
developer. For example, certain applications (such as AI machine
learning inference) can be coded at the framework level (e.g.,
Caffe, TensorFlow); others can be coded in C using pre-optimized
libraries (e.g., filters for 5G radio). Traditional hardware evelopers
can still port their existing RTL to ACAP via the traditional RTL
entry flow.

This talk reviews the needs driving the change from the traditional
CPU-based compute model, explores the alternative options, and
unveils the Xilinx Versal ACAP, the industry's first heterogeneous
compute platform.

CCS CONCEPTS

• Computer systems organization ~ Reconfigurable computing

• Computer systems organization ~ Heterogeneous (hybrid)
systems • Hardware ~ Hardware accelerator

• Hardware ~Programmable logic elements

• Hardware ~ Programmable interconnect

• Hardware ~ Reconfigurable logic applications

• Hardware ~ Evolvable hardware

KEYWORDS Adaptive Compute Acceleration Platform;
ACAP; ADAS; AI; DSA; DSA; FPGA; NOC; NIC; PL.

BIOGRAPHY

Amit Gupta, Vice President, FPGA Implementation software at
Xilinx. In this role, he oversees all physical designs software
development from RTL to bitstream, databases and HW-SW
handoff automation. Amit's team is responsible for all compilers
within Vivado, an award winning, industry best FPGA compilation
software. With 20 years of overall experience, Amit has held
senior technical positions at Xilinx for nine years. Previously, he

was Director, Backend Software,
for eASIC, Senior Staff Engineer at
Tabula, and held several
engineering positions at Mentor
Graphics. Amit received his master
of science from the University of
Massachusetts at Amherst and his
bachelor of science from the
Indian Institute of Technology,
Kharagpur.

REFERENCES

[1] Versal: The First Adaptive Compute Acceleration Platform
(ACAP),
https://www.xilinx.com/support/documentation/white_paper
s/wp505-versal-acap.pdf", Xilinx Inc., October 2018.

[2] J. Hennessy, D. Patterson, "Computer Architecture: A
Quantitative Approach,: 6th Edition, November, 2017.

[3] "Nvidia AI Inference Platform: Giant Leaps in Performance
and Efficiency for AI Services, from the Data Center to the
Network's Edge", https://www.nvidia.com/en-us/data-
center/resources/inference-technical-overview/, Nvidia Inc.,
2018.

[4] N. Jouppi, C. Young, N. Patil, et al., "In-Datacenter
Performance Analysis of a Tensor Processing Unit,™ 44th In
Proc. Of ACM/IEEE International Symposium on Computer
Architecture (ISCA) Proceedings, pp. 1-12, JJune, 2017.

[5] S. Kanev, J. Darago, K. Hazelwood, et al., "Profiling a
warehouse-scale computer,"
https://pdfs.semanticscholar.org/9395/5f44974ac8b525bcb429f
0a8ddc2e6f0fcb8.pdf, June 2015.

Improving Programmability and Efficiency of Large-Scale Graph Analytics for FPGA Platforms

Muhammet Mustafa Ozdal
Bilkent University
Ankara, Turkey
mustafa.ozdal@cs.bilkent.edu.tr

ABSTRACT

Large-scale graph analytics has gained importance due to emergence of new applications in different contexts such as web, social networks, and computational biology. It is known that typical CPU/GPU implementations for sparse graph applications cannot efficiently utilize the available compute resources [1, 2]. In our previous work, we have shown that significant performance and energy efficiency improvements can be achieved using custom hardware accelerators for graph applications [3, 4, 5]. On the other hand, designing application-specific hardware is expensive in terms of engineering, manufacturing, and maintenance costs. Since FPGAs are known to provide a good tradeoff between customizability and efficiency, several prominent vendors have started offering data-center solutions with FPGAs.

In this talk, we present our recent and ongoing work on FPGA accelerators for graph analytics. Specifically, we propose a template-based optimized architecture that is targeted for both standalone FPGA and integrated CPU+FPGA platforms with coherent shared memory space.

For easier programmability, we propose a vertex-centric template model where the high-level application-specific data structures and functions are separated from low-level hardware-specific optimizations. Our methodology includes source-to-source transformation of user-defined graph data structures so that they can be shared by the host software and the FPGA hardware. We also propose several low-level architectural optimizations to improve both throughput of computation and work efficiency of graph applications. Our initial results show that these optimizations can lead to significant improvements with respect to state-of-the-art implementations.

CCS Concepts/ACM Classifiers

• Hardware~Hardware accelerators

BIOGRAPHY

Mustafa Ozdal is an Associate Professor in the Computer Engineering Department of Bilkent University. He received his PhD in Computer Science from the University of Illinois at Urbana-Champaign in 2005. He worked at Intel Corporation between 2005-2015, most recently as a Research Scientist in the Strategic CAD Labs, Hillsboro, OR. He has served in the executive and technical program committees of several conferences. He was the Program/General Chair of ISPD 2016/2017. He is a recipient of the IEEE/ACM William J. McCalla ICCAD Best Paper Award (2011), ACM SIGDA Technical Leadership Award (2012), and the European Commission MSCA Individual Fellowship (2016). His research interests include high performance computing, parallel and heterogeneous computing, computer-aided design algorithms, and hardware/FPGA accelerators for large-scale problems.

REFERENCES

[1] S. Beamer, K. Asanovic, and D. Patterson, "Locality exists in graph processing: Workload characterization on an Ivy Bridge server," in Proc. of IISWC, pp. 56–65, October 2015.

[2] Q. Xu, H. Jeon, and M. Annavaram, "Graph processing on GPUs: Where are the bottlenecks?," in Proc. of IISWC, pp. 140–149, October 2014.

[3] M. M. Ozdal, S. Yesil, T. Kim, A. Ayupov, J. Greth, S. Burns, and O. Ozturk, "Energy efficient architecture for graph analytics accelerators", in Proc. of ACM/IEEE International Symposium on Computer Architecture (ISCA), pp. 166-177, June 2016.

[4] M. M. Ozdal, S. Yesil, T. Kim, A. Ayupov, J. Greth, S. Burns, and O. Ozturk, "Graph analytics accelerators for cognitive systems". IEEE Micro, 37(1), pp.42-51, January 2017.

[5] A. Ayupov, S. Yesil, M. M. Ozdal, T. Kim, S. Burns, and O. Ozturk, "A Template-Based Design Methodology for Graph-Parallel Hardware Accelerators". IEEE Transactions on Computer-Aided Design of Integrated Circuits and Systems, 37(2), pp.420-430, Feb 2018.

Pin Access-Driven Design Rule Clean and DFM Optimized Routing of Standard Cells under Boolean Constraints

Nikolay Ryzhenko
Intel Corporation
Hillsboro, OR, USA
nikolai.v.ryzhenko@intel.com

Steven Burns
Intel Corporation
Hillsboro, OR, USA
steven.m.burns@intel.com

Anton Sorokin
Intel Corporation
Hillsboro, OR, USA
anton.a.sorokin@intel.com

Mikhail Talalay
Intel Corporation
Hillsboro, OR, USA
mikhail.s.talalay@intel.com

ABSTRACT

In this paper, we propose a routing flow for nets within a standard cell that generates layout of standard cells without any design rule violations. Design rules, density rules for metal fill, and pin-access requirements are modeled via Boolean formulas for discrete layout objects on grids. Formulas are translated into a single Boolean satisfiability problem (SAT). Having constraints on net connectivity and candidate routes, the SAT solver produces legal and complete routing concurrently for all nets satisfying mandatory pin-access and density requirements. A SAT-based optimization engine minimizes undesired layout patterns such as DFM (design-for-manufacturing) hot spots.

CCS CONCEPTS

• Hardware~Standard cell libraries   • Hardware~Physical synthesis

KEYWORDS

Standard cell libraries, routing, DFM, layout, FinFET, SAT, Boolean satisfiability, metal fill

ACM Reference format:
Nikolay Ryzhenko, Steven Burns, Anton Sorokin, Mikhail Talalay. 2019. Pin Access-Driven Design Rule Clean and DFM Optimized Routing of Standard Cells under Boolean Constraints. *In Proceedings of ACM International Symposium on Physical Design (ISPD'19). April 14–17, 2019, San Francisco, CA, USA,* ACM, New York, NY, USA, *7 pages.* https://doi.org/10.1145/3299902.3309744

Introduction

Given a placement of legged transistors, *the routing task for nets within a standard cell* is to connect drains, sources, and gates of transistors by wires and vias according to the netlist. Power/ground (P/G) nets must be connected to appropriate rails. Input/output (I/O) nets must have a specified number of feasible intersections with the upper metal layer. Layout must satisfy

design rules (be DR-clean). Routing should be optimized for DFM and performance. Some layers may require a metal fill [1].

Challenges of the optical lithography enforce various forms of layout regularity [2, 3]. Unidirectional layers without jogs, fixed pitches, and regular metal templates become a common practice, both at base and lower metal layers. In such conditions, solving technologies are used for routing standard cells on regular grids.

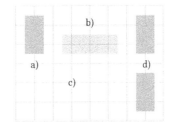

a) Length of a vertical wire is at least 2 grids.
b) Length of a horizontal wire is at least 3 grids.
c) Two vias must be separated by 1 grid.
d) Wire line ends must be separated by 1 grid.

Figure 1: Layout rules obeyed by the router [11].

In [4], integer linear programming (ILP) is used to route standard cells optimizing the via count between metal layers on a gridded layout fabric as shown in Fig. 1. The router [4] supports four gridded design rules (Fig. 1). Another ILP-based approach optimizes the wire length and I/O pin access [5]. Point-to-point (PtP) routes are enumerated and violations of design rules are modeled as conflicts between pairs of routes: two conflicting routes cannot appear simultaneously. In [6], conflicts between PtP routes are used both to model DRs and to prune unfeasible routes to simplify the Boolean satisfiability problem (SAT). In addition, the SAT router [6] supports forbidden combinations of ≤ 4 vias. In [7], basic design rules for a 7nm fabric are modeled as constraints for edges of the 3D routing graph. Mixed integer programming (MIP) constructs a routing from fixed-sized wire segments. A greedy post routing approach adds extra constraints and re-solves the whole problem to optimize DFM. In [8], forbidden layout patterns are hard-coded in a C++ library and translated directly into SAT clauses. The strongest point of [8] is that it allows coding arbitrary strict layout rules. Pin-access is modeled in [8] by forcing the router to create floating terminals. However, a post routing ILP-based net-by-net rip-up-and-reroute can handle very few types of optimizations. More practical multi-net rip-up-and-reroute is used in [9]. Given a layout with manufacturing hot spots, a SAT solver substitutes undesired topologies in a moving window by legal patterns from a pre-built library. However, larger searching windows cause an exponential growth of possible legal layout variants. We can highlight modern routing challenges at the standard cell level as follows:

- The wavelength of optical lithography 193nm has remained unchanged for many years and it is one order of magnitude larger than the feature size of modern ICs. This gap makes design rules non-local and extremely complex because of the tradeoff between density and manufacturability. Regular patterns make lithography easier [2] but conservative fabrics cause area growth [3, 10] that reduces the process profitability. A design rule may involve several layout objects on different wire tracks and layers. Evidently, conflicts between pairs of routes [5, 6] cannot model DRs that involve more than two layout objects, for example, forbidden placements of 3+ vias or forbidden configurations of 3+ wire cuts.

- Optimization of *soft rules of different criticality* becomes vital, especially for DFM. Minimization of layout hot spots increases the yield and increases the process marginality [2, 8, 9]. Post-routing window-based and rip-up-and-reroute heuristics and especially net-by-net approaches can provide only sub-optimal solutions.

- *Metal fill* (MF) is another aspect of DFM. During MF, dummy wires are inserted and signal wires are extended to satisfy the required layout density. MF rules are not trivial. For example, minimal wire length may vary for different combinations of wires and vias around. Window-based ILP algorithms are most common for this task [1, 13]. A limitation is that starting layouts are modified in windows. Ideally, MF should be done concurrently with routing.

To solve the old and highlighted problems, we propose a comprehensive routing flow. Our contributions are listed as follows.

- The routing flow supports arbitrary design rules of any complexity. Rules are expressed via Boolean formulas for discrete layout objects on grids [11]. SAT produces 100% DR-clean layouts by construction. The router creates the necessary number of pin-access points for I/O nets. Special pin-access rules model various blockages and forbidden pin configurations.

- The flow produces routing concurrently for all nets and simultaneously with the metal fill. Layout density rules are modeled by special Boolean patterns.

- We propose a universal approach that optimizes soft layout rules of any nature: DFM, pin-access, density, reliability, performance, etc. We employ Boolean counters and SAT assumptions. Groups of undesired layout patterns are minimized lexicographically according to the predefined criticality. Concurrent routing, metal fill, and Boolean counters guarantee that every group of soft rules gets an optimal solution for the current constraints.

- To the best of our knowledge, this is the first work that addresses 100% DR-clean routing, metal fill, pin-accessibility, and comprehensive optimization as a common Boolean task. Sub-optimal interleaving flows such as rip-up-and-reroute and net-by-net fixes are not used.

The rest of the paper is organized as follows. In Section 2, we start with modeling layout rules as a SAT problem. In Section 3.1, we describe the generation of candidate routes and detail the SAT formulation. Then, we describe pin-access rules (3.2), performance aspects (3.3), routing optimizations (3.4), metal fill (3.5), and removal of the redundant layout (3.6). Experimental results are presented in Section 4. We conclude in Section 5.

2. Layout Modeling

2.1 Layout Patterns and SAT Formulation

In this work, a *layout discrete* is a via or a piece of a wire located on rectangular grid lines. A layout discrete has a fixed shape and a fixed position. A binary decision variable is created for every discrete. If this variable is $TRUE$, it means that the discrete is present in the layout. If it is $FALSE$, that layout discrete is absent. Fig.2a depicts a regular grid S where two wires $S(0,0)$ and $S(1,1)$ touch each other. $S(0,1)$ and $S(1,0)$ are empty regions – the corresponding wires are absent (shown as white rectangles). Formula (1) represents this layout. Similarly, formulas (2) and (3) express the wire "knots" of Fig. 2b and of Fig. 2c.

$$F_1 = S(0,0) \land S(1,1) \land \overline{S(0,1)} \land \overline{S(1,0)} \tag{1}$$

$$F_2 = S(0,0) \land S(1,0) \land S(0,1) \land S(1,1) \tag{2}$$

$$F_3 = S(0,0) \land S(1,0) \land S(1,1) \land S(2,1) \tag{3}$$

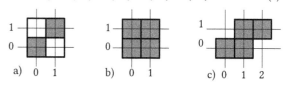

Figure 2: Examples of patterns on a regular grid.

In this work, Boolean formulas express *illegal layout patterns*. When a formula F_i evaluates to $TRUE$ that means there is a DRV in the layout. Thus, for example, in case of (3) (layout of Fig. 2c), presence or absence of $S(2,0)$ or $S(0,1)$ do not matter. If $S(0,0)$, $S(1,0)$, $S(1,1)$, and $S(2,1)$ are all present, the layout is illegal.

In [11], an API is proposed between layout tools and such Boolean formulas to answer questions like: *"Is this layout object correct?"*, *"Is the layout in this region correct"*, *"How can I correct this incorrect layout by addition?"*, etc. In our flow, we do not use this type of API. The strict constraint (4) is added to the SAT problem directly. Since Boolean satisfiability is an exact technology, the SAT solver either finds a routing without DRVs or reports $UNSAT$ meaning that a legal solution does not exist.

$$\bigvee F_i = FALSE \tag{4}$$

In routing, every layout object belongs to a particular signal, power, ground, or a dummy net. In our SAT formulation, a Boolean literal $S(x, y)$ of a fixed discrete layout object is a disjunction of N literals $\{v\}$, where N is the number of nets in the cell (5).

$$S(x, y) = \bigvee_{i=1}^{N} v_i \tag{5}$$

If after SAT, all variables $\{v\}$ are $FALSE$, it means that the corresponding discrete $S(x, y)$ is absent in the layout. If one of variables v_i is $TRUE$, it means that $S(x, y)$ is present and belongs to the net n_i. Other variables of this layout discrete $\{v_{j \neq i}\}$ must be

FALSE. The constraint (6) is added into the problem. Similarly to (6), variables v_i and v_j of two *electrically connected* discretes belonging to different nets n_i and n_j cannot be both *TRUE*.

$$\bigvee_{i=1, j=1, i \neq j}^{N} (v_i \wedge v_j) = FALSE \qquad (6)$$

N is relatively small. A simple inverter has four nets: input, output, power, and ground, plus an optional dummy net for dummy objects. Most complex cells have less than 20-30 nets.

2.2 Design Rules via Boolean Expressions

To model a design rule, we code by Boolean functions all possible layout cases that lead to corresponding DRVs. For example, functions (7), (8), (9) assert *TRUE* when design rules of Fig 1a, 1b, 1c are violated. As for the rule of Fig. 1d, smaller than one grid unit is only zero grid units but there are no shorts by construction.

$$F_7 = \overline{M_v(x, y)} \wedge M_v(x, y+1) \wedge \overline{M_v(x, y+2)} \qquad (7)$$

$$F_8 = \overline{M_h(x, y)} \wedge M_h(x+1, y) \wedge (\overline{M_h(x+2, y)} \vee \overline{M_h(x+3, y)}) \qquad (8)$$

$$F_9 = Via(x, y) \wedge Via(x+1, y) \qquad (9)$$

In our model, every layer has own grid. Grid lines of different grids may not coincide. A *Via*1, its minimal *Metal*1 landing, and its minimal *Metal*2 enclosure are shown in Fig. 3. This design rule, usually with little variations, is common for any technology. We have chosen this simple example to illustrate that an expression can bind objects from different grids. Complex via enclosure rules such as several sets of values in x- and y-directions rules are supported by corresponding grids and gridded layout shapes.

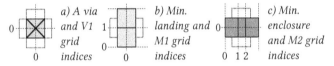

Figure 3: Mandatory M1 landing and M2 enclosure for V1.

In the router, we use the following convention. For a *via layer*, the intersection of grid lines defines the location of a via center. For a *vertical routing layer*, x defines the center vertical grid line; y defines the horizontal grid line where the wire discrete starts; the discrete ends at the next grid line $y + 1$ (Fig. 3b). A *horizontal routing layer* is defined similarly (Fig. 3c). We found that this scheme is most convenient for grids with non-uniform stopping points of wire line ends as shown for $M2$ grid. In such a formulation, formula (10) evaluates to *TRUE* when the via $V1(0,0)$ is present but at least one of five mandatory wire segments is missing.

$$F_{10} = V1(0,0) \wedge \left(\overline{M1(0,0)} \vee \overline{M1(0,1)} \vee \overline{M2(0,0)} \vee \overline{M2(1,0)} \right. \\ \left. \vee \overline{M2(2,0)} \right) \qquad (10)$$

A *bidirectional routing layer* can be modeled by two grids. One corresponds to vertical segments, another one corresponds to horizontal segments. A common grid also can be used.

Note. *We want to emphasize that any design rule can be expressed by Boolean expressions if layout is gridded. Examples of Boolean expressions for different DRs can be found in [8, 9]. More formulas*

are presented in this paper. Grids in the most pictures are uniform and indexed as in Fig. 2 for illustration purposes only.

2.3 Lithography-Aware Rules

Below we demonstrate a design rule corresponding to side-to-side minimal spacing and its related soft DFM rules using a hypothetical example. Shapes of nanometer objects in optical lithography heavily depend on the layout around them [2]. Fig. 4 shows two instances of the same topology (some via V and a piece of metal M) placed the minimal distance L_0 from each other. Assume this topology is not friendly for optical lithography, so the shapes get deformed. L_0 is a strict design rule on side-to-side wire spacing. The actual distance between wires L_1 is smaller than L_0. It makes the layout more sensitive to variations. A random fluctuation may result in a short between wires with a low but non-zero probability.

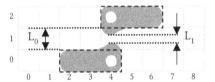

Figure 4: Adjacent layout patterns: $L_1 < L_0$.

The lower wire is extended to the right in Fig. 5. Assume this topology reduces the wire deformation. The distance between wires increases to $L_2 > L_1$. The layout becomes more robust.

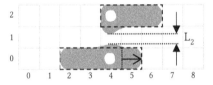

Figure 5: Lower wire extended to the right: $L_2 > L_1$.

In Fig. 6, the upper wire is extended to the left. The distance between wires becomes even larger: $L_3 > L_2$. The topologies of Fig. 4, 5, 6 are DR-clean. However, the last pattern is the most sustainable for process variations. The pattern of Fig. 4 is marked as a litho-unfriendly pattern (a hot spot) with the highest criticality. The pattern of Fig. 5 is marked as a litho-unfriendly pattern with lower priority. The pattern of Fig. 6 is not constrained.

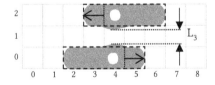

Figure 6. Upper wire extended to the left: $L_3 > L_2$.

Formula (11) models a pattern of Fig. 4. A sub-expression $V(4,0) \wedge V(4,2)$ models two vias, $M(4,0) \wedge \overline{M(5,0)}$ and $M(4,2) \wedge \overline{M(3,2)}$ model line-ends of wires, and $\overline{M(4,1)}$ says that wires are not connected. More discretes are not needed to model this hot spot. Similarly, formula (12) is constructed for the pattern of Fig. 5.

$$F_{11} = V(4,0) \wedge V(4,2) \wedge M(4,0) \wedge \overline{M(5,0)} \wedge M(4,2) \wedge \overline{M(3,2)} \qquad (11)$$
$$\wedge \overline{M(3,1)}$$

$$F_{12} = V(4,0) \wedge V(4,2) \wedge M(4,0) \wedge M(5,0) \wedge \overline{M(6,0)} \wedge M(4,2) \qquad (12)$$
$$\wedge \overline{M(3,2)} \wedge \overline{M(3,1)}$$

3. SAT Routing

3.1 DR-Clean Routing

In this work, routing of nets is constructed from pre-built routes rather than from wire segments. Segment-based approaches [7, 8] require complex techniques to control segmentation, via count, and scenic routing. It is difficult to build a tradeoff with other performance-aware aspects and soft rules. At the same time, for regular layouts, reasonable pre-computed routes provide predicted quality without loss of routability [5, 6]. Routes are limited by a particular bounding box around the terminals. By default, a route may have one wire segment of the highest allowed routing layer and up to two segments per layer for layers below. We observed that finer segmentation does not increase routability much because of limited size of the routing problem.

Candidate routes are constructed as follows. 1) Nets are split into two-terminal connections. 2) A global router selects reasonable connections based on minimal spanning trees. 3) A maze router constructs several candidate routes $\{R\}$ for every signal connection as well as routes between transistors and P/G rails. 4) In addition, routes with default *seed pins* (see Section 3.2) are created for I/O nets. 5) If a technology has *non-discrete contacts*, we use gridded virtual contacts. An additional expression assigns to a virtual contact all physical contacts in a corresponding region. When SAT selects a route with a virtual contact, it also selects at least one real physical contact satisfying design rules. 6) Two routes are marked as conflicting if they create an electrical short or a DRV. 7) Pair conflicts between routes help to prune unfeasible candidates. However, opposing to [5, 6], conflicts are not used to model DRVs during solving. In our flow, a route R_k (13) of a net n is a conjunction of Boolean literals $\{v_s^n\}$, where every v_s^n belongs to the unique layout discrete S attached to net n, where Boolean literals $\{v\}$ obey (5)-(6) and discretes $\{S\}$ constitute formulas (4). If the SAT solver selects a route R_k then formula (13) evaluates to TRUE.

$$R_k = \bigwedge v_s^n \qquad (13)$$

A SAT solver finds such a combination of routes (13) that realizes all required connections and at the same time sets to FALSE all strict Boolean formulas that express illegal layout patterns (4). Thus, a complete DR-clean routing is constructed.

3.2 Satisfying Pin-Access Requirements

Architectures have additional layout requirements [17]. They depend on interaction of DRs, P/G rails, boundaries. Thus, I/O nets must have a minimal number (typically 2-4) of *pin-access points*, feasible intersections with the upper routing layer. For example, in Fig. 7, all vertical shapes except 7c have 2 feasible intersections with the horizontal *metal2*. Pins are shown as they belong to the same net to demonstrate interactions with various blockages.

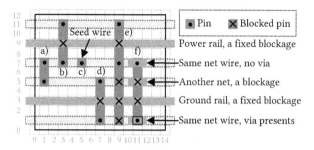

Figure 7: All metal1 pins except (c) have 2 access points.

There are several constraint-reasoning studies [5, 8, 14, 15] addressing this problem. Our router creates pins of the required length concurrently with the signal routing as follows. 1) First, the router has a built-in constraint that every I/O net must be connected to a piece of wire of a pin layer. It can be a general PtP route that just uses the pin layer for routing. Also it can be a special route that connects a transistor with a seed pin wire. 2) Second, extra Boolean formulas define extensions of the seed pin wire forcing them to intersect the necessary number of tracks. 3) Formulas take into account P/G rails and blockages (Fig. 7e, 7f).

As a result, SAT solver creates a required number of seed wires; then it extends the wires to the required minimal length obeying all rules and taking into account pin blockages.

The next section illustrates pin-access formulas for the cell in Fig. 7. (14) expresses blockages at *metal1* grid point (x, y), where objects $V1^{sn}$ are *sameNet* vias, $M2^{dn}$ are *differentNet metal2* wires. Formula (15) expresses a solid *metal1* wire at track x between y_{start} and y_{target}. We use Boolean counters to count blockages on top of pin wires. Here, a Boolean counter $C_\geq(\{p\}, Q)$ is a function of P literals $\{p\}$; the function returns $TRUE$ when the number of $TRUE$ literals among $\{p\}$ $P_{TRUE} \geq Q$. A Boolean counter consists of $O(P)$ AND and OR operands [6, 16]. $O(N_{M2})$ formulas are created for a wire $M1(x, y)$, where N_{M2} is the number of available *metal2* tracks within the cell height: formulas (16) define illegal pin-access cases if a wire comes from the top and ends at $M1(x, 7)$; formulas (17) define illegal pin-access cases if a wire comes from the bottom and ends at $M1(x, 7)$. Similar formulas are constructed for all wires $1(x, y)$, $y \in [1,11]$. Obeying the formulas, SAT will create at least 2 access points for every I/O net or report $UNSAT$ if it is impossible. Formulas for access points > 2 are built similarly.

$$B(x,y) = V1^{sn}(x-2,y) \vee V1^{sn}(x+2,y) \vee \left(\vee_{i=x-2}^{i=x+2} M2^{dn}(i,y) \right) \qquad (14)$$
, where $x = 2*n+1$, $y = 2*m+1$, n and m are integers.

$$W(x, y_{start}, y_{target}) = \bigwedge_{y=y_{start}}^{y=y_{target}} M1(x, y) \qquad (15)$$

$$F_{16}^{up,1} = M1(x,7) \wedge \overline{M1(x,6)} \wedge C_\geq(B(x,7), B(x,11), 1) \qquad (16a)$$

$$F_{16}^{up,2} = M1(x,7) \wedge \overline{M1(x,6)} \wedge \overline{W(x,7,11)} \qquad (16b)$$

$$F_{17}^{dn,1} = M1(x,7) \wedge \overline{M1(x,8)} \wedge C_\geq(B(x,7), B(x,5), B(x,1), 2) \qquad (17a)$$

$$F_{17}^{dn,2} = M1(x,7) \wedge \overline{M1(x,8)} \wedge C_\geq(B(x,7), B(x,5), 1) \wedge \overline{W(x,7,1)} \qquad (17b)$$

$$F_{17}^{dn,3} = M1(x,7) \wedge \overline{M1(x,8)} \wedge \overline{W(x,7,5)} \qquad (17c)$$

For pins, there can be a strict rule that every pin must have at least N access points and a recommendation to have $N + 1$ access points if possible. Another example: four pins cannot be in adjacent *metal*1 tracks if they share only three unique *metal*2 tracks. A unique advantage of our approach is that any forbidden or undesired layout can be coded as an abstract Boolean expression and solved as a strict rule or as a soft rule.

3.3   Performance-Driven Patterns

As we mentioned in the introduction, [5, 6, 7, 8] address total wire-length minimization and via count. However, many other metrics make sense for the performance. Fig. 8 depicts a few most common examples:

- Contact 8a is worse than 8b because of a long high-resistance poly wire.
- Peripheral contact 8c is worse than a central contact 8d between two transistors.
- A contact with two uniformly placed vias 8f is more reliable than a single-via contact 8e at the diffusion side.
- A power rail hook-up 8i is better than the long one 8h but worse than the shortest one 8j.

Poly jumpers between metal wires, long coupled wires also affect electrical properties.

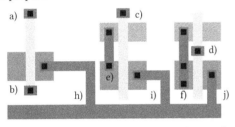

Figure 8: Examples of patterns important for performance.

In addition to traditional wire length and via count, we model performance-unfriendly layouts. Some formulas are made *strict* to forbid unacceptable cases. Others are marked as *undesired*. An expression and even a sub-expression can be assigned to a certain net type: I/O, clock, P/G, regular net, etc. Such formulas are straightforward to express (the cases in Fig. 8) but lengthy enough that we will omit them here (long coupled wires are considered in Section 3.5).

3.4   Minimization of Undesired Patterns

We use Boolean counters to minimize undesired layout patterns. Here, a Boolean counter $C_{\leq}(\{p\}, Q)$ is a function of P literals $\{p\}$; the function returns *TRUE* when the number of *TRUE* literals among $\{p\}$ $P_{TRUE} \leq Q$. Optimizations start after the initial routing guaranteeing that at least one satisfiable solution exists. Given a pattern F_i, all $\{p(F_i)\}$ are found which represent the pattern at different grid locations and a maximal $Q_{max} \leq P$ is estimated.

SAT solvers can specify assumptions: it is possible to assign *temporary* values to literals. A bisection search sequentially imposes several assumptions $C_{\leq}(p(F_i), Q) = TRUE$, where $Q \in [0, Q_{max}]$. It finds a $Q_{min} \leq Q_{max}$ such that $C_{\leq}(p(F_i), Q_{min}) = TRUE$ is *SAT* (satisfiable) while $C_{\leq}(p(F_i), Q_{min} + 1) = TRUE$ is *UNSAT*. The temporary assumption $C_{\leq}(p(F_i), Q_{min}) = TRUE$ is made a permanent strict constraint and the flow proceeds to another undesired pattern with lower priority.

Note. *During optimizations of undesired patterns, layout remains DR-clean because the same SAT problem is solved but with extra constraints. All strict layout rules are satisfied. It is not a net-by-net rip-up-and-reroute approach. A full problem is solved from scratch but with a new added SAT assumption in each run.*

An example in Fig. 9 illustrates the algorithm. An uniform routing grid S is used to route three nets a, b, and c (Fig. 9a). Formulas (1)-(3) act as design rules in this example. Formula (18) expresses an undesired pattern, a line-end attacker on a wire side (Fig. 9b).

$$F_{18} = S(1,0) \wedge S(2,0) \wedge \overline{S(1,1)} \wedge \overline{S(0,2)} \wedge S(1,2) \wedge \overline{S(2,2)} \quad (18)$$

The initial layout in Fig. 9a is clean; it has zero instances of patterns (1)-(3) at any grid point. However, the layout has six instances of undesired pattern (18) in four regions marked by dotted rectangles; it defines the upper bound $Q_{max} = 6$. A bisection search applies assumptions $C_{\leq}(p(F_{18}),3) = TRUE$, $C_{\leq}(p(F_{18}),1) = TRUE$, and $C_{\leq}(p(F_{18}),0) = TRUE$. Fig. 9d, 9e, and 9f depict corresponding layouts. In this example, we can reach $Q_{min} = 0$. By applying $C_{\leq}(p(F_{18}),0) = TRUE$, the soft rule (18) becomes strict.

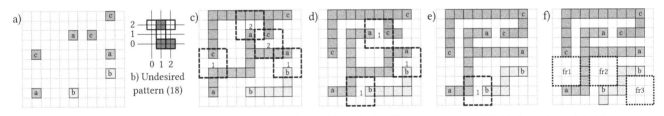

Figure 9: Evolution of the routing. a) Terminals of nets. b) Undesired layout pattern. c) Initial routing with 6 layout instances of (18). d) Applied an assumption $C_{\leq}(p(F_{18}), 3) = TRUE$; no more than 3 instances of (18) can appear. e) Applied $C_{\leq}(p(F_{18}), 1) = TRUE$; no more than 1 instance of (18) can appear. f) Pattern (18) is forbidden; in addition, 3 fill regions (fr) are shown (see Section 3.5).

3.5 Metal Fill Insertion

During metal fill (MF), dummy wires are inserted. Signal wires can also be extended to achieve the required density. In our flow, density rules are solved together with the signal routing. A large amount of inserted dummy wires may affect electrical properties [13]. Extra soft rules control the electrical quality of layout.

A Boolean counter $C_<(\{S\}, D)$ returns $TRUE$ when less than D literals $\{S\}$ are $TRUE$. Using the counter, we can specify a target wire density for an arbitrary region. A density rule (19) is shown in Fig. 10; any region 2x2 must have at least one wire, i.e. when F_{19} is $TRUE$ it is illegal. Regions are larger in real cases. Two more rules forbid a hole 1x1 (20) and a single wire 1x1 (21). With these constraints, any post-routing MF flow would not avoid the undesired pattern (18) in a region *fr2* in Fig. 9f. Fig. 10 depicts an optimal layout re-solved with strict rules (1)-(3) and (18)-(21). A soft pattern (22) in Fig. 10 models undesired long coupled wires but does not affect this example. Formula for (22) is omitted.

$$F_{19} = C_<(S(0,0), S(0,1), S(1,0), S(1,1), 1) \qquad (19)$$

$$F_{20} = S(1,0) \wedge S(0,1) \wedge \overline{S(1,1)} \wedge S(2,1) \wedge S(1,2) \qquad (20)$$

$$F_{21} = \overline{S(1,0)} \wedge \overline{S(0,1)} \wedge S(1,1) \wedge \overline{S(2,1)} \wedge \overline{S(1,2)} \qquad (21)$$

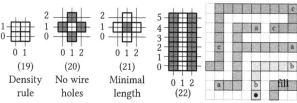

Figure 10: Signal routing with metal fill.

3.6 Removal of Redundant Layout

Even in constrained layouts, it is quite usual when discretes do not violate DRs and do not influence any quality constraints. If a decision variable does not affect anything, SAT solvers do not prefer 0 or 1. Useless *active fill* may appear, for example, such as a wire *b* marked by the dot "●" in Fig. 10. A final SAT procedure eliminates redundant layout objects as follows.

V are all literals which belong to layout discretes. The task is to find literals $V' \subseteq V$ which are superfluously present. V is separated into three groups. Group V_1 contains all literals which are $FALSE$. Literals $TRUE$ which belong to selected PtP routes (13) constitute group V_2. Remaining $TRUE$ literals come into group V_3. These V_3 are potentially superfluous layout discretes. Literals V_1 are made constant $FALSE$ to prohibit the appearance of new objects on the next SAT runs. Literals V_2 are made constant $TRUE$ to fix the signal routing.

A heuristic starts. On the first iteration, all $v_i \in V_3$ are *temporary* assigned to $FALSE$. SAT solver runs. It either finds a new solution without these layout discretes or reports $UNSAT$. $UNSAT$ means that some literals are mandatory. In this case, V_3 is randomly split into equal groups V_3' and V_3'' and the procedure repeats for the new groups. If necessary, a bisection algorithm continues to split literals. A splitting stops when the solver finds

a satisfiable solution; then current literals are set to constant $FALSE$. A splitting also stops when a group has *only one* literal and SAT solver still reports $UNSAT$. This is a mandatory piece of layout, and the literal is set to constant $TRUE$. After the procedure, all literals V become either constant $TRUE$ or constant $FALSE$.

Redundant signal wires introduce extra capacitance and should be removed before others. In our flow, redundant routes are actually eliminated in 3 stages. *Stage1*: Signal antennas are examined while P/G and dummy objects are not constrained – new dummy wires may appear and P/G wires may be extended. *Stage2*: Signal routing is fixed; P/G antennas are examined while dummy layout is not constrained. *Stage3*: Signal and P/G wires are fixed; dummy layout is examined. Experiments demonstrated that *random* bisection of literals into equal groups V_3' and V_3'' works well. All *custom* "smart" separation techniques resulted in similar layouts.

Note. *The procedure leaves the layout DR-clean and optimized because the same SAT problem is solved with all design rules and quality constraints. The SAT verifies removal of every discrete. Constraints trim useless layout incrementally.*

4. Experimental Results

We have implemented our algorithm in C++ and tested it using a commercial 10nm standard cell library [18]. We used one core of Intel® Xeon® CPU 3.00GHz and an industrial single-core SAT solver. In this experiment, results are presented for routing. Both transistor legging and placement are beyond the scope of this work. Implementation details of the placer are presented in [19].

Table 1 contains results for most complex combinational and sequential cells from the library. All cells by construction are DR-clean and have the required number of pin-access points. Cell were optimized for DFM, performance, and power. In Table 1, *"#routes"* is the number of feasible candidates that reached the SAT stage. Peak values are shown for *"#literals"* and *"#clauses"*.

"SAT runtime" represents accumulated runtime spent for initial routing, minimization of undesired patterns, and antenna removal. SAT runtime did not dominate in the reported runs. The rest of the runtime was spent for generation of candidate routes, detection of pair conflicts between candidates, pruning of unfeasible routes, optimization of formulas, and building the SAT problem. *"Total runtime"* is quite practical. All cells were routed in minutes. A mask designer would spend several days to create all these cells of the same quality.

Patterns for design rules and for DFM hot spots are relatively compact. Pin-access patterns use a full cell height. Density-, electrical-, and performance-aware patterns are the most geometrically extended. However, we did not see that size of formulas affected the SAT runtime. For reasons of proprietary information, we cannot show commercial layouts and expose design rules. However, we can report that in this experiment 46 types of soft rules for DFM, power, and performance were separated onto 15 groups and optimized group by group by predefined criticality.

Table 1. Table 1. Routing results for combinational and sequential cells from a 10 nm standard cell library [18].

Cell type	#transistors	#nets	#routes	#literals	#clauses	Total runtime, m:ss.	SAT runtime, m:ss.
XOR	13	8	2,533	486,338	1,217,752	1:14	0:06
2-to-1 multiplexer	13	10	1,677	519,607	776,481	0:57	0:07
Half adder	18	12	2,002	681,392	1,144,917	1:37	0:12
High-strength AND-OR	22	13	1,180	679,452	614,128	0:43	0:04
Flip-flop	28	16	3,822	982,610	1,851,459	2:56	0:32
Full adder	32	17	3,797	1,236,482	2,713,914	5:45	2:14
Scanable Flip-flop	38	25	4,160	1,826,160	3,266,194	6:19	1:00

To test an alternative routing approach, we emulated [5] and [6] in our implementation. To do this, we modeled as pair conflicts between routes: shorts between wires, forbidden pairs of vias, and end-to-end wire spacing rules. All other manufacturing rules, DFM and MF rules were disabled inasmuch [5, 6] originally support only pair conflicts between routes and simple via rules. As expected, generated cells had multiple DR- and DFM-violations. These results demonstrate that our approach gives clear added value in industrial settings.

5. Conclusion

We presented a routing flow at the standard cell level. The flow uses a tandem approach of accurate SAT solving and modeling rules via Boolean formulas. Design rules and pin-access constraints are correct by construction. The router uses Boolean counters to produce optimized layout for DFM, performance, wire length, via count, and other soft rules. In addition, we presented examples of Boolean expressions for pin-access rules, density rules, DFM-aware rules, and for several design rules. To the best of our knowledge, this is the first work that address simultaneous DR-clean routing, metal fill, pin-access problem, comprehensive routing optimizations, and antenna removal by solving a single Boolean formulation. Runtime and quality of layouts make the approach practical for industrial standard cell design. It has been successfully applied to 22nm, 14nm, 10nm, and 7nm commercial libraries. The capacity of the approach grows with the regularity of every new technology node. In our manufacturing organization, generated layouts are delivered to mask designers. Usually, low-priority cells are accepted for the production without modifications. High-priority cells, those that are utilized in designs most frequently, are sometimes further improved manually, but using the synthesized layout as a starting point.

References

[1] Y. Lin, B. Yu, D. Z. Pan, High performance dummy fill insertion with coupling and uniformity constraints, Design Automation Conference, June 7-11, 2015.

[2] T. Jhaveri, et al., Co-optimization of circuits, layout and lithography for predictive technology scaling beyond gratings, IEEE Tran. on CAD of ICs and S. 29(4), May 2010, pp. 509-527.

[3] V. D. Bem, P. Butzen, F. S. Marranghello, A. I. Reis, R.P. Ribas, Impact and optimization of lithography-aware regular layout in digital circuit design, Int. Conf. on Comp. Design: VLSI in Computers and Proc., 2011, pp. 279-284

[4] H.-J. Lu, et al., Practical ILP-based routing of standard cells, Conference on Design, Automation and Test in Europe, 2016.

[5] Wei Ye, et al., Standard cell layout regularity and pin access optimization considering middle-of-line, Great Lakes Symposium on VLSI, 2015, pp. 289-294.

[6] N. Ryzhenko, S. Burns, Standard cell routing via Boolean satisfiability, Design Automation Conf., DAC 2012, pp. 603–612.

[7] P. Cremer, S. Hougardy, J. Schneider, J. Silvanus, Automatic Cell Layout in the 7nm Era, ISPD, USA, March 19-22, 2017.

[8] J. Cortadella, J. Petit, S. Gomez, F. Moll, A Boolean rule-based approach for manufacturability-aware cell routing, IEEE Trans. On CAD, Vol. 33, No. 3, pp. 409-422, March 2014.

[9] F. Yang, Y. Cai, Q. Zhou, J. Hu, SAT based multi-net rip-up-and-reroute for manufacturing hotspot removal, Conference on Design, Automation and Test in Europe, DATE 2010.

[10] N. Ryzhenko, S. Burns, Physical synthesis onto a layout fabric with regular diffusion and polysilicon geometries, The 48th Design Automation Conference, June 5–9, DAC 2011.

[11] G. Suto, Rule agnostic routing by using design fabrics, Design Automation Conference, June 3–7, 2012.

[12] W. C. Tam, S. Blanton, To DFM or not to DFM? The 48th Design Automation Conference, June 5-9, 2011, pp. 65-70.

[13] H. Xiang, L. Deng, R. Puri, K.-Y. Chao, M. D. Wong, Fast dummy-fill density analysis with coupling constraints, IEEE Transactions on CAD, vol. 27, no. 4, pp. 633-642, 2008.

[14] X. Xu, B. Cline, G. Yeric, B. Yu, and D. Z. Pan, Self-aligned double patterning aware pin access and standard cell layout co-optimization, Int. Symp. on Physical Design, USA, 2014.

[15] X. Xu, Y. Lin, V. Livramento, D. Z. Pan, Concurrent pin access optimization for unidirectional routing, The 54th Design Automation Conference, USA, June 18–22, 2017.

[16] C. E. Shannon, A symbolic analysis of relay and switching circuits. Thesis, MIT, Dept. of Electrical Engineering, 1940.

[17] S. Bykov, N. Ryzhenko, A. Sorokin, Automated solution for preventing design rules violations at abutment stage for standard cells synthesis flow, Proc. of the 14th IEEE East-West Design & Test Symposium, Armenia, October 14-17, 2016.

[18] X. Wang, et al., Design-technology co-optimization of standard cell libraries on Intel 10nm process, 2018 IEEE International Electron Devices Meeting, San Francisco, USA, December 1-5, 2018.

[19] A. Sorokin, N. Ryzhenko, SAT-Based Placement Adjustment of FinFETs inside Unroutable Standard Cells Targeting Feasible DRC-Clean Routing, In Proceedings of the 29th ACM Great Lakes Symposium on VLSI (GLSVLSI'19), May 9 – 11, Washington, D.C., USA.

PSION: Combining Logical Topology and Physical Layout Optimization for Wavelength-Routed ONoCs

Alexandre Truppel
Faculdade de Engenharia,
Universidade do Porto
Porto, Portugal
alex.truppel@fe.up.pt

Tsun-Ming Tseng
Chair of Electronic Design
Automation, TUM
München, Germany
tsun-ming.tseng@tum.de

Davide Bertozzi
University of Ferrara
Ferrara, Italy
davide.bertozzi@unife.it

José Carlos Alves
Faculdade de Engenharia,
Universidade do Porto
Porto, Portugal
jca@fe.up.pt

Ulf Schlichtmann
Chair of Electronic Design
Automation, TUM
München, Germany
ulf.schlichtmann@tum.de

ABSTRACT

Optical Networks-on-Chip (ONoCs) are a promising solution for high-performance multi-core integration with better latency and bandwidth than traditional Electrical NoCs. Wavelength-routed ONoCs (WRONoCs) offer yet additional performance guarantees. However, WRONoC design presents new EDA challenges which have not yet been fully addressed. So far, most topology analysis is abstract, i.e., overlooks layout concerns, while for layout the tools available perform Place & Route (P&R) but no topology optimization. Thus, a need arises for a novel optimization method combining both aspects of WRONoC design. In this paper such a method, PSION, is laid out. When compared to the state-of-the-art design procedure, results show a 1.8× reduction in maximum optical insertion loss.

CCS CONCEPTS

• **Theory of computation → Integer programming**; • **Hardware → Emerging optical and photonic technologies**.

KEYWORDS

optical networks-on-chip; silicon photonics; physical layout; design optimization; placement & routing

ACM Reference Format:
Alexandre Truppel, Tsun-Ming Tseng, Davide Bertozzi, José Carlos Alves, and Ulf Schlichtmann. 2019. PSION: Combining Logical Topology and Physical Layout Optimization for Wavelength-Routed ONoCs. In *2019 International Symposium on Physical Design (ISPD '19), April 14–17, 2019, San Francisco, CA, USA*. ACM, New York, NY, USA, 8 pages. https://doi.org/10.1145/3299902.3309747

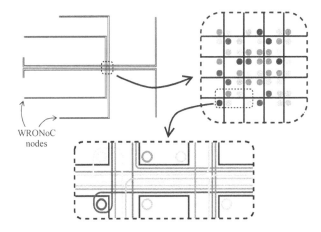

Figure 1: Final design of a WRONoC router for 8 nodes given by PSION. A portion of some message paths is shown (color indicates wavelength).

1 INTRODUCTION

Optical Networks-on-Chip (ONoCs) have been proposed as a solution for the ever-increasing integration requirements of large System-on-Chip designs. Compared to traditional Electrical Networks-on-Chip, ONoCs present not only lower dynamic power consumption but also extremely low signal delay and higher bandwidth [9].

The use of light as opposed to electrical signals to send information between network nodes requires the following four main components on the optical routing plane: 1) *modulators* to convert electrical signals into optical signals at every node (electrical-optical interface) of the optical network, 2) *demodulators* to do the opposite, 3) *waveguides* acting as optical wires and 4) *optical routing elements* to transfer optical signals between waveguides [7].

ONoCs can be organized into two main categories: **1)** *active networks* [3, 12, 17] and **2)** *passive networks*. Active networks require a control layer for routing. Passive networks use routing elements which resonate with different frequencies such that a message is passively routed according to the wavelength of the carrier light. Hence, a message's path is completely defined, at design time, by its origin

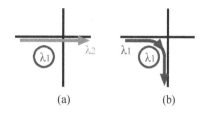

Figure 2: Wavelength routing using an MRR. (a) The light signal is not routed because it has a different wavelength than the MRR. (b) The light signal is routed through the MRR to another waveguide.

and wavelength alone (Figure 1 shows an example of wavelength routing). Thus, passive ONoCs are also termed Wavelength-Routed ONoCs (WRONoCs) [8]. This eliminates network delay resulting from path setup and dynamic power consumption required for the extra control layer.

Multiple light sources of different wavelengths can be used to transmit separate information streams on the same waveguide without interference (wavelength-division multiplexing). This enables conflict-free communications with increased bandwidth. The only requirement is to make sure at design time that no two messages with the same wavelength are allowed to share the same waveguides.

The optical switching element in ONoCs is the Micro-Ring Resonator (MRR). It has a circular silicon structure whose radius defines the resonance frequency. A light signal with a certain wavelength propagating on a waveguide close to an MRR with a matching resonance frequency will be coupled to the MRR and moved onto another waveguide also close to that MRR [10]. Figure 2 shows an example of this behaviour.

The design of a WRONoC router is an optimization process with *two aspects* to consider: the logical topology and the physical layout of the router. The former assigns a wavelength to each message and each MRR and also connects the nodes through waveguides and MRRs such that the communication matrix, which specifies the communication requirements between nodes, is fulfilled. The latter optimally places and routes those elements on the optical plane while considering the physical positions of the nodes and constraints related to the physical placement of the waveguides.

So far both aspects have only been considered separately or with restrictions. Various works have presented specific topologies with few concerns about their layout [7, 13, 14]. Ramini et al. [11] present a topology designed in tandem with placement constraints, yet it results from a manual optimization effort for one set of node positions. Ortín-Obón et al. [9] take into consideration physical constraints, but analyze only the ring topology. Few attempt to optimize for non-complete communication matrices [1, 5]. P&R tools to optimize the second aspect have been developed [2, 15, 16], but all take a topology as input, forcing the designer to choose the topology beforehand.

However, neither aspect can be considered in isolation, as each influences the other [11, 13, 15]. During generation of the logical topology we are unable to accurately predict important physical characteristics, e.g. the number of waveguide crossings, of the final

design after P&R. Furthermore, during P&R, if the logical topology has already been chosen and fixed, any subsequent optimization is being done only around a local minimum of the solution space.

Ideally, a design tool would take as inputs the communication matrix and the physical positions of the nodes and, by working on both aspects simultaneously, produce a fully-optimized fully-custom logical topology and matching physical layout [13]. In reality, the problem space of such an optimization is discouragingly vast for any but the simplest cases. Thus, in this paper we propose and solve a constrained version of the complete problem. In this version – PSION – a physical layout template is also given as an input to the optimization. The template mainly consists of MRR placeholders and waveguides already placed and routed on the optical plane, and connects all nodes.

We define the optimization problem in Section 2. Physical layout templates are described in Section 3 and the Mixed Integer Programming (MIP) model used to optimize them is presented in Section 4. Section 5 explains a fast technique to verify the model's feasibility and Section 6 then proposes a 3-step algorithm to efficiently solve it. Finally, Section 7 reveals three layout templates and tests them against the state-of-the-art P&R PROTON+ [15] and PlanarONoC [2] tools.

2 WRONOC DESIGN PROBLEM

We formally define the optimization problem for the design of WRONoC routers as follows:

Input data:

- Communication matrix: a square binary matrix $CM_{i,j} \in \mathbb{R}^{N \times N}$ with N equal to the number of nodes and where $CM_{i,j} = 1$ if node i sends a message to node j.
- Physical positions of the modulators and demodulators of each node on the optical plane.
- Technology parameters: power loss values.

Output data:

- Wavelength of each message and MRR.
- Placement of each MRR.
- Routing of each waveguide.

Minimization objectives. Their choice depends on the technology and the needs of the design. We consider **1)** number of wavelengths, **2)** message insertion loss and **3)** number of MRRs, as in previous publications [9–11, 13–15]. With PSION, the weighting coefficient for each objective can be freely adjusted to meet different designer demands.

Message insertion loss is the sum of seven types of losses: **1)** crossing loss, **2)** drop loss, **3)** through loss, **4)** bending loss, **5)** propagation loss, **6)** modulator loss and **7)** demodulator loss [6, 15]. We consider all except the last two, which are constant and equal for all messages and thus can be ignored from an optimization perspective.

3 PHYSICAL LAYOUT TEMPLATE

We consider a constrained version of the complete problem, where an extra input is required. This input, called a **physical layout template**, consists of a collection of WRONoC router elements

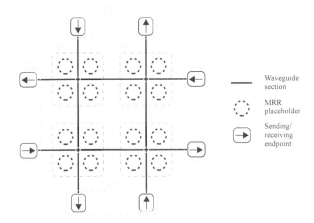

Figure 3: Generalizing the 4x4 GWOR topology [14] using endpoints, GRUs and waveguide sections.

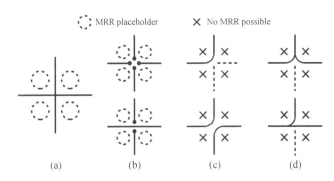

Figure 4: Internal structure of a GRU. (a) 4 MRR placeholders and a crossing. (b) Avoiding the crossing, when possible (c) Valid corner bending states. (d) Invalid corner bending states.

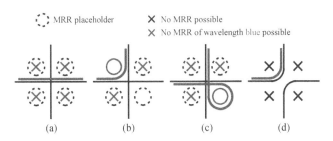

Figure 5: Routing possibilities through a GRU. (a) Direct path. (b)(c) Routing through an MRR. (d) Routing through a bend.

(modulators, demodulators, waveguides and MRR placeholders) already placed and routed on the optical plane.

The role of the solver with this new input is to optimally route the messages defined in the communication matrix through the template and to activate the necessary routing features for the chosen paths.

This way we significantly reduce the complexity of the complete problem while still improving upon the state-of-the-art solutions. Nevertheless, this template does not need to be intricate or sophisticated. In fact, the intuitive knowledge of the designer about the structure of the router to be created is more than enough to provide a good template.

3.1 Template elements

We model layout templates with three layout elements. Together they allow for the design of any WRONoC topology (an example is shown in Figure 3).

Endpoints represent modulators and demodulators. They are placed wherever the (de)modulators for each node are and connect to one waveguide section.

General Routing Units (GRUs) are elements that connect to multiple waveguide sections (the *edges* of the GRU) and contain MRR placeholders, to be populated by the solver as needed. They are the routing building blocks of the template and are described further in the next section.

Waveguide sections connect two GRUs or a GRU and an endpoint. Each section has two associated parameters: *length* and *extraloss*. The latter is used to describe sections with other constant sources of insertion loss besides length, such as sections with 90° bends.

Our method can solve for any template, i.e., any arrangement of endpoints, GRUs and waveguide sections.

3.2 General Routing Unit

Photonic Switching Elements (PSEs) are commonly applied in WRONoC routers [7, 11, 13, 14]. For PSEs, MRR locations and wavelengths are explicitly specified and the waveguide structure is fixed.

GRUs are the routing building blocks for the proposed layout template and, in contrast to PSEs, GRUs are not inherently constrained to a specific internal structure. Instead, only MRR placeholders are predefined in a GRU. Thus, different MRR placement and wavelength configurations can happen for each GRU, as well as different edge connection arrangements. This provides more flexibility in the resulting WRONoC design.

3.2.1 Structure. Figure 4(a) shows the structure of a GRU: the four waveguide sections form a crossing where any of the four corners on that crossing can have an MRR. Sometimes the crossing can be avoided, leading to the variations in Figure 4(b).

We also consider an additional structure variation called *corner bending*. When active, the GRU contains no MRRs and some corners may be replaced by a bend between the two edges in that corner, as in Figure 4(c).

Note that two corners connected to the same edge of a GRU *cannot* be both bent. Therefore, if two edges are connected through a corner bend, the other two edges must be bent through the opposite corner if they have messages going through. Figure 4(d) shows two invalid configurations.

This extra variation proves useful for sparser templates (low ratio of the number of messages to the number of MRR positions), or in cases where multiple messages must be routed through the same corner.

3.2.2 Routing. Figure 5 shows the routing possibilities through a GRU. If no MRRs of the same wavelength as the message are present and corner bending is not activated, the message will have no direction change, as shown in Figure 5(a).

For wavelength routing, the message can be routed through an MRR with the same wavelength in the closest corner, as shown in Figure 5(b), or in the opposite corner, as shown in Figure 5(c).

With corner bending, since the two waveguides become connected, all messages in any of the two waveguides are routed through that corner, regardless of wavelength, as shown in Figure 5(d).

A message's path through a GRU is always independent of its direction, i.e., all routing features are bidirectional. Also, the four MRRs on a GRU can have different wavelengths (examples are shown in Figure 1). This allows for intricate multi-message routing capabilities per waveguide crossing which have not yet been optimized to their full potential.

3.3   Communication Matrix

Given a layout template, the communication matrix can be translated into a set of messages (one for each nonzero entry), where each message is associated with two endpoints on that template: the sender and the receiver.

4   MATHEMATICAL MODEL

We solve the constrained problem using a Mixed Integer Programming model. Advantages of MIP models include:

(1) A MIP model can give optimal solutions, or at least an upper/lower bound to the optimal value of the optimization function.
(2) The same MIP can be used to optimize different objectives, therefore giving the designer more flexibility.
(3) MIP models are flexible, so new GRU designs, routing features or other modifications can easily be added.

The model constants and indices are outlined in Table 1. Constants L_{wg}, L_{wg}^E and indices W_i^* collectively describe the physical layout template and indices E_m^* define the communication matrix. Table 2 lists all model variables.

We now specify the constraints and the optimization function (note that similar constraints for multiple directions or corners are omitted). Finally, we present some model reduction techniques.

4.1   Constraints

Message routing. A path with the correct beginning and end must be guaranteed for each message. For that we apply the following three sets of constraints:

(1) A message must be on the waveguide of the endpoints it is sent from and received by.

$$mwg_{m, W_{E_m^S}^E} = 1 \quad mwg_{m, W_{E_m^R}^E} = 1 \qquad \forall m = 1...N_m$$

(2) If an endpoint does *not* send or receive a given message, that message *cannot* be present on its waveguide section.

$$mwg_{m, W_{ep}^E} = 0 \quad \forall ep = 1...N_{ep} \setminus \{E_m^S, E_m^R\}$$
$$\forall m = 1...N_m$$

Table 1: Model constants & indices

Constants

N_{gru}, N_{wg},	Total number of GRUs, waveguide
N_m, N_{ep},	sections, messages, endpoints and
N_λ	wavelengths
L^P, L^C, L^B,	Values for propagation, crossing,
L^D, L^T	bending, drop and through loss
L_{wg}, L_{wg}^E	Length and extra loss of waveguide
	section wg

Indices

W_g^T, W_g^B,	Waveguide section connected to GRU g
W_g^L, W_g^R	to the top, bottom, left and right
W_{ep}^E	Waveguide section connected to
	endpoint ep
E_m^S, E_m^R	Sending and receiving endpoints for
	message m

(3) A message is exactly on 0 or 2 edges of a GRU.

$$mwg_{m, W_g^T} + mwg_{m, W_g^R} + mwg_{m, W_g^B} + mwg_{m, W_g^L} \in \{0, 2\}$$
$$\forall m = 1...N_m, g = 1...N_{gru}$$

It is possible for a message to be on all four edges of a GRU, but this was neglected because it appearing on an optimized solution is highly unlikely, and not including it simplifies the model and the problem space. The reason is that a message routing through all 4 edges (enter through edge 1, leave through 2, enter through 3, leave through 4) can also route through 2 edges (enter through 1, leave through 4) with half the loss on that GRU and a shorter path.

Wavelength exclusion. Each waveguide section has at most one message going through it for each wavelength. First, each message must use exactly one wavelength:

$$\sum_{\lambda=1}^{N_\lambda} mwl_{m, \lambda} = 1 \qquad \forall m = 1...N_m$$

Then the value of mwe_{m_1, m_2} is set accordingly:

$$mwl_{m_1, \lambda} \wedge mwl_{m_2, \lambda} \Rightarrow mwe_{m_1, m_2}$$
$$\forall \lambda = 1...N_\lambda$$
$$\forall m_1, m_2 = 1...N_m : m_2 \neq m_1$$

Now enforce exclusivity of wavelengths on all waveguides:

$$mwe_{m_1, m_2} \Rightarrow (mwg_{m_1, wg} + mwg_{m_2, wg} \leqslant 1)$$
$$\forall m_1, m_2 = 1...N_m : m_1 \neq m_2$$
$$\forall wg = 1...N_{wg}$$

Activation of routing features. A path is chosen for each message but, to make that path take effect, constraints are needed to enforce the activation of the routing features responsible for it.

If a message takes the direct path through a GRU, no features need to be turned on. However, if a message is present on adjacent edges of a GRU, then one of the three options from Figure 5(b-d)

Table 2: Model variables

Binary

$cb_{g,p}$	Corner p on GRU g is bent
wlu_λ	At least one message uses wavelength λ
$mwl_{m,\lambda}$	Message m uses wavelength λ
mwe_{m_1,m_2}	Messages m_1 and m_2 use the same wavelength
$mwg_{m,wg}$	Message m goes through waveguide section wg
$cl_{g,m}, bl_{g,m}$	Message m has crossing/bending loss on GRU g
$tl_{g,p,m}$	Message m has through loss due to MRR p in GRU g
$rum_{g,p,m}$	MRR on GRU g, corner p, used by message m
$ru_{g,p}$	MRR on GRU g, corner p, used by a message
mch_g, mcv_g	GRU g has at least one message going through the center crossing horizontally/vertically

Integer

nwl	Number of used wavelengths

Continuous

mil_m	Insertion loss for message m
$maxil$	Maximum insertion loss over all messages

Index $p \in \mathbb{P}$, $\mathbb{P} = \{TL : $ Top-Left, $TR :$ Top-Right, $BL :$ Bottom-Left, $BR :$ Bottom-Right$\}$.

must be active:

$$mwg_{m,W_g^T} \wedge mwg_{m,W_g^L} \Rightarrow rum_{g,TL,m} \vee rum_{g,BR,m} \vee cb_{g,TL}$$
$$\forall\ 4\ \text{corners}, m = 1...N_m, g = 1...N_{gru}$$

Each MRR can only be used for one message. The following constraints both set the value of $ru_{g,p}$ and enforce that restriction:

$$ru_{g,p} = \sum_{m=1}^{N_m} rum_{g,p,m} \qquad \forall g = 1...N_{gru}, p \in \mathbb{P}$$

Corner bending. The following three sets of constraints are required[1]:

(1) A GRU cannot have corners bent and MRRs active.

$$cb_{g,p_1} + ru_{g,p_2} \leqslant 1 \qquad \forall p_1, p_2 \in \mathbb{P}, g = 1...N_{gru}$$

(2) Corners for the same edge cannot be bent at the same time for the same GRU.

$$cb_{g,TL} + cb_{g,TR} \leqslant 1 \qquad cb_{g,TR} + cb_{g,BR} \leqslant 1$$
$$cb_{g,TL} + cb_{g,BL} \leqslant 1 \qquad cb_{g,BL} + cb_{g,BR} \leqslant 1$$
$$\forall g = 1...N_{gru}$$

---

[1] This feature can be turned off, if needed, by adding constraints to set all $cb_{g,p}$ variables to zero.

(3) If a corner is bent then messages present on one of the edges of that corner must be present on the other.

$$cb_{g,TL} \Rightarrow mwg_{m,W_g^T} = mwg_{m,W_g^L}$$
$$\forall\ 4\ \text{corners}, m = 1...N_m, g = 1...N_{gru}$$

Crossing loss. A message suffers crossing loss when going through a crossing with a perpendicular waveguide. Two things must happen for a message to have crossing loss on a GRU: **1)** the message must take a direct path through the GRU and **2a)** the perpendicular direct path must be taken by at least one other message *or* **2b)** there must be at least one message taking the path on Figure 5(c). For any other case the crossing on the GRU can be avoided, as exemplified in Figure 4(b), and no crossing loss exists.

First set the values of the variables mch_g and mcv_g:

$$mwg_{m,W_g^L} \wedge mwg_{m,W_g^R} \Rightarrow mch_g$$
$$\forall\ 2\ \text{directions}, m = 1...N_m, g = 1...N_{gru}$$
$$mwg_{m,W_g^T} \wedge mwg_{m,W_g^L} \wedge rum_{g,BR,m} \Rightarrow mch_g \wedge mcv_g$$
$$\forall\ 4\ \text{corners}, m = 1...N_m, g = 1...N_{gru}$$

The value of $cl_{g,m}$ follows:

$$mwg_{m,W_g^T} \wedge mwg_{m,W_g^B} \wedge mch_g \Rightarrow cl_{g,m}$$
$$\forall\ 2\ \text{directions}, m = 1...N_m, g = 1...N_{gru}$$

Through loss. If a message is going through the direct path on a GRU, then it has through loss for each MRR present on that GRU.

$$mwg_{m,W_g^L} \wedge mwg_{m,W_g^R} \wedge ru_{g,p} \Rightarrow tl_{g,p,m}$$
$$\forall\ 2\ \text{directions}, m = 1...N_m, p \in \mathbb{P}, g = 1...N_{gru}$$

Bending loss. A message has bending loss on a GRU if it routes through a corner that is bent.

$$mwg_{m,W_g^T} \wedge mwg_{m,W_g^L} \wedge cb_{g,TL} \Rightarrow bl_{g,m}$$
$$\forall\ 4\ \text{corners}, m = 1...N_m, g = 1...N_{gru}$$

Drop loss. Proportional to the number of MRRs used by each message.

Propagation loss. Proportional to the length of the waveguides the message goes through.

Message insertion loss. The total insertion loss of a message over all waveguides and GRUs is a weighted sum.

$$mil_m = \sum_{i=1}^{N_{wg}} (L^P * L_i + L_i^E) * mwg_{m,i} + L^T * \sum_{g=1}^{N_{gru}} \sum_{p \in \mathbb{P}} tl_{g,p,m}$$
$$+ \sum_{g=1}^{N_{gru}} (L^C * cl_{g,m} + L^B * bl_{g,m} + L^D * \sum_{p \in \mathbb{P}} rum_{g,p,m})$$
$$\forall m = 1...N_m$$

4.2 Objective function

Calculating the number of wavelengths is done with the following constraints:

$$wlu_\lambda \geqslant mwl_{m,\lambda} \qquad \forall m = 1...N_m, \lambda = 1...N_\lambda$$

$$nwl = \sum_{\lambda=1}^{N_\lambda} wlu_\lambda$$

Determining the maximum insertion loss over all messages is done with the following constraints:

$$maxil \geqslant mil_m \qquad \forall m = 1...N_m$$

Finally, the following objective function is minimized:

$$\alpha_1 * nwl + \alpha_2 * maxil + \alpha_3 * \sum_{m=1}^{N_m} mil_m + \alpha_4 * \sum_{g=1}^{N_{gru}} \sum_{p\in\mathbb{P}} ru_{g,p}$$

where α_i are optimization weights chosen by the designer.

Since the value for the insertion loss of each message is available through the mil_m variables, functions other than the maximum or the sum of the insertion loss can also be added to the model and used for optimization.

4.3 Model reduction techniques

4.3.1 Restrictions on usage of wavelengths. The following constraints can be added:

$$mwl_{m,\lambda} = 0 \qquad \forall \lambda = (m + 1)...N_\lambda \qquad \forall m = 1...N_m$$

They restrict the possible wavelengths for each message: message 1 uses wavelength 1, message 2 uses wavelengths 1 or 2, etc. This way, some meaningless variations around the same effective solution are removed. The optimal solution, however, is not removed from the solution space.

4.3.2 Restrictions on usage of MRRs. Empirically we find that minimizing the insertion loss favors optimal solutions where each message uses a low total number of MRRs. Following this reasoning, constraints can be added to the model that force a maximum number of MRRs per message (R^{max}):

$$\sum_{g=1}^{N_{gru}} \sum_{p\in\mathbb{P}} rum_{g,p} \leqslant R^{max} \qquad \forall m = 1...N_m$$

This reduces the set of paths considered by the solver by removing poor, convoluted paths while keeping the more direct paths between endpoints.

5 PROOF OF FEASIBILITY

It is possible that the chosen layout template cannot satisfy the entire communication matrix (for example, if the template is too small). For those cases, the model above will be unfeasible. Verifying the existence of a solution can be done much faster using a simplified version of the model. For that we consider $N_\lambda = N_m$ and uniquely assign a wavelength to each message by adding these constraints:

$$mwl_{m,\lambda} = 1 \qquad \forall m = 1...N_m, \lambda = m$$
$$mwl_{m,\lambda} = 0 \qquad \forall m = 1...N_m, \lambda \neq m$$

The resulting model can be solved much faster but, if the solver is unable to find a feasible solution for this simplified model, the complete model is also unfeasible.

PROOF. Assume a feasible solution exists. It will have $nwl \leqslant N_m$. From that solution build another where each message uses its own wavelength (thus either maintaining or increasing nwl). Any message that changes its wavelength must also change the wavelength of the MRRs it uses. This is always possible because each MRR routes only one message. Furthermore, the wavelength exclusion rule is always satisfied. Hence, the feasibility of the complete model implies the existence of a solution for the simplified version. □

6 3-STEP OPTIMIZATION

Section 4 introduced a MIP model that is capable of solving the constrained problem for *any* layout template. Therefore, programming the model as presented on any MIP solver and solving it directly for the chosen minimization objective is enough to obtain the optimal solution. However, due to the nature of the problem, it is possible to slightly alter the optimization process yielding more control and faster results. This leads to the proposed 3-step optimization process used in PSION, where each step optimizes a slightly different version of the model and produces a solution used at the start of the next step.

In the **first step** we consider $N_\lambda = N_m$ and apply the feasibility proof from Section 5. In this way we can generate the first feasible solution much faster if one exists. It can then be used as a warm start, which decreases optimization times substantially. This has the added bonus of stopping the process as quickly as possible if unfeasible.

In the **second step** we only minimize the number of wavelengths, for two reasons. Firstly, the designer will most likely want to use fewer wavelengths than the number of messages, thus making this optimization problem hierarchical, i.e., minimizing wavelengths has a higher priority than minimizing insertion loss or #MRRs. Secondly, because, after completing this step, a feasible solution for a smaller number of wavelengths is then available, so the model can again be simplified by eliminating from it the $N_m - nwl$ unused wavelengths. To make this simplification, the following constraints are added:

$$mwl_{m,\lambda} = 0 \qquad \forall m = 1...N_m, \text{ unused wavelengths } \lambda$$

The designer might be willing to use more wavelengths than the minimum needed. In that case it is up to the designer to know the maximum acceptable number of wavelengths. The second step can be stopped earlier once a solution is found within that acceptable range.

In the **third step** we consider the model with the needed amount of wavelengths only and further optimize the last solution using the chosen function ($maxil$, for example). We have now reached the final solution.

Using this process we can notably simplify the problem space during the optimization. However, because the model reductions are always done according to the hierarchical characteristics of the optimization goals, the optimal solution is never missed.

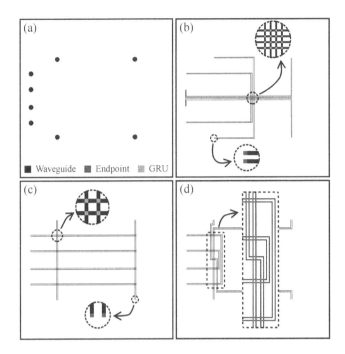

Figure 6: (a) Location of the eight nodes that produces the best result in PROTON+. (b) A centralized grid template connecting those nodes. (c) A distributed grid template. (d) A custom template.

Table 3: Results for 8 nodes, 44 messages

	#WLs	Max IL	#MRRs	Time	
PROTON+				T_{total}	
λ-Router	8	6.6 - 9.0	56	134	
GWOR	7	8.1 - 11.3	48	79	
Std. crossbar	8	10.5 - 13.0	64	602	
PlanarONoC				T_{total}	
λ-Router	8	5.2	56	<1	
GWOR	7	6.4	48	<1	
Std. crossbar	8	7.4	64	<1	
PSION				T_{opt}	T_{total}
Centralized	8	3.1	52	178	271
Distributed	8	3.6	48	37	376
Custom	7	4.1	40	<1	6

T_{opt} is time to find the optimal solution, T_{total} is total execution time (for PSION: $T_{total} = T_{opt}$ + time to prove optimality; for others: the time that produces the best result). Time in seconds, insertion loss in dB.

7   RESULTS

The MIP model and 3-step optimization algorithm are programmed in C++ and make use of Gurobi [4], a MIP solver, on a 2.6 GHz CPU.

We tested our model and optimization procedure against the state-of-the-art PROTON+ and PlanarONoC P&R tools. Most of their result analysis is dedicated to an 8 node test case with 44 messages. We solved the same test case considering the same communication matrix, node placement, die size, crossing size and loss parameters.

PROTON+ and PlanarONoC compare results originating from P&R of three logical topologies (8x8 λ-Router, 8x8 GWOR and 8x8 Standard Crossbar). PROTON+ also considers five different sets of node positions and various permutations of solver parameters, which results in a range of values for the results. We used the node positions that produced the best result over all presented in PROTON+, shown in Figure 6(a). We manually designed three simple layout templates, presented in Figure 6(b-d), that connect to these node positions. The last step of the optimization was set to minimize the max. insertion loss (*maxil*), just like PROTON+ and PlanarONoC.

7.1   Physical templates

All templates share some common features:

(1) Each node has two endpoints: a modulator and a demodulator.
(2) The power distribution network – not shown in these templates – can always be routed from the outside such that no

other crossings in the router exist besides those considered by the template.

The **centralized grid** template is a $w \times h$ grid of GRUs where $w + h$ equals the number of nodes. Each node is connected with waveguides to two ports on the grid (one for sending, the other for receiving), which are next to each other. This router can be thought of as a different generalization of the 4x4 GWOR router in Figure 3. The grid itself was placed on the center of the die, the ports used by each node were chosen as to remove any crossings external to the grid and the waveguides connecting the nodes to the grid were manually routed to minimize bends.

The **distributed grid** template was built by placing horizontal or vertical pairs of waveguides starting at each node, with a GRU on each crossing.

The **custom** template was built specifically for this test case (i.e., these node positions and communication matrix). In particular, no message needs to use more than one MRR. Therefore, R^{max} was set to 1 for this template while the grid templates were solved with $R^{max} = 2$.

7.2   Comparison to the state-of-the-art

Figure 1 shows the result for the centralized grid router and Table 3 presents the various comparisons. Most important are the number of wavelengths and maximum insertion loss, but #MRRs and execution time are also given. Results from PSION are optimal solutions for the given templates.

Number of wavelengths. The communication matrix in these tests requires an absolute minimum of 7 wavelengths when using one modulator per node. The custom template matches this value, but the grid templates require an actual minimum of 8. However, PSION can reduce this number if given a smaller communication matrix, in contrast to the presented logical topologies.

Max. insertion loss. PSION produces results that are **2.7×** better compared to PROTON+ and **1.8×** better compared to PlanarONoC. Some intuitive reasons are available to justify these outcomes:

- We combined logical topology and physical layout optimization.
- We used templates, which automatically removes many sub-optimal solutions compared to a conventional P&R solution space.
- We used GRUs, which support up to four MRRs per crossing, whereas PSEs only support two. Thus, fewer GRUs are used in our templates than PSEs are used in logical topologies such as the λ-Router. This increases the density of our designs which decreases the total number of crossings.
- We drastically reduced the number of crossings outside PSEs/GRUs.
- We obtain the optimal solution within the specified template.

MRR usage. This was not an optimization objective in these tests, but the comparison to both PROTON+ and PlanarONoC remains favourable.

Time. Grid templates have a total execution time comparable with PROTON+. PlanarONoC is still two orders of magnitude faster. The custom template is much better, however, mostly because of the technique from Section 4.3.2.

Furthermore, the optimal solution is consistently reached in half or less than the total execution time. Thus, a designer not requiring proof of optimality can end the optimization once a satisfactory solution is found which, based on these results, is likely to appear quickly and be close to optimal.

7.3 Further comments

We also solved the MIP models from these tests by directly minimizing $100 \times nwl + 1 \times maxil$ – which assures the same hierarchical optimization – and got the same final results, but found that using the 3-step procedure is **2.5×** faster on average. Likewise, we ran the same tests without any of the reduction techniques from Section 4.3. The results were the same, but using the techniques was **4.5×** faster on average.

Finally, the grid templates are entirely straightforward and can be used in virtually any WRONoC, which speaks to the potential of PSION even when no effort is spent in designing the template. The custom template, however, was built for this case. The fact that it achieves even better results in some areas also shows the promising possibilities available through careful template synthesis.

8 CONCLUSION

In this work we defined the WRONoC design problem and presented PSION, a novel method for solving it. This method uses a physical layout template to combine logical topology and physical layout optimization. We also presented a new, flexible, routing element, the GRU. We used a MIP model and a 3-step optimization procedure to solve for the optimal solution. These combined efforts produce results superior to the state of the art. In future work the proposed method can be extended to include optimization of the power distribution network and other GRU designs. Also, the run-time characteristics of MIP modelling may yet be improved with

further reduction techniques. Finally, template synthesis methods should also be explored.

REFERENCES

[1] Sébastien Le Beux, Ian O'Connor, Gabriela Nicolescu, Guy Bois, and Pierre Paulin. 2013. Reduction methods for adapting optical network on chip topologies to 3D architectures. *Microprocessors and Microsystems* 37, 1 (2013), 87 – 98. https://doi.org/10.1016/j.micpro.2012.11.001

[2] Yu-Kai Chuang, Kuan-Jung Chen, Kun-Lin Lin, Shao-Yun Fang, Bing Li, and Ulf Schlichtmann. 2018. PlanarONoC: Concurrent Placement and Routing Considering Crossing Minimization for Optical Networks-on-chip. In *Proceedings of the 55th Annual Design Automation Conference*. ACM, Article 151, 6 pages.

[3] H. Gu, K. H. Mo, J. Xu, and W. Zhang. 2009. A Low-power Low-cost Optical Router for Optical Networks-on-Chip in Multiprocessor Systems-on-Chip. In *2009 IEEE Computer Society Annual Symposium on VLSI*. 19–24. https://doi.org/10.1109/ISVLSI.2009.19

[4] Gurobi Optimization, Inc. 2018. *Gurobi Optimizer Reference Manual*. http://www.gurobi.com.

[5] Mengchu Li, Tsun-Ming Tseng, Davide Bertozzi, Mahdi Tala, and Ulf Schlichtmann. 2018. CustomTopo: A Topology Generation Method for Application-Specific Wavelength-Routed Optical NoCs. In *Proceedings of the 37th International Conference on Computer-Aided Design*.

[6] M. Nikdast, J. Xu, L. H. K. Duong, X. Wu, X. Wang, Z. Wang, Z. Wang, P. Yang, Y. Ye, and Q. Hao. 2015. Crosstalk Noise in WDM-Based Optical Networks-on-Chip: A Formal Study and Comparison. *IEEE Transactions on Very Large Scale Integration (VLSI) Systems* 23, 11 (Nov 2015), 2552–2565. https://doi.org/10.1109/TVLSI.2014.2370892

[7] I. O'Connor, M. Brière, E. Drouard, A. Kazmierczak, F. Tissafi-Drissi, D. Navarro, F. Mieyeville, J. Dambre, D. Stroobandt, J.-M. Fedeli, Z. Lisik, and F. Gaffiot. 2005. Towards reconfigurable optical networks on chip. *ReCoSoC'05* (2005), 121–128.

[8] Marta Ortín-Obón, Luca Ramini, Herve Tatenguem Fankem, Víctor Viñals, and Davide Bertozzi. 2014. A Complete Electronic Network Interface Architecture for Global Contention-free Communication over Emerging Optical Networks-on-chip. In *Proceedings of the 24th Edition of the Great Lakes Symposium on VLSI*. ACM, 267–272. https://doi.org/10.1145/2591513.2591536

[9] M. Ortín-Obón, L. Ramini, V. Viñals Yúfera, and D. Bertozzi. 2017. A tool for synthesizing power-efficient and custom-tailored wavelength-routed optical rings. In *Asia and South Pacific Design Automation Conference (ASP-DAC)*. 300–305. https://doi.org/10.1109/ASPDAC.2017.7858339

[10] A. Peano, L. Ramini, M. Gavanelli, M. Nonato, and D. Bertozzi. 2016. Design technology for fault-free and maximally-parallel wavelength-routed optical networks-on-chip. In *2016 IEEE/ACM International Conference on Computer-Aided Design (ICCAD)*. 1–8. https://doi.org/10.1145/2966986.2967023

[11] L. Ramini, P. Grani, S. Bartolini, and D. Bertozzi. 2013. Contrasting wavelength-routed optical NoC topologies for power-efficient 3d-stacked multicore processors using physical-layer analysis. In *2013 Design, Automation & Test in Europe Conference & Exhibition (DATE)*. 1589–1594. https://doi.org/10.7873/DATE.2013.323

[12] M. Ashkan Seyedi, Antoine Descos, Chin-Hui Chen, Marco Fiorentino, David Penkler, François Vincent, Bertrand Szelag, and Raymond G. Beausoleil. 2016. Crosstalk analysis of ring resonator switches for all-optical routing. *Opt. Express* 24, 11 (May 2016), 11668–11676. https://doi.org/10.1364/OE.24.011668

[13] M. Tala, M. Castellari, M. Balboni, and D. Bertozzi. 2016. Populating and exploring the design space of wavelength-routed optical network-on-chip topologies by leveraging the add-drop filtering primitive. In *2016 Tenth IEEE/ACM International Symposium on Networks-on-Chip (NOCS)*. 1–8. https://doi.org/10.1109/NOCS.2016.7579331

[14] X. Tan, M. Yang, L. Zhang, Y. Jiang, and J. Yang. 2011. On a Scalable, Non-Blocking Optical Router for Photonic Networks-on-Chip Designs. In *2011 Symposium on Photonics and Optoelectronics (SOPO)*. 1–4. https://doi.org/10.1109/SOPO.2011.5780550

[15] Anja von Beuningen, Luca Ramini, Davide Bertozzi, and Ulf Schlichtmann. 2015. PROTON+: A Placement and Routing Tool for 3D Optical Networks-on-Chip with a Single Optical Layer. *J. Emerg. Technol. Comput. Syst.* 12, 4, Article 44 (Dec. 2015), 28 pages. https://doi.org/10.1145/2830716

[16] Anja von Beuningen and Ulf Schlichtmann. 2016. PLATON: A Force-Directed Placement Algorithm for 3D Optical Networks-on-Chip. In *Proceedings of the 2016 on International Symposium on Physical Design*. ACM, 27–34. https://doi.org/10.1145/2872334.2872356

[17] Yiyuan Xie, Mahdi Nikdast, Jiang Xu, Wei Zhang, Qi Li, Xiaowen Wu, Yaoyao Ye, Xuan Wang, and Weichen Liu. 2010. Crosstalk Noise and Bit Error Rate Analysis for Optical Network-on-chip. In *Proceedings of the 47th Design Automation Conference*. ACM, 657–660. https://doi.org/10.1145/1837274.1837441

Construction of All Multilayer Monolithic Rectilinear Steiner Minimum Trees on the 3D Hanan Grid for Monolithic 3D IC Routing

Sheng-En David Lin
dl23ee.lin@wsu.edu
Washington State University
Pullman, Washington

Dae Hyun Kim
daehyun@eecs.wsu.edu
Washington State University
Pullman, Washington

ABSTRACT

Monolithic three-dimensional (3D) integration enables stacking multiple ultra-thin silicon tiers in a single package, thereby providing smaller footprint area, shorter wirelength, higher performance, and lower power consumption than conventional planar fabrication technologies. Physical design of monolithic 3D integrated circuits (ICs) requires several design steps such as 3D placement, 3D clock-tree synthesis, 3D routing, and 3D optimization. Among the steps, 3D routing is very time-consuming due to numerous routing blockages. Thus, 3D routing is typically performed in two sub-steps, monolithic inter-layer via (MIV) insertion and tier-by-tier routing. In this paper, we propose an algorithm to build a routing topology database that can be used to construct all multilayer monolithic rectilinear Steiner minimum trees on the 3D Hanan grid. The database will help 3D routers reduce the runtime of the MIV insertion step and improve the quality of the 3D routing.

CCS CONCEPTS

• **Hardware** → **3D integrated circuits**; **Wire routing**.

KEYWORDS

Monolithic 3D Integrated Circuits, Rectilinear Steiner Minimum Tree, RSMT, Routing, Wirelength, Congestion

ACM Reference Format:
Sheng-En David Lin and Dae Hyun Kim. 2019. Construction of All Multilayer Monolithic Rectilinear Steiner Minimum Trees on the 3D Hanan Grid for Monolithic 3D IC Routing. In *2019 International Symposium on Physical Design (ISPD '19), April 14–17, 2019, San Francisco, CA, USA*. ACM, New York, NY, USA, 8 pages. https://doi.org/10.1145/3299902.3309749

1 INTRODUCTION

Monolithic three-dimensional (3D) integration stacks very thin silicon tiers and electrically connects transistors in different tiers by monolithic inter-layer vias (MIVs). An MIV is similar to a through-silicon via (TSV), but the width and the z-directional length of an MIV are much shorter than those of a TSV. Thus, MIV insertion has

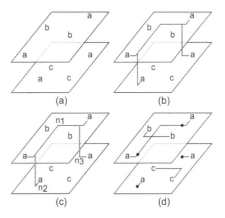

Figure 1: 3D-net-first routing. (a) Three nets to route. (b) 3D routing topology generation for the 3D net. (c) MIV insertion. (d) Tier-by-tier routing.

almost negligible area and capacitance overheads in the monolithic 3D integrated circuit (IC) layout design. However, inserting too many MIVs into a 3D IC layout causes serious routing congestion because planar wires should be connected to the MIVs and routing of the planar wires requires much larger area than the MIV area. Thus, 3D placement in general tries to minimize the number of MIVs inserted into a layout [1, 10] and 3D routing should also minimize the number of MIVs.

3D routing routes 2D and 3D nets.[1] 3D routing algorithms could route all the 2D and 3D nets in a given design separately or simultaneously. For example, the routing methodology in [3] routes 3D nets first, then routes 2D nets. On the other hand, the routing methodology used in [9] routes 2D and 3D nets simultaneously by using a commercial tool and modified library files. The latter, however, has some drawbacks compared to the former. According to our own routing simulations using modified library files, the runtime of the simultaneous routing of 2D and 3D nets increases significantly as the complexity (the average net degree, the number of tiers, and the number of instances) of a given design goes up. On the other hand, if 3D nets are routed first, we can route 2D nets in each tier separately (tier-by-tier routing). Thus, the 3D-net-first routing methodology has been used extensively in the literature [3, 5, 10, 11].

The 3D-net-first routing methodology finds MIV locations for each 3D net, inserts MIVs into the locations, and decomposes the 3D

[1]A 2D (3D) net is a net connecting instances placed in a tier (different tiers).

net into multiple 2D nets. Figure 1 shows an example. In Figure 1(a), eight pins are spread out in two tiers. The net connecting four a pins is a 3D net, whereas the other two nets connecting two b and two c pins are 2D nets. In Figure 1(b), a 3D routing topology using two z-directional edges is constructed for the 3D net. The z-directional edges are replaced by MIVs and the 3D net is decomposed into three 2D nets, n_1, n_2, and n_3 in Figure 1(c). By the decomposition of the 3D net into the three 2D nets, routing of the 3D net is converted into routing of the three 2D nets, two in the bottom tier and one in the top tier. Finally, the 2D nets are routed in each tier in Figure 1(d).

As mentioned above, 3D routing should minimize the number of MIVs used to route 3D nets. In addition, 3D routing should evenly distribute the MIVs over the entire layout area to minimize routing congestion around the MIVs. At the same time, 3D routing should evenly distribute planar wires routing 3D nets over the layout area so that routing of 2D nets does not suffer from serious routing congestion in specific tiers. The MIV insertion methodologies used in the literature, however, do not control the MIV count, MIV locations, and planar wires of 3D nets effectively. For example, the 3D rectilinear Steiner tree (RST) algorithms used in [4, 5, 10, 11] do not guarantee the minimization of the MIV count. The MIV insertion algorithm used in [3] minimizes the MIV count, but fails to minimize the planar wirelength. It is also possible to use multilayer obstacle-avoiding rectilinear Steiner tree (MLOARST) construction algorithms to minimize both the planar wirelength and the number of MIVs [6, 8]. However, the MLOARST construction algorithms do not generate multiple topologies having different MIV locations and planar wire distributions.

In this paper, we propose an algorithm to build a database that can be used to construct all multilayer monolithic rectilinear Steiner minimum trees (MMRSMTs) on the 3D Hanan grid for given pin locations for up to six-pin nets and four tiers. MMRSMTs have the shortest planar wirelength with the minimum number of MIVs, so MIV insertion algorithms can use the database to effectively optimize MIV locations and planar wires of 3D nets. We also propose database size reduction techniques for practical use of the database in academia and industry. To the best of our knowledge, this is the first work on constructing all MMRSMTs on the 3D Hanan grid.

2 PRELIMINARIES AND PROBLEM FORMULATION

In this section, we explain terminologies used in this paper, review the construction of an RSMT in FLUTE [2] and construction of all RSMTs in [7], and formulate the problem we solve in this paper.

2.1 Terminologies

2.1.1 2D and 3D Hanan Grids. Suppose a finite set S of points are given in the 2D plane. The **2D Hanan grid** constructed from S is a graph $G_S = (V_S, E_S)$. The vertex set of G_S is $V_S = \{(x, y) | x \in X_S, y \in Y_S\}$ where $X_S = \{x_1, ..., x_L\}(x_1 < ... < x_L)$ and $Y_S = \{y_1, ..., y_M\}(y_1 < ... < y_M)$ are the sets of the x- and y-coordinates of all the points in S, respectively. The edge set of G_S is $E_S = E_{S,X} \cup E_{S,Y}$ where

$$E_{S,X} = \{(v_1, v_2) | v_1 = (x_{i<L}, y_j) \in V_S, v_2 = (x_{i+1}, y_j) \in V_S\},$$
$$E_{S,Y} = \{(v_1, v_2) | v_1 = (x_i, y_{j<M}) \in V_S, v_2 = (x_i, y_{j+1}) \in V_S\}.$$

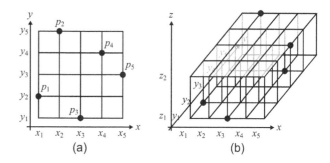

Figure 2: 2D and 3D Hanan grids.

In other words, $E_{S,X}$ and $E_{S,Y}$ are the sets of the x- and y-directional edges of G_S, respectively. Figure 2(a) shows the 2D Hanan grid constructed for the five points located at (x_1, y_2), (x_2, y_5), (x_3, y_1), (x_4, y_4), and (x_5, y_3).

Suppose a finite set T of points are given in the 3D space. The **3D Hanan grid** constructed from T is a graph $G_T = (V_T, E_T)$. The vertex set of G_T is $V_T = \{(x, y, z) | x \in X_T, y \in Y_T, z \in Z_T\}$ where $X_T = \{x_1, ..., x_L\}(x_1 < ... < x_L)$, $Y_T = \{y_1, ..., y_M\}(y_1 < ... < y_M)$, and $Z_T = \{z_1, ..., z_N\}(z_1 < ... < z_N)$ are the sets of the x-, y-, and z-coordinates of all the points in T, respectively. The edge set of G_T is $E_T = E_{T,X} \cup E_{T,Y} \cup E_{T,Z}$ where

$$E_{T,X} = \{(v_1, v_2) | v_1 = (x_{i<L}, y_j, z_k) \in V_T, v_2 = (x_{i+1}, y_j, z_k) \in V_T\},$$
$$E_{T,Y} = \{(v_1, v_2) | v_1 = (x_i, y_{j<M}, z_k) \in V_T, v_2 = (x_i, y_{j+1}, z_k) \in V_T\},$$
$$E_{T,Z} = \{(v_1, v_2) | v_1 = (x_i, y_j, z_{k<N}) \in V_T, v_2 = (x_i, y_j, z_{k+1}) \in V_T\}.$$

In other words, $E_{T,X}$, $E_{T,Y}$, and $E_{T,Z}$ are the sets of the x-, y-, and z-directional edges of G_T, respectively. Figure 2(b) shows the 3D Hanan grid constructed for the five points located at (x_1, y_2, z_1), (x_2, y_5, z_2), (x_3, y_1, z_1), (x_4, y_4, z_1), and (x_5, y_3, z_2).

2.1.2 Position Sequence. x_+- and x_--directions are the directions along which x-coordinates increase and decrease, respectively. y_+-, y_--, z_+-, and z_--directions are defined similarly.

Suppose a finite set $P = \{p_1, ..., p_n\}$ of n distinct pins[2] are given in an $n \times n$ grid. Let the x-coordinates of the y-directional edges be x_1 to x_n from the left and the y-coordinates of the x-directional edges be y_1 to y_n from the bottom as shown in Figure 2(a). Then, we denote sorting the pins in the increasing (+) and decreasing (−) order of their c-coordinates (c is x or y) by c_+ and c_-, respectively. In Figure 2(a), for example, y_+ sorting leads to the ordered list $L_1 = (p_3, p_1, p_5, p_4, p_2)$ and x_- sorting leads to the ordered list $L_2 = (p_5, p_4, p_3, p_2, p_1)$. Suppose we obtain an ordered list $L = (l_1, ..., l_n)$ from c_+ or c_- sorting. Then, we can obtain the $\bar{c}$-coordinates (if c is x (or y), $\bar{c}$ is y (or x)) of the pins in the $\bar{c}_+$- or $\bar{c}_-$-direction from L. For example, we obtain (31542) and (35124) if we extract the x-coordinates of the pins in L_1 in the x_+ and x_- directions, respectively. The **position sequence** $\Gamma_{(R,C)}$ for P is a sequence $(s_1 s_2 ... s_n)$ where $R \in \{c_+, c_-\}$, $C \in \{\bar{c}_+, \bar{c}_-\}$, and s_i is the $\bar{c}$-coordinate of the i-th pin in the $\bar{c}_+$ or $\bar{c}_-$-direction in the list of the pins sorted by c_+ or c_- sorting. For example, assume that (R, C) is (y_+, x_+) and P is the set of pins in Figure 2(a). Then, we first sort the pins along the y_+-direction, which leads to the ordered list

---

[2]If the coordinate of p_i is (x_{p_i}, y_{p_i}), $x_{p_i} \neq x_{p_j}$ and $y_{p_i} \neq y_{p_j}$ for any i and j ($i \neq j$).

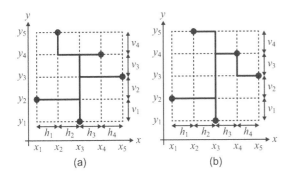

Figure 3: Two trees constructed on the 2D Hanan grid.

$(p_3, p_1, p_5, p_4, p_2)$, and obtain $\Gamma_{(y_+, x_+)} = (31542)$. Similarly, $\Gamma_{(y_+, x_-)}$ is (35124), $\Gamma_{(y_-, x_+)}$ is (24513), $\Gamma_{(y_-, x_-)}$ is (42153), $\Gamma_{(x_+, y_+)}$ is (25143), $\Gamma_{(x_+, y_-)}$ is (41523), $\Gamma_{(x_-, y_+)}$ is (34152), and $\Gamma_{(x_-, y_-)}$ is (32514).

2.1.3 Potentially Optimal Wirelength Vector and Potentially Optimal Steiner Tree. The wirelength of an RST on the 2D Hanan grid can be expressed as a linear combination of the x- and y-directional edge vectors representing the tree as explained in [2]. For example, the wirelength of the tree in Figure 3(a) is

$$L = 1 \cdot h_1 + 2 \cdot h_2 + 2 \cdot h_3 + 1 \cdot h_4 + 1 \cdot v_1 + 1 \cdot v_2 + 1 \cdot v_3 + 1 \cdot v_4, \quad (1)$$

which can also be expressed as

$$L = (1, 2, 2, 1, 1, 1, 1, 1) \cdot (h_1, h_2, h_3, h_4, v_1, v_2, v_3, v_4). \quad (2)$$

The first vector $(1, 2, 2, 1, 1, 1, 1, 1)$ is called a ***coefficient vector*** and the second vector $(h_1, h_2, h_3, h_4, v_1, v_2, v_3, v_4)$ is called an ***edge length vector***. The edge length vector is a constant vector for a given set of pin locations. However, the coefficient vector is dependent on the topology of the constructed tree. For example, the wirelength of the tree in Figure 3(b) is

$$L = 1 \cdot h_1 + 2 \cdot h_2 + 1 \cdot h_3 + 1 \cdot h_4 + 1 \cdot v_1 + 1 \cdot v_2 + 2 \cdot v_3 + 1 \cdot v_4, \quad (3)$$

whose coefficient vector is $(1, 2, 1, 1, 1, 1, 2, 1)$. Thus, the two trees in Figure 3(a) and (b) have the same edge length vector, but different coefficient vectors.

For a given set of pin locations, a coefficient vector $V = (c_1, ..., c_k)$ becomes a ***potentially optimal wirelength vector (POWV)*** if it satisfies the following conditions [2]:

- There exists an RST that connects all the pins and uses the edges specified in the coefficient vector V on the Hanan grid constructed for the pins.
- For the same pin locations, there is no other coefficient vector $V' = (c'_1, ..., c'_k)$ satisfying $c'_i \le c_i$ for all $i = 1, ..., k$.

An RST corresponding to a POWV is called a ***potentially optimal Steiner tree (POST)*** [2]. The RST shown in Figure 3(a) is a POST for POWV $(1, 2, 2, 1, 1, 1, 1, 1)$, which belongs to position sequence (31542). Similarly, the RST shown in Figure 3(b) is a POST for POWV $(1, 2, 1, 1, 1, 1, 2, 1)$, which belongs to the same position sequence.

2.2 Construction of an RSMT and All RSMTs on the Hanan Grid

FLUTE constructs an RSMT by a lookup table [2]. The lookup table consists of all position sequences, all POWVs belonging to each

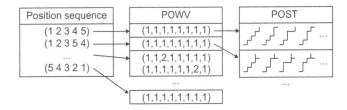

Figure 4: An overview of the lookup table of all POSTs in [7].

position sequence, and one POST for each POWV. Whenever a set of pin locations is given, FLUTE first finds the position sequence of the pin locations, then compares the wirelengths of all the POWVs belonging to the position sequence by calculating the inner product of each POWV and the edge length vector for the given pin locations. Then, FLUTE returns the POST of the POWV having the minimum wirelength. If multiple POWVs have the same wirelength, FLUTE can return the POSTs of all the POWVs having the minimum wirelength. The returned POSTs are RSMTs for the pin locations. For more details, we refer readers to [2].

FLUTE contains only one POST per POWV, but a POWV can have multiple POSTs. If the lookup table contains all POSTs for each POWV, numerous CAD algorithms can also benefit from the POSTs. For example, congestion-aware global routing can reduce routing congestion by finding all RSMTs and choosing the best one for each net. Thus, Lin generated a lookup table storing all POSTs in [7]. Figure 4 shows an overview of the lookup table of all POSTs. The algorithm of finding all POSTs uses a binary decision tree with several speed-up techniques to reduce the runtime. For more details, we refer readers to [7].

2.3 Multilayer Monolithic Rectilinear Steiner Minimum Trees

The following three definitions define a 3D rectilinear tree, a 3D rectilinear Steiner tree, and a 3D rectilinear Steiner minimum tree.

DEFINITION 1. *A **3D rectilinear tree** is a tree having only x-, y-, and z-directional edges and connecting all given pins.*

DEFINITION 2. *A **3D rectilinear Steiner tree (3D RST)** is a 3D rectilinear tree with Steiner points. A Steiner point is a non-pin vertex having more than two edges.*

DEFINITION 3. *A **3D rectilinear Steiner minimum tree (3D RSMT)** is a 3D RST having the minimum wirelength.*

The wirelength of a 3D rectilinear tree is computed by the sum of the lengths of all the x-, y-, and z-directional edges in the tree. When 3D RSTs or 3D RSMTs are used for routing of 3D IC layouts, the length of a vertical via is adjusted so that the actual overhead of the vertical via can be properly taken into account in the design. In the monolithic 3D IC layout design, the area and capacitance overhead of an MIV is negligible, so we can set the length of an MIV to zero during 3D routing. However, minimizing the number of MIVs inserted in the layout is still crucial. Thus, we define a multilayer monolithic rectilinear Steiner minimum tree as follows:

DEFINITION 4. *A **multilayer monolithic rectilinear Steiner minimum tree (MMRSMT)** is a 3D RSMT using the minimum number of z-directional edges with zero z-directional edge length.*

Since an MMRSMT is a 3D RSMT, it has the shortest planar wirelength. Thus, if we project all the edges in an MMRSMT onto the xy plane, the projection becomes a 2D RSMT. In other words, *an MMRSMT can be constructed from a 2D RSMT by properly placing x- and y-directional edges of the 2D RSMT in a 3D grid and inserting z-directional edges.* In addition, we obtain 2D RSMTs from POSTs as mentioned in the previous section. Thus, we can construct an MMRSMT from a POST. We define a 3D potentially optimal Steiner tree as follows:

DEFINITION 5. *Suppose a set of xy-distinct[3] pin locations is given. Let the set be $P = \{(x_1, y_1, z_1), ..., (x_n, y_n, z_n)\}$. Let the set of the projections of the pins onto the xy plane be $P' = \{(x_1, y_1), ..., (x_n, y_n)\}$. Let a POST constructed for P' be $G' = (V', E')$. Let the coordinate of e' in E' be $e'(i, j)$. A **3D potentially optimal Steiner tree (3D POST)** is a tree T that connects all the pins in P, uses the minimum number of z-directional edges in the 3D Hanan grid G constructed from P, and uses one of the edges among $e(i, j, k = 0, ..., t-1)$ in G for each $e'(i, j) \in E'$. t in the definition is the number of tiers.* From now, we denote the POSTs in the database of all POSTs in [7] by 2D POSTs to distinguish them from 3D POSTs.

In summary, if we have a database of all 3D POSTs, we can build all MMRSMTs for a given set of pin locations in a very short period of time. In this paper, we build a database of all 3D POSTs for all possible relative pin locations in two, three, and four tiers.

3 CONSTRUCTION OF ALL 3D POSTS

In this section, we present an algorithm to construct all 3D POSTs on the 3D Hanan grid for a given set of pin locations and a 2D POST for them. Figure 5 shows a 3D grid, pin and non-pin vertices, x-, y-, and z-directional edges, and notations used in this paper.

3.1 Construction of All 3D POSTs

The input to the algorithm is a set P of pin locations and a 2D POST, $G_2 = (V_2, E_2)$ constructed for the projections of the pins onto the xy plane. In Figure 6(a), for example, the coordinates of the three pins are $(0, 0, 0)$, $(1, 2, 2)$, and $(2, 1, 1)$. The position sequence $\Gamma_{(y_+, x_+)}$ of the projections is (132) and the 2D POST shown in Figure 6(a) belongs to the position sequence.

Algorithm 1 shows the algorithm for constructing all 3D POSTs. We first set the *visited* variables of all the edges in E_2 to false (Line 1). Then, we sort the edges in E_2 and store the result in an ordered set E'_2 (Line 2). The function **sort_edges** chooses a pin vertex in G_2 and performs the breadth-first search starting from the pin vertex until all the pin vertices are reached. Whenever it goes through an edge, the function inserts the edge into E'_2. This order reduces the runtime of the algorithm. For example, the sort_edges function starts from the pin vertex $(0, 0, 0)$ in Figure 6(a). Then, E'_2 becomes $(e_x(0, 0), e_y(0, 1), e_x(1, 1), e_y(1, 1))$. Then, we construct a 3D grid $G_3 = (V_3, E_3)$ from G_2 and P (Line 3). The **construct_3D_grid** function expands the 2D graph G_2 to a 3D graph G_3 as shown in Figure 6(b). The expansion adds vertices $v(i, j, k = 0, ..., t-1)$ to G_3 for each vertex $v'(i, j)$ in G_2 where t is the number of tiers. Similarly, the expansion adds $e_x(i, j, k = 0, ..., t-1)$ to G_3 for each

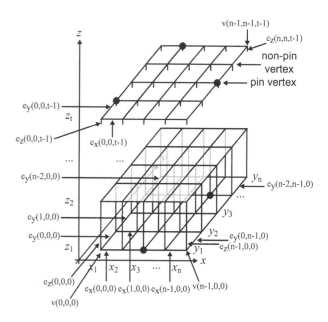

Figure 5: An $n \times n \times t$ 3D grid, pin and non-pin vertices, and indices for x-, y-, and z-directional edges.

$e'_x(i, j)$ in G_2, $e_y(i, j, k = 0, ..., t-1)$ to G_3 for each $e'_y(i, j)$ in G_2, and $e_z(i, j, k = 0, ..., t-2)$ to G_3 for each $v'(i, j)$ in G_2. Then, we set the *used* variables of all the edges in E_3 to false, which means that the edges are not used yet (Line 4). T is a set of graphs storing all the 3D POSTs, nr_MIVs is a variable storing the number of MIVs used in G_3, and min_nr_MIVs is a variable storing the minimum number of MIVs used in the 3D POSTs (Line 5). Then, we call the **recur_con** function to recursively construct all 3D POSTs for the given pin locations and the 2D POST (Line 6). Once the algorithm ends, we return T (Line 7).

The **recur_con** function starts from checking the given index, which is used to access the edges in E'_2. The edge index is greater than the number of edges in E'_2 when there is no more edge to process in G_3 (Line 1), which means that G_3 is a 3D graph connecting all the pins. In this case, if the total number of MIVs used in G_3 is equal to the minimum number of MIVs used in the best graphs found until now, we add it to T (Line 3). However, if the total number of MIVs used in G_3 is less than the minimum number of MIVs used in the best graphs found until now, all the graphs in T use more MIVs than G_3, so we empty T (Line 5), add G_3 to T, and update min_nr_MIVs (Line 6).

If the edge index is less than than the size of E'_2 (Line 10), we visit the edge in E'_2 indexed by the edge index variable (Line 11) and try using edges in G_3 corresponding to the indexed edge (Line 12 to Line 32). First, suppose $e'_d(i, j)$ is $E'_2[index]$ where d is either x or y. Then, we try using $e_d(i, j, k)$ in G_3 for each $k = 0, ..., t-1$ (Line 14). In Figure 6(c), $e_x(0, 0, 0)$ in G_3, which corresponds to the first edge $e_x(0, 0)$ in E'_2, is used. Then, if e is x-directional, we obtain its left vertex in G_2, otherwise we obtain its bottom vertex in G_2 and assign it to v (Line 15). Then, we find the bottommost and topmost tiers that should be connected along the z-axis through v in G_3 by the **get_min_max_tier** function (Line 16 to Line 19). The function

---

[3]If the coordinate of p_i is $(x_{p_i}, y_{p_i}, z_{p_i})$, $x_{p_i} \neq x_{p_j}$ and $y_{p_i} \neq y_{p_j}$ for any i and j $(i \neq j)$.

Function: Construct all 3D POSTs for P and G_2.
Input: Pin locations (P) and a 2D POST $G_2 = (V_2, E_2)$.
1: $e.$visited = false for all $e \in E_2$;
2: Ordered set E_2' = **sort_edges** (G_2);
3: $G_3 = (V_3, E_3)$ = **construct_3D_grid** (G_2, P);
4: $e.$used = false for all $e \in E_3$;
5: $T = \{\}$; nr_MIVs = 0; min_nr_MIVs = ∞;
6: Call **recur_con** (T, G_2, G_3, E_2', 0, nr_MIVs, min_nr_MIVs);
7: Return T;

Function: recur_con (T, G_2, G_3, E_2', index, nr_MIVs, min_nr_MIVs)
1: **if** index $\geq |E_2'|$ **then**
2:   **if** nr_MIVs == min_nr_MIVs **then**
3:     Add G_3 to T;
4:   **else if** nr_MIVs < min_nr_MIVs **then**
5:     Clear T;
6:     Add G_3 to T; min_nr_MIVs = nr_MIVs;
7:   **end if**
8:   return;
9: **end if**
10: $e = E_2'[$index$]$;
11: $e.$visited = true;
12: **for** tier = 0 ; tier < # tiers ; tier = tier + 1 **do**
13:   $e_3 = E_3[e.x][e.y][tier]$;
14:   $e_3.$used = true;
15:   $v = e.$left (or $e.$bottom);
16:   min_t1 = max_t1 = 0;
17:   **if** All the edges connected to v in G_2 have been visited **then**
18:     min_t1, max_t1 = **get_min_max_tier** (v, G_2, G_3);
19:   **end if**
20:   $v = e.$right (or $e.$top);
21:   min_t2 = max_t2 = 0;
22:   **if** All the edges connected to v in G_2 have been visited **then**
23:     min_t2, max_t2 = **get_min_max_tier** (v, G_2, G_3);
24:   **end if**
25:   delta = (max_t1 - min_t1) + (max_t2 - min_t2);
26:   nr_MIVs = nr_MIVs + delta;
27:   **if** nr_MIVs $\leq$ min_nr_MIVs **then**
28:     **recur_con** (T, G_2, G_3, E_2', index+1, nr_MIVs, min_nr_MIVs);
29:   **end if**
30:   nr_MIVs = nr_MIVs - delta;
31:   $e_3.$used = false;
32: **end for**
33: $e.$visited = false;

Algorithm 1: Construction of all 3D POSTs for a given 2D POST and pin locations in 3D.

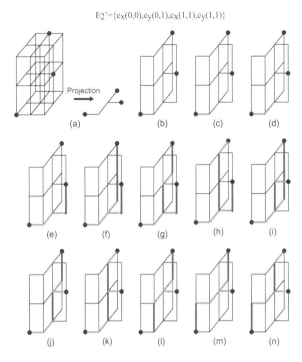

$E_2' = \{e_x(0,0), e_y(0,1), e_x(1,1), e_y(1,1)\}$

(a)   (b)   (c)   (d)

(e)   (f)   (g)   (h)   (i)

(j)   (k)   (l)   (m)   (n)

Figure 6: Construction of all 3D POSTs in three tiers for pins $(0,0,0)$, $(1,2,2)$, $(2,1,1)$. **(a) A 2D POST is given. (b) The construct_3D_grid function creates a 3D grid structure. (c)-(n) 3D POST construction. The red edges are used planar edges and the blue edges are used z-directional edges.**

finds all the visited edges connected to e in G_2, obtains the tiers of the edges in G_3 corresponding to the visited edges, and finds the bottommost and topmost tiers. In addition, if v is a pin vertex, the z-coordinate of the pin should be included in the computation of the range of the tiers. We repeat the same process for the right vertex of e (or top vertex if e is y-directional) (Line 20 to Line 24).

If we have visited all the edges connected to the left (bottom) and/or right (top) vertices of e, we can find the z-directional edges required to connect to the pin and the edges along the z-axis at the vertices. From the z-directional edges, we obtain the number of MIVs (Line 25). If the total number of MIVs currently used in G_3 is less than or equal to the minimum number of MIVs used in the best graphs found until now, we move on to the next edge in

E_2' (Line 28). Otherwise, the current graph uses more MIVs than the best graphs found until now, so we do not need to proceed to the next edge. Once the recursive function call ends (Line 28), we readjust the number of MIVs used in G_3 (Line 30) and try using the edge above e (Line 31 and Line 32).

In Figure 6(c), for example, $e_x(0,0,0)$ is in Tier 0 and the left vertex of $e_x(0,0,0)$ is a pin vertex, which is also in Tier 0. Thus, both the bottommost and topmost tiers for the vertex are Tier 0. Then, we move on to $e_y(0,1)$ in E_2' and try using $e_y(0,1,0)$ in G_3 in Figure 6(d). The *used* variables of all the edges connected to the bottom vertex of $e_y(0,1)$ are *true* at this point and all the edges are placed in Tier 0. Thus, we do not need to add any z-directional edges above the vertex. Then, we process the next edge $e_x(1,1)$ in E_2' in Figure 6(e). The right vertex of $e_x(1,1)$ is connected to the pin located at $(2,1)$, which corresponds to the pin located at $(2,1,1)$ in G_3, so the bottommost and topmost tiers at the vertex are Tier 0 and Tier 1, respectively. Thus, we use $e_z(2,1,0)$ in G_3, which is inserting an MIV into the location. When we also try using $e_y(1,1,0)$ in Figure 6(f), we finally construct a 3D graph connecting all the pins. The total number of MIVs is three. Similarly, the total numbers of MIVs in the 3D graphs in Figure 6(g), (h), and (i) are all three. However, the 3D graph in Figure 6(j) uses two MIVs. At this time, T contains all the 3D graphs found in Figure 6(f), (g), (h), and (i), so we delete all of them from T and add the 3D graph found in Figure 6(j) to T. There are four more 3D graphs using two MIVs as shown in Figure 6(k), (l), (m), and (n). Thus, when the algorithm finishes, T contains the five 3D graphs found in Figure 6(j), (k), (l), (m), and (n). All of them become 3D POSTs for the given pin locations and 2D POST.

3.2 Congruence of 3D POSTs

The runtime of the algorithm shown in Algorithm 1 is prohibitively long. In addition, there are numerous 3D POSTs in the database, so it is crucial to reduce the runtime and the size of the database. In this section, we show congruent properties of the 3D POSTs, which are used to skip generating and storing some 3D POSTs.

3.2.1 Congruence of Position Sequences. As mentioned in [2], two position sequences are congruent if rotating one of them leads to the other. For example, Figure 7(a) shows position sequence (31542). If we rotate it counterclockwise by 90, 180, and 270 degrees, we obtain position sequences (41523), (42153), and (34152) as shown in Figure 7(b), (c), and (d), respectively. If two position sequences are congruent to each other, a 2D POST constructed for one of them can be for the other position sequence. Thus, we do not need to generate 2D POSTs for some position sequences.

In addition to the rotation, reflection also generates congruent position sequences. If we reflect the pin locations in Figure 7(a) over a y-directional line results in position sequence (35124) shown in Figure 7(e). Now, rotating the position sequence counterclockwise by 90, 180, and 270 degrees leads to position sequences (32514), (24513), and (25143) shown in Figure 7(f), (g), and (h), respectively.

Rotating and reflecting a position sequence has the same effect as generating position sequences by $\Gamma_{(d_1,d_2)}$. For example, generating the position sequence in Figure 7(a) is the same as generating the position sequence $\Gamma_{(y_+,x_+)}$. The position sequences obtained by rotating the position sequence $\Gamma_{(y_+,x_+)}$ by 90, 180, and 270 degrees are the same as the position sequences $\Gamma_{(x_+,y_-)}, \Gamma_{(y_-,x_-)}$, and $\Gamma_{(x_-,y_+)}$, respectively. Similarly, reflecting $\Gamma_{(y_+,x_+)}$ over a y-directional line is the same as generating the position sequence $\Gamma_{(y_+,x_-)}$. Then, rotating $\Gamma_{(y_+,x_-)}$ by 90, 180, and 270 degrees are the same obtaining the position sequences $\Gamma_{(x_-,y_-)}, \Gamma_{(y_-,x_+)}$, and $\Gamma_{(x_+,y_+)}$, respectively.

If multiple position sequences are congruent, we can store POSTs for only one (called a *base position sequence*) of them. Then, we can obtain POSTs for the other position sequences by properly transforming the POSTs stored for their base position sequences. Notice that a position sequence can be congruent to multiple position sequences as shown in Figure 7, so we need a rule to choose a base position sequence among congruent position sequences. In this paper, we use the following rule to determine base position sequences. Suppose a set of pin locations is given in the 2D plane. Then, we find all the eight position sequences $\Gamma_{(y_\pm,x_\pm)}$ and $\Gamma_{(x_\pm,y_\pm)}$ and choose the smallest position sequence for their base sequence. In Figure 7, for example, (24513) in Figure 7(g) is the smallest number, so (24513) becomes the base position sequence for all the position sequences in Figure 7.

3.2.2 Congruence of 3D POSTs. Suppose pin locations are given in the 3D space. Then, we can characterize the pin locations by two sequences, a position sequence and a tier sequence. The position sequence $PS = (s_1...s_n)$ is based on the projections of the pins onto the xy plane and the tier sequence $TS = (t_1...t_n)$ is a sequence of the z-coordinates of the pins where t_i corresponds to s_i. Figure 8

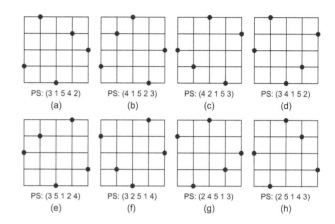

PS: (3 1 5 4 2) (a)
PS: (4 1 5 2 3) (b)
PS: (4 2 1 5 3) (c)
PS: (3 4 1 5 2) (d)
PS: (3 5 1 2 4) (e)
PS: (3 2 5 1 4) (f)
PS: (2 4 5 1 3) (g)
PS: (2 5 1 4 3) (h)

Figure 7: Congruence of eight position sequences.

shows an example. In Figure 8(a), the z-coordinates of the pins corresponding to the position sequence elements 3, 1, 5, 4, 2 are 0, 1, 0, 1, 0, respectively. Thus, the tier sequence for the pin locations is $TS = (01010)$.

If we rotate the two tiers in Figure 8(a) counterclockwise by 90, 180, and 270 degrees around the z-axis, we obtain the position and tier sequences shown in Figure 8(b), (c), and (d), respectively. In addition, if we reflect the two tiers in Figure 8(a) over a plane parallel to the yz plane, we obtain the position and tier sequences in Figure 8(e). Rotating the two tiers in Figure 8(e) counterclockwise by 90, 180, and 270 degrees around the z-axis leads to the position and tier sequences in Figure 8(f), (g), and (h), respectively. Moreover, reflecting the two tiers in Figure 8(a) and (e) over a plane parallel to the xy plane generates the position and tier sequences in Figure 8(i) and (m), respectively. Rotating the position and tier sequences in Figure 8(i) and (m) counterclockwise by 90, 180, and 270 degrees around the z-axis generates the position and tier sequences in Figure 8(j), (k), and (l), and Figure 8(n), (o), and (p), respectively.

To find a congruence between two sets of position and tier sequences, we define a *3D position sequence* $\Gamma_{(R,C,T)}$, which consists of a pair of sequences. The first sequence is the 2D position sequence $(s_1...s_n)$ obtained from $\Gamma_{(R,C)}$. The second sequence is the tier sequence along the T-direction ($T \in \{z_\pm\}$) as defined above. Then, the 3D position sequence for the pins in Figure 8(a) is denoted by $\Gamma_{(y_+,x_+,z_+)}$. Similarly, 3D position sequences for the pins in Figure 8(b), (c), (d), (e), (f), (g), and (h), are $\Gamma_{(x_+,y_-,z_+)}, \Gamma_{(y_-,x_-,z_+)}$, $\Gamma_{(x_-,y_+,z_+)}, \Gamma_{(y_+,x_-,z_+)}, \Gamma_{(x_-,y_-,z_+)}, \Gamma_{(y_-,x_+,z_+)}$, and $\Gamma_{(x_+,y_+,z_+)}$, respectively. Since the reflection over a plane parallel to the xy plane reverses the tier sequence, 3D position sequences for the pins in Figure 8(i), (j), (k), (l), (m), (n), (o), and (p) are $\Gamma_{(y_+,x_+,z_-)}, \Gamma_{(x_+,y_-,z_-)}$, $\Gamma_{(y_-,x_-,z_-)}, \Gamma_{(x_-,y_+,z_-)}, \Gamma_{(y_+,x_-,z_-)}, \Gamma_{(x_-,y_-,z_-)}, \Gamma_{(y_-,x_+,z_-)}$, and $\Gamma_{(x_+,y_+,z_-)}$, respectively. If two sets of pin locations are congruent, we can use the 3D POSTs belonging to one of them for the other by properly transforming the 3D POSTs.

We also define a *3D base position sequence* as follows. Suppose a set of pin locations is given in the 3D space. Then, we find all the 16 3D position sequences $\Gamma_{(y_\pm,x_\pm,z_\pm)}$ and $\Gamma_{(x_\pm,y_\pm,z_\pm)}$ for them and choose the smallest 3D position sequence. If multiple 3D position sequences have the same 2D position sequence, we choose

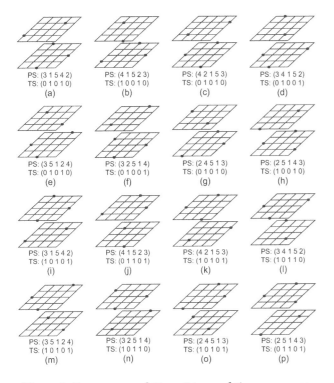

PS: (3 1 5 4 2)
TS: (0 1 0 1 0)
(a)

PS: (4 1 5 2 3)
TS: (1 0 0 1 0)
(b)

PS: (4 2 1 5 3)
TS: (0 1 0 1 0)
(c)

PS: (3 4 1 5 2)
TS: (0 1 0 0 1)
(d)

PS: (3 5 1 2 4)
TS: (0 1 0 1 0)
(e)

PS: (3 2 5 1 4)
TS: (0 1 0 0 1)
(f)

PS: (2 4 5 1 3)
TS: (0 1 0 1 0)
(g)

PS: (2 5 1 4 3)
TS: (1 0 0 1 0)
(h)

PS: (3 1 5 4 2)
TS: (1 0 1 0 1)
(i)

PS: (4 1 5 2 3)
TS: (0 1 1 0 1)
(j)

PS: (4 2 1 5 3)
TS: (1 0 1 0 1)
(k)

PS: (3 4 1 5 2)
TS: (1 0 1 1 0)
(l)

PS: (3 5 1 2 4)
TS: (1 0 1 0 1)
(m)

PS: (3 2 5 1 4)
TS: (1 0 1 1 0)
(n)

PS: (2 4 5 1 3)
TS: (1 0 1 0 1)
(o)

PS: (2 5 1 4 3)
TS: (0 1 1 0 1)
(p)

Figure 8: Congruence of 16 position and tier sequences.

the smallest tier sequence among them. In Figure 8, for example, the smallest 2D position sequence is (24513) in Figure 8(g) and (o). Between these two, the tier sequence (01010) in Figure 8(g) is smaller than (10101) in Figure 8(o), so the 3D position sequence of Figure 8(g) becomes the base 3D position sequence for all the 3D position sequences in Figure 8.

4 SIMULATION RESULTS

In this section, we present simulation results obtained from the construction of all 3D POSTs on the 3D Hanan grid. We implemented the proposed algorithm using C/C++ and ran the code in an Intel Core i5-6600K 3.3GHz CPU system with 64GB memory. We used the 2D POST database in [7].

Table 1 shows statistics of the construction of all 3D POSTs for two- to six-pin nets and two to four tiers. The number of position sequences is $n!$ where n is the number of pins. The number of 2D POSTs comes from the database of all 2D POSTs in [7].

Our first observation is that as the tier count goes up from two to four, the total number of 3D POSTs increases exponentially. This is because the number of combinations of placing pins in different tiers increases exponentially as the tier count goes up. The recurrent relation for counting the number of the combinations is as follows:

$$f(n, t) = t^n - \sum_{i=1}^{t-1}\{(t - i + 1) \cdot f(n, i)\} \qquad (4)$$

where $f(n, t)$ is the number of combinations of placing n pins in t consecutive tiers. A closed-form expression for $f(n, t)$ is as follows:

$$f(n, t) = t^n - 2 \cdot (t - 1)^n + (t - 2)^n, \qquad (5)$$

$$f(n, 1) = 1. \qquad (6)$$

Thus, as t increases, $f(n, t)$ goes up exponentially. In addition, as the pin count goes up, the number of 2D POSTs also increases exponentially as shown in the table. Thus, the total number of 3D POSTs increases extremely fast as the pin and tier counts go up.

We also observe that the number of generated 3D POSTs is approximately 16% of the total 3D POSTs. As explained in Section 3.2, using the congruence properties of position sequences and 3D POSTs significantly reduces the number of 3D POSTs actually generated from the proposed algorithm. Thus, we reduce the construction time and the database size effectively. The database contains the generated 3D POSTs for all the 3D base position sequences. For non-base topologies, the database contains their base topologies and rules transforming the non-base topologies to their base topologies.

The construction efficiency measured by the ratio between the number of generated 3D POSTs and the total construction time decreases almost exponentially as the pin count and the tier count go up. The proposed algorithm can still construct approximately 130,000 3D POSTs for the six-pin four-tier case. However, there are almost 15-billion 3D POSTs to generate for the case, so the construction time is about 30 hours. The table size is approximately 135 GB, which can be easily handled in server computers.

Figure 9 shows two 3D POSTs constructed for pin locations $(0, 0, 0)$, $(3, 1, 3)$, $(2, 2, 2)$, $(5, 3, 1)$, $(1, 4, 0)$, $(4, 5, 3)$ and the same 2D POST. The red edges are planar wires and the blue edges are MIVs. The 3D POST in Figure 9(a) has five planar edges in Tier 0 (the bottommost tier) and eight planar edges in Tier 1, respectively. On the other hand, the 3D POST in Figure 9(b) has 12 planar edges in Tier 2 and a planar edge in Tier 3 (the topmost tier). In addition, the planar coordinates of the MIVs in Tier 1 in Figure 9(a) are $(2, 1)$ and $(2, 3)$, whereas those in Tier 1 in Figure 9(b) are $(0, 0)$ and $(1, 4)$. Similarly, the planar coordinates of the MIVs in Tier 2 in Figure 9(a) are $(3, 1)$, $(2, 2)$, and $(4, 5)$, whereas those in Figure 9(b) are $(0, 0)$, $(1, 4)$, and $(5, 3)$. The planar coordinates of the MIVs in Tier 3 in Figure 9(a) are $(3, 1)$ and $(4, 5)$, whereas those in Figure 9(b) are $(2, 1)$ and $(4, 5)$. Thus, among the seven MIVs inserted in the two 3D POSTs, only one MIV located at $(4, 5, 3)$ is common and the other six MIVs are located at different locations. We have also compared various 3D POSTs and found similar trends. Overall, we expect that the database of the 3D POSTs can be used for 3D routing to evenly distribute planar wires and MIVs across the tiers in a given layout.

5 CONCLUSION

Monolithic 3D integration uses ultra-small MIVs, so routing of 3D nets in the design of monolithic 3D IC layouts should minimize the planar wirelength and the number of MIVs at the same time while evenly distributing planar wires across tiers. In this paper, therefore, we have developed an algorithm to build a database of 3D POSTs, which can help routers generate MMRSMTs in no time and use them to route monolithic 3D ICs and optimize 2D and 3D interconnects. The database size is manageable for up to four-tier

Table 1: Statistics of the construction of all 3D POSTs for two- to six-pin nets for two, three, and four tiers. "# PS" is the number of 2D position sequences for projected pins. "# all 3D POSTs" is the total number of 3D POSTs and "# gen. 3D POSTs" is the number of 3D POSTs generated from the proposed algorithm. r is the ratio between the number of generated 3D POSTs and the total number of 3D POSTs. "Con. time" is the construction time for all the generated 3D POSTs. "Con. eff." is the construction efficiency, which is measured by the ratio between the number of generated 3D POSTs and the construction time in seconds.

# pins (n)	# PS ($n!$)	# 2D POSTs	# tiers	# all 3D POSTs	# gen. 3D POSTs	r	Con. time	Con. eff.	Table size
2	2	4	2	24	12	0.5	0.0 s	-	< 1 KB
			3	48	24	0.5	0.0001 s	-	< 1 KB
			4	80	40	0.5	0.0001 s	-	< 1 KB
3	6	16	2	224	84	0.375	0.0001 s	-	1 KB
			3	896	336	0.375	0.0003 s	-	2 KB
			4	2,352	888	0.378	0.0006 s	-	4 KB
4	24	284	2	20,056	5,372	0.268	0.0043 s	1,249,302	35 KB
			3	226,800	60,120	0.265	0.0457 s	1,315,536	313 KB
			4	1,396,944	367,424	0.263	0.3465 s	1,060,387	2 MB
5	120	4,260	2	719,864	125,360	0.174	0.1484 s	844,744	850 KB
			3	14,876,928	2,575,092	0.173	5.2478 s	490,699	16 MB
			4	142,195,680	24,482,354	0.172	95.77 s	255,637	167 MB
6	720	120,212	2	85,530,040	13,831,206	0.162	20.13 s	687,094	93 MB
			3	4,318,826,472	697,355,262	0.161	42.2 m	275,417	5.1 GB
			4	90,473,628,112	14,586,090,890	0.161	30.2 h	134,162	129 GB

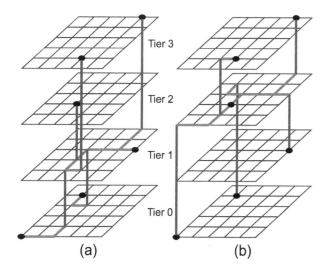

Figure 9: Comparison of two 3D POSTs constructed for pin locations $(0,0,0)$, $(3,1,3)$, $(2,2,2)$, $(5,3,1)$, $(1,4,0)$, $(4,5,3)$. 3D position sequence: $PS = (143625)$, $TS = (032103)$.

six-pin 3D POSTs. Thus, the proposed algorithm and the database of 3D POSTs will help various VLSI CAD algorithms optimize 3D IC layouts more effectively and serve as a baseline algorithm for better monolithic 3D IC routing algorithms.

ACKNOWLEDGMENTS

This work was supported by the Defense Advanced Research Projects Agency Young Faculty Award under Grant D16AP00119 and the New Faculty Seed Grant (125679-002) funded by the Washington State University.

REFERENCES

[1] Yiting Chen and Dae Hyun Kim. 2017. A Legalization Algorithm for Multi-Tier Gate-Level Monolithic Three-Dimensional Integrated Circuits. In *Proc. Int. Symp. on Quality Electronic Design*. 277–282.
[2] Chris Chu and Yiu-Chung Wong. 2008. FLUTE: Fast Lookup Table Based Rectilinear Steiner Minimal Tree Algorithm for VLSI Design. In *IEEE Trans. on Computer-Aided Design of Integrated Circuits and Systems*, Vol. 27. 70–83.
[3] Dae Hyun Kim, Krit Athikulwongse, and Sung Kyu Lim. 2013. Study of Through-Silicon-Via Impact on the 3D Stacked IC Layout. In *IEEE Trans. on VLSI Systems*, Vol. 21. 862–874.
[4] Dae Hyun Kim, Rasit Onur Topaloglu, and Sung Kyu Lim. 2012. Block-level 3-D IC Design with Through-Silicon-Via Planning. In *Proc. Asia and South Pacific Design Automation Conf.* 335–340.
[5] Bon Woong Ku, Kyungwook Chang, and Sung Kyu Lim. 2018. Compact-2D: A Physical Design Methodology to Build Commercial-Quality Face-to-Face-Bonded 3D ICs. In *Proc. Int. Symp. on Physical Design*. 90–97.
[6] Chung-Wei Lin, Shih-Lun Huang, Kai-Chi Hsu, Meng-Xiang Lee, and Yao-Wen Chang. 2008. Multilayer Obstacle-Avoiding Rectilinear Steiner Tree Construction Based on Spanning Graphs. In *IEEE Trans. on Computer-Aided Design of Integrated Circuits and Systems*, Vol. 27. 2007–2016.
[7] Sheng-En David Lin and Dae Hyun Kim. 2018. Construction of All Rectilinear Steiner Minimum Trees on the Hanan Grid. In *Proc. Int. Symp. on Physical Design*. 18–25.
[8] Chih-Hung Liu, Chun-Xun Lin, I-Che Chen, D. T. Lee, and Ting-Chi Wang. 2014. Efficient Multilayer Obstacle-Avoiding Rectilinear Steiner Tree Construction Based on Geometric Reduction. In *IEEE Trans. on Computer-Aided Design of Integrated Circuits and Systems*, Vol. 33. 1928–1941.
[9] Shreepad Panth, Kambiz Samadi, Yang Du, and Sung Kyu Lim. 2014. Design and CAD Methodologies for Low Power Gate-level Monolithic 3D ICs. In *Proc. Int. Symp. on Low Power Electronics and Design*. 171–176.
[10] Shreepad Panth, Kambiz Samadi, Yang Du, and Sung Kyu Lim. 2015. Placement-Driven Partitioning for Congestion Mitigation in Monolithic 3D IC Designs. In *IEEE Trans. on Computer-Aided Design of Integrated Circuits and Systems*, Vol. 34. 540–553.
[11] Shreepad Panth, Kambiz Samadi, Yang Du, and Sung Kyu Lim. 2017. Shrunk-2D: A Physical Design Methodology to Build Commercial-Quality Monolithic 3D ICs. In *IEEE Trans. on Computer-Aided Design of Integrated Circuits and Systems*, Vol. 36. 1716–1724.

ROAD: Routability Analysis and Diagnosis Framework Based on SAT Techniques

Dongwon Park
Electrical and Computer Engineering,
UC San Diego
La Jolla, California
dwp003@ucsd.edu

Ilgweon Kang
Cadence Design Systems, Inc.
San Jose, California
ikang@cadence.com

Yeseong Kim
Computer Science and Engineering,
UC San Diego
La Jolla, California
yek048@ucsd.edu

Sicun Gao
Computer Science and Engineering,
UC San Diego
La Jolla, California
sicung@ucsd.edu

Bill Lin
Electrical and Computer Engineering,
UC San Diego
La Jolla, California
billlin@ucsd.edu

Chung-Kuan Cheng
Computer Science and Engineering,
UC San Diego
La Jolla, California
ckcheng@ucsd.edu

ABSTRACT

Routability diagnosis has increasingly become the bottleneck in detailed routing for sub-$10nm$ technology due to the limited tracks, high density, and complex design rules. The conventional ways to examine the routability of detailed routing are ILP- and SAT-based techniques. However, once we identify the routability, the diagnosis remains an open problem for physical designers. In this paper, we propose a novel framework, called *ROAD*, which diagnoses explicit reasons for routing failures. The proposed ROAD framework utilizes a diagnosis-friendly SAT formulation to represent design's layout and diagnoses the routability with SAT solving techniques. Based on the diagnosis, ROAD provides human-interpretable explanations for conflicted routing conditions. To show the practical value of our framework, we also generate comprehensive test-sets that enable exhaustive exploration of layouts based on Rent's rule. We demonstrate that ROAD successfully examines conflict causes for diverse pin layouts. Throughout extensive diagnosis, we also present several key findings for design failure. ROAD performs routability diagnosis within 2 minutes on average for 90 grids test-sets, while diagnosing the exact causes of routing failures in terms of congestion and conditional design rules.

KEYWORDS

Physical Design, Detailed Routing, Routability, Diagnosis, SAT, MUS, Longest Path, BCP, PIG

ACM Reference Format:
Dongwon Park, Ilgweon Kang, Yeseong Kim, Sicun Gao, Bill Lin, and Chung-Kuan Cheng. 2019. ROAD: Routability Analysis and Diagnosis Framework Based on SAT Techniques. In *2019 International Symposium on Physical Design (ISPD '19), April 14–17, 2019, San Francisco, CA, USA*. ACM, New York, NY, USA, 8 pages. https://doi.org/10.1145/3299902.3309752

1 INTRODUCTION

As manufacturing technology nodes are continuously evolved into sub-$10nm$, the detailed routing has been more challenging [1]. One of the major difficulties in the detailed routing is exposed by the resolution limitations coming from the diffraction limit of optical lithography which has $193nm$ (i.e., $193i$) wavelength [11, 12, 23]. Although recent multi-patterning techniques [4, 18, 19] enable to deliver $10nm$ and sub-$10nm$ technology nodes to foundries, they induce more complex conditional design rules for manufacturability which are new hurdles in the detailed routing procedure [2]. Routability becomes a critical bottleneck in detailed routing due to less number of routing tracks, higher pin density, and smaller pin geometry [23, 25]. Moreover, many layout revisions are urgently required during engineering change order (ECO) procedure since the mismatch between a global-route congestion map and detailed-route violations(i.e., design-rule violations) is growing [15].

For the detailed routability problem, several ILP-based approaches are proposed to achieve design rule-correct routability analysis [10, 12, 14]. SAT (Boolean satisfiability) techniques are widely utilized for efficient routability estimation [3, 9, 22], but they only focus on routing for standard cell designs, rather than layout design. Recently, a fast routability analysis technique based on a SAT formulation for the detailed routing is proposed [16]. However, even if we achieve the routability analysis successfully, the diagnosis for the routing failure remains an open question in the detailed routing.

In this paper, we propose a novel framework which diagnoses explicit reasons for the detailed routing failure while efficiently estimating the routability of layout architectures. To identify conflict geometry and design rules, ROAD converts design constraints of pin layouts to SAT clauses. It then diagnoses design conflicts based on several SAT techniques, such as Minimal Unsatisfiable Subset (MUS), Boolean Constraint Propagation (BCP) and Partial Implication Graph (PIG). Using the MUS technique [6, 27] identifying a minimum unsatisfiable subset of conflicting clauses, we first extract partial layouts that include the causes of conflicts in the unroutable case. BCP [17] is a simplification procedure for clauses using unit clauses. We iteratively perform BCP procedures until either there are no more remained unit clauses or any conflict is found. ROAD then represents variable nodes and clause edges generated by the

BCP procedure as a directed acyclic graph (DAG). This subprocedure is conducted by the PIG technique [17], and we exploit the PIG to produce diagnosis results of the conflict layouts.

The main contributions of this paper are listed as follows:

- We propose a fast and intuitive routability diagnosis framework, called *ROAD*, by utilizing the routability analysis technique based on SAT formation [16].
- ROAD provides comprehensive information of unroutable layouts, e.g., conflict geometries and design rules. This information is useful to layout designers for fast trouble-shooting and to design-rule managers for fine-grained decisions of design rule priority.
- We demonstrate that our diagnosis procedures are suitable to identify the causes of unroutable pin layouts.
- ROAD utilizes an automated technique [16] which generates pin layout testsets based on *Rent's Rule* [26]. It enables comprehensive exploration of conflicting cases which layout designers encounter in practice.

Our ROAD framework allows designers to diagnose the causes of routing failure cases and provides useful insights with enhancement of understanding for the unroutablity. In this paper, we also present several key findings. We find that layout conflicts happen due to two main factors: (i) pin-shape pattern and (ii) routing resource shortages (i.e., routing congestion). The pin-shape pattern is the main concern of pin accessbility problems. When the resource is insufficient, technology limitation may hinder layout routability, e.g., due to insufficient tracks and metal layers about pin layout. We find the exact geometry and design rules related to the conflict, and thus it can be a guideline how to resolve the conflict.

2 ROAD : ROUTABILITY ANALYSIS AND DIAGNOSIS

In this section, we describe the detailed procedures of ROAD: (i) Overview of ROAD, (ii) SAT formulation, (iii) Diagnosis Procedure, (iv) Diagnosis Result Report and (v) Automated Pin Layout Generation.

2.1 Overview of ROAD

Figure 1 shows the overview of the ROAD framework. The ROAD framework first performs the routability analysis based on the SAT formulation presented in [16]. If it is unroutable, we diagnose causes of the unroutablity. As the first step of the diagnosis procedure, we extract MUS (Minimal Unsatisfiable Subset), i.e., the subset of clauses including the conflict region and design rules which require a careful attention during the diagnosis. In the next initial propagation phase, we construct geometric information of switch-boxes by simplifying the extracted MUS. The key diagnosis steps are the iterative decision and propagative procedures. We decide appropriate via positions (Decision) and execute BCP (Boolean Constraint Propagation) with partial assignments (Propagation). The BCP procedure generates PIGs (Partial Implication Graphs), i.e., a DAG including variable nodes and clause edges. By combining multiple PIGs, we obtain a designer-friendly interpretation of the conflict geometry and design rules.

2.2 SAT Formulation

SAT formulation is derived on top of the multi-commodity network flow theory and conditional design rules [8, 16]. Among several

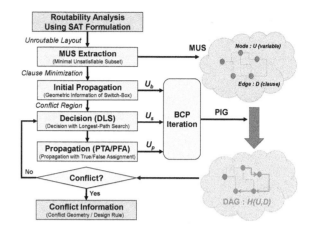

Figure 1: An overview of ROAD framework.

Table 1: Notations for SAT formulation.

Term	Description
$G(V, E)$	Three-dimensional (3-D) routing graph
V	Set of vertices in the routing graph G
V_i	Set of vertices in i^{th} metal layer of the routing graph G
v	A vertex at the coordinate (x_v, y_v, z_v)
v_d	0-1 indicator if d-directional adjacent vertex about v
$a(v)$	Set of adjacent vertices of v
E	Set of edges in the routing graph G
$e_{v,u}$	An edge between v and u, $u \in a(v)$
N	Set of multi-pin nets in the given routing box
n	n^{th} multi-pin net
s^n	A source of n
T^n	Set of sinks in n
t_m^n	m^{th} sink of n
f_m^n	m^{th} commodity flow of n heading to t_m^n
$e_{v,u}^n$	0-1 indicator if $e_{v,u}$ is used for n
$f_m^n(v, u)$	0-1 indicator if $e_{v,u}$ is used for commodity t_m^n
$m_{v,u}$	0-1 indicator if there is a metal segment on $e_{v,u}$
$g_{d,v}$	0-1 indicator if v forms d-side EOL of a metal segment

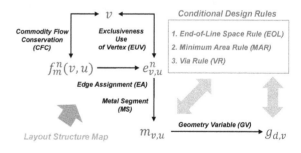

Figure 2: Constraint relations of the proposed SAT formulation.

kinds of SAT encoding methods, our formulation is a kind of the "muldirect" method, which is a directly encoding method of constraint satisfaction problem. It allows multiple assignments for the multi-commodity network to represent the detailed routing problem [20, 24].

The formulation consists of three subgroups, *(i) flow formulation, (ii) design rule formulation* and *(iii) layout structure map*. The notations and relations between constraints and variables are shown in Table 1 and Figure 2. The formulated subgroups create the foundation for the SAT framework. The SAT framework identifies if there are violations for the formulation, deciding the routability of the given layout.

Most of our formulation is composed by the Exactly-One (EO) constraint which is related to the flow formulation, or the At-Most-One (AMO) constraints which are related to design rules and exclusiveness. ROAD adopts the "pair-wise" and "commander" encoding methodology for EO and AMO constraints [21].

2.2.1 Flow Formulation (F).
We use a multi-commodity flow foundation to represent routing flows for a given layout. We achieve more efficient formulation by reducing CNF (conjunctive normal form) representation, i.e., regarding the flows as an undirected graph (1). This simplification still holds the correct representation since we only need to consider the source-sink connectivity.

$$f_m^n(v, u) = f_m^n(u, v), \ No \ Direction \tag{1}$$

Commodity Flow Conservation (CFC). Logical Expressions $(3, 4)$ represent the constraint of CFC, describing the commodity flow constraint on each vertex at a per-net and per-commodity granularity. $\mathbf{F}_{CFC}$ (2) is either $\mathbf{F}_{CFC_1}$ or $\mathbf{F}_{CFC_2}$ depending on the vertex type.

$$\mathbf{F}_{CFC}(v, n, m) = \begin{cases} \mathbf{F}_{CFC_1}(v, n, m), & \text{if } v \neq s^n, \ t_m^n \\ \mathbf{F}_{CFC_2}(v, n, m), & \text{if } v = s^n, \ t_m^n \end{cases} \tag{2}$$

$\mathbf{F}_{CFC_1}$ (3) represents the flow feasibility, i.e., either no flow passes or the flow of commodity m is connected between a pair of edges $(e_{v,p}$ and $e_{v,q})$, when a vertex v is neither a source nor a sink.

$$\mathbf{F}_{CFC_1}(v, n, m) = \bigwedge_{u \in a(v)} \neg f_m^n(v, u) \vee \bigvee_{p, q \in a(v), p \neq q} \left(f_m^n(v, p) \wedge f_m^n(v, q) \wedge \right.$$
$$\left. \bigwedge_{u \in a(v), u \neq p, u \neq q} \neg f_m^n(v, u) \right), \ \forall v \in V, \ \forall n \in N, \ \forall t_m^n \in T^n \tag{3}$$

$\mathbf{F}_{CFC_2}$ (4) represents the flow feasibility of the commodity m on a vertex v using an EO constraint [21] of commodity flow indicators $f_m^n(v, u)$, when v is either a source or a sink.

$$\mathbf{F}_{CFC_2}(v, n, m) = \text{EO}\left(\left\{ f_m^n(v, p) \mid p \in a(v) \right\} \right), \ \forall v \in V, \ \forall n \in N, \ \forall t_m^n \in T^n \tag{4}$$

Exclusiveness Use of Vertex (EUV). Logical Expressions $(6, 7)$ represent the constraint of EUV, ensuring that there are no intersecting nets on any vertex. $\mathbf{F}_{EUV}$ (5) is either $\mathbf{F}_{EUV_1}$ or $\mathbf{F}_{EUV_2}$ depending on the vertex type as well.

$$\mathbf{F}_{EUV}(v) = \begin{cases} \mathbf{F}_{EUV_1}(v), & \text{if } v \neq s^n, \ t_m^n \\ \mathbf{F}_{EUV_2}(v), & \text{if } v = s^n, \ t_m^n \end{cases} \tag{5}$$

$\mathbf{F}_{EUV_1}$ (6) represents the exclusiveness feasibility on each vertex v using an AMO net constraint [21], when the vertex v is neither a source nor a sink.

$$\mathbf{F}_{EUV_1}(v) = \text{AMO}\left(\left\{ \bigvee_{p \in a(v)} e_{v,p}^n \mid n \in N \right\} \right), \ \forall v \in V \tag{6}$$

$\mathbf{F}_{EUV_2}$ (7) represents the exclusiveness feasibility on each vertex v using an EO constraint of edge indicators $e_{v,u}^n$, when v is either a source or sink.

$$\mathbf{F}_{EUV_2}(v) = \text{EO}\left(\left\{ e_{v,p}^n \mid p \in a(v), \ n \in N \right\} \right), \ \forall v \in V \tag{7}$$

Figure 3: An example to determine GV.

Edge Assignment (EA). Logical Expression (8) represents the constraint of Edge Assignment (EA), ensuring the multi-commodity flow of net n. If the flow indicator $f_m^n(v, u)$ is 1, then the edge $e_{v,u}$ is 1.

$$\mathbf{F}_{EA}(e_{v,u}, n, m) = e_{v,u}^n \vee \neg f_m^n(v, u), \ \forall e_{v,u} \in E, \ \forall n \in N, \ \forall t_m^n \in T^n \tag{8}$$

Metal Segment (MS). Logical Expression (9) represents the constraint of Metal Segment (MS) using an EO constraint, i.e., either exclusiveness use of edge for certain net or no edge uses. The expression is a part of the AMO commander encoding [21] whose commander is the metal segment.

$$\mathbf{F}_{MS}(e_{v,u}) = \text{EO}\left(\left\{ \neg m_{v,u} \right\} \cup \left\{ e_{v,u}^n \mid n \in N \right\} \right), \ \forall e_{v,u} \in E \tag{9}$$

The flow feasibility $\mathbf{F}$ is represented by a conjunction of each sub-formulation as Expression (10).

$$\mathbf{F} = \bigwedge_{v \in V} \left(\mathbf{F}_{EUV}(v) \wedge \bigwedge_{n \in N} \bigwedge_{t_m^n \in T^n} \mathbf{F}_{CFC}(v, n, m) \right) \wedge$$
$$\bigwedge_{e_{v,u} \in E} \left(\mathbf{F}_{MS}(e_{v,u}) \wedge \bigwedge_{n \in N} \bigwedge_{t_m^n \in T^n} \mathbf{F}_{EA}(e_{v,u}, n, m) \right) \tag{10}$$

2.2.2 Design Rule Formulation (D).
The detailed routing procedure, several critical conditional-design rules come from the gap between the technology node and the diffraction limitation of optical lithography source. The gap perpetually increases because the technology node is continuously shrinking while the resolution limitation is fixed. Our proposed SAT formulation adopts representative conditional design rules such as *Minimum Area Rule, End-of-Line Spacing Rule*, and *Via Rule* from [10, 14, 16].

Geometric Variable (GV). Logical Expressions (11-13) represent the feasibility of Geometric Variable (GV) determined by the EOL of a metal segment as shown in Figure 3. Each geometric-directional feasibility is determined by a linear representation, $g_{d,v}$, converted from a logical AND of metal segments (i.e., $\mathbf{D}_{GV_L}(v)$ is converted from $g_{L,v} = \neg m_{v_L,v} \wedge m_{v,v_R}$) [12, 16]. The geometry feasibility $\mathbf{D}_{GV}$ (13) is the conjunction of each directional GV representation $\mathbf{D}_{GV_L}(v), \mathbf{D}_{GV_R}(v), \mathbf{D}_{GV_F}(v), \mathbf{D}_{GV_B}(v)$ for all vertices. The front- and back-directional GV are derived by changing L and R to F and B, respectively.

$$\mathbf{D}_{GV_L}(v) = (g_{L,v} \wedge \neg m_{v_L,v} \wedge m_{v,v_R}) \vee (\neg g_{L,v} \wedge \neg m_{v,v_R}) \vee (\neg g_{L,v} \wedge m_{v_L,v}),$$
$$\forall v \in V_2 \tag{11}$$

$$\mathbf{D}_{GV_R}(v) = (g_{R,v} \wedge m_{v_L,v} \wedge \neg m_{v,v_R}) \vee (\neg g_{R,v} \wedge \neg m_{v_L,v}) \vee (\neg g_{R,v} \wedge m_{v,v_R}),$$
$$\forall v \in V_2 \tag{12}$$

$$\mathbf{D}_{GV} = \bigwedge_{v \in V_2} \left(\mathbf{D}_{GV_L}(v) \wedge \mathbf{D}_{GV_R}(v) \right) \wedge \bigwedge_{v \in V_1, V_3} \left(\mathbf{D}_{GV_F}(v) \wedge \mathbf{D}_{GV_B}(v) \right) \tag{13}$$

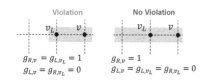

Figure 4: An example of MAR.

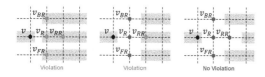

Figure 5: An example of EOL.

Based on GV, we formulate conditional design rules as follows.

Minimum Area Rule (MAR). Logical Expressions (14,15) represent MAR using a simple AMO constraint for GVs. Figure 4 depicts an example of MAR. Each disjoint metal segment should be no smaller than the resolution limitation. In our formulation, a metal segment must cover at-least three vertices. The MAR feasibility formulation for M_1 and M_3 ($\mathbf{D}_{MAR_{FB}}(v)$) are derived by changing L and R to F and B, respectively. The MAR feasibility $\mathbf{D}_{MAR}$ (15) is the conjunction of $\mathbf{D}_{MAR_{LR}}$ and $\mathbf{D}_{MAR_{FB}}$.

$$\mathbf{D}_{MAR_{LR}}(v) = \mathbf{AMO}(g_{L,v}, g_{R,v}, g_{L,v_R}, g_{R,v_R}), \ \forall v \in V_2 \quad (14)$$

$$\mathbf{D}_{MAR} = \bigwedge_{v \in V_2} \mathbf{D}_{MAR_{LR}}(v) \wedge \bigwedge_{v \in V_1, V_3} \mathbf{D}_{MAR_{FB}}(v) \quad (15)$$

End-of-Line(EOL) Space Rule. Logical Expressions (16,17) represent EOL Spacing Rule related to the distance between any of two opposite EOLs (i.e., "tips") using simple AMO constraints for GVs. The minimum distance between each of the tips depends on the design rule, we assume that it has to be larger than two Manhattan distance (i.e., L^1 Norm) as depicted in Figure 5. The other cases, i.e., $\mathbf{D}_{EOL_L}$, $\mathbf{D}_{EOL_F}$, and $\mathbf{D}_{EOL_B}$ are derived in similar ways to $\mathbf{D}_{EOL_R}$.

$$\mathbf{D}_{EOL_R}(v) = \mathbf{AMO}(g_{R,v}, g_{L,v_{FR}}) \wedge \mathbf{AMO}(g_{R,v}, g_{L,v_R}) \wedge$$
$$\mathbf{AMO}(g_{R,v}, g_{L,v_R}, g_{L,v_{RR}}), \ \forall v \in V_2 \quad (16)$$

$$\mathbf{D}_{EOL} = \bigwedge_{v \in V_2} \left(\mathbf{D}_{EOL_L}(v) \wedge \mathbf{D}_{EOL_R}(v) \right) \wedge \bigwedge_{v \in V_1, V_3} \left(\mathbf{D}_{EOL_F}(v) \wedge \mathbf{D}_{EOL_B}(v) \right) \quad (17)$$

Via Rule (VR). Logical Expression (18) represents VR related to restriction rules of inter-layer via (i.e., via) locations. In our formulation, the distance between two vias should be larger than $\sqrt{2}$ Euclidean distance (i.e., L^2 Norm) as shown in Figure 6(a) (i.e., via-to-via spacing rule). The via placement on the top of another via is not allowed as shown in Figure 6(b) (i.e., stacked-via regulation). The expression of VR feasibility can be represented by the conjunction of simple AMO constraints for GVs as well.

$$\mathbf{D}_{VR}(v) = \mathbf{AMO}(m_{v,v_U}, m_{v_R,v_{UR}}, m_{v_B,v_{UB}}, m_{v_{BR},v_{UBR}}) \wedge$$
$$\mathbf{AMO}(m_{v_D,v}, m_{v,v_U}), \ \forall v \in V \quad (18)$$

The design rule correctness $\mathbf{D}$ is represented by the conjunction of each design rule subset (19).

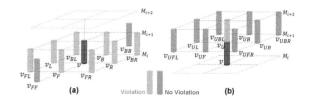

Figure 6: VR rule. (a) via-to-via spacing rule. (b) stacked-via regulation.

$$\mathbf{D} = \mathbf{D}_{GV} \wedge \mathbf{D}_{MAR} \wedge \mathbf{D}_{EOL} \wedge \bigwedge_{v \in V} \mathbf{D}_{VR}(v) \quad (19)$$

2.2.3 Layout Structure Map (L). Layout structure map is composed by unit clauses determined by the geometry of the switchbox, e.g., the information of prohibited power rail track in M_2, the pin allocation in M_1 and the boundary condition of the switchbox.

2.2.4 Design Rule-Correct Routability Analysis. The design rule-correct routability $\mathbf{R}$ can be derived by combining all sub formation $\mathbf{F}$, $\mathbf{D}$ and $\mathbf{L}$ as shown in Expression (20).

$$\mathbf{R} = \mathbf{F} \wedge \mathbf{D} \wedge \mathbf{L} \quad (20)$$

Through the SAT analysis, we evaluate if the expression is true, i.e., all the given design rules are correct. When it calls "unroutable", we proceed our diagnosis procedure discussed in the next section.

2.3 Diagnosis Procedure

The diagnosis procedure consists of four phases, *(i) MUS Extraction, (ii) Initial Propagation, (iii) Decision,* and *(iv) Propagation phase.* The key diagnosis steps are the iterative Decision and Propagation until we face conflicting clauses as shown in Figure 1. The diagnosis using clauses is similar to one of the longest-path-search problem for a DAG [5, 13]. In this paper, the DAG is defined as follows:

Definition 2.1. (Diagnosis DAG) The DAG $H(U, D)$ is defined as
(1) D is a set of clauses in an MUS.
(2) $U = \{U_b, U_s, U_p\} \subset V$ is a set of variables involving the conflict. U_b is a set of input layout variables ($U_b \subset I$), U_s is the variables selected by the decision procedure of an iteration and U_p is the variables determined in an iteration of BCP.
(3) $H(U, D) = PIG(U_b \cup U_s \cup U_p, D)$, where $PIG(U, D)$ is generated in each propagation step with BCP.

2.3.1 MUS Extraction Phase. For the unroutable pin layout, we first extract the MUS which is the minimal unsatisfiable set if all its proper subsets are satisfiable. It significantly contributes the diagnosis time reduction by replacing the diagnosis target with the very small number of clauses. ROAD uses one of the state-of-the-art MUS Extractor *MUSer2* [7].

2.3.2 Initial Propagation Phase. Based on the MUS, ROAD executes initial BCP using the clauses of $\mathbf{L}$. It restricts the design-conflict region of the unroutable layout. Figure 7 shows an example $(9\_13\_100)^1$ of restricted conflict region. The estimated conflict region is the target range of the next iterative decision and propagation phases.

---

[1]The naming convention for a switchbox is <1>_<2>_<3>, where < 1 − 3 > are the number of vertical tracks, horizontal tracks and pin density, respectively.

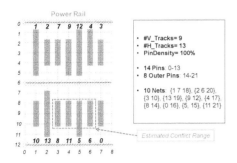

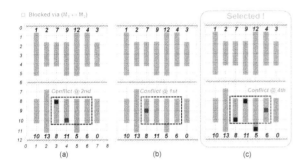

Figure 7: An example of unroutable layout (9_13_100).

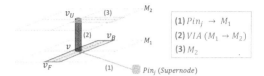

Figure 9: PTA phase for M_1 vertex v.

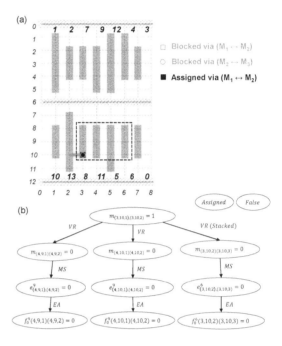

Figure 8: Path length. (a) 2 @ (3,8,1). (b) 1 @ (3,9,1), (c) 4 @ (3,10,1).

2.3.3 Decision with Longest-path Search (DLS) Phase.

In DLS phase, ROAD selects a certain via position for the next propagation phase. A technical challenge for the explanation of practical design failure is that there are too many ways to explain the design-rule conflicts. We address this issue by adopting a longest-path search algorithm. The underlying intuition is that the longest routing path usually represents the causes of the routability failure in a comprehensive manner.

Figure 8 shows that the 9_13_100 layout has three possible via positions ($m_{(3,8,1),(3,8,2)}$, $m_{(3,9,1),(3,9,2)}$ and $m_{(3,10,1),(3,10,2)}$) in the first iteration. The designer would consider that the short paths depicted in Figure 8(a), (b) are obvious to avoid, while the longest path in Figure 8(c) provides the intrinsic problem caused by the design rules. The DLS phase thus selects a via which initiates the maximum path length of $H(U, D)$.

2.3.4 Propagation with True Assignment (PTA) Phase.

We then execute the propagation by assigning 1 for the selected via position. As illustrated in Figure 9, there are three kinds of variables assigned with 1 for a certain via position. For the vertex v, the variables between Pin_j[2] to M_1 are set as True (step (1)). The via elements between v and vertex v_U are also set as True (step (2)). Finally, the M_2 elements connected with v_U are set as True (step(3)). We also choose the direction of variables on the M_2 layer so that its PIG can have the longest path as well.

Figure 10 shows an example of the PTA results for via#1 of 9_13_100 layout with its PIG. Three via positions ($m_{(4,9,1)(4,9,2)}$, $m_{(4,10,1)(4,10,2)}$ and $m_{(3,10,2)(3,10,3)}$) are blocked by the VR rule. The direction of the variables at the M_2 layer is determined by "left" to find the longest path.

---
[2]Pin_j is a supernode which covers vertices of the pin on M_1.

Figure 10: Via#1 of 9_13_100. (a) PTA result. (b) Some part of PIG.

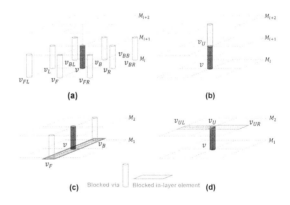

Figure 11: PFA phase for v. (a) Via-to-via spacing. (b) Stacked-via. (c) Vias in the same pin. (d) In-layer variables with direction against PTA.

2.3.5 Propagation with False Assignment (PFA) Phase.

The PFA phase executes the propagation with 0 value for the selected via position. The false assignment happens to cover four reasons: via-to-via spacing void, stacked-via void, void of vias in the same pin and void of the in-layer variables with direction against forcing. Figure 11 describes each reason.

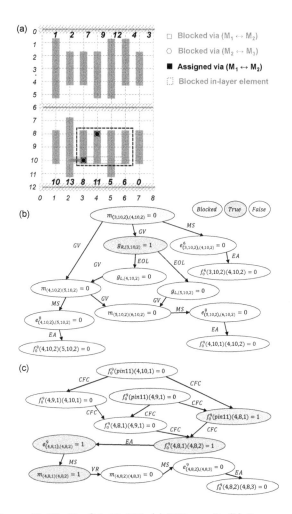

Figure 12: Via#1 of 9_13_100. (a) PFA result. (b) Some part of PIG for in-layer element with direction against PTA. (c) Some part of PIG for via-to-via spacing void.

By the via-to-via spacing PFA case as depicted in Figure 11(a), vias within $\sqrt{2}\ L^2$ Norm from the v are blocked. The stacked-via PFA case (Figure 11(b)) blocks via positions which are on the top of another via. In Figure 11(c), only one via is allowable in a pin. In-layer variables, which direction is against PTA, are blocked from Figure 11(d) rule.

Figure 12 illustrates an example with the via at the first iteration(i.e., via#1= $m_{(3,10,1)(3,10,2)}$). The elements between (3,10,2) and (4,10,2) are blocked by PFA phase as depicted in Figure 12(a). Figure 12(b)-(c) are some parts of PIG related to this PFA case. The detailed blocking procedure of M_2 layer's elements is found in Figure 12(b). With PTA phase result, PFA blocks two via positions in $pin11$ and so the only $m_{(4,8,1)(4,8,2)}$ is selected as also shown in Figure 12(c). The selected via is accepted as the output of the DLS phase in the following iteration.

2.4 Diagnosis Result Report

We perform the iterative procedures until it has a conflict. ROAD provides precise information for conflicts in terms of geometry and conflicted conditional design rules. Figure 14 shows that, e.g.,

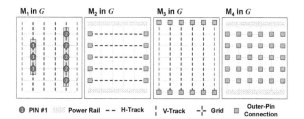

Figure 13: Pin layout configuration.

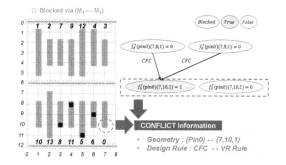

Figure 14: Diagnosis result of 9_13_100.

the conflict of the 9_13_100 layout occurs at the PFA phase when the path length is 4, i.e., the fourth iteration. The cause of the unroutability is the conflict between VR and CFC rules due to $f_0^7(pin0)(7,10,1)$ variable. From VR rule, all possible via locations in $pin0$ vertices are blocked in the PFA phase (i.e., $f_0^7(pin0)(7,10,1)$ is set as False). However, since at-least one vertex must have a via for $pin0$ connection due to CFC rule (i.e., $f_0^7(pin0)(7,10,1)$ is set as True), we can identify the variable values are conflicted each other.

2.5 Automated Pin Layouts Generation

ROAD has a feature of an automated test-sets generation which creates practical pin layouts based on *Rent's Rule* [26]. For a test-set generation, we specify the inputs as the number of vertical tracks (V-tracks) and horizontal tracks (H-tracks), and pin density for the switchbox. The number of Grids is defined by the number of intersection between V-tracks and H-tracks. As depicted in Figure 13, we assume 7-track cell library, which means five tracks for each routing row are eligible for detailed routing, and total four metal layers are in the switchbox. M_1 is only for pin placement and each pin cover 3-5 vertices. We don't use any detailed-placement refinements (e.g., cell padding) in the pin layout generation since this refinement affects quantification results.

3 EXPERIMENTS

In this section, we describe the experimental results of ROAD, i.e., the analysis and diagnosis. ROAD provides the routability analysis through the routing assessment using SAT formulation and the causes of unroutable layouts through the novel diagnosis procedure. The diagnosis procedure is built on the longest path search-based decision and BCP-based propagation technique. Our ROAD is implemented and validated on 2.6GHz Intel Xeon E5-2640 Linux workstation with 128GB memory.

Table 2: Unroutable layout examples. #N=#Nets, #P=#Pins.

SwitchBox	Spec. #N	Spec. #P	SAT Formulation #Variable	SAT Formulation #Clauses	MUS #Clauses	Conflict Cause
11_7_80	6	12	16,776	378,551	215	Simple-CP
9_19_100	13	29	101,943	5,368,125	234	Simple-CP
9_13_100	10	22	54,884	2,280,223	272	Simple-CP
12_13_70	10	23	79,471	3,478,371	446	Propagated-CP
11_7_90	7	14	21,014	580,925	514	Propagated-CP
7_7_100	4	9	7,972	110,389	1,194	Routing Congestion
7_13_100	7	15	24,236	595,898	4,060	Routing Congestion
15_7_90	9	20	45,782	1,725,676	6,579	Routing Congestion
19_13_70	15	33	171,092	11,287,222	19,375	Routing Congestion

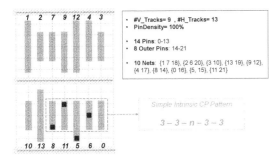

Figure 15: 9_13_100 : Simple-CP pattern (3-3-n-3-3).

3.1 Unroutable layout classification

Based on our diagnosis procedure, we show a couple of findings regarding the causes of the conflicts. Table 2 summarizes unroutable layouts with their conflict causes. The causes are classified into the three categories: *Simple-*, *Propagated-Conflict Pin-shape (CP) Pattern* and *Routing Congestion*. In our SAT formulation, the number of clauses is determined by the number of V-tracks, H-tracks, nets, and pins. On the other hand, the number of MUS is highly related to the conflict causes rather than the specification of the layout.

3.1.1 Simple-CP Pattern. We classify an unroutable layout into the Simple-CP type if it has an intrinsic CP pattern, while it is obviously infeasible without any further investigation in terms of pin accessibility. The conflict of the Simple-CP type is only related to the region inside the pattern. For example, the layout in Figure 15 is a Simple-CP type since it has a $3 - 3 - n - 3 - 3$ CP pattern, where $n > 3$.

3.1.2 Propagated-CP pattern. We classify an unroutable layout into the Propagated-CP type if it has no intrinsic CPs but a CP can be found after multiple-sequential propagations. For example, as shown in Figure 16(a), the 12_13_70 layout has no intrinsic CPs to explicitly identify from the pin-shape. However, we can find a simple "3-3-3" CP pattern after the propagation of the fourth via as depicted in Figure 16(b) since the via at (5,7,1) is blocked the by the EOL rule.

3.1.3 Routing Congestion. The unroutable layout that has no violations in locating vias on the pins in M_1 is the Routing Congestion type. The cause of this type is related to the lack of routing resources. For example, Figure 17(b) shows the 15_7_90 layout has no violations in locating vias between M_1 and M_2 layers. This means that there must be a conflict in either M_2 / M_3 layers or vias between M_2 and M_3 layers. Net 5 of the 15_7_90 is one of the in-switchbox connections (i.e., Pin 1 and 4 in net 5). Pin 1 and 4 should be connected through the inside routing tracks. However, all tracks of

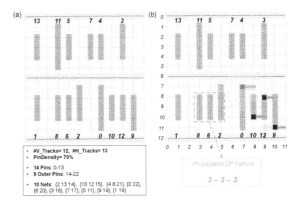

Figure 16: An example of propagated-CP pattern. (a) Given layout. (b) Propagated-CP pattern(3-3-3).

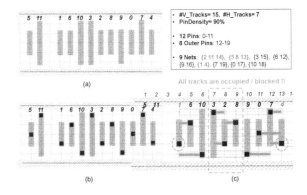

Figure 17: An example of Routing Congestion. (a) Given layout. (b) No violation in locating vias between M_1 and M_2. (c) Lack of routing tracks.

which x coordinates are between 7 and 9 on M_2 layer are either already occupied by other connections or blocked by design rules (e.g., VR and EOL rule) after several propagations as shown in Figure 17(c). In this case, there are no ways to connect pin 1 to pin 4 since the connection between two pins needs at least one track in any x coordinates.

3.2 Experimental Results

Table 3 presents our diagnosis experimental statistics with comparisons for each conflict type. Each row in Table 3 reports the average results. The result shows that ROAD can give the detailed diagnosis results with an efficient runtime cost. For example, the total diagnosis time, including the MUS Extraction and the iterative diagnosis procedure (Decision & Propagation), is finished with 21.1 seconds on average for CP pattern cases. Even the routing congestion cases, the run-time for the MUS Extraction and the Decision & Propagation is 72.9 and 33.4 seconds on average, respectively. Within 2 minutes (strictly, 106.3 seconds), the routability analysis and diagnosis are completed with exact conflict reasoning.

As mentioned in Section 2.3, this diagnosis efficiency is achieved by adopting MUS clauses for the diagnosis target. As shown in Table 3, the amount of MUS for the CP pattern and routing congestion is 0.010 and 0.086% of original representation, respectively.

Table 3: Experiment statistics of routability diagnosis (94 pin layouts @ 90 grids). In the table, #N=#Nets, #P=#Pins.

Conflict Type	#N (avg.)	#P (avg.)	#Variable (avg.)	#Clauses (avg.)			Diagnosis Time [s] (avg.)		
				Original	MUS	Ratio [%]	MUS Extraction	Decision & Propagation	Total
CP pattern (80 cases)	10.2	22.4	68,954.6	3,068,017.3	291.5	0.010	17.0	4.1	21.1
Routing Congestion (14 cases)	10.0	22.5	68,803.3	3,049,687.6	2,627.8	0.086	72.9	33.4	106.3

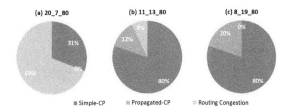

Figure 18: Unroutable cause classification of layout with 90 grids, 80% density and (a) one row, (b) two rows, (c) three rows of pins.

From the statistics, the number of MUS clauses and the diagnosis time for routing congestion type is about nine and five times those of CP pattern type, respectively. It demonstrates that routing congestion type requires more iterations of Decision & Propagation to verify the conflicting clauses even though the specification of the layout is similar between two types as mentioned in Section 3.1.

The composition of unroutable causes fully vary depending on the row number of pins (e.g., the number of routing tracks). Figure 18 summarizes the findings for 90 grids. As shown in Figure 18(a), 69% of pin layouts with one row is classified into the Routing Congestion type, while there is no Propagated-CP type. The Routing Congestion type's potion is significantly reduced by 8% for cases with two pin rows as shown in Figure 18(b). Unlike the Routing Congestion, the portion of the Propagated-CP and Simple-CP type increase to 80% and 12%, respectively. Figure 18(c) shows that, for the pin layouts with three rows, no routing congestion type occurs and all cases are CP pattern type (80% simple-CP, 20% propagated-CP).

4 CONCLUSION

We have described our ROAD, a new analysis and diagnosis framework that examines routing feasibility for the detailed pin layout architecture. Our diagnosis procedure performs iterative procedures of decision and propagation to identify the longest path of the conflicted pin layouts. It provides useful insight into the causes of the conflict design rule, unlike existing ILP-based routability analysis methodologies. Throughout a comprehensive diagnosis, we also identify three categories of conflict causes, Simple-CP, Propagated-CP pattern and Routing Congestion. We demonstrate the diagnosis results with 6,000 pin layouts, and 165 selected unroutable pin layouts. Our ROAD suggests strong theoretical background towards diverse pin pattern exploration for unroutability. Our future plan includes applying machine learning techniques in the detailed routing.

REFERENCES

[1] 2015. ITRS Report 2015. http://www.itrs2.net/itrs-reports.html
[2] 2018. Design Rule Complexity Rising. https://semiengineering.com/design-rule-complexity-rising/.
[3] Charles J Alpert and Gustavo E Tellez. 2010. The importance of routing congestion analysis. *DAC Knowledge Center Online Article* (2010).
[4] Yasmine A Badr, Ko-wei Ma, and Puneet Gupta. 2014. Layout pattern-driven design rule evaluation. *Journal of Micro/Nanolithography, MEMS, and MOEMS* 13, 4 (2014), 043018.
[5] Oliver Bastert and Christian Matuszewski. 2001. Layered drawings of digraphs. In *Drawing graphs*. Springer, 87–120.
[6] Anton Belov and EPCL Basic Training Camp. 2012. Minimal Unsatisfiability: Theory, Algorithms and Applications. (2012).
[7] Anton Belov and Joao Marques-Silva. 2012. MUSer2: An efficient MUS extractor. *Journal on Satisfiability, Boolean Modeling and Computation* 8 (2012), 123–128.
[8] RC Carden, Jianmin Li, and Chung-Kuan Cheng. 1996. A global router with a theoretical bound on the optimal solution. *IEEE Transactions on Computer-Aided Design of Integrated Circuits and Systems* 15, 2 (1996), 208–216.
[9] Jian Chen, Jun Wang, ChengYu Zhu, Wei Xu, Shuai Li, Eason Lin, Odie Ou, Ya-Chieh Lai, and Shengrui Qu. 2018. Pin routability and pin access analysis on standard cells for layout optimization. In *Design-Process-Technology Co-optimization for Manufacturability XII*, Vol. 10588. International Society for Optics and Photonics, 105880D.
[10] Pascal Cremer, Stefan Hougardy, Jan Schneider, and Jannik Silvanus. 2017. Automatic Cell Layout in the 7nm Era. In *International Symposium on Physical Design*. ACM, 99–106.
[11] Yixiao Ding, Chris Chu, and Wai-Kei Mak. 2017. Pin Accessibility-Driven Detailed Placement Refinement. In *International Symposium on Physical Design*. ACM, 133–140.
[12] Kwangsoo Han, Andrew B Kahng, and Hyein Lee. 2015. Evaluation of BEOL design rule impacts using an optimal ILP-based detailed router. In *the 52nd Annual Design Automation Conference*. ACM, 68.
[13] T.C. Hu and M.T. Shing. 2002. *Combinatorial Algorithms 2nd Ed.* Dover Publications.
[14] Xiaotao Jia, Yici Cai, Qiang Zhou, Gang Chen, Zhuoyuan Li, and Zuowei Li. 2014. MCFRoute: a detailed router based on multi-commodity flow method. In *IEEE/ACM International Conference on Computer-Aided Design*. IEEE Press, 397–404.
[15] Andrew B Kahng. 2018. Machine Learning Applications in Physical Design: Recent Results and Directions. In *International Symposium on Physical Design*. ACM, 68–73.
[16] Ilgweon Kang, Dongwon Park, Changho Han, and Chung-Kuan Cheng. 2018. Fast and precise routability analysis with conditional design rules. In *Proceedings of the 20th System Level Interconnect Prediction Workshop*. ACM, 4.
[17] Daniel Kroening and Ofer Strichman. 2016. *Decision Procedures: An Algorithmic Point of View*. Springer.
[18] Kevin Lucas, Chris Cork, Bei Yu, Gerard Luk-Pat, Ben Painter, and David Z Pan. 2012. Implications of triple patterning for 14nm node design and patterning. In *Design for Manufacturability through Design-Process Integration VI*, Vol. 8327. International Society for Optics and Photonics, 832703.
[19] Yuangsheng Ma, Jason Sweis, Hidekazu Yoshida, Yan Wang, Jongwook Kye, and Harry J Levinson. 2012. Self-aligned double patterning (SADP) compliant design flow. In *Design for Manufacturability through Design-Process Integration VI*, Vol. 8327. International Society for Optics and Photonics, 832706.
[20] G-J Nam, Fadi Aloul, Karem A Sakallah, and Rob A Rutenbar. 2004. A comparative study of two Boolean formulations of FPGA detailed routing constraints. *IEEE Trans. Comput.* 53, 6 (2004), 688–696.
[21] Van-Hau Nguyen. 2014. SAT Encodings of Finite CSPs. (2014).
[22] Nikolai Ryzhenko and Steven Burns. 2012. Standard cell routing via boolean satisfiability. In *the 49th Annual Design Automation Conference*. ACM, 603–612.
[23] Jaewoo Seo, Jinwook Jung, Sangmin Kim, and Youngsoo Shin. 2017. Pin accessibility-driven cell layout redesign and placement optimization. In *the 54th Annual Design Automation Conference 2017*. ACM, 54.
[24] Miroslav N Velev. 2007. Exploiting hierarchy and structure to efficiently solve graph coloring as SAT. In *Proceedings of the 2007 IEEE/ACM international conference on Computer-aided design*. IEEE Press, 135–142.
[25] Xiaoqing Xu, Bei Yu, Jhih-Rong Gao, Che-Lun Hsu, and David Z Pan. 2016. PARR: Pin-access planning and regular routing for self-aligned double patterning. *ACM Transactions on Design Automation of Electronic Systems (TODAES)* 21, 3 (2016), 42.
[26] Payman Zarkesh-Ha, Jeffrey A Davis, William Loh, and James D Meindl. 2000. Prediction of interconnect fan-out distribution using Rent's rule. In *System-level interconnect prediction*. ACM, 107–112.
[27] Jianmin Zhang, Tiejun Li, and Sikun Li. 2015. Application and analysis of unsatisfiable cores on circuits synthesis. In *Advanced Computational Intelligence (ICACI), 2015 Seventh International Conference on*. IEEE, 407–410.

A Perspective on Security and Trust Requirements for the Future

Kenneth Plaks
DARPA
Arlington, VA, USA
kenneth.plaks@darpa.mil

ABSTRACT

As integrated circuit manufacturing becomes increasingly global and the availability of domestically produced advanced transistor nodes shrinks, security vulnerabilities within the supply chain become a significant issue for IC defense applications. In this talk, we will present some of DARPA's efforts towards creating an active community and tool library for circuit design obfuscation in an effort to achieve trusted-by-design IC manufacturing at international foundries. By using a combination of techniques, our goal is to make the placement and triggering of hardware Trojans more difficult and their detection easier, and to make reverse engineering intractable within the window of vulnerability. We will discuss the development of obfuscation assessment metrics and tradeoffs in power, area, and timing overhead, and the creation of an obfuscation technique library to help identify optimal obfuscation strategies in future IC design.

Author Keywords

Obfuscation; Supply Chain; Hardware Security; Logic Locking; ASIC

BIOGRAPHY

Dr. Plaks retired from the US Air Force in 2014. He was the director for Special Programs and was the principal advisor to the Secretary of the Air Force and Chief of Staff for all aspects of Special Access Program (SAP) governance, budgeting, research, development, acquisition, production, sustainment, security classification, execution and congressional engagement. Prior to that, he commanded the USAF's largest test squadron. He is a graduate of USAF Test Pilot School and has flown more than 40 different types of aircraft.

Dr. Plaks was the top academic graduate from the USAF Academy in 1989 with bachelor degrees in physics and mathematics. He was a Hertz Fellow at the Massachusetts Institute of Technology and received a master's in physics in 1991. After a break for military service, he finished his doctorate in physics as a Hertz Fellow at University of Nevada, Las Vegas in 2003.

Dr. Ken Plaks joined DARPA in January 2015 as a program manager. His research interests include stealth aircraft, electronic warfare, weapons research and cybersecurity.

ISPD '19, April 14–17, 2019, San Francisco, CA, USA.
© 2019 Copyright is held by the owner/author(s).
ACM ISBN 978-1-4503-6253-5/19/04.
DOI: https://doi.org/10.1145/3299902.3311059

Declarative Language for Geometric Pattern Matching in VLSI Process Rule Modeling

Gyuszi Suto
Intel Corporation
Hillsboro, OR, USA
gyuszi.suto@intel.com

Geoff S. Greenleaf
Intel Corporation
Hillsboro, OR, USA
geoffrey.s.greenleaf@intel.com

Phanindra Bhagavatula
Intel Corporation
Santa Clara, CA, USA
phanindra.bhagavatula@intel.com

Heinrich R. Fischer
Intel Corporation
Hillsboro, OR, USA
heinrich.r.fischer@intel.com

Sanjay K. Soni
Intel Corporation
Hillsboro, OR, USA
sanjay.k.soni@intel.com

Brian H. Miller
Intel Corporation
Hillsboro, OR, USA
brian.h.miller@intel.com

Renato F. Hentschke
Intel Corporation
Hillsboro, OR, USA
renato.f.hentschke@intel.com

ABSTRACT

This paper presents a formal (machine readable) declarative language developed for the specific reason of modeling physical design process rules of any complexity. Case studies are presented on synthetic as well as industry known design rules of simple complexity (two objects, pair-wise relationship) as well as multi-object complex rules (n-wise relationship). The building blocks of the language are presented and a comparison is drawn between declarative and imperative (general industry practice) implementation of a rule. Automatic test layout generation is presented that would not be possible on an imperative model. Advanced language concepts are also described, including patterns – that can be embedded in each other – as well as rule exceptions using the logical NOT in conjunction with patterns. Further advanced language features are presented, including grids (discretization) and sets – all crucial elements for implementing a wide variety of rules. A strong argument is made for the advantages of this language being the precise and unambiguous description of the intent of the rule with immediate access to a rule checker as well as automatic test layout generator that can test the boundaries of the process node.

CCS CONCEPTS

• Hardware~Physical synthesis • Hardware~Design rule checking

Keywords

Process Rules; Rule Modeling; Declarative; Formal

ISPD '19, April 14–17, 2019, San Francisco, CA, USA.
© 2019 Association of Computing Machinery.
ACM ISBN 978-1-4503-6253-5/19/04...$15.00.
DOI: https://doi.org/10.1145/3299902.3309745

ACM Reference Format:
Gyuszi Suto, Geoff S. Greenleaf, Phanindra Bhagavatula, Heinrich R. Fischer, Sanjay K. Soni, Brian H. Miller, Renato F. Hentschke. 2019. Declarative Language for Geometric Pattern Matching in VLSI Process Rule Modeling. *In Proceedings of ACM International Symposium on Physical Design (ISPD'19). April 14–17, 2019, San Francisco, CA, USA.* ACM, New York, NY, USA, *8 pages.* https://doi.org/10.1145/3299902.3309745

1. INTRODUCTION

One of the most critical complexities of physical design in the modern processes is to cope with design rules. Design rules come from different sources, such as lithography limitations, design and architecture decisions, yield and DFM guidelines, etc. In the early years of VLSI, most design rules were simple two object relationships that could be categorized into a small set of primitives such as edge-to-edge distance, via enclosure, etc. That complexity gradually increased to encompass multiple object relationships, multi-patterning, gridding. As we walk into 10nm, 7nm and 5nm technology nodes there is a clear trend into multiple objects pattern descriptions and non-trivial exceptions. Today the task of describing, checking and synthesizing layout for a design rule is extremely complex. In this paper we tackle the description and checking of state-of-the-art VLSI technology and design constraints.

The description of a design rule comes in different flavors. One can describe a layout pattern for human consumption with sentences in English and drawings. In many cases, and especially with the complexities of 10 nm and beyond, this didactic approach fails to provide an accurate description of the geometric pattern that the rule is actually modeling. At the same time, the same rule is implemented in a checker such as [2] or [1] and can easily be out-of-sync with the "human consumable" description. Clearly it is desired that a design rule description is accurate and readable to humans and checkers. At the same time, the language must be rich and powerful to model any design rules.

We can categorize design rule modeling languages into imperative and declarative languages. Most streamline commercial tools such as [2] and [1] support an imperative language (e.g. a procedural program) that checks for such violations. While that language is accurate to the programmers intent, it will hardly be human readable, nor will it be able to automatically generate test layout. A declarative language, as used in [7] describes the rule in terms of logic and mathematical equations and can efficiently be consumed by a machine. While [7] can be efficient to encode many modern design rules, we found that it does not cover all complexities of modern process nodes in a simple and practical way.

The language presented in this paper has full support of boolean expressions (*AND, OR, XOR*, etc.), geometric types ranging from point, rectangle all the way to polygon sets with holes, a large collection of functions on these geometric types (*join, intersection, subtraction, bloat, distances*, etc.). The language also supports higher level concepts such as (single, or multi-level) *patterns*, custom functions, *sets, elements* of *sets* and rule exceptions. The declarative nature of the language allows the automatic creation of sample layouts exercising and violating a rule. These layouts can be created at the conceptual boundaries specified in the constraints of the rule.

2. General description of physical design rules

During the manufacturing process of the VLSI chips, several rules (aka. constraints) need to be obeyed. These constraints are imposed by lithography, etching and other steps in manufacturing. They usually involve multiple layout objects, (like wires, vias, and devices) and there are spatial, pair-wise or n-wise geometric constraints. A simple pair-wise rule (involving two objects) is an end-to-end spacing constraint on a metal layer (ex. Metal2), described in plain English in the following way: If two Metal2 wires of any width have their ends facing each other at a distance less than 60nm or a distance between 100 and 120nm, then it is a violation.

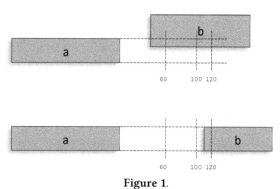

Figure 1.

Figure 1 shows two violations (aka. matching) of the rule. In the bottom layout *a* and *b* are aligned on the vertical dimension and are within 100 to 120 horizontal spacing of each other. In the top

layout, they're not aligned on the vertical dimension, but they do have vertical projection overlap, and are between 0 and 60 horizontal spacing of each other.

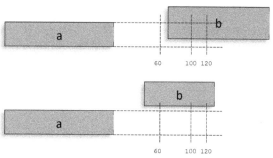

Figure 2.

The two examples in Figure 2 do not violate the rule (no matching), either because the distance is not in the constraints (top case), or there is no face to face vertical overlap (bottom case).

3. Introduction to declarative language

The above rule, described in the declarative language presented in this paper looks like the following:

```
Rule Metal2_End_to_End
AND
    a, b Metal2 |
        a.intersects(b, V)
        a.distance(b, H) in { (0, 60), (100, 120)}
```

In the first line we're defining a rule with the name Metal2_End_to_End: Rule Metal2_End_to_End. The second line contains *AND*, it means that the subsequent clauses are *AND*-ed together. When the rule matches then the *AND* will evaluate to Boolean true. The third line *a, b Metal2 |* means that there exist two objects *a* and *b* of type *Metal2*, such that (| is the guard expression), followed by two lines by default *AND*'d together, describing the conditions of the guard expression that govern the selection of objects *a* and *b*. The fourth line: *a.intersects(b, V)* describes the constraint for *a* and *b* to intersect in the vertical (V) projection. The last line *a.distance(b, H) in {(0, 60), (100, 120)}* states that the horizontal distance (let's call it d) between the objects *a* and *b* needs to be in the interval set of *{(0, 60), (100, 120)}*, which is equivalent to: *(0 < d AND d < 60) OR (100 < d AND d < 120)*.

```
Rule Airplane
AND
    f Fuselage |                    ; there exists a fuselage f
        f.delta(H) in {[70, 90], 100}  ;   such that its horizontal dimension is in the given interval set
    w Wing |                        ; there exists a wing w
        w.delta(V) in {44, [48, 56], 90} ;   such that its vertical dimension is in the given interval set
        f.contains(w, H)            ;   and the fuselage f contains w in the horizontal projection
        w.contains(f, V)            ;   and the wing w contains the fuselage f in the vertical projection
    t Tail |                        ; there exists a tail t
        f.contains(t, H)            ;   such that fuselage f contains tail t in the horizontal projection
        w.contains(t, V)            ;   and the wing w contains tail t in the vertical projection
    c Cockpit |                     ; there exists a cockpit c
        f.contains(c)               ;   such that the fuselage f contains the cockpit c
    c.xc < w.xc                     ; the cockpit's x center coordinate is left of the wing's x center
    w.xc < t.xc                     ; the wing's x center coordinate is left of the tail's x center
    c.yc == f.yc                    ; cockpit's y center same as fuselage y center
    w.yc == f.yc                    ; wing's y center same as fuselage y center
    t.yc == f.yc                    ; tail's y center same as fuselage y center
```

The indentations in the rule description denote the scope of the various operators. Next we're introducing an example of a multi-object (n-wise) Airplane rule. It is a made-up rule, but the geometrical relationships it describes are similar to those found in advanced process technologies. The types used like Fuselage and Wing are made-up also, but one can think of them as horizontal or vertical metal wires and the Cockpit type could be a Via. The letters *H* and *V* are abbreviations of *HORIZONTAL* and *VERTICAL*.

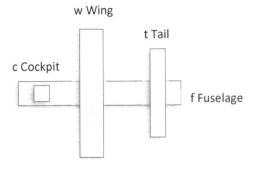

Figure 3.

Figure 3 shows a layout that is matching the constraints in the Airplane rule. All the four building blocks *f, w, t and c* do exist, their dimensions comply and the relationships between the objects are also correct. In general, when rules are written, they're written as bad layout, layout to avoid. The language does not enforce that matching layout should be bad or good. It just describes the pattern of interest, and then the user will decide what to do with that layout. In this respect it's similar to regular expressions and searching for special patterns in a text. Once the rule is parsed and a memory model is built, it can be used to check (match) layout configurations that comply with the described airplane.

4. Automatic Test Layout Generator

In addition to the checker, we also implemented a test layout generator that synthesizes (creates) layout that matches the rule. In Figure 4 we're showing automatically generated airplane layout. All of these comply with the Airplane rule, and when the checker is run on this layout, each of these will match the rule. The colors of the rectangles in this figure are not relevant.

Figure 4.

The test layout generator can also generate non-matching layout, where one or more clauses in the rule are disobeyed. In Figure 5 below the Airplane rule will not match at all for various reasons, either the fuselage is of the wrong size, or the wing is of the wrong size, or the cockpit is in the wrong position, etc.

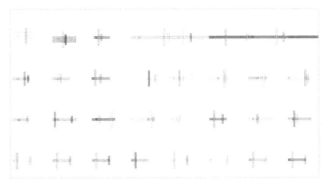

Figure 5.

The test layout in Figure 6 was also generated with the automatic test layout generator and we allowed it to occasionally drop the existence of some of the components, for example some don't have the fuselage or the cockpit present. None of these layouts match the Airplane rule.

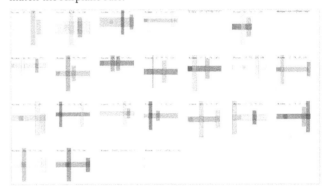

Figure 6.

5. The Building Blocks of the Declarative Language

The language has the following foundations:

1. Basic type system supporting *integers, intervals, interval sets*, geometric types like: *point, line, rectangle, rectangle set, polygon sets* (with *holes*) and polygon *edges* and *corners*

2. It supports expressions and operators like addition (+), subtraction (-), multiplication (*), modulo (%), part of a set (in), comparators (==, <, <=, >, >=, !=)

3. It supports all Boolean logic operators (*AND, OR, XOR, NOT*, etc.)

4. It has an extensive library of generic functions (geometric and logical) like: *abuts, area, bloat, bounding_box, contains, convolve, delta, fracture, generalized_intersection, is_visible, distance, projection_overlap, shrink, bloat* to name a few. It also has Boolean operators on polygon sets (* for *intersection AND*, - for *subtraction*, + for *union OR*, ^ for *XOR*).

5. It has higher level concepts like *Pattern* (embedded), *Set, Element* of Set, custom functions.

6. Declarative versus Imperative language for design rule modeling and checking

If we write the following C code:

```
int a = 7, b = 15; // State0 a:7  b:15
a = a ^ b;         // State1 a:8  b:15
b = b ^ a;         // State2 a:8  b:7
a = a ^ b;         // State3 a:15 b:7
```

With a sequence of bitwise *XOR* operations we achieved a swap between the two variables *a* and *b*. This is a classic example of imperative language, where a sequence of commands change the state from State0 all the way to State3 to achieve the final goal of the swap. A different example of swap can be achieved with the use of a temporary variable, this is a more common (and less obfuscated) way:

```
int a=7, b=15, t=0; // State0 a:7  b:15 t:0
t = a;              // State1 a:7  b:15 t:7
a = b;              // State2 a:15 b:15 t:7
b = t;              // State3 a:15 b:7  t:7
```

In contrast, a declarative way of stating the above would be *swap(a, b)* where the implementation (how) is not clearly stated, instead the goal (what) is stated. It is important to note that typically there's a straightforward path to convert an algorithm from declarative to imperative, but the opposite conversion (from imperative to declarative) - though theoretically possible - in practice is not possible.

Let's consider another rule's implementation. This rule is a complicated attacker rule inspired by MinEndOfLineSpacing rule [6] page 602.

```
Rule AttackerComplicated
Constant EOL_WITHIN = 30
Constant EOL_SPACE  = 40
Constant PAR_SPACE  = 28
AND
  mid    Metal2 xl = 0 yh = 0
  top    Metal2 | xl < 0
                  xh > mid.xh
                  yl in (0, EOL_SPACE)
  left   Metal2 |
    AND
      distance(left, mid, H) < PAR_SPACE
      OR
        abs(left.yh - mid.yh) < EOL_WITHIN
        abs(left.yl - mid.yh) < EOL_WITHIN

  right  Metal2 |
    AND
      distance(mid, right, H) < PAR_SPACE
      OR
        abs(right.yh - mid.yh) < EOL_WITHIN
        abs(right.yl - mid.yh) < EOL_WITHIN
```

The rule states that there is an attacker violation between the north edge of the *mid* wire wrt. *top* wire if the *left* wire has a north

or south edge intersecting the rectangle labeled *ll*, and the *right* wire has a north or south edge intersecting the rectangle labeled *rr* (Figure 7 below). Rectangles *ll* and *rr* have a height of 2xEOL_WITHIN and width of PAR_SPACE.

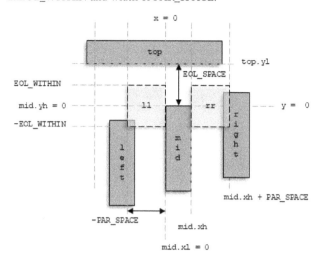

Figure 7.

Once the rule is parsed and its model is built in memory, all the commands and relationships are stored in a tree structure that, when visualized, looks like this (see Figure 8) generated using [5]:

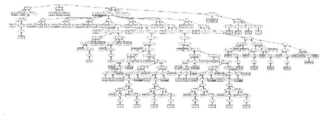

Figure 8.

Each of the nodes of the tree represents either a variable, a coordinate, a constant, a comparison, or a Boolean function. This zoomed in branch of the tree in Figure 9 corresponds to the last line in the rule:

```
abs(right.yl - mid.yh) < EOL_WITHIN
```

One can notice the nodes in the tree with references to the right and mid objects, their *yl* and *yh* coordinates, the *subtraction* function and the *abs()* function:

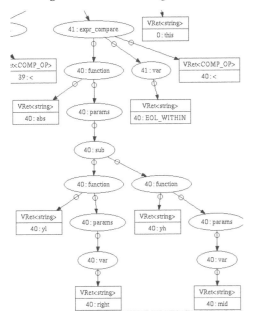

Figure 9.

Since this is a declarative language, the tree model in the memory contains all the declarations and relationships stated in the rule. How the rule is actually checked is dependent on the implementation that is outside of the scope of this paper. Suffice to say, that our implementation is finding the proper objects of appropriate type in the layout database (binding) and then it evaluates the tree from bottom up. If the tree returns true, then the rule is matched.

The same data model in memory is used to automatically generate test layout. We achieved this by using an SMT (Satisfiability Modulo Theory) [3] based implementation that creates a variety of test layout that matches the rule and another set that does not match the rule (but is very close to matching it – we call this on boundary).

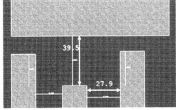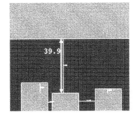

Figure 10.

In figure 10 we're showing two examples of the thousands of test layouts we automatically generate from the *AttackerComplicated* rule. Both of these examples do match the rule. We can optionally ask the test layout generator to generate cases close to constraint boundaries in the rule. The left figure shows that two of the highlighted distances are within a very close value of the boundary condition (39.5 is on boundary of the *EOL_SPACE* 40 value, 27.9 is on the boundary of the *PAR_SPACE* 28 value). In the figure on the right only one distance is in the boundary value of *EOL_SPACE*.

7. Comparing declarative versus imperative implementations of a design rule

Typical signoff checkers would implement this very rule in an imperative fashion, as a sequence of polygon set operations. In

step 1 (Figure 11) we would generate a thin rectangle at the bottom and top edges of all vertical wires (red).

```
wires := LAYER                          ; all wires in the layer
vWires := subset(wires, orient=VERTICAL) ; all vertical wires
hWires := wires NOT vWires               ; all wires not vertical
; generating top and bottom edges of vertical wires
; by shrinking all vertical wires by a tiny amount
; then doing a polygon set subtraction
vWireEdges := vWires - shrink(vWires, VERTICAL, epsilon)
```

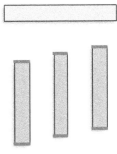

Figure 11.

In step 2 (Figure 12) we would find all vertical candidates that are close enough to a horizontal wire (within *EOL_SPACE*), their relevant edges are colored purple:

```
; find all attacking regions b/w vertical and horizontal wires
; that are facing each other at less than EOL_SPACE
attackingLocations :=externalSpacing( hWires, vWires, VERTICAL, dy
< EOL_SPACE)
; find all edges of vertical wires that are involved in the attack
attackingLocationsEdges := bloat( attackingLocations, VERTICAL,
epsilon) * vWires
```

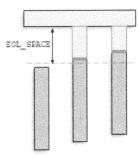

Figure 12.

In Step 3 (Figure 13) we would bloat all *attackingLocationsEdges* vertically by *EOL_WITHIN* (red) and also find neighboring top or bottom edges of vertical wires closer than *PAR_SPACE*:

```
; bloat attacking edges vertically by EOL_WITHIN
bloatedAttackingEdges := bloat( attackingLocationsEdges, VERTICAL,
EOL_WITHIN - epsilon)
; find all relevant wire edges within PAR_SPACE
lrWireEdgesNearby := externalSpacing( vWireEdges,
bloatedAttackingEdges, HORIZONTAL, dx < PAR_SPACE)
```

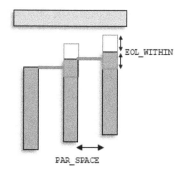

Figure 13.

In the final step (Figure 14) we would generate the one (grey) marker with the following operation:

```
violations := attackingLocations interacting
   (bloatedAttackingEdges interacting(count >=2)
lrWireEdgesNearby)
```

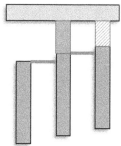

Figure 14.

Notice that in this imperative way, we altered the state of the polygon set(s) with a series of operations, and at the end we found the only one marker of interest that is the remnant of all these operations and signifies a match of the rule. The downside of doing it in imperative way is that the code is hard to read and does not resemble the original human thought/logic of the rule. Also, it does not build a memory model of the logic of the rule (expression) and cannot be used for further services like test layout generation or conversions of the rule to other models serving layout synthesis tools.

In contrast, the advantages of doing it in a declarative fashion are:

1. The source code more closely resembles the human logic and original spirit of the rule
2. The source code can be written by non-programmers also, who don't need to be versed in polygon-set-based runset languages.
3. The declarative model can be used for checking the rule (finding matches in the layout) as well as for automatic test layout generation. The latter cannot be done with imperative implementations.
4. Additionally, the declarative model, when matched against the layout knows which objects were involved in the evaluation, what conditions were (or were not) satisfied, what would it take to modify the layout to change the match into a non-match. None of these can be achieved with an imperative implementation.

8. A closer look at automatic test layout generation

Let's reconsider the end to end rule from the beginning of the paper:

```
Rule Metal2_End_to_End
AND
   a, b Metal2 | a.intersects(b, VERTICAL)
                a.distance(b, HORIZONTAL) in {(0, 60), (100, 120)}
```

After the rule is parsed, we build a tree-like memory model of the rule. Figure 15 shows a rough approximation of the expression tree. The variables v1 – v7 represent Boolean true/false values. The sub-tree below the *OR* node represents the guard expression from line 4 of the rule.

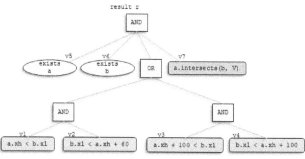

Figure 15.

When we're trying to check existing layout, we bind two objects of type Metal2 to *a* and *b*, evaluate the tree on these two layout objects. If the result *r* evaluates to true, we have a match, else we don't have a match. Obviously, for *r* to be true, v5, v6 and v7 all need to be true and also the *OR* node needs to evaluate to true.

In the case of automatic test layout generation (synthesis), we don't have any layout to start with. To generate test layout, all we need to do is somehow come up with the bottom left and upper right corner coordinates of objects a and b: *a.xl, a.yl, a.xh, a.yh, b.xl, b.yl, b.xh, b.yh*. To do that, we ask SMT to generate these eight variables with the condition that result *r* needs to evaluate to true. Obviously there could be many (millions) of layouts generated that match the rule. The SMT tries to solve the following two equations:

```
1) to generate matching cases:
V5 & V6 & ((V1 & V2) | (V3 & V4)) & V7 == TRUE
2) to generate non matching cases:
V5 & V6 & ((V1 & V2) | (V3 & V4)) & V7 == FALSE
```

Some test layouts are more interesting than others. For example, if the end to end distance is 1nm or 59nm is more interesting than say 23nm, because the former two are on the boundary of matching. We can guide SMT to generate these more interesting "boundary" cases by adding additional constraints in the tree, for example the *AND* above *v1* and *v2* can be modified to:

OR ((a.xh == b.xl-1), (b.xl == a.xh+59))

These boundary cases can be added on all or just some branches of the tree, depending on the objective of the test layout generation. In general, we see the most value in generating a wide spread of testcases that are close to the border separating legal (process node compliant) layout from illegal (non-compliant and/or low yield) layout.

Non process compliant
(illegal)

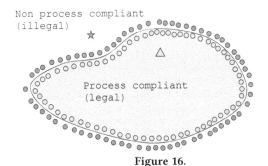

Figure 16.

In Figure 16 we're showing the conceptual boundary separating process compliant from non-process compliant layout. We're directing the test layout generator the generate the layouts corresponding to the red balls, these are illegal layout on the outside and close to the boundary of legality, as well as the green balls, these are legal layouts on the inside and close to the border of illegality. We can also generate the red star (illegal) and green triangle (legal) test layouts, but those are of lesser value in general. The design space is near-infinite, especially with more complex rules, so one needs to be careful how and how many test layouts to generate to be meaningful and relevant. We are achieving this by manipulating the boundary conditions in the expression tree and also imposing certain constraints on the results of the subtrees to produce meaningful and varied combinations of layouts.

9. Advanced Language Concepts

The language described in this paper supports Patterns. Patterns are structures that are pre-defined that are then used in rule(s) later with the advantage of re-using common patterns and simplifying the rule.

```
Constant EOL_WITHIN = 30 ; constants defined outside,
                         ; used both by pattern and rule
Constant EOL_SPACE  = 40
Constant PAR_SPACE  = 28

Pattern P ; describes a general pattern P
         ; with 2 elements middle and side
AND
  middle Metal2   ; there exists a middle
  side   Metal2 | ; there exits a side, such that:
    AND           ; conditions b/w middle and side
      distance(side, middle, H) < PAR_SPACE
    OR
      abs(side.yh - middle.yh) < EOL_WITHIN
      abs(side.yl - middle.yh) < EOL_WITHIN


; re-implementing the rule from Figure 7,
; this time using pattern P
Rule AttackerComplicatedWithPattern
AND
  l, r P | l.middle == r.middle ; there exists two
                                ; instances of P l and r
                     ; such that their middle is identical
  ; there exists a top, with conditions wrt. l.middle
  top   Metal2 |
    xl < l.middle.xl
    xh > l.middle.xh
    yl in (l.middle.yh, l.middle.yh + EOL_SPACE)
```

Patterns make the definition of complex rules easier. In the example above, we used the pattern P twice, thus making the rule terser. In some cases the usage of patterns can make the rules four to eight times shorter. In addition to making the rules more concise, the patterns allow us to define absence of certain objects as part of the rule. Consider the following example:

```
; describes a v1 object enclosed by m1 and m2
Pattern R1
AND
  m1 Metal1Wire
  v1 Via1        | m1.contains(v1)
  m2 Metal2Wire  | m2.contains(v1)
```

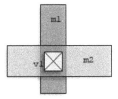

Figure 17.

```
; describes a pattern that has an me1, and two
; vias v0a and v0b, and it does not have a
; pattern R1 whose m1 member is same as me1
Pattern R2
AND
  v0a, v0b Via0
  me1 Metal1Wire | me1.contains(v0a)
                   me1.contains(v0b)
  ; does not exist a pattern R1 such that
  ; its m1 is same as me1
  NOT p R1 | p.m1 == me1 ;
```

Figure 18.

```
Rule R3
AND
  m0a, m0b Metal0Wire
  m0a.net == m0b.net
  NOT b R2 | m0a.contains(b.v0a)
             m0b.contains(b.v0b)
```

Rule R3 is trying to make sure that if there are two *Metal0Wire* objects with the same net, then they need to be connected by a *Metal1* wire (using two *Via0s*) and that *Metal1* wire object may not have *Via1* connecting it to *Metal2*. In Figure 19, the first example on the left does not match rule R3 because the nets are different. The second example does match R3, because the two *Metal0* wires have the same net and not connected by a *Metal1* wire. The third example does not match, because it's correctly connecting two *Metal0* wires. The rightmost (fourth) example does match R3 because even though it's connecting the two *Metal0* wires it is violating rule R3's requirement that the *Metal1* object may not have a connection to *Metal2*.

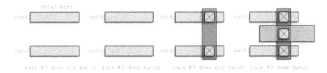

Figure 19.

Our declarative language also supports the concept of Set and Grids. The following example shows a made-up rule using both of these language features:

```
; vertical grid for Metal1
Grid M1_Grid offset=0 period=200 pitches={0, 60, 120}
orientation=V
; horizontal grid for Metal2
Grid M2_Grid offset=0 period=160 pitches={0, 70}
orientation=H

Rule Made_Up_Via_Rule
Constant D1 = 50 ; constants used later in the rule
Constant D2 = 100
Constant LL = 2
Constant HH = 4
AND
  a Via1 | xc on M1_Grid ; there exists a Via1
                        ; with x center on M1_Grid
            yc on M2_Grid ; and y center on M2_Grid
  ; temporary set of these 2 types, with these conditions
  let neighbors_in_the_doughnut = Set{Via1, Via2} |
    ; set element's center distance to a's center
    a.c.euclidean_distance(this.c) in [D1, D2]
    ; set element's x center on M1_Grid
    this.xc on M1_Grid
    ; set element's y center on M2_Grid
    this.yc on M2_Grid
  ; count b/w 2-4
  count(neighbors_in_the_doughnut) in [LL, HH]
  ; there exists an M2Wire b that intersects circle D2
  b M2Wire | a.c.euclidean_distance(this) < D2
```

M1_Grid defines the vertical (blue) grid, *M2_Grid* defines the horizontal (orange) grid. We start the rule by stating that there exists *Via1 a*, such that its x center is on the vertical grid and its y center is on the horizontal grid. Then we build a set that contains *Via1* and/or *Via2* objects such that their center to center distance from *a* is within the *[D1, D2]* interval and said set needs to have 2, 3 or 4 members. In our example the set will contain *Via1* objects *m* and *n*, and *Via2* object *r*. The other vias are not in the set because, *o* is not on grid, *q* is not on grid (only on the vertical, but not on horizontal grid), *p* is outside of the *[D1, D2]* donut. So our set has 3 members. Additionally, we have an *M2Wire b* poking its bottom right corner into the *[D1, D2]* donut. The layout in Figure 20 matches the rule from above.

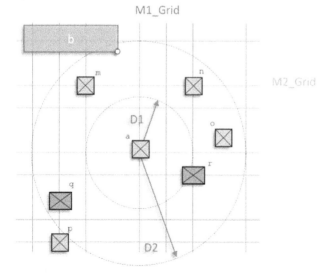

Figure 20.

10. Conclusion

We present a declarative, formal language for modeling layout rules of arbitrary complexity. This model provides several advantages over previous alternatives. This language is complete over its problem domain: future rules can be modeled without need of language extensions. Unlike rule definitions in human language, a formal language definition of a rule is unambiguous and formally verifiable. Definition of a rule in this language provides immediate access to a rule checker and a test layout generator.

Such a language can provide significant benefit during process definition and layout construction. Rapid prototyping of candidate rules enables faster iteration by both process and design. Test layout generation is immediate, automatic, and expansive, resulting in increased confidence that the rule accurately captures the design intent. A clear, unambiguous definition of the layout constraints reduces communication overhead between engineering teams.

11. REFERENCES

[1] Synopsys IC Validator DOI= https://www.synopsys.com/content/dam/synopsys/impleme ntation&signoff/datasheets/ic-validator-ds.pdf

[2] Mentor Graphics Calibre Pattern Matching DOI=https://www.mentor.com/products/ic_nanometer_desi gn/verification-signoff/physical-verification/calibre-pattern-match/

[3] Alexander Nadel. Bit-vector rewriting with automatic rule generation. In Armin Biere and Roderick Bloem, editors, Computer Aided Verification – 26th International Conference, CAV 2014, Held as Part of the Vienna Summer of Logic, VSL 2014, (Vienna, Austria, July 18-22, 2014). Proceedings, volume 8559 of Lecture Notes in Computer Science, pages 663–679. Springer, 2014.

[4] Boost Polygon DOI=https://www.boost.org/doc/libs/1_68_0/libs/polygon/d oc/index.htm

[5] Graphviz Linux DOI=https://graphviz.gitlab.io/documentation/

[6] Si2 Open Access API Tutorial DOI=http://vsevteme.ru/attachments/show?content=8292

[7] Sage Design Automation DOI= http://www.sage-da.com/images/doc/sage_iDRM_WP1_R2_15062017.pdf

Electromigration-Aware Interconnect Design

Sachin S. Sapatnekar
Department of Electrical and Computer Engineering
University of Minnesota
Minneapolis, MN (USA)
sachin@umn.edu

ABSTRACT

Electromigration (EM) is seen as a growing problem in recent and upcoming technology nodes, and affects a wider variety of wires (e.g., power grid, clock/signal nets), circuits (e.g., digital, analog, mixed-signal), and systems (e.g., mobile, server, automotive), touching lower levels of metal than before. Moreover, unlike traditional EM checks that were performed on each wire individually, EM checks must evolve to consider the system-level impact of wire failure. This requires a change in how interconnect design incorporates this effect. This paper overviews the root causes of EM, its impact on high-performance designs, and techniques for analyzing, working around, and alleviating the effects of EM.

CCS CONCEPTS

• **General and reference** → **Reliability**; • **Hardware** → **Metallic interconnect**; **Very large scale integration design**; **Electronic design automation**; **Physical design (EDA)**; **Aging of circuits and systems**; *Analog and mixed-signal circuits*.

KEYWORDS

Electromigration, stress, reliability, power grids, clock networks

ACM Reference Format:
Sachin S. Sapatnekar. 2019. Electromigration-Aware Interconnect Design. In *2019 International Symposium on Physical Design (ISPD '19), April 14–17, 2019, San Francisco, CA, USA*. ACM, New York, NY, USA, 8 pages. https://doi.org/10.1145/3299902.3313156

1 INTRODUCTION

Electromigration (EM) in metal wires is a serious reliability problem in deeply-scaled technologies. EM is induced in wires with high current densities, and can result in an increase in wire resistance over time, eventually leading to an effective open-circuit. EM has long been a significant issue that impacts physical design, and analysis and simulation papers in the EDA community have targeted this phenomenon for many years [11, 37]. It is well known that the impact of EM can be mitigated by using wider wires that reduce the average current density in the wire. The causes and impact of

EM are documented in the physical design literature [21, 22], and several physical design techniques are outlined in these papers.

For recent and upcoming technology nodes, several changes have made EM considerations different and more important. First, the emergence of FinFETs and gate all-around FETs, coupled with reduced wire cross sections, has resulted in two factors that exacerbate EM: increased wire current densities and elevated temperatures. Second, in the past, EM checks were primarily directed at the uppermost metal layers, but EM has now become increasingly important in lower metal layers as well. Third, EM is no longer considered to be a problem primarily for long-lifetime parts, e.g., in the automotive market, but is also a serious consideration over shorter lifetimes, e.g., in the mobile market. Fourth, unlike traditional EM checks that are performed on a per-wire basis, system failure analysis must incorporate the inherent redundancy of many EM-sensitive interconnect systems.

2 EM ANALYSIS

When a sufficiently high current flows through an on-chip wire over a long period of time, it can cause a physical migration of atoms in the wire. The current-conducting electrons form an "electron wind," which leads to momentum exchange with the constituent atoms of metal. This effect will result in a net flux of metal atoms in the direction of electron flow (opposite of current direction), creating voids (depletion of material) upstream and hillocks (accumulation of material) downstream at locations of atomic flux divergence. EM can cause uneven redistribution of resistance, dielectric cracking, and undesired open circuits. EM is witnessed most notably in supply (power and ground) wires, where the flow of current is mostly unidirectional, but AC EM has been reported in signal wires [19, 38].

We will first overview the basics of EM and then outline both *empirical* EM models based on characterization, and *physics-based* models that capture the dynamics of EM.

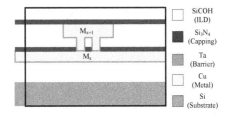

Figure 1: Schematic of dual damascene copper interconnect.

2.1 The roots of EM

The schematic in Fig. 1 illustrates a copper dual-damascene (Cu DD) interconnect structure used in modern integrated-circuits. The interconnect is made up of copper and is cladded with Ta barrier layer on the sides and bottom. The top surface is bounded by the Si_3N_4 capping layer, while the inter layer dielectric (ILD), made of low-k material, such as SiCOH lies between the copper lines. The entire structure rests on a silicon substrate that is a few hundreds of microns thick.

EM degradation in Cu wires occurs due to the nucleation and growth of voids [12, 29], which results in an increase in the wire resistance and ultimately causes functional failure. Fig. 2 illustrates the two driving forces for EM for a wire of length L – the electron wind force due to the flow of a current density j, and the back-stress force generated due to the stress gradient caused by EM-induced mass redistribution. As the movement of migrated atoms is blocked at either end due to the atom-impermeable barrier layer, the electron wind force causes atomic depletion near the cathode, and the resulting tensile stress generated leads to *void nucleation* when the stress exceeds a critical stress, σ_c. Further electron wind force leads to *void growth*, at a rate dictated by drift velocity.

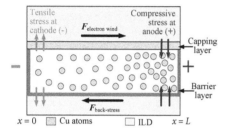

Figure 2: Cross section of a Cu wire indicating the back-stress and the electron wind force.

Korhonen's equation [18] models the temporal evolution of stress, i.e., the interaction between electron wind and back-stress:

$$\frac{\partial \sigma}{\partial t} = \frac{\partial}{\partial x}\left[\kappa\left(\frac{\partial \sigma}{\partial x} + G\right)\right] \quad (1)$$

Here, the term involving G corresponds to the electron wind force driven by j, $\partial \sigma / \partial x$ relates to the back-stress force, x is the distance from the cathode, and t is the time variable. Other terms are:

$$\kappa = \frac{D_{eff}\, B\, \Omega}{k_B T} \quad ; \quad G = \frac{eZ_{eff}^\star\, \rho\, j}{\Omega}$$

in which $D_{eff} = D_0 \exp(-E_a/k_B T)$ is the EM effective diffusivity, D_0 is the diffusivity constant, E_a is the activation energy, k_B is Boltzmann's constant, T is the temperature, B is the effective bulk modulus for the metal-ILD system, Ω is the atomic volume for the metal, e is the elementary electron charge, $Z_{eff}^\star$ the effective charge number, and ρ is the resistivity.

For the current-carrying line in Fig. 2, the boundary condition is that the net atomic flux at the endpoints enclosed by vias is zero, since the Ta barrier at the vias in a Cu DD process blocks the flow of metal atoms, i.e., $\frac{\partial \sigma}{\partial x} + G = 0$, at $x = 0, x = L$, for all t.

2.2 The Blech criterion

A wire is immortal to EM when the back-stress and electron wind forces are in equilibrium in the steady state, i.e., $\frac{\partial \sigma}{\partial t} = 0$ [6]. Using

this condition in (1), if there is no initial stress at $t = 0$,

$$\frac{\partial \sigma}{\partial x} + G = 0 \quad (2)$$

For a constant current flow (i.e., constant G), the slope of the stress profile at steady state is a constant, i.e., $G = \left|\frac{\partial \sigma}{\partial x}\right| = \left|\frac{\Delta \sigma}{L}\right| = \frac{2\sigma}{L}$ [12]. If $\sigma < \sigma_c$, the critical stress that creates a void, the wire will be immortal to EM damage. Therefore,

$$G = \frac{2\sigma}{L} \le \frac{2\sigma_c}{L} \quad (3)$$

$$\text{i.e., } (j\,L) \le \frac{2\sigma_c\,\Omega}{eZ_{eff}^\star\, \rho} = (jL)_{\text{crit}} \quad (4)$$

This is the Blech criterion: the product of the current density j and wire length L must not exceed a threshold, $(jL)_{\text{crit}}$.

2.3 Empirical modeling

2.3.1 Black's equation. EM is a statistical process due to variations in the activation energy, E_a, associated with (1). It has been demonstrated that the probability of failure, referred to as the failure fraction FF, follows a lognormal dependency on the time to failure, t_f [5]. Industrial markets demand low failure rates (e.g., 100 defective parts per million (DPPM) over the chip lifetime). Chip reliability engineers translate this chip-level specification to specific fail fraction (FF) targets, in units of failures-in-time (FITs), on individual resistors. The classic Black's equation [5] relates the mean time to failure, t_{50}, to the average current density j across the interconnect cross-section and the wire temperature T as:

$$t_{50} = \frac{A}{j^n} \exp \frac{E_a}{k_B T} \quad (5)$$

Here, A and n are constants and typical values of n are between 1 and 2, since void nucleation and void growth accelerate as $j = 2$ and $j = 1$, respectively [23]. Industry practice involves setting up a current density limit using the above equation for a given target mean time to failure, t_{50}.

It is important to note that the temperature T corresponds to contributions from the ambient temperature as well as RMS-current-induced temperature rise due to Joule heating [14]. Thus the average current determines j, and the RMS current influences T. Before this fact was realized, it was sometimes stated that the exponent n varied between 1 and 3, instead of 1 and 2 as is now accepted.

2.3.2 Using Black's equation. To translate the mean time to failure predicted by Black's equation, the underlying lognormal is used to determine the average current density thresholds to meet a target FF. This is achieved by defining the lognormal transformation parameter (z), which relates t_{50} to the time to failure, t_f, for a specific FF as follows:

$$z = \frac{\ln(t_f) - \ln(t_{50})}{\sigma}, \quad \text{i.e., } t_f = t_{50}e^{\sigma z} \quad (6)$$

$$FF = \int_{-\infty}^{z} \frac{e^{-x^2/2}}{\sqrt{2\pi}}\,dx \quad (7)$$

where the standard deviation of the distribution, σ, is process-dependent. The transformation variable z helps in directly representing the cumulative failure rate with a normal distribution.

For a given design, the specification provides the acceptable FF and the lifetime of the part, t_{life}. This is translated into a maximum average current density j_{max} as follows:

- The specification is first translated to $t_f \geq t_{life}$. This is a lower bound on t_f.
- Next, the one-to-one mapping between FF and z in Eq. (7) is used to infer z.
- For this z, Eq. (6) translates the lower bound t_{life} on t_f to a lower bound on t_{50}.
- Finally, Black's equation converts the lower bound on t_{50} to an upper bound, j_{max} on the current density j in the wire.

In summary, the conventional empirical method for EM analysis for interconnects involves a two-step process:

- Filtering out EM-immortal wires using the Blech criterion [6]: mortal wires may potentially cause EM failure.
- Checking the current density through these wires against a global limit determined by Black's equation [5].

2.3.3 Pitfalls in characterizing Black's equation. The distribution of t_f is characterized through experiments on interconnect test structures [3], stressed at elevated temperature (typically $300°C$ [13]) and voltage values, to induce EM failure. The failure times are then mapped back to normal chip operating conditions [23]. The statistical distributions of these test structures capture the variations in EM failure times due to variations in grain structure or activation energy, but fail to capture layout-dependent effects.

Void nucleation occurs when the stress in a wire exceeds σ_c. This stress in a wire could have contributions not only from the electron wind and back stress forces, but also from thermomechanical stress, which is generated due to a mismatch in the coefficient of thermal expansion (CTE) of the metallization and the surrounding dielectric [30]. The CTE differential results in compressive/tensile stresses when the wafer is annealed from high-temperature $(300 - 350°C)$ manufacturing conditions to normal operating temperatures. Characterization structures may fail to capture this effect, which a function of the layout and the CTE differentials with the surrounding layers, because (a) they may not be sufficiently diverse to capture all configurations of on-chip interconnects (b) the elevated temperature conditions used during characterization are closer to those at manufacturing [13], due to which thermomechanical stresses are greatly reduced from normal operating temperatures.

2.4 Physics-based modeling

Unlike empirical EM models, physics-based models solve Korhonen's equation, (1). However, the solution takes the form of an infinite series that is expensive to compute. To identify EM-susceptible wires, [27] proposes an efficient filter-based approach.

To present this solution, we consider the solution of Korhonen's equation to compute the stress at the cathode $(x = 0)$ for two cases: a finite (F) line, as in Fig. 2, and a semi-infinite (SI) line where $L \to \infty$. The solutions are:

$$\sigma_{SI}(0, t) = 2G \sqrt{\frac{\kappa t}{\pi}} \tag{8}$$

$$\sigma_F(0, t) = GL \left(\frac{1}{2} - 4 \sum_{i=0}^{\infty} \frac{e^{-m_i^2(\kappa t / L^2)}}{m_i^2} \right) \tag{9}$$

where $m_i = (2i + 1)\pi$. The solution to the SI case is provably an upper bound for the F case: intuitively, this is because the back-stress is lower when the anode is at ∞, which leads to a larger net stress at the cathode. As illustrated in Fig. 3, the two curves closely track each other initially and diverge as t increases. This is explained by the observation in [18] that the steady state for a line of length, L, can be achieved in time $t \approx \frac{L^2}{4\kappa}$. The F and SI curves differ significantly at this time, but are close for smaller values of t, before sufficient back-stress is built up. For long wires (e.g., in power grids in upper level metals), the SI approximation is accurate.

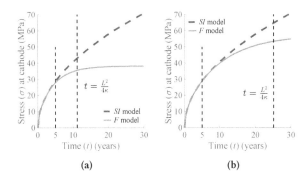

Figure 3: Stress $\sigma(0, t)$ at the cathode for (a) $L = 50\mu$m and (b) $L = 75\mu$m, as predicted by SI and F model for two values of L.

The approach in [27] successively identifies EM-safe wires using three successive filters, where earlier filters are computationally cheaper, and typically capable of filtering out more wires:

Filter 1 uses the Blech criterion to identify immortal wires. This eliminates the largest number of wires that are short and/or have low j.

Filter 2 uses the SI formula (8) to identify whether $\sigma_{SI}(0, t_{life}) < \sigma_{crit}$ where t_{life} is the chip lifetime; since σ_F is upper-bounded by σ_{SI}, this implies that these wires will not nucleate during the lifetime of the chip.

Filter 3 uses the most computationally expensive analysis, to verify whether the remaining wires are EM-safe. This finds a Newton-Raphson solution of the equation $\sigma_F(0, t_{nuc}) = \sigma_c$, where σ_F is truncated to 20 terms, to compute the nucleation time, t_{nuc}.

This approach is efficient because identifies a large fraction of wires as EM-safe through Filters 1 and 2 in a computationally cheap manner, and only a small fraction of wires require the expensive Newton-Raphson computation. This can be extended to capture the statistical nature of EM through the statistical nature of effective diffusity [24], as in [26, 28].

2.5 Flux divergence in multisegment nets

Fundamentally, EM is induced by divergence of atomic flux, which is typically highest at sites such as vias, contacts, or points where the leads merge. Much of the analysis above is presented for two-terminal lines in a single layer, but real interconnects often have multiple branches, segments, metal layers, and fanouts. For Cu DD interconnect, each change of metal layer constitutes a barrier to the migration of atoms, resulting in localized effects and boundary conditions that require solutions to Korhonen's equation.

Further, it has been reported in literature that even if the incoming atomic flux (signified by high current density) is high at such sites, the site itself may not fail due to low atomic flux divergence, but a simple, individual-lead based Black's equation continues to predict failure for such a structure. This inefficiency has been recently revisited by various researchers resulting into evolution of alternative paradigms in EM checking [1, 7, 10, 31, 36]. Such alternative methods rely on computing some form of atomic flux divergence at EM-probable sites and subsequently comparing them against set thresholds.

One computationally simple method, reported in [31], is the vector via-node based method, wherein the physical and directional interactions amongst various leads are incorporated to perform the reliability verification. Notably, however, the fundamental inputs required to perform these calculations still remain the individual current density in every single interconnect of the circuit, along with additional information like the circuit topology.

2.6 Signal EM

The preceding approaches assume a current density j in a wire, which is appropriate for power grid wires that largely have a unidirectional current flow. Currents in signal wires flow in both directions, and the reversal of direction leads to some damage recovery. To model this, we define an effective j as:

$$j = j_{avg}^+ - \mathcal{R} j_{avg}^- \qquad (10)$$

where $\mathcal{R}$ is an empirical recovery factor for EM (typically 0.7–0.95), and j_{avg}^+ and j_{avg}^- indicate the average current density in each of the two directions. There is some controversy as to whether EM recovery is significant or not, or whether a value of $\mathcal{R} \approx 1$ can be used. Even for $\mathcal{R} = 1$, it should be noted that if the PMOS and NMOS strengths driving a signal line are different, then $|j_{avg}^+| \neq |j_{avg}^-|$, and the value of j is nonzero.

3 EM IN NANOSCALE TECHNOLOGIES

3.1 Thermally-induced EM acceleration

Designs at advanced nodes are based on FinFETs that provide improved electrostatic control over the channel. These device topologies help reduce short channel effects, increase the drive current, enable the use of lower supply voltages, and provide superior scalability, but also suffer from significant self-heating (SH) issues. The high transistor density results in high heat flux, and inefficient heat-removal paths to the thermal ambient. The thermal conductivity in the confined region of the fin is degraded due to lattice vibrations (phonons), and the addition of buried oxide (BOX) in SOI FinFETs, or the oxide that surrounds nanowires in gate all-around FETs (GAAFETs), further degrades the thermal conduction path [8].

Figs. 4(a)–(c) show the heat transfer paths in a bulk FinFET, an SOI FinFET, and a lateral GAAFET, and Figs. 4(d)–(f) illustrate the cross-sectional thermal profiles due to SH for an array of three fins and two gates, in series, of a cell from a FinFET library. The bulk FinFET, which has the easiest path to thermal ground through the substrate, has the lowest temperatures, followed by the SOI FinFET, where the bulk path is impeded by BOX, and then the GAAFET,

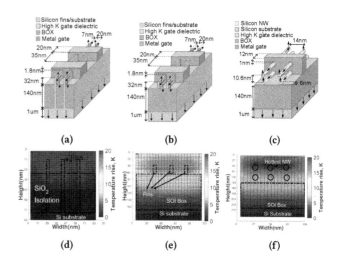

Figure 4: Structure and the paths of heat dissipation in (a) 7nm bulk FinFET, (b) 7nm SOI FinFET, and (c) 5nm lateral GAAFET with arrows that indicate the paths to thermal ground, and thermal contours under a power dissipation of 0.1μW for (d) a bulk FinFET with 3 fins/2 gates (e) an SOI FinFET with 3 fins/2 gates (f) a lateral GAAFET with 3 NW stacks/2 gates.

where thermal paths must negotiate both BOX and the oxide around the NWs, and more heat is conducted through the interconnects. In all these structures, SH can accelerate EM.

In [8], thermal analysis is performed on a set of benchmark circuits. Temperature distributions from thermal analysis are used to estimate the impact on EM using Black's law, and the percentage EM lifetime degradation due to SH is shown in Fig. 5. Degradations in SOI and GAAFET technologies are particularly large, so that wider wires must be used for non-Blech interconnects in these technologies to be EM-safe.

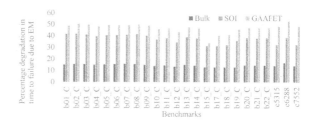

Figure 5: EM-induced time to failure, on benchmark circuits for bulk FinFETs, SOI FinFETs, and GAAFETs.

3.2 EM in lower metal layers

Due to high heat flux and/or high current densities driven in advanced designs, EM can be much more of a problem even in lower metal layers. For instance, cell-internal EM is expressed in signal and power lines within standard cells with high current densities [15, 16, 32, 33]. The signal and power lines could be connected to global interconnects, and thus are not filtered out by the Blech criterion. Similarly, EM may be seen in lower-level metals, an effect that is exacerbated by thermal effects.

The problem of cell-internal EM is illustrated using the INV_X4 (inverter with size 4) cell, shown in Fig. 6(a), from a 45nm library. The input signal A is connected to the polysilicon structure. The layout uses four parallel transistors for the pull-up (poly over p-diffusion, upper half of the figure) and four for the pull-down (poly over n-diffusion, lower half of the figure), and the output signal can be tapped along the H-shaped metal net in the center of the cell. The positions where the output pin can be placed are numbered 1 through 7, and the edges of the structure are labeled e_1 through e_6, as shown in the figure. Since the four PMOS transistors are all identical, by symmetry, the currents injected at nodes 1 and 5 are equal; similarly, the NMOS currents at nodes 3 and 7 are equal.

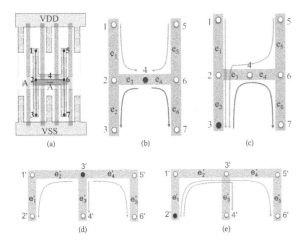

Figure 6: (a) The layout and output pin position options for INV_X4. Charge/discharge currents when the output pin is at (b) node 4 and (c) node 3. The red [blue] lines represent rise [fall] currents. (d) The Vdd pin position options for INV_X4 and the currents when the Vdd pin is at node $3'$ and (e) node $2'$.

For signal EM, depending on whether the pin is at node 4 (Fig. 6(b)) or node 3 (Fig. 6(c)), the current distribution through the wires within the cell is different. In [32, 33], based on exact parasitic extraction of the layout, fed to SPICE (thus including short-circuit and leakage currents), the average effective EM current through e_2 is found to be 1.17× larger than when the pin is at node 4. Accounting for Joule heating, this results in a 19% lifetime reduction. For the Vdd pin (and similarly for Vss pins), a similar effect occurs when the pin position is changed, as shown in Figs. 6(d) and (e).

3.3   EM in analog circuits

EM is becoming an increasing concern not just in digital circuits, but also in analog designs. Many fundamental analog components carry large currents for long periods of time, e.g., a standard structure is a differential pair connected to a current mirror. Unlike signal wires in digital circuits, these "signal" wires carry unidirectional currents. When coupled with narrowing interconnects in advanced process generations, this implies that the wires connected to these components, even in low metal layers, correspond to a significant current density. This requires the use of wider wires to meet EM

lifetime constraints, and this poses a significant issue in analog layout, whereby wire widths must be set based on current densities.

4   ANALYSIS OF INTERCONNECT SYSTEMS

4.1   The weakest link model

A typical EM failure criterion for a wire is a resistance increase of 10%. To translate wire failure to system failure, the weakest link model [9, 20] has been widely used for EM analysis. This is based on the idea that a chip fails on the first EM event, i.e., the chip-level EM failure probability corresponds to the case where no wire experiences EM. At time t, if the failure probability of the ith of K elements is $F_i(t)$, then the probability, $F_{chip}(t)$, of chip failure is:

$$F_{chip}(t) = 1 - \Pi_{i=1}^{K}(1 - F_i(t)) \qquad (11)$$

Variations of this approach have been extensively used for on-chip EM analysis [20], but they are largely dependent on making the method simple to use by decoupling the failure of each element from that of other elements. This allows a separate maximum current density check on every wire in the system. However, in many instances, a circuit has inherent resilience that permits it to continue functioning even after an EM event. Fundamentally, the concept of redundancy is a reliability engineer's friend as it enables such resilience. For example, while a tree-structured interconnect may become nonfunctional due to a EM-induced wire break, connectivity in a mesh structure will be maintained even after the first EM failure. In this section, we will first analytically examine the impact of EM failure on system failure, and then provide several examples where the weakest link assumption is invalid.

4.2   Reliability under changing stress

In an interconnect system with redundancy, when one component fails, the current is redistributed to the other wires. This results in higher current densities, and therefore, increases the risk of EM failure in those wires. In this section, we provide a mathematical treatment of this scenario, based on the work in [17].

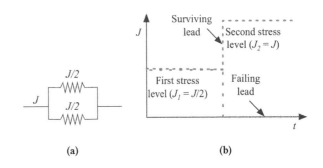

Figure 7: (a) Schematic showing a parallel two-component system (b) Current profile evolution, with first failure occurring at time t1.

Consider a system comprising two components (Fig. 7(a)), where both components initially carry a current density $J_1 = J/2$ (Fig. 7(b)). When one of them fails at time t_1, the current in the surviving component changes to $J_2 = J$. After the first component fails, the current through the second component rises, altering its failure statistics. The initial failure rate, $f(t)$, of each component is lognormal,

$$f(t) = \frac{1}{t\sigma\sqrt{2\pi}} e^{\left(-\frac{1}{2}\left(\frac{\ln t - \ln t_{50}}{\sigma}\right)\right)} \tag{12}$$

with a cumulative probability distribution function (CDF) given by

$$F(t) = \Phi\left(\frac{\ln t - \ln t_{50}}{\sigma}\right) \tag{13}$$

where $\Phi(x)$ as the standard normal CDF. Until time t_1, the reliability CDF of each component is described by

$$F_1(t) = \Phi\left(\frac{\ln t - \ln t_{50,1}}{\sigma}\right) \tag{14}$$

where $t_{50,1}$ is the mean time to failure for J_1, as in Fig. 8. For a general component that carries current corresponding to second stress level, J_2, the reliability is represented by a CDF, $F_2(t)$, and the associated $t_{50,2}$. For the case of Fig. 7(b), the CDF trajectory for the surviving component at t_1 therefore must change from F_1 to F_2. After the step jump in the current, we shift F_2 by time δ_1 to ensure continuity with F_1 at time t_1, i.e.,

$$F_2(t_1 - \delta_1) = F_1(t_1) \tag{15}$$

This equivalence implies that the curve follows the trajectory of F_2, starting at the same fraction of the failed population under the two stresses, but that the failure rate increases after t_1. For example, for a ξ_{ij} fail probability, shown in Fig. 8, the TTF changes from t_{ijh} (if only the first stress were applicable) to a lower value, t_{ijk} (under the new stress condition). The effective CDF curve (Fig. 8) is

$$F_1(t) = \Phi\left(\frac{\ln t - \ln t_{50,1}}{\sigma}\right) 0 \leq t \leq t_1 \tag{16}$$

$$F_2(t - \delta_1) = \Phi\left(\frac{\ln(t - \delta_1) - \ln t_{50,2}}{\sigma}\right) t \geq t_1 \tag{17}$$

$$\text{where} \quad \delta_1 = t_1\left(1 - \frac{t_{50,2}}{t_{50,1}}\right) \tag{18}$$

For a system where components undergo a change in stress multiple times, we can generalize the formulation to account for k changes in current, from J_1 to $J_2 \cdots$ to J_k:

$$\delta_k = \left(t_k - \sum_{i=1}^{k-1} \delta_i\right)\left(1 - \frac{t_{50,k}}{t_{50,k-1}}\right) \tag{19}$$

We now apply this idea and basic formulation to analyze the system reliability for the structure in Fig. 7(a). We define the system to be functional as long as there is a valid electrical connection between the two terminals of the parallel system. If both components are from the same process population (Fig. 7(b)), the reliability of the case when both are simultaneously functional is given by:

$$R_{11}(t) = (1 - F_1(t))^2 \tag{20}$$

Next, the reliability for the case when the first component fails at an arbitrary time t_1, and the second component works successfully till time t, is computed. The probability that the first component fails between time t_1 and $(t_1 + \Delta t_1)$ is $f_1(t_1)\Delta t_1$, where $f_1(t)$ is the probability density function associated with $F_1(t)$. After the current redistribution at t_1, the failure statistics of the surviving component are given by the CDF $F_2(t - \delta_1)$. Thus, the probability of the second component working when the first has failed is:

$$[1 - F_2(t - \delta_1)]f_1(t_1)\Delta t_1. \tag{21}$$

Integrating over all possible failure times from 0 to t, the reliability for this case at time t is:

$$R_{12}(t) = \int_{t_1=0}^{t_1=t} [1 - F_2(t - \delta_1)]f_1(t_1)dt_1 \tag{22}$$

The effective failure probability of the parallel configuration is:

$$F_{||}(t) = 1 - [R_{11}(t) + 2R_{12}(t)] \tag{23}$$

For this two-component system, another alternative is to use a single component of twice the width to carry the entire current, $2J_1 = J$. Such a component has the same current density as each of the parallel leads and its failure probability is the single component CDF, F_1, in Fig. 8, which is significantly worse. This margin arises from EM stochasticity, since the probability of two narrower wires failing simultaneously is smaller than that for a single wide wire.

4.3 Power grid IR drop analysis

The power grid is designed as a mesh so that there are multiple paths from the supply/ground pins to any gate. This naturally implies redundancy: even with the loss of a wire segment due to EM failure, there are other current paths to a gate. As in Section 4.2, when a wire fails, the currents to the gate are redistributed along these other paths. While this creates larger EM stress on the wires on these paths, the circuit often functions well after the first failure.

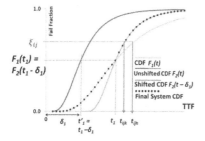

Figure 8: Analytically estimated CDF evolution of a single component when it undergoes a stress change. The dotted line is the effective CDF, when stress change occurs at t_1.

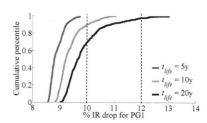

Figure 9: CDF plots for IR drop of the benchmark PG1 for different circuit lifetimes, t_{life}.

The work in [26, 28] presents an analysis of the impact of EM, using probabilistic physics-based models, on the performance of a power grid. Results are shown on the IBM power grid benchmarks, and the cumulative distribution function of the IR drop for PG1 is shown in Fig. 9. It is seen here that as the life of the chip (t_{life}) is increased in simulation, the curves shift to the right, indicating a larger probability of failing an IR drop constraint. The scenarios where the IR drop crosses a threshold are found to correspond to multiple EM failures, rather than a weakest-link failure. The worst-case resistance increase on any wire for the 10- and 20-year lifetime plots is found to be 124% and 297%; in contrast, recall that the basic weakest-link model may pessimistically pronounce system failure when wire resistance increases by 10%.

4.4 Via arrays and thermomechanical stress

Metal lines in the upper metal layers may use wires as wide as 2–$3\mu m$, and interconnections between metal layers involve an array of vias instead of a single via. These via arrays have complex geometrical and electrical characteristics that can affect EM, and also contain inherent redundancy as the failure of one via of the array does not imply an open circuit between the connected wires.

Since thermomechanical stress is a function of the layout and the composition of the surrounding layers, the stress in via arrays is position-dependent: vias on the edge of the array see a different CTE environment as compared to vias in the interior. As a result, the critical stress due to EM that causes nucleation is different for vias in the array. This section summarizes the work in [25].

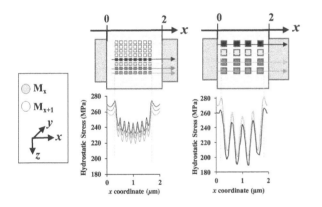

Figure 10: FEA simulation 8×8 vs. 4×4 via array.

Fig. 10 shows two via configurations, corresponding to an 8×8 via array, and another to a 4×4 via array same effective cross section area. The vias connect an upper level of metal M_{x+1} with the next lower level, M_x, and the metal layer heights correspond to M7 and M8 in a 32nm technology node. The wire widths are chosen as $2\mu m$ for the interconnects, and are representative of wires in a power grid. Both vias have an effective area of $1\mu m^2$, corresponding to the same resistance between M_x and M_{x+1}.

The figure also shows the results of a finite element analysis (FEA) simulation of the thermomechanical stress through each via. The four curves (black, yellow, green, and red) in each figure represent the hydrostatic stress as a function of distance x, along an arrow of the same color in the figure above. The local minima of

stress occur in the interior of each via, and the local maxima occur in the regions between the vias. The stress profile is different for the two scenarios, and although the largest stress in two cases is similar, the inner vias see different stresses.

Current-induced EM stress adds to this residual stress, and voids are formed when the net stress reaches a threshold value [13, 18]. The lower preexisting thermomechanical stress values in the inner vias result in a lower likelihood of achieving the critical threshold value needed for void formation. Moreover, for the 4×4 via array, even if a void does form, its impact may be mitigated by the fact that the via array has more redundancy than a single via. Together, these two factors imply that the choice of the via array dimension can alter interconnect lifetimes.

It is shown in [25] that the thermomechanical stress differences lead to significant lifetime differences for various vias. Additionally, the invalidity of the weakest-link approximation is quite visible in a via array that has a large degree of redundancy. For a 4×4 via ($n = 16$), the failure of one via ($n_F = 1$) results in a 6.7% resistance change, and the failure of eight vias will result in a 100% increase.

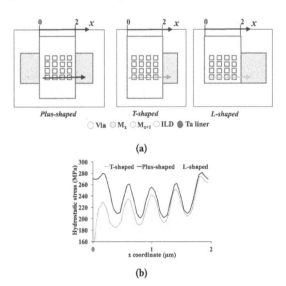

Figure 11: (a) The plus-shaped (left), T-shaped (centre), and L-shaped (right) patterns, illustrated with a 4×4 via array. (b) Thermal stress for these intersection patterns.

The level of thermomechanical stress depends on other factors. For an M_x–M_{x+1} metal layer pair, where x and x+1 may be either intermediate or top layers [2] (with three combinations: intermediate–intermediate, intermediate–top, and top–top), an interconnect in a power grid consists of three patterns of via array structures, corresponding to the structure of the wires in the two metal layers: *Plus-shaped* patterns, *T-shaped* patterns, and *L-shaped* patterns. These patterns are illustrated in Fig. 11(a). Fig. 11(b) shows the thermomechanical stress under the first row of vias (indicated by the arrows in figure above) in the M_x metal layer of a 4×4 via array for each of these patterns. The difference in stress due to the structure of each pattern can be attributed to a larger CTE for Cu relative to ILD: in these cases, the amount of ILD near the via changes the magnitude of CTE mismatch.

4.5 Clock distribution networks

Signal interconnects can be affected by EM over the chip lifetime, subject to the notion of recovery described in Section 2.6. In particular, EM concerns in wires in clock networks, which carry high amounts of current, can be a serious concern. Therefore, much of the chip-level signal EM analysis is focused on ensuring safety of clock nets, even though they are physically routed at non-default widths due to delay considerations. Mesh-structured clock networks [4, 34, 35] are used because of their robustness to clock skew, but they are also inherently resilient to EM due to the presence of multiple paths to each sink node, and multiple driving buffers that are inserted to maintain clock system performance. Due to this redundancy, the clock skew and slew rate can remain robust after some failures in the grid, and a weakest link approach is pessimistic.

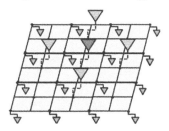

Figure 12: A one-level clock grid schematic with multiple drivers.

These factors were studied in [17] using a Monte Carlo analysis built upon the techniques of Section 4.2. The work considers a one-level clock grid (Fig. 12), with an exemplary buffer and its four identical neighbors to the north, south, east, and west, implemented in a commercial 28nm node, at 1GHz. In our example, wire widths in the clock grid are large so that the likelihood of EM failure is negligible and we focus on failures that may occur in within-cell wires [32] that drive large external wires, or in the power grid. It is shown (Fig. 13) that the weakest link approximation (WLA) significantly underestimates failure, and using a skew-based criterion instead of the WLA results in a ∼ 2× lifetime improvement.

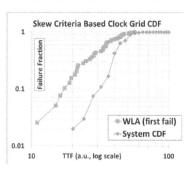

Figure 13: The CDF of lifetime using skew-based criteria based CDF, as against the weakest link approximation (WLA) on a clock grid shows the high level of pessimism of the latter.

5 CONCLUSION

EM is an increasingly significant problem in nanometer-scale designs. The primary message of this paper is that reliable interconnect design requires an understanding not only of the physics that

drives EM, but also circuit-level insights into the impact of EM on performance, and scenarios that cause circuits to fail due to EM.

ACKNOWLEDGMENTS

This work was supported in part by the NSF under awards CCF-1421606, CCF-1714805, and by the DARPA IDEA program. The author gratefully acknowledges the work of Dr. Vivek Mishra, Dr. Palkesh Jain, and Vidya Chhabria that led to many of the insights in this paper.

REFERENCES

[1] S. M. Alam, C. L. Gan, F. L. Wei, C. V. Thompson, and D. Troxel. 2005. Circuit-level reliability requirements for Cu metallization. *IEEE T. Device Mater. Rel.* 5, 3 (2005), 522–531.
[2] C. J. Alpert, Z. Li, M. Moffitt, G.-J. Nam, J. Roy, and G. Tellez. 2010. What makes a design difficult to route?. In *Proc. ISPD*. ACM, New York, NY, 7–12.
[3] JEDEC Solid State Technology Association. 2018. Foundry process qualification guidelines (Wafer fabrication manufacturing sites) – Backend of line. JEP001-1A.
[4] D. W. Bailey and B. J. Benschneider. 1998. Clocking design and analysis for a 600-MHz alpha microprocessor. *IEEE J. Solid-St. Circ.* 3, 11 (Nov. 1998), 1627–1633.
[5] J. R. Black. 1969. Electromigration failure modes in aluminum metallization for semiconductor devices. *Proc. IEEE* 57, 9 (1969), 1587–1594.
[6] I. A. Blech. 1976. Electromigration in thin aluminum films on titanium nitride. *J. Appl. Phys.* 47, 4 (1976), 1203–1208.
[7] S. Chatterjee, V. Sukharev, and F. N. Najm. 2018. Power grid electromigration checking using physics-based models. *IEEE T. Comput. Aid D.* 37, 7 (July 2018), 1317–1330.
[8] V. Chhabria and S. S. Sapatnekar. 2019. Impact of self-heating on performance and reliability in FinFET and GAAFET designs. In *Proc. ISQED*. IEEE, Piscataway, NJ.
[9] D. F. Frost and K. F. Poole. 1989. Reliant: a reliability analysis tool for VLSI interconnect. *IEEE J. Solid-St. Circ.* 24, 2 (April 1989), 458–462.
[10] Z. Guan, M. Marek-Sadowska, S. Nassif, and B. Li. 2014. Atomic flux divergence based current conversion scheme for signal line electromigration reliability assessment. In *Proc. IEEE International Interconnect Technology Conference*. IEEE, Piscataway, NJ, 245–248.
[11] J. E. Hall, D. E. Hocevar, Ping Yang, and M. J. McGraw. 1987. SPIDER – A CAD system for modeling VLSI metallization patterns. *IEEE T. Comput. Aid D.* 6, 6 (Nov. 1987), 1023–1031.
[12] C. S. Hau-Riege, S. P. Hau-Riege, and A. P. Marathe. 2004. The effect of interlevel dielectric on the critical tensile stress to void nucleation for the reliability of Cu interconnects. *J. Appl. Phys.* 96, 10 (2004), 5792–5796.
[13] A. Heryanto, K. L. Pey, Y. K. Lim, W. Liu, N. Raghavan, J. Wei, C. L. Gan, M. K. Lim, and J. B. Tan. 2011. The effect of stress migration on electromigration in dual damascene copper interconnects. *J. Appl. Phys.* 109, 1 (2011), 013716-1–013716-9.
[14] W. Hunter. 1997. Self-consistent solutions for allowed interconnect current density. II. Application to design guidelines. *IEEE Transactions on Electron Devices* 44, 2 (Feb. 1997), 310–316.
[15] P. Jain, J. Cortadella, and S. S. Sapatnekar. 2016. A fast and retargetable framework for logic-IP-internal electromigration assessment comprehending advanced waveform effects. *IEEE T. VLSI Syst* 24, 6 (June 2016), 2345–2358.
[16] P. Jain and A. Jain. 2012. Accurate current estimation for interconnect reliability analysis. *IEEE T. VLSI Syst* 20, 9 (Sept. 2012), 1634–1644.
[17] P. Jain, S. S. Sapatnekar, and J. Cortadella. 2015. Stochastic and topologically aware electromigration analysis for clock skew. In *Proc. IRPS*. IEEE, Piscataway, NJ, 3.D.4-1–3.D.4–6.
[18] M. A Korhonen, P. Borgesen, K. N. Tu, and C. Y. Li. 1993. Stress evolution due to electromigration in confined metal lines. *J. Appl. Phys.* 73, 8 (1993), 3790–3799.
[19] K.-D. Lee. 2012. Electromigration recovery and short lead effect under bipolar- and unipolar-pulse current. In *Proc. IRPS*. IEEE, Piscataway, NJ, 6B.3.1–6B.3.4.
[20] B. Li, P. S. McLaughlin, J. P. Bickford, P.Habitz, D. Netrabile, and T. D. Sullivan. 2011. Statistical evaluation of electromigration reliability at chip level. *IEEE T. Device Mater. Rel.* 11, 1 (March 2011), 86–91.
[21] J. Lienig. 2013. Electromigration and its impact on physical design in future technologies. In *Proc. ISPD*. ACM, New York, NY, 33–40.
[22] J. Lienig and M. Thiele. 2018. The pressing need for electromigration-aware physical design. In *Proc. ISPD*. ACM, New York, NY, 144–151.
[23] J.R. Lloyd. 2007. Black's law revisted—Nucleation and growth in electromigration failure. *Microelectron. Reliab.* 47, 9 (2007), 1468–1472.
[24] J. R. Lloyd and J. Kitchin. 1991. The electromigration failure distribution: The fine-line case. *J. Appl. Phys.* 69, 4 (1991), 2117–2127.
[25] V. Mishra, P. Jain, S. K. Marella, and S. S. Sapatnekar. 2016. Incorporating the role of stress on electromigration in power grids with via arrays. In *Proc. DAC*. ACM, New York, NY, 21:1–21:6.
[26] V. Mishra and S. S. Sapatnekar. 2013. The impact of electromigration in copper interconnects on power grid integrity. In *Proc. DAC*. ACM, New York, NY, 88:1–88:6.
[27] V. Mishra and S. S. Sapatnekar. 2016. Predicting electromigration mortality under temperature and product lifetime specifications. In *Proc. DAC*. ACM, New York, NY, 43:1–43:6.
[28] V. Mishra and S. S. Sapatnekar. 2017. Probabilistic wire resistance degradation due to electromigration in i power grids. *IEEE T. Comput. Aid D.* 36, 4 (April 2017), 628–640.
[29] A. S. Oates. 2015. Strategies to ensure electromigration reliability of Cu/Low-k interconnects at 10 nm. *ECS J. Solid State Sc. Tech.* 4, 1 (2015), N3168–N3176.
[30] J.-M. Paik, H. Park, and Y.-C. Joo. 2004. Effect of low-k dielectric on stress and stress-induced damage in Cu interconnects. *Microelectron. Eng.* 71, 3–4 (2004), 348–357.
[31] Y. J. Park, P. Jain, and S. Krishnan. 2010. New electromigration validation: Via node vector method. In *Proc. IRPS*. IEEE, Piscataway, NJ, 698–704.
[32] G. Posser, V. Mishra, P. Jain, R. Reis, and S. S. Sapatnekar. 2014. A systematic approach for analyzing and optimizing cell-internal signal electromigration. In *Proc. ICCAD*. IEEE, Piscataway, NJ, 486–491.
[33] G. Posser, V. Mishra, P. Jain, R. Reis, and S. S. Sapatnekar. 2016. Cell-internal electromigration: Analysis and pin placement based optimization. *IEEE T. Comput. Aid D.* 35, 2 (Feb. 2016), 220–231.
[34] H. Qian et al. 2012. Subtractive router for tree-driven-grid clocks. *IEEE T. Comput. Aid D.* 31, 6 (June 2012), 868–877.
[35] H. Su and S. S. Sapatnekar. 2001. Hybrid structured clock network construction. In *Proc. ICCAD*. IEEE, Piscataway, NJ, 333–336.
[36] Z. Sun, E. Demircan, M. D. Shroff, C. Cook, and S. X.-D. Tan. 2018. Fast electromigration immortality analysis for multisegment copper interconnect wires. *IEEE T. Comput. Aid D.* 37, 12 (Dec. 2018), 3137–3150.
[37] C.-C. Teng, Y.-K. Cheng, E. Rosenbaum, and S.-M. Kang. 1997. iTEM: A temperature-dependent electromigration reliability diagnosis tool. *IEEE T. Comput. Aid D.* 16, 8 (Aug. 1997), 882–893.
[38] L. M. Ting, J. S. May, W. R. Hunter, and J. W. McPherson. 1993. AC electromigration characterization and modeling of multilayered interconnects. In *Proc. IRPS*. IEEE, Piscataway, NJ, 311–316.

Toward Intelligent Physical Design: Deep Learning and GPU Acceleration

Haoxing Ren

NVIDIA Corporation

Austin, TX

haoxingr@nvidia.com

ABSTRACT

Deep learning (DL) has achieved tremendous success in computer vision, natural language processing and gaming. The key drivers for this success are increasing dataset sizes, increasing model sizes, and faster GPU computing powers with better software infrastructure to enable the processing of larger models and datasets [3]. Would the same drivers help push physical design toward a more intelligent paradigm to meet the post-Moore era design automation challenges? The applications of conventional machine learning (ML) methods such as regressions, decision trees and support vector machines in physical design have been studied extensively in previous years [5]. ML often performs tasks such as prediction and correlation. The complexity of deep learning models, together with the availability of large datasets and computing power enables DL to achieve dramatic improvements in prediction accuracy compared to conventional ML methods. DL also enables applications that cannot be easily formulated with conventional ML methods.

We will first discuss three DL models and our works applying these models to physical design and related EDA domains. The first model is Convolutional Neural Network (CNN) based classification or regression model. CNNs have achieved huge successes in building classifiers for computer vision and many other domains when processing structured 2D data. Clearly, we should apply CNN model in our design automation problems whenever we can as a low hanging fruit. A significant benefit of CNN is that there are many well-known pretrained CNN models in the public domain. We leveraged a pretrained VGG net [10] to predict power from register traces [13]. Mapping register traces to an image that VGG net can handle is a feature encoding problem. We experimented with several encoding methods, but it turns out that VGG is complex enough that it is almost insensitive to the encoding strategy.

The second model is a Fully Convolutional Network (FCN) [9]. This model was commonly used for image segmentation in the compute vision community. It is good at predicting a target image from an input image, as compared to the CNN based classification or regression model which only predicts one number or category from an input image. We developed a model called RouteNet [11] based on FCN, which predicts DRC hotspots from placement stage using this model. Because it can capture the global influence on the local region from the entire design, its prediction accuracy is better than the local window-based approach.

The third model is a Graph Convolution Network (GCN) [6]. CNN models are only suitable for data on the Euclidian space, however design automation problems are often based on a netlist, which is commonly represented as a graph. There is a growing body of research in the DL community focusing on graph-based models. GCN is one of the newer graph-based models that is suitable for EDA. We applied a GCN to predict testability of a gate and inserted test points to improve testability based on the model prediction [8]. We also improved the performance of this model to scale to millions of gates and developed multi-stage classification flow to deal with data imbalance issue.

These three examples of DL are applications of supervised learning, where labeled data is used to train a model in order to perform a prediction on new data. However, these models can also be used in Reinforcement learning (RL) to solve optimization as well. Most physical design problems are NP-hard optimization problems. They are often solved by simulated annealing methods or various heuristics. RL leveraging DL models, i.e. Deep Reinforcement Learning (DRL), has the capability to handle complex optimization scenarios beyond these conventional methods. Recent work has leveraged DRL to solve combinatorial optimization problems such as the Traveling Salesman Problem (TSP) [1]. DRL has also shown great potential when applied to logic circuits optimization[4].

Looking into the future, to overcome the difficulty of getting training labels for supervised learning, unsupervised learning (UL) will also play a big role. With deep learning models, UL learns the distributions of the datasets in their latent space and generates new data samples by interpolation among the latent space. Furthermore, the learned latent space can be used to assist classification or optimization tasks. Generative models such as Generative Adversarial Network (GAN) and autoregressive models are key deep learning models used in UL. Although recent work leveraging GAN to generate optical proximity correction (OPC) masks [12] is still supervised learning, it sheds light on how a generative model can be utilized to solve an EDA problem.

The latest advancements in GPU hardware have has created unprecedented computing power. The NVIDIA DGX2 system has 16 fully interconnected Volta GPUs with 512GB GPU memory and can deliver 2 Peta FLOPS [2]. Indeed, as one of the three drivers of Deep learning revolution, GPU computing power is one key to the success of deep learning. Can we unleash the same power in physical design directly instead of through deep learning indirectly? Fortunately, the ability to harness GPU performance for optimization problems has also continued to improve over recent years. In particular, the DL community has created several GPU

ISPD '19, April 14–17, 2019, San Francisco, CA, USA

© 2019 Copyright held by the owner/author(s).

ACM ISBN 978-1-4503-6253-5/19/04...$15.00

https://doi.org/10.1145/3299902.3311066

enabled frameworks such as TensorFlow, PyTorch and MxNet to improve algorithm development productivity beyond the CUDA development environment. The physical design community can leverage these frameworks as well to build GPU accelerated algorithms. We built GPU accelerated placement engines based on TensorFlow and PyTorch. The PyTorch based placer [7] achieved over 30X speedup on a GV100 GPU in global placement without quality degradation compared to a state-of-the-art multi-threaded placer. Since GPUs require exploiting significantly more parallelism than multi-core CPUs for good performance and contain specialized accelerator blocks such as TensorCores [2], novel parallelization schemes should be invented for EDA problems.

Deep learning and GPU acceleration can also work together. On the one hand, GPU accelerated algorithms can help provide a large amount of training data required for DL models quickly; On the other hand, iterative algorithms such as RL or simulated annealing will require fast turnaround time for each iteration which can be speedup by GPU acceleration. We will illustrate an idea of integrated DL and GPU acceleration to produce better quality floorprlans.

KEYWORDS

Deep Learning; Machine Learning; Electronic Design Automation; GPU; Accelerated Computing

ACM Reference Format:
Haoxing Ren. 2019. Toward Intelligent Physical Design: Deep Learning and GPU Acceleration. In *2019 International Symposium on Physical Design (ISPD '19), April 14–17, 2019, San Francisco, CA, USA.* ACM, New York, NY, USA, 2 pages. https://doi.org/10.1145/3299902.3311066

 Haoxing Ren is a principal research scientist at NVIDIA. His current research interests are machine learning application in design automation and GPU accelerated EDA. He worked at IBM EDA Lab from 2000 to 2006 where he was a key developer of placement tools. He joined IBM Research in 2007 where he led the development of logic ECO synthesis tools and high-level synthesis tools. Prior to joining NVIDIA in May 2016, he was a technical executive at PowerCore, a startup developing server-class CPUs licensing IBM OpenPower technology. Mark holds over twenty patents and co-authored many papers including several book chapters in physical design and logic synthesis. He is an IEEE senior member and served as a TPC member for ICCAD and DAC. Mark earned a PhD degree in Computer Engineering from University of Texas at Austin, a M.S. degree in Computer Engineering from Rensselaer Polytechnic Institute, and M.S/B.S. degrees in Electrical Engineering from Shanghai Jiao Tong University.

REFERENCES

[1] Irwan Bello, Hieu Pham, Quoc V. Le, Mohammad Norouzi, and Samy Bengio. 2016. Neural Combinatorial Optimization with Reinforcement Learning. *CoRR* abs/1611.09940 (2016). arXiv:1611.09940 http://arxiv.org/abs/1611.09940

[2] NVIDIA Corporation. 2018. NVIDIA DGX-2. hhttps://www.nvidia.com/en-us/data-center/dgx-2/

[3] Ian Goodfellow, Yoshua Bengio, and Aaron Courville. 2016. *Deep Learning.* MIT Press. http://www.deeplearningbook.org.

[4] W. Haaswijk, E. Collins, B. Seguin, M. Soeken, F. Kaplan, S. SÄijsstrunk, and G. De Micheli. 2018. Deep Learning for Logic Optimization Algorithms. In *2018 IEEE International Symposium on Circuits and Systems (ISCAS).* 1–4. https://doi.org/10.1109/ISCAS.2018.8351885

[5] Andrew B. Kahng. 2018. Machine Learning Applications in Physical Design: Recent Results and Directions. In *Proceedings of the 2018 International Symposium on Physical Design (ISPD '18).* ACM, New York, NY, USA, 68–73. https://doi.org/10.1145/3177540.3177554

[6] Thomas N. Kipf and Max Welling. 2016. Semi-Supervised Classification with Graph Convolutional Networks. *CoRR* abs/1609.02907 (2016). arXiv:1609.02907 http://arxiv.org/abs/1609.02907

[7] Yibo Lin, Shounak Dhar, Wuxi Li, Haoxing Ren, Brucek Khailany, and David Z. Pan. 2019. DREAMPlace: Deep Learning Toolkit-Enabled GPU Acceleration for VLSI Analytical Placement. *To Appear.* In *Proceedings of the 56th Annual Design Automation Conference (DAC '19).* ACM, New York, NY, USA.

[8] Yuzhe Ma, Haoxing Ren, Brucek Khailany, Harbinder Sikka, Lijuan Luo, Karthikeyan Natarajan, and Bei Yu. 2019. High Performance Graph Convolutional Networks with Applications in Testability Analysis. *To Appear.* In *Proceedings of the 56th Annual Design Automation Conference (DAC '19).* ACM, New York, NY, USA.

[9] Evan Shelhamer, Jonathan Long, and Trevor Darrell. 2017. Fully Convolutional Networks for Semantic Segmentation. *IEEE Trans. Pattern Anal. Mach. Intell.* 39, 4 (2017), 640–651. https://doi.org/10.1109/TPAMI.2016.2572683

[10] Karen Simonyan and Andrew Zisserman. 2014. Very Deep Convolutional Networks for Large-Scale Image Recognition. *CoRR* abs/1409.1556 (2014). http://arxiv.org/abs/1409.1556

[11] Zhiyao Xie, Yu-Hung Huang, Guan-Qi Fang, Haoxing Ren, Shao-Yun Fang, Yiran Chen, and Nvidia Corporation. 2018. RouteNet: Routability Prediction for Mixed-size Designs Using Convolutional Neural Network. In *Proceedings of the International Conference on Computer-Aided Design (ICCAD '18).* ACM, New York, NY, USA, Article 80, 8 pages. https://doi.org/10.1145/3240765.3240843

[12] Haoyu Yang, Shuhe Li, Yuzhe Ma, Bei Yu, and Evangeline F. Y. Young. 2018. GAN-OPC: Mask Optimization with Lithography-guided Generative Adversarial Nets. In *Proceedings of the 55th Annual Design Automation Conference (DAC '18).* ACM, New York, NY, USA, Article 131, 6 pages. https://doi.org/10.1145/3195970.3196056

[13] Yan Zhou, Haoxing Ren, Yanqing Zhang, Ben Keller, Brucek Khailany, and Zhiru Zhang. 2019. PRIMAL: Power Inference using Machine Learning. *To Appear.* In *Proceedings of the 56th Annual Design Automation Conference (DAC '19).* ACM, New York, NY, USA.

Multiple Patterning Layout Compliance with Minimizing Topology Disturbance and Polygon Displacement*

Hua-Yu Chang
Synopsys, Inc.
Taipei 11012, Taiwan
huayu.chang@gmail.com

Iris Hui-Ru Jiang
National Taiwan University
Taipei 10617, Taiwan
huiru.jiang@gmail.com

ABSTRACT

Multiple patterning lithography (MPL) divides a layout into several masks and manufactures them by a series of exposure and etching steps. As technology advances, MPL is still indispensable because of its cost effectiveness and hybrid lithography capability. Producing a layout by MPL relies on layout decomposition and layout compliance. The former reports conflicts (i.e., identifies undecomposable polygons), and the latter further modifies the layout to clean conflicts. As long as a layout has unresolved conflicts, it cannot be manufactured by MPL. Hence, layout compliance is crucial for MPL. This task, however, becomes more complicated and challenging because of more masks used and design rule explosion at advanced technology nodes. Semi-automation or manual fixing is thus no longer applicable. Moreover, from a designer's perspective, layout modification is desired to preserve interconnect correctness, not to create new conflicts, and to minimize topology disturbance and polygon displacement. Therefore, in this paper, we propose the first fully automatic approach for multiple patterning layout compliance. For achieving this goal, we extract topology relations of polygons and model the layout correction as a polygon legalization problem. Experimental results demonstrate the superior efficiency and effectiveness of our approach. With topology awareness, our spacing constraint handling is general and can be applied to other layout fixing problems.

ACM Reference format:
Hua-Yu Chang and Iris Hui-Ru Jiang. 2019. Multiple Patterning Layout Compliance with Minimizing Topology Disturbance and Polygon Displacement. In *Proceedings of 2019 International Symposium on Physical Design (ISPD '19)*. ACM, New York, NY, USA, 8 pages.
https://doi.org/10.1145/3299902.3309755

1 INTRODUCTION

As technology advances, multiple patterning lithography (MPL) continues to play an important role because of its cost

*This work was supported in part by Synopsys, TSMC, and MOST of Taiwan under Grant MOST 106-2628-E-002-019-MY3.

effectiveness and hybrid lithography capability [1]. MPL possesses a flexibility to integrate with next generation lithography techniques such as directed self-assembly, extreme ultraviolet lithography, and electron beam lithography [2]–[5].

MPL divides a layout into several masks (colors) and manufactures them through a series of exposure and etching processes. When the Euclidean distance between two polygons is less than the minimum same color spacing, they should be assigned to different masks to prevent a coloring conflict. Producing a layout by MPL relies on two major tasks: Layout decomposition reports coloring conflicts (indicating polygons which cannot successfully be decomposed), and layout compliance modifies the layout to remove conflicts. Layout compliance is critical for MPL because once a layout has unresolved conflicts, it cannot be manufactured.

Prior research endeavors mainly focused on layout decomposition, e.g., [6]–[10]. Conventionally, layout decomposition is reduced to graph coloring on a conflict graph, where each mask corresponds to a color, each vertex represents a polygon, and each edge indicates the same color spacing violation between the corresponding two polygons (see Fig. 1(a)). Double patterning lithography (DPL) is the simplest form of MPL. Based on two-colorability, odd cycles in the conflict graph can automatically be reported in linear time. For triple patterning lithography (TPL) and beyond, however, identifying native conflict graph patterns is still an open problem.

On the other hand, there is a paucity of literature on layout compliance. For DPL, existing polygon edge shifting approaches are developed based on two-colorability [11][12]. So far, this task for general MPL has not been automated very well. Due to the lack of knowledge of MPL conflict patterns, existing studies are restricted to fix only few special patterns, e.g., four-cliques (K_4) for TPL, five-cliques (K_5) for quadruple patterning lithography (QPL) [13]–[15]. Yu *et al.* presented a semi-automatic approach for TPL [15]: They first performed fast coloring to report likely conflicts, then manually modified the layout to remove K_4, and finally verified remaining conflicts by incremental coloring. Non-four-clique conflicts may still remain afterwards. As MPL uses more masks and design rules explode in size and complexity at advanced technology nodes [16][17], layout compliance becomes more complicated and challenging. Thus, either semi-automation or laborious manual intervention is time consuming and no longer applicable.

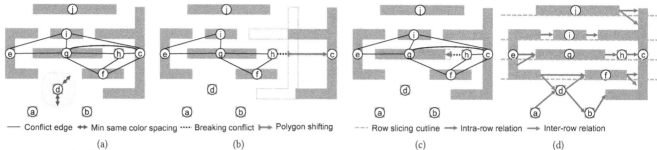

Figure. 1: Multiple patterning layout compliance for TPL. (a) Conflict graph of a layout. (b) One possible fix with a large shift on polygon *c*. (c) A better fix with a small shift on *g*. (d) Row slicing scheme for topology extraction.

From a designer's perspective, since an input layout has been optimized for power, timing, and area, layout compliance is expected to be done with least layout change. Moreover, modern design rules are strongly correlated to topology and polygon shapes; topology change or polygon distortion may induce unwanted new violations. Most prior studies cannot guarantee not to create new conflicts and not to alter polygon shapes.

Therefore, in this paper, we propose the first fully automatic approach for interconnect correct multiple patterning layout compliance. For accelerating design closure, our goal is shifting polygons to fix coloring conflicts without creating new ones under minimized topology disturbance and polygon displacement. For easier visualization, Fig. 1 shows a single-layer sample layout with a K_4 containing polygons *c*, *f*, *g*, *h* for TPL. A naïve solution is to shift polygon *c* rightwards with a large displacement. In contrast, we may wisely shift polygon *g* to resolve the conflict with a small layout change.

For achieving this goal, we extract topology relations of polygons and model the layout correction as a polygon legalization problem. First, we construct the conflict graph for a given layout. Second, we extend exact conflict reporting to collect multiple edges involved in an arbitrary conflict pattern. Third, for facilitating topology extraction, we perform row/column slicing for each layer. We then construct a topology graph to represent intra-layer and inter-layer topology relations among polygons. Fourth, for selecting proper breaking conflict edges with least influence, we estimate the induced displacements, identify influenced regions, and set spacing budgets for involved edges. Fifth, we perform polygon legalization to realize conflict breaking with minimizing topology disturbance and polygon displacement. Our approach can handle multi-layer layouts and is not limited to specific conflict patterns. Our contributions are summarized as follows:

1) We propose the first fully automatic interconnect correct multiple patterning layout compliance approach, which is advantageous from a designer's perspective.

2) Because polygons usually have arbitrary rectilinear shapes, we devise a novel row slicing scheme to facilitate extracting topology relations of polygons (see Fig. 1(d)).

3) We first model multiple patterning layout compliance as a polygon legalization problem. Because most polygons have already satisfied spacing constraints, the corresponding quadratic program can be solved efficiently.

4) Different from existing studies, which are restricted to fix only specific conflict patterns, we collect multiple edges from an arbitrary conflict pattern, thus enhancing the fixing flexibility.

5) We present a novel polygon displacement estimation technique, slack absorption, to identify the influenced region of breaking a conflict edge. By doing so, we can select proper breaking edges to minimize layout change. (see Fig. 1(c).)

Experiments are conducted on the benchmark suite used in state-of-the-art multiple patterning layout decomposition works [6]–[10]. Experimental results show that our approach has superior efficiency and effectiveness. With topology awareness, our spacing constraint handling is general and can easily be extended to other layout fixing problems.

The remainder of this paper is organized as follows. Section 2 introduces spacing constraints, conflict graph construction, and the problem formulation. Section 3 details our multiple patterning layout compliance approach. Section 4 reports experimental results. Finally, Section 5 concludes this work.

2 PRELIMINARIES

2.1 Design Rules and Spacing Constraints

Design rules specify geometric and connectivity restrictions to ensure sufficient margins to account for process variations. Three basic design rules are width, spacing, and enclosure rules.

For manufacturing a single layer by MPL, each polygon has its own minimum different color spacing and minimum same color spacing, forming its spacing territory. As shown in Fig. 2(a), fat polygons require larger spacing than narrow polygons. If two polygons violate minimum different color spacing, they cannot be manufactured by MPL; if they violate minimum same color spacing, they should be assigned to different masks (colors). For a given layout, there is a slack for moving two polygons without affecting their mask assignment flexibility. Shape change may cause the switching between narrow and fat spacing thus inducing unexpected violations.

Minimum via-metal enclosure requires a via/contact to be covered by connected polygons at adjacent layers with additional margins. (see Fig. 2(b).)

It can be seen that these intra-layer and inter-layer rules can be converted to *spacing constraints* between polygon edges/corners. Most of other rules not mentioned here can be converted similarly.

2.2 Conflict Graph Construction

Assume that polygons in an input layout have satisfied minimum different color spacing and shape related rules (e.g., minimum width, minimum area, etc.). Prior layout decomposition work, e.g., [6]–[10], constructs a **conflict graph** $G_C = (V_C, E_C)$ to interpret color spacing relations of polygons: Each vertex represents a polygon, and an *undirected* edge $\{u, v\} \in E_C$ exists when the Euclidean distance between polygons u and v is less than the minimum same color spacing.

2.3 Problem Formulation

Multiple patterning layout compliance is desired to be completed with least layout change without creating new conflicts. In addition, we would like to maintain polygon shapes and topology relations during layout compliance for keeping designer's intent and avoiding unwanted design rule violations (e.g., narrow spacing switched to fat spacing). Therefore, the problem addressed in this paper can be formulated as follows.

The Multiple Patterning Layout Compliance Problem: Given a layout represented by a set of polygons, the number of available masks, the minimum different color spacing, and the minimum same color spacing of each polygon, our goal is to shift polygons so that the number of coloring conflicts is minimized without creating new conflicts under minimized topology disturbance and minimum polygon displacement.

3 OUR APPROACH

Herein, we propose the first fully automatic approach of interconnect correct multiple patterning layout compliance with minimizing topology disturbance and polygon displacement.

3.1 Overview

In this work, we shift polygons to fulfill layout compliance using as little layout change as possible. In general, a polygon shift can be viewed as a horizontal shift and/or a vertical shift.

Fig. 3 shows the algorithm flow of our approach. 1) We construct the conflict graph for an input layout. 2) We extend exact conflict reporting to collect multiple edges involved in each undecomposable graph pattern. 3) For facilitating topology extraction, we perform row/column slicing for each layer. We

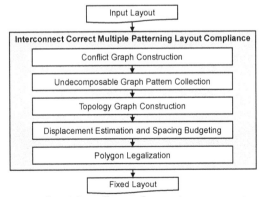

Figure. 3. Algorithm flow of our interconnect correct multiple patterning layout compliance approach.

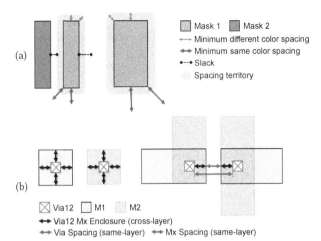

Figure 2: Spacing constraints. (a) Color spacing constraints in MPL: Narrow spacing vs. fat spacing. (b) Via-metal enclosure related spacing constraints: Via12 vs. M1/M2.

then construct a topology graph to represent intra-layer and inter-layer topology relations of polygons. 4) For selecting proper breaking conflict edges with least influence, we propose slack absorption to estimate the induced displacements, identify influenced regions, and set spacing budgets for horizontal and vertical shifts. 5) We perform polygon legalization to realize conflict breaking with minimizing topology disturbance and polygon displacement.

3.2 Undecomposable Graph Pattern Collection

An undecomposable graph pattern involves multiple conflict edges (e.g., K_4 contains six conflict edges in TPL). Due to the lack of knowledge of native conflict patterns in MPL, existing layout decomposition algorithms report only one conflict edge from them [6]–[10]. Sometimes, the reported conflict edge cannot be resolved because of no room for polygon shifting (e.g., polygon f in Fig. 1). Hence, we try to collect multiple edges from an undecomposable graph pattern to provide fixing flexibility.

3.2.1 Exact Conflict Reporting

In [10], an exact conflict reporting scheme is proposed along with layout decomposition. "Exact" means each reported conflict belongs to an undecomposable graph pattern. The framework in [10] contains Dancing Links data structure [18] plus Algorithm X*. Algorithm X* is a recursive backtracking procedure for finding a layout decomposition solution and reporting all exact conflicts. Vertices are visited basically in breadth-first search (BFS) order starting with the vertex of maximum degree, unless some vertex has only one possible color assignment during the traversal, e.g., vertex 4 is visited before vertex 5 in Fig. 4(a).

3.2.2 Pattern Collection

Although identifying native conflict graph patterns is an open problem, we attempt to identify partial undecomposable graph patterns by extending the exact conflict reporting in this paper.

Based on different traversal orders of vertices in an undecomposable graph pattern, Algorithm X* reports different conflict edges, and all of these edges belong to the same pattern.

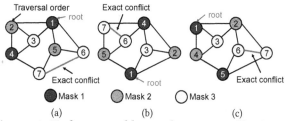

Figure. 4. Undecomposable graph pattern collection. (a) The first run of exact conflict reporting for TPL. (b)(c) More conflict edges can be quickly collected by setting different BFS roots (and/or traversal orders).

Starting with the exact conflict edge reported in the first run of Algorithm X*, we set the final visited vertex of this conflict edge as the BFS root and/or adopt a different traversal order in the second run of Algorithm X*. Because the edge reported in the first run belongs to an undecomposable pattern, an exact conflict can be quickly concluded in the second run with another conflict edge. Repeating this process collects more conflict edges from a pattern. (see Fig. 4(b)(c).) The collection has not to be complete; thus, the collection process terminates when some previously collected edge is reported again or the number of collected edges reaches a user-specified bound. In real cases, undecomposable patterns are usually small. Hence, pattern collection has low runtime overhead compared with a single run of Algorithm X*.

3.3 Topology Graph Construction

In addition to conflict graph, we construct a topology graph to record topology relations of polygons for protecting polygon shifting against new spacing violations. Because polygons in a layout usually have arbitrary rectilinear shapes (not restricted to rectangles), topology extraction is not trivial. Topology can be classified into intra-layer and inter-layer relations. We focus on intra-layer relations here and inter-layer relations in Section 3.6.

In this paper, we propose a principle for topology extraction:

"Two polygons have a topology relation if polygon shifting may alter and worsen the coloring condition between them."

The coloring condition of two polygons falls into three cases: 1) Their Euclidean distance is greater than or equal to the minimum same color spacing (i.e., no conflict edge between them). 2) Their Euclidean distance is in between the minimum same color spacing and the minimum different color spacing (i.e., a conflict edge between them). 3) Their Euclidean distance is smaller than the minimum different color spacing (i.e., a hard spacing violation between them). Their coloring condition worsens as switching from case 1 to case 2 or from case 2 to case 3. However, if their condition remains unchanged or is improved (i.e., switching from case 2 to case 1) during polygon shifting, they have no topology relation.

In general, a polygon shift can be viewed as a horizontal shift and/or a vertical shift. Thus, a topology graph contains a horizontal topology graph for horizontal shifting and a vertical topology graph for vertical shifting. In the following, we explain horizontal topology graph construction. The vertical topology graph can be constructed similarly.

Exhaustive testing every two polygon edges/corners to extract all topology relations is time consuming and may over-constrain the subsequent polygon shifting. Layout slicing is helpful for capturing local topology, especially when some polygons span over a large area in a layout. Once we capture local topology, global topology is maintained as well.

Conventional layout slicing is cutting along polygon corners. Fig. 5(a) shows the conventional slicing on the layout given in Fig. 1. It can be seen that this slicing generates numerous narrow rows. Many of them are redundant because of containing duplicated or only partial topology information of other rows. Therefore, we devise a novel row slicing scheme for facilitating horizontal topology extraction.

Assume the lower left corner of a polygon i is originally located at (x_i', y_i'). We sort all polygons in the non-decreasing lexicographic order of (y_i', x_i'). Polygons in Fig. 5(b) are ordered as $(a, b, c, ..., j)$. According to the order, we compare an investigated polygon with visited polygons that their projections overlap in x or y axis. If their projections overlap only in x axis, but not in y axis, we place the investigated polygon at the next row and create a cutline along its lower left corner; otherwise, the investigated polygon inherits the current row number.

Based on row slicing, we construct the horizontal **topology graph** $G_T = (V_T, E_T)$, where each vertex represents a polygon $(V_T = V_C)$, and each *directed* arc $(u, v) \in E_T$ describes one of the following relations:

1) Intra-row relation: Polygons in the same row are sorted in non-decreasing order of the lower left corner coordinates of their parts resided in the row. We maintain the linear order of polygons for keeping designer's intent; $(u, v) \in E_T$ exists when u, v are adjacent in a row.

2) Inter-row relation: In each row, we visit polygon parts in the linear order used by intra-row relation. As described in Section 2.1, each polygon has its own color spacing territory. For inter-row relation, we check each polygon part with other polygon parts in its upper rows based on our coloring condition worsening principle. By shifting the investigated polygon part u leftwards, we identify the first polygon part v that u enters v's territory or v enters u's territory, and $(v, u) \in E_T$. By shifting u rightwards, we identify the first encountered polygon part w, and $(u, w) \in E_T$. If a polygon part u is inside t's territory at the original location and polygon shifting would not worsen their coloring condition, $(u, t) \notin E_T$ and $(t, u) \notin E_T$.

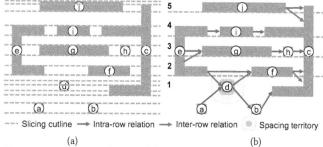

--- Slicing cutline ⟶ Intra-row relation ⟶ Inter-row relation ● Spacing territory

(a)   (b)

Figure. 5. Layout slicing. (a) Conventional row slicing. (b) Our row slicing with intra-row and inter-row relations.

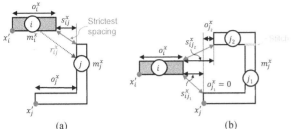

(a)   (b)

Figure. 6. (a) Generic spacing constraint. (b) Stitch handling.

These arcs are further merged such that two polygons have at most one arc, preserving the strictest spacing requirement. For example, polygons f and c in Fig. 5(b) have both intra-row and inter-row relations, and only the intra-row relation remains.

In addition to row slicing, column slicing is also performed for vertical topology graph similarly.

3.4 Displacement Estimation and Spacing Budgeting by Slack Absorption

Breaking any edge within a conflict pattern resolves this conflict. After identifying multiple conflict edges for an undecomposable pattern, we estimate the influenced region of each edge, and attempt to break the edge with sufficient shifting room and with least influence. For the example given in Fig. 1, breaking the edge between polygons h and g (by shifting g) is preferable to breaking the edge between c and h (by shifting c). To do so, we estimate the induced displacement and influenced region of each collected conflict edge and then determine target breaking conflict edges with spacing budgets.

To break a conflict edge, we may shift the corresponding pair of polygons horizontally and/or vertically. Once a polygon is moved, other neighboring polygons are probably forced to move for maintaining topology and spacing constraints. In this section, we estimate the total displacement of a chain move and its influenced region. We derive four independent estimates: Left-shifting and right-shifting on horizontal topology graph; up-shifting and down-shifting on the vertical topology graph.

Notation for displacement estimation is as shown in Fig. 6(a). Let (x_i', y_i') and (x_j', y_j') be the original lower left corners of polygons i, j, respectively, o_i^x and o_j^x i's and j's effective spacing offsets in x with respect to x_i' and x_j', respectively, s_{ij}^x effective spacing constraint in x between i and j, d_{ij}^x effective distance requirement between x_i' and x_j', r_{ij}^x spacing slack (residual), m_i^x movement (accumulated slack) of i with respect to x_i'. o_i^x, o_j^x, and s_{ij}^x are computed based on the polygon edges/corners contributing the strictest spacing requirement between i and j.

First, we analyze the topology graph to compute spacing violations according to the original polygon coordinates. For any arc $(i, j) \in E_T$, the *generic spacing constraint* between i and j is:

$$x_j' + o_j^x \geq x_i' + o_i^x + s_{ij}^x$$

$$x_j' - x_i' \geq d_{ij}^x = o_i^x - o_j^x + s_{ij}^x. \tag{1}$$

If $\{i, j\} \in E_C$, the Euclidean distance between i and j should be larger than or equal to their minimum different color spacing. s_{ij}^x is computed to reflect the effective spacing requirement in x.

Otherwise ($\{i, j\} \notin E_C$), s_{ij}^x is computed based on their minimum same color spacing. The spacing slack between i and j is:

$$r_{ij}^x = (x_j' - x_i') - d_{ij}^x. \tag{2}$$

A spacing violation occurs when $r_{ij}^x < 0$.

Second, considering to break $\{i, j\} \in E_C$ and assuming i is to the left of j, we temporarily add $(i, j) \in E_T$ and modify s_{ij}^x. For breaking $\{i, j\} \in E_C$, the Euclidean distance between i and j should be larger than or equal to their minimum same color spacing, and s_{ij}^x is adjusted accordingly.

Considering r_{ij}^x of each arc in E_T, if negative cycles exist, there is no feasible solution for fixing spacing violations under the investigated shifting direction (horizontal or vertical).

Third, we devise *slack absorption* to estimate total displacement and influenced region of shifting j rightwards, where $(i, j) \in E_T$ is the added arc. Sometimes, cycles exist in the topology graph. For facilitating slack absorption, we temporarily break directed cycles by ignoring back arcs marked by depth first search starting with i. With cycle breaking, the topology graph becomes a directed acyclic graph, and we have topological ordering starting with j.

As listed in Fig. 7, slack absorption computes movements for influenced polygons by slack propagation. As shown in Fig. 8, to resolve the spacing violation between i and j by shifting j rightwards, we set $m_i^x = 0$ and propagate slack to j:

$$m_j^x = m_i^x + r_{ij}^x. \tag{3}$$

We continue slack propagation until the movement is nonnegative. $m_j^x = -3$ in Fig. 8 means j should be shifted rightwards with displacement 3 to resolve the spacing violation, $m_n^x = 1$ means n is safe and does not need to move. Total negative movement is the estimated displacement (nonnegative movements are not counted). The influenced region covers polygons with negative movements (j, k, p in Fig. 8). There is no feasible solution for the investigated shifting direction when the procedure ends with no nonnegative movements. The estimates of other three shifting directions can also be obtained.

Procedure SlackAbsorption

Input: Topology graph G_T, target breaking arc (i, j)
Output: Movement (estimated displacement)
1. $m_i^x = 0$, $m_j^x = m_i^x + r_{ij}^x$, $m_k^x = \infty$ for other vertices k
2. **if** $m_j^x \geq 0$ **then return**
3. **for each** j' in topological order starting from j **do**
4.   **if** $m_{j'}^x < 0$ **then**
5. $M = M \cup \{m_{j'}^x\}$ // collect
6.   **for each** $(j', k) \in E_T$ **do**
7. $m = m_{j'}^x + r_{j'k}^x$
8.   **if** $m < m_k^x$ **then**
9. $m_k^x = m$

Figure. 7. Slack absorption procedure.

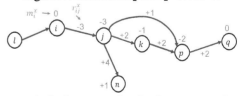

Figure. 8. Slack absorption for displacement estimation.

Finally, we collect target breaking conflict edges in E_B. For an undecomposable graph pattern, based on the estimated displacements for each collected conflict edge, we select the edge with the best displacement as the target breaking edge. Fig. 9 depicts examples when the best displacement contributed by a horizontal shift (left-shifting or right-shifting). We include the selected breaking edge in E_B and update the corresponding horizontal/vertical spacing constraint. Once an undecomposable pattern cannot be resolved by single-direction shifting, we split the spacing slack to one horizontal shift plus one vertical shift (see Fig. 9(d)). In addition, Fig. 9(f) shows an unsolvable case.

3.5 Polygon Legalization

Multiple patterning layout compliance tries to fix coloring conflicts by shifting polygons without creating new conflicts and with least layout change (topology disturbance and polygon displacement). After topology extraction, E_T contains all topology relations to be maintained. After displacement estimation and spacing budgeting, E_B contains target breaking conflict edges. E_T and E_B can be interpreted as spacing constraints. Hence, based on E_T and E_B, we model the layout compliance as a polygon legalization problem as follows.

The Polygon Legalization Problem: Given a layout of n polygons, where the lower left corner of each polygon i is located at (x'_i, y'_i), the goal is to move each polygon to some coordinate (x_i, y_i) such that the total displacement is minimized and the spacing constraints between polygons are satisfied.

The polygon legalization problem has two counterparts, one for horizontal shifting, and the other for vertical shifting. For horizontal shifting, polygons are shifted horizontally, i.e., $y_i = y'_i, \forall 1 \le i \le n$. Thus, the polygon legalization problem of horizontal shifting can be formulated as a quadratic program:

$$
\begin{aligned}
\min \quad & \tfrac{1}{2}\sum_{i=1}^n (x_i - x'_i)^2 \\
\text{s.t.} \quad & x_j - x_i \ge d_{ij}^x, \text{ if } (i,j) \in E_T \cup E_B. \\
& x_i \ge 0. \quad\quad\quad\quad\quad\quad\quad\quad (4)
\end{aligned}
$$

Each topology relation in E_T or a target breaking edge in E_B corresponds to a spacing constraint. Based on our coloring condition worsening principle, E_T covers all topology relations to be considered. For any other conflict edge neither in E_T nor in E_B, its coloring condition would not change or worsen during polygon shifting; thus, it is not included in the quadratic program. The right boundary of a layout is relaxed in the program for preventing infeasibility in some extreme case.

Because most polygons in the input layout satisfy spacing constraints, the quadratic program formulated here can be solved efficiently.

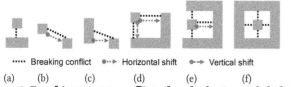

┈┈┈ Breaking conflict   ●┈●> Horizontal shift   ●─●> Vertical shift

(a)   (b)   (c)   (d)   (e)   (f)

Figure. 9. Breaking target conflict edges by horizontal shifting.

3.6 Multilayer and Stitch Handling

3.6.1 Multilayer Handling

Based on intra-layer topology relation discussed in Section 3.4, we construct a topology graph G_T for each layer of an input layout. In this section, we further handle inter-layer topology relation to guarantee interconnect correctness.

In a layout, vias/contacts are used to connect different layers. Each via layer corresponds to a single layer topology graph. Moreover, via-metal enclosure is an inter-layer design rule that requires each via/contact should be covered by connected polygons at adjacent layers with additional margins as shown in Fig. 2(b). The enclosure rule can be converted to a spacing constraint between two polygons (a via/contact is also a polygon).

At a metal layer, when a polygon connects with a via/contact, we introduce a vertex to represent this via/contact and create the corresponding enclosure relation into the topology graph G_T of the metal layer. This added relation is associated with a spacing constraint.

Other inter-layer rules can be considered similarly, e.g., metal-metal clearance (spacing between polygons at different metal layers). With interconnect correctness and topology awareness, our spacing constraint handling is general and can be applied to other layout fixing problems.

3.6.2 Stitch Handling

Stitches can be handled in our framework natively. A polygon with k stitches can be viewed as additional k slicing cutlines on the polygon at the layout slicing stage (Section 3.3). As shown in Fig. 6(b), polygon j are sliced into two parts j_1 and j_2 by one stitch. j_1 and j_2 have their own spacing constraints to i and build their relations independently. Then, same as the process for sliced parts, these relations are merged at the end of topology graph construction.

4 EXPERIMENTAL RESULTS

We implemented our approach in C++ programming language on a platform with a 2.9 GHz Intel Core under Windows OS. We adopted GUROBI [19] as the quadratic programming (QP) solver. Our experiments were conducted on the ISCAS-85 & 89 benchmark suite used by state-of-the-art multiple patterning layout decomposition works [6]–[10]. For the first ten cases listed in Table 1, the minimum different color spacing was set as to 40, while the minimum same color spacing was set as to 120. For the final five cases, 35 and 100 were used, respectively. Table 1 provides the conflict graph information. '$|V_C|$' denotes the number of vertices (polygons), '$|E_C|$' the number of conflict edges, '$|C|$' the number of coloring conflicts reported by [10].

Thus far, layout compliance has not been automated very well for general MPL. Existing methods are semi-automatic or manual; there are *no* prior automatic approaches available for comparison.

In this paper, we propose the first fully automatic approach, and Table 2 lists our results. '$|C|$' denotes the number of remaining coloring conflicts, '$|E_x|$' the number of conflicts

Table 2. Multiple Patterning Layout Compliance Results.

Circuit	Direct Fixing							Complete						
	$|C|$	$|E_x|$	$|E_y|$	#Constraints	Displacement	CPU$_{OT}$	CPU$_{QP}$	$|C|$	$|E_x|$	$|E_y|$	#Constraints	Displacement	CPU$_{OT}$	CPU$_{QP}$
C432	0	3	1	6,447	10,649	0.054	0.17	0	1	3	6,445	183	0.047	0.15
C499	0	0	0	0	0	0.085	0.00	0	0	0	0	0	0.093	0.00
C880	0	6	1	13,283	2,147	0.084	0.24	0	4	3	13,283	282	0.078	0.31
C1355	0	3	0	17,906	453	0.138	0.17	0	2	1	17,906	288	0.125	0.27
C1908	0	0	1	27,872	88	0.210	0.20	0	1	0	27,872	26	0.203	0.12
C2670	0	6	0	43,618	5,183	0.322	0.39	0	4	3	43,618	202	0.329	0.95
C3540	0	7	2	55,315	3,700	0.510	0.94	0	4	6	55,316	323	0.500	1.98
C5315	0	7	2	83,954	5,637	0.635	2.94	0	3	6	83,953	275	0.640	3.27
C6288	1	153	53	80,661	94,602	0.673	5.81	0	128	80	80,656	12,196	0.750	3.12
C7552	0	15	7	119,658	21,267	0.904	5.81	0	16	7	119,657	5,666	0.907	4.19
S1488	0	2	0	28,167	127	0.231	0.29	0	0	2	28,167	12	0.360	0.26
S38417	1	41	32	371,102	19,507	3.654	14.16	0	30	47	371,104	521	3.757	16.16
S35932	1	36	51	876,664	10,221	9.280	36.07	0	39	50	876,859	873	10.048	35.71
S38584	0	81	71	920,196	20,989	9.460	35.06	0	73	79	920,195	1,968	11.063	35.38
S15850	1	76	56	876,323	36,099	9.351	35.28	0	69	65	876,319	1,190	10.762	37.19
Ratio					16.11	1.01	0.96					1.00	1.00	1.00

Direct Fixing: Our approach without undecomposable graph pattern collection, fixing conflict edges reported by the first run of Algorithm X*.
Complete: Our complete approach.   Displacement: $\sum_{i=1}^{n}(|x_i - x_i'| + |y_i - y_i'|)$.

solved by horizontal shifting, '$|E_y|$' the number of conflicts solved by vertical shifting, '#Constraints' the number of constraints in the quadratic programs of polygon legalization, 'Displacement' the total polygon Manhattan displacement in x and y calculated by $\sum_{i=1}^{n}(|x_i - x_i'| + |y_i - y_i'|)$, 'CPU$_{QP}$' QP solving time (second), and 'CPU$_{OT}$' runtime (second) of the first four steps in Fig. 3. (Total runtime CPU$_{TOTAL}$ = CPU$_{OT}$ + CPU$_{QP}$.)

'Complete' in Table 2 means our complete approach. Overall, our complete approach cleans all coloring conflicts in a cost-effective way, with very small polygon displacement and topology disturbance. By a manual or semi-automatic method, it is impossible to resolve tens or hundreds of conflicts in such a short time.

Furthermore, we evaluate the impact of undecomposable graph pattern collection. 'Direct Fixing' in Table 2 means our approach without pattern collection, which directly breaks the conflict edges reported by layout decomposition engine [10] (i.e., the first run of Algorithm X* in Section 3.2). Because some reported conflict edges have no room for polygon shifting, in some cases, direct fixing cannot resolve all conflicts. In contrast, with pattern collection, displacement estimation, and spacing budgeting, our complete approach can wisely select target breaking conflict edges. Compared with direct fixing, on average, our complete approach reduces total displacement by 16.11X with almost no runtime overhead for pattern collection.

Fig. 10 shows our triple patterning layout compliance result of C432; the final influenced regions and total displacement are very small. Fig. 11 illustrates our partial multilayer layout compliance result for an industrial design, where M1 layer is manufactured by TPL. One reported conflict at M1 layer is cleaned by slightly shifting polygons on M1, M2, and Via12.

5 CONCLUSION

In this paper, we have presented the first fully automatic approach for interconnect correct multiple patterning layout compliance with several delicate techniques: The novel row slicing scheme facilitates topology extraction on polygons with arbitrary rectilinear shapes. The modeled polygon legalization

problem can be solved efficiently. Collecting undecomposable patterns, not restricted to only special conflict patterns, enhances the fixing flexibility. Slack absorption quickly estimates polygon displacement and identifies the influenced region of breaking a conflict edge. Experimental results have shown that our approach has superior efficiency and effectiveness. With interconnect correctness and topology awareness, our spacing constraint handling is general and can easily be extended to other layout fixing problems.

REFERENCES

[1] D. Abercrombie. 2017. Will EUV kill multi-patterning? (January 2017). Semiconductor Engineering. Retrieved from https://semiengineering.com/will-euv-kill-multi-patterning/

[2] M. Neisser, S. Wurm. 2015. ITRS lithography roadmap: 2015 challenges. *Adv. Opt. Techn.* 4, 4 (August 2015), 235-240.

[3] M. van den Brink. 2014. Many ways to shrink: the right moves to 10 nanometer and beyond. (November 2014). Retrieved from https://staticwww.asml.com/doclib/investor/asml_3_Investor_Day-Many_ways_to_shrink_MvdBrink1.pdf

[4] Y. Badr, A. Torres, Y. Ma, J. Mitra, P. Gupta. 2015. Incorporating DSA in multipatterning semiconductor manufacturing technologies. In *Proc. SPIE* 9427, Design-Process-Technology Co-optimization for Manufacturability IX, Article 94270P, 8 pages.

[5] Y. Yang, W.-S. Luk, D.Z. Pan, H. Zhou, C. Yan, D. Zhou, X. Zeng. 2016. Layout decomposition co-optimization for hybrid e-beam and multiple patterning lithography. *IEEE Trans. on Computer-Aided Design of Integrated*

Table 1. Benchmark Statistics.

Circuit	Conflict Graph Information		
	$|V_C|$	$|E_C|$	$|C|$
C432	1,109	1,222	4
C499	2,216	2,817	0
C880	2,411	2,686	7
C1355	3,262	3,326	3
C1908	5,125	5,598	1
C2670	7,933	9,336	6
C3540	10,189	11,968	9
C5315	14,603	16,881	9
C6288	14,575	15,605	206
C7552	21,253	24,372	22
S1488	4,611	5,504	2
S38417	67,696	79,527	73
S35932	157,455	186,052	84
S38584	168,319	196,072	152
S15850	159,952	190,796	131

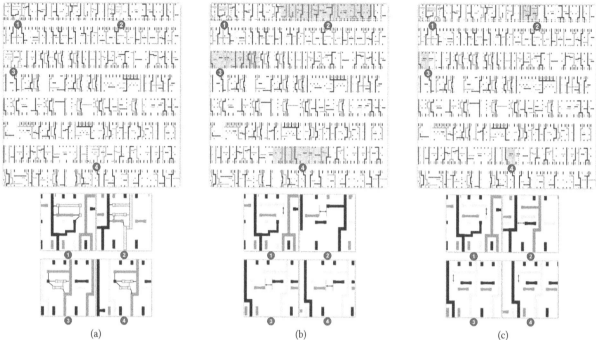

(a)   (b)   (c)

Figure. 10. Our layout compliance result of C432 for TPL. (a) Four coloring conflicts (highlighted polygons in labeled dotted boxes) reported by layout decomposition. (b) Direct fixing and its influenced regions (shaded area): displacement = 10,649. Double-headed arrows indicate fixed spacing constraints. (c) Complete and its influenced regions: displacement = 183.

Circuits and Systems (TCAD) 35, 9 (September 2016), 1532-1545.

[6]   J. Kuang, E. F.Y. Young. 2013. An efficient layout decomposition approach for triple patterning lithography. In *Proc. Design Automation Conference (DAC '13)*. ACM, New York, NY, USA, Article 69, 6 pages.

[7]   S.-Y. Fang, Y.-W. Chang, W.-Y. Chen. 2014. A novel layout decomposition algorithm for triple patterning lithography. *IEEE Trans. on Computer-Aided eDesign of Integrated Circuits and Systems (TCAD)* 33, 3 (March 2014), 397-408.

[8]   B. Yu, K. Yuan, D. Ding, D.Z. Pan. 2015. Layout decomposition for triple patterning lithography. *IEEE Trans. on Computer-Aided Design of Integrated Circuits and Systems (TCAD)* 34, 3 (March 2015), 433-446.

[9]   B. Yu, D.Z. Pan. 2014. Layout decomposition for quadruple patterning lithography and beyond. In *Proc. Design Automation Conference (DAC '14)*. ACM, New York, NY, USA, Article 53, 6 pages.

[10]   I. H.-R. Jiang, H.-Y. Chang. 2017. Multiple patterning layout decomposition considering complex coloring rules and density balancing. *IEEE Trans. on Computer-Aided Design of Integrated Circuits and Systems (TCAD)* 36, 12 (December 2017), 2080-2092. Also see in *Proc. Design Automation Conference (DAC '16)*. ACM, New York, NY, USA, Article 40, 6 pages.

[11]   R.S. Ghaida, K.B. Agarwal, S.R. Nassif, X. Yuan, L.W. Liebmann, P. Gupta. 2013. Layout decomposition and legalization for double-patterning technology. *IEEE Trans. on Computer-Aided Design of Integrated Circuits and Systems (TCAD)* 32, 2 (February 2013), 202-215.

[12]   S. Bhattacharya, S. Rajagopalan, S. H. Batterywala. 2014. Fixing double patterning violations with look-ahead. In *Proc. Asia and South Pacific Design Automation Conference (ASP-DAC '14)*, IEEE, Piscataway, NJ, USA, 149-154.

[13]   J. Dorsc. 2015. Changes and challenges abound in multi-patterning lithography. (February 2015). Semiconductor Manufacturing and Design (SemiMD). Retrieved from http://www.semi.org/en/node/54491

[14]   M. White. 2014. A look behind the mask of multi-patterning. (October 2014) Electronic Design. Retrieved from http://www.electronicdesign.com/eda/look-behind-mask-multi-patterning

[15]   B. Yu, G. Garreton, D. Z. Pan. 2014. Layout compliance for triple patterning lithography: an iterative approach. In *Proc. SPIE* 9235, Photomask Technology, Article 923504, 13 pages.

[16]   D. Payne. 2014. Design rule checking (DRC) meets new challenges. (December 2014). SemiWiki. Retrieved from https://www.semiwiki.com/forum/content/4062-design-rule-checking-drc-meets-new-challenges.html

[17]   E. Sperling. 2018. Design rule complexity rising. (April 2018). Manufacturing & Process Technology, Semiconductor Engineering. Retrieved from https://semiengineering.com/design-rule-complexity-rising/

[18]   D.E. Knuth. 2000. Dancing links. arXiv:cs/0011047. Retrieved from https://arxiv.org/abs/cs/0011047

[19]   Gurobi Optimization Inc. 2014. Gurobi Optimizer 7.5.1.

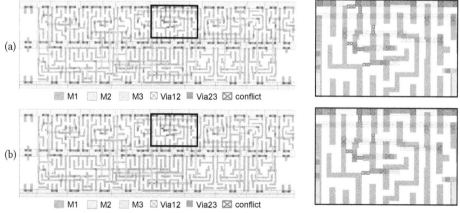

Figure 11. Our multilayer layout compliance result for TPL. (a) Before fixing. Collected multiple conflict edges for a reported conflict are highlighted. (b) After fixing. One conflict edge is broken by slightly shifting polygons on M1, M2, and Via12.

From Electronic Design Automation to Automotive Design Automation

Chung-Wei Lin

cwlin@csie.ntu.edu.tw

Department of Computer Science and Information Engineering

Graduate Institute of Networking and Multimedia

National Taiwan University

ABSTRACT

Advanced driver assistance systems (ADAS), autonomous functions, and connected applications bring a revolution to automotive systems, but they also make automotive design, especially software and electronics, more complex than ever. The complexity introduces significant challenges to automotive industry, and thus design automation, model-based design, and platform-based design can assist system designers to verify design correctness, improve design quality, accelerate design development, reduce design cost, and prevent redesign or recall. Sharing similar concepts with electronic design automation, automotive design automation can be categorized into three core parts: *modeling*, *design* (including synthesis and optimization), and *analysis* (including verification, simulation, and testing).

In this talk, we first go through some examples of modeling, design, and analysis in both of electronic design automation and automotive design automation. Next, we present two *routing* problems, one applicable to circuit physical design and automotive harness design and the other one applicable to microfluidic biochip design and intersection management, and discuss their similarities and differences. Then, we bring out four design-time problems in the automotive domain: (1) *placement* which allocates tasks onto automotive systems, edges, and the cloud, (2) *verification* which checks the compatibility of automotive sub-systems, (3) *software integrity* which aims to comply with an automotive functional safety standard, ISO 26262, and (4) *security-aware design and analysis* which provide decisions at the early stages in the V-model.

Besides the existing solutions and research challenges of these problems, how the techniques in electronic design automation can facilitate addressing these problems is also covered. We believe that the techniques can not only contribute solutions to integrated circuit design and automotive design but also give insights to the design of embedded systems, cyber-physical systems, and other complex systems.

CCS CONCEPTS

• **Computer systems organization** → **Embedded and cyber-physical systems**; • **Hardware** → **Electronic design automation**; **Physical design (EDA)**.

KEYWORDS

Automotive; design automation; model-based design; physical design; placement; routing; security; software integrity; verification

ACM Reference Format:
Chung-Wei Lin. 2019. From Electronic Design Automation to Automotive Design Automation. In *2019 International Symposium on Physical Design (ISPD '19), April 14–17, 2019, San Francisco, CA, USA*. ACM, New York, NY, USA, 1 page. https://doi.org/10.1145/3299902.3311061

BIOGRAPHY

Chung-Wei Lin is an Assistant Professor at the Department of Computer Science and Information Engineering at the National Taiwan University. He received his Ph.D. degree in electrical engineering and computer sciences from the University of California, Berkeley. He received his M.S. degree in electronics engineering and his B.S. degree in computer science and information engineering from the National Taiwan University. His early research included electronic design automation, especially physical design, advised by Prof. Yao-Wen Chang, at the National Taiwan University and then moved to automotive model-based design, advised by Prof. Alberto Sangiovanni-Vincentelli, at the University of California, Berkeley. He was a summer intern at the General Motors in 2011, 2012, and 2013, and a researcher at the Toyota InfoTechnology Center, USA, from 2015 to 2018. He won the 2016 Best Paper Award of ACM Transactions on Design Automation of Electronic Systems (TODAES). His current research covers diverse topics including cyber-physical systems, connected and autonomous vehicles, security, and system design methodology.

ACKNOWLEDGMENTS

This work is partially supported by Moxa Inc., MediaTek Inc., and Ministry of Education of Taiwan under Grant Number NTU-107V0901.

Enterprise-wide AI-enabled Digital Transformation

Mehdi Maasoumy
Lead Data Scientist
C3, Inc.
mehdi.maasoumy@c3.ai

ABSTRACT

Building a modern, big-data, AI application is a challenge for any organization. The number of languages, technologies, and data sources that need to be stitched together is massive. Research and Data Scientists spend majority of their time bringing together data files from multiple data sources and joining them together. Developers on the other hand, spend significant amounts (if not most) of their time just stitching together infrastructure and keeping it running day-to-day. In doing so, most of the time on solving a machine learning or in general AI problem at scale in an organization is spent on solving the technology problems as opposed to the business problems. We will discuss how the "Type System", an abstraction layer between all infrastructure components, and components built by the developer and data scientists acts as a meet-in-the-middle layer to solve this problem.

Having solved the data integration problem, we discuss how convergence of 4 technology vectors, namely Big Data, Artificial Intelligence, Cloud Computing, and Internet of Things (IoT) has, for the first time, enabled us to solve a class of problems previously deemed as unsolvable at massive scales. AI applications such as predictive maintenance, fraud detection, sensor network health, supply chain optimization, energy management, anti-money laundering, and customer engagement are among the set of problems that are now solvable at enterprise scale. This is possible, thanks to the platform that brings together all infrastructure, micro services, data sources and research and data scientist on the same platform, and in doing so improves the productivity of the development team by a factor of 10-100x.

We will discuss the "Predictive Maintenance" problem applied to distribution networks, aircraft systems and oil and gas assets, "Inventory Optimization" problem solved in the manufacturing

industry, and "Fraud Detection" in the electricity space as well as banking space.

CCS CONCEPTS

• Machine learning, supervised learning, deep learning, cloud computing, stochastic control and optimization

KEYWORDS

Predictive Maintenance, Fraud detection. Inventory Optimization

Biography

Mehdi Maasoumy is a Lead Data Scientist at C3 (c3.ai), where he has been developing machine learning algorithms for Industrial IoT applications including predictive maintenance, fraud detection, anomaly detection, and customer segmentation. Dr.

Maasoumy received his PhD from University of California at Berkeley. His research interests include Model Predictive Control, Machine Learning and Optimization, applied to Cyber-Physical Systems (CPS). He has authored more than 50 peer-reviewed publications and two book chapters in optimal control and machine learning. His PhD work has won several awards. He won 3 Best Student Paper Awards at the International Conference on Cyber-Physical Systems in 2013, the ASME Dynamic Systems and Control Conference in 2013, and the IEEE American Control Conference in 2014. He received the Award of Excellence for outstanding performance in the Global Energy Forecasting Competition (GEFCom) 2014 from the IEEE Power & Energy Society.

ISPD '19, April 14–17, 2019, San Francisco, CA, USA.
© 2019 Copyright is held by the owner/author(s).
ACM ISBN 978-1-4503-6253-5/19/04.
DOI: https://doi.org/10.1145/3299902.3311062

Secure and Trustworthy Cyber-Physical System Design: A Cross-Layer Perspective

Pierluigi Nuzzo

Ming Hsieh Department of Electrical and Computer Engineering,
Viterbi School of Engineering, University of Southern California
Los Angeles, California, USA
nuzzo@usc.edu

ABSTRACT

This talk discusses some of the design challenges posed by cyber-physical system security at different abstraction layers, from algorithm design to the realization of trusted hardware platforms. We introduce two design problems, namely, detecting sensor attacks in large-scale cyber-physical systems, and systematic design of circuit obfuscation schemes to satisfy system-level security requirements. We then summarize some of the approaches pursued by the research community to address these problems, with the potential of fostering new methodologies, algorithms, and tools for the design of secure and trustworthy cyber-physical systems.

KEYWORDS

Electronic Design Automation; System Level Design; Cyber-Physical Systems; Security; Trust; Secure State Estimation; Integrated Circuit Obfuscation

BIOGRAPHY

Pierluigi Nuzzo is an Assistant Professor in the Department of Electrical and Computer Engineering of the University of Southern California, Los Angeles. He received the Ph.D. in Electrical Engineering and Computer Sciences from the University of California at Berkeley in 2015, the Laurea degree in Electrical Engineering (summa cum laude) from the University of Pisa, Italy, and the Diploma in Engineering (summa cum laude) from the Sant'Anna School of Advanced Studies, Pisa. Before joining the University of California at Berkeley, he held research positions at the University of Pisa and IMEC, Leuven, Belgium, working on the design of energy-efficient A/D converters, frequency synthesizers for reconfigurable radio, and design methodologies for mixed-signal integrated circuits. His current research interests include: methodologies and tools for cyber-physical system and mixed-signal system design; contracts, interfaces, and compositional methods for embedded system design; the application of formal methods and optimization theory to problems in embedded and cyber-physical systems, electronic design automation, and hardware security.

Prof. Nuzzo received the Best Submission in the Design Automation Conference (DAC) and International Solid State Circuit Conference (ISSCC) Design Competition in 2006, and the Best Paper Award from the International Conference on Cyber-Physical Systems (ICCPS) in 2016. His awards and honors also include a Marie Curie Fellowship from the European Union, the University of California at Berkeley EECS departmental fellowship, the University of California at Berkeley Outstanding Graduate Student Instructor Award, the IBM Ph.D. Fellowship, and the University of California at Berkeley EECS David J. Sakrison Memorial Prize.

ACKNOWLEDGMENTS

The author acknowledges the partial support by the Air Force Research Labs (AFRL) and the Defense Advanced Research Projects Agency (DARPA) under agreement number FA8560-18-1-7817.

The Slow Start of Fast Spice: A Brief History of Timing

Jacob K. White
white@mit.edu
EECS, M. I. T.
Cambridge, MA

ABSTRACT

The list of Professor Alberto Sangiovanni-Vincentelli's research contributions is astounding in length and breadth, yet does not entirely capture what this author believes is his true genius. In so many areas of computer-aided design, Sangiovanni-Vincentelli provided the intellectual framework, often nucleating a research community in the process. Of personal familiarity is the area of transistor-level timing simulation, now better known as "Fast SPICE". In the decades since Sangiovanni-Vincentelli's papers on circuit simulation, relaxation, and third generation techniques, simulation sizes have grown from thousands to millions of transistors, vectorized main frames have given way to GPUs and multicores and clouds, yet his papers are still the defining taxonomy for the field.

ACM Reference Format:
Jacob K. White. 2019. The Slow Start of Fast Spice: A Brief History of Timing. In *2019 International Symposium on Physical Design (ISPD '19), April 14–17, 2019, San Francisco, CA, USA.* ACM, New York, NY, USA, 2 pages. https://doi.org/10.1145/3299902.3311068

1 TALK OVERVIEW

Much has changed in the half century since circuit simulators helped launch the field of electronic design automation[9, 11, 16]. Transient simulation of dozen transistor circuits, once a premiere capability, is now effectively free [4], and even on-line (fig.1)[8]; specialized RF techniques, once limited to a few dozen devices, now routinely simulate thousand-transistor communication subsystems[6, 15]; and the capacity of the latest "fast SPICEs" are in the millions of transistors[12]. Faster computers deserve much of the credit for this remarkable progress, but so does the transition to an abstraction hierarchy popularized by Professor Sangiovanni-Vincentelli, his colleagues and his students.

Early descriptions of circuit simulation relied on circuit interpretations of numerical algorithms, and were effective at developing insight. For example, the node-by-node algorithm in the seminal timing simulator, MOTIS [1], is most easily described using a circuit equivalent, as in fig.2). Many of the early circuit simulators embraced this circuit interpretation, leading somewhat inflexible

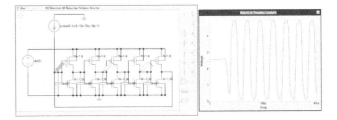

Figure 1: On-line Javascript Circuit Simulator (from http://scripts.mit.edu/ white/newtlines/schvsp.cgi?file=vsr5s).

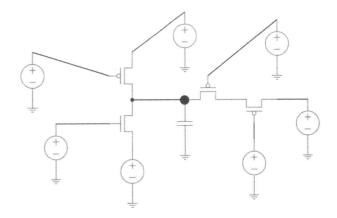

Figure 2: Circuit interpretation of the grounded-capacitor node update.

software, as every element (resistor, capacitor, inductor, diode, transistor, etc) needed a "companion model" for every solution algorithm (linear solution, nonlinear solution, backward-difference integration, trapezoidal rule integration, etc)[3].

In this talk we will show that [5, 10, 14] formed a nucleating taxonomy for the development and analysis of strategies for timing simulation including: waveform relaxtion and multirate integration (in programs RELAX), iterated timing analysis (in programs like SPLICE), and block-partitioning (in programs like MOSTIS2)[2, 7, 13]. And even though problem size and computational technology have changed dramatically,the fast SPICEs of today fit neatly in to that timing simulation taxonomy.

REFERENCES

[1] B. Chawla, H. Gummel, and P. Kozak. 1975. MOTIS-An MOS timing simulator. *IEEE Transactions on Circuits and Systems* 22, 12 (December 1975), 901–910. https://doi.org/10.1109/TCS.1975.1084003
[2] Chin-Fu Chen, C-Y Lo, Hao N Nham, and Prasad Subramaniam. 1984. The second generation MOTIS mixed-mode simulator. In *21st Design Automation Conference Proceedings.* IEEE, 10–17.

[3] Leon O Chua and Pen-Min Lin. 1975. Computer-aided analysis of electronic circuits: algorithms and computational techniques. (1975).

[4] Wikipedia contributors. 2019. List of free electronics circuit simulators — Wikipedia, The Free Encyclopedia. https://en.wikipedia.org/w/index.php?title= List_of_free_electronics_circuit_simulators&oldid=882864511. [Online; accessed 17-February-2019].

[5] G. D. Hachtel and A. L. Sangiovanni-Vincentelli. 1981. A survey of third-generation simulation techniques. *Proc. IEEE* 69, 10 (Oct 1981), 1264–1280. https://doi.org/10.1109/PROC.1981.12166

[6] Kenneth S Kundert. 1999. Introduction to RF simulation and its application. *IEEE Journal of Solid-State Circuits* 34, 9 (1999), 1298–1319.

[7] E. Lelarasmee, A. E. Ruehli, and A. L. Sangiovanni-Vincentelli. 1982. The Waveform Relaxation Method for Time-Domain Analysis of Large Scale Integrated Circuits. *IEEE Transactions on Computer-Aided Design of Integrated Circuits and Systems* 1, 3 (July 1982), 131–145. https://doi.org/10.1109/TCAD.1982.1270004

[8] Piotr F Mitros, Khurram K Afridi, Gerald J Sussman, Chris J Terman, Jacob K White, Lyla Fischer, and Anant Agarwal. 2013. Teaching electronic circuits online: Lessons from MITx's 6.002 x on edX. In *2013 IEEE International Symposium on Circuits and Systems (ISCAS2013)*. IEEE, 2763–2766.

[9] Laurence W Nagel and Omega Enterprises. 1996. The life of SPICE. In *1996 Bipolar Circuits and Technology Meeting*.

[10] A Richard Newton and Alberto L Sangiovanni-Vincentelli. 1983. Relaxation-based electrical simulation. *IEEE Transactions on Electron Devices* 30, 9 (1983), 1184–1207.

[11] Lawrence T Pillage, Ronald A Rohrer, and Chandramouli Visweswariah. 1995. *Electronic circuit and system simulation methods.* McGraw-Hill New York.

[12] Michał Rewieński. 2011. A perspective on fast-SPICE simulation technology. In *Simulation and Verification of Electronic and Biological Systems.* Springer, 23–42.

[13] Resve A Saleh, James E Kleckner, and A Richard Newton. 1984. *Iterated timing analysis and SPLICE1.* Electronics Research Laboratory, College of Engineering, University of âĂę.

[14] Alberto L Sangiovanni-Vincentelli. 1984. Circuit simulation. In *Computer Design Aids for VLSI Circuits.* Springer, 19–112.

[15] P. Wambacq, G. Vandersteen, J. Phillips, J. Roychowdhury, W. Eberle, , D. Long, and A. Demir. 2001. CAD for RF circuits. In *Proceedings Design, Automation and Test in Europe. Conference and Exhibition 2001.* 520–527. https://doi.org/10.1109/ DATE.2001.915073

[16] W Weeks, A Jimenez, G Mahoney, Deepak Mehta, Hassan Qassemzadeh, and T Scott. 1973. Algorithms for ASTAP–A network-analysis program. *IEEE Transactions on Circuit Theory* 20, 6 (1973), 628–634.

Basic and Advanced Researches in Logic Synthesis and their Industrial Contributions

Masahiro Fujita
fujita@ee.t.u-tokyo.ac.jp
University of Tokyo
Tokyo, Japan

ABSTRACT

We first present historical view on the techniques for two-level and multi-level logic optimizations, and discuss the practical issues with respect to them. Then the techniques for sequential optimizations are briefly reviewed. Based on them, a new approach which formulates ECO (Engineering Change Order) as partial logic synthesis is discussed. Finally a new formulation of an automatic generation of parallel/distributed computing from sequential one is introduced with an application example.

CCS CONCEPTS

• **Hardware** → **Logic synthesis**.

KEYWORDS

two-level logic optimization, multi-level logic optimization, Engineering Change Order, logic debugging, sequential optimization, automatic test pattern generation

ACM Reference Format:
Masahiro Fujita. 2019. Basic and Advanced Researches in Logic Synthesis and their Industrial Contributions. In *2019 International Symposium on Physical Design (ISPD '19), April 14–17, 2019, San Francisco, CA, USA*. ACM, New York, NY, USA, 8 pages. https://doi.org/10.1145/3299902.3311069

1 INTRODUCTION

Logic synthesis is to convert specifications in logic formulae into networks of logic gates including flipflops if the target circuit is a sequential one. In that process, various logic optimizations are applied so that the generated logic circuits becomes smaller, faster, and/or less power consuming. There are basically two categories in logic optimization: two-level logic optimization and multi-level logic optimization. Two-level logic optimization is to minimize the numbers of products in Sum-of-Products (SOP) representations whereas multi-level logic optimization is to minimize the numbers of wires (or literals in logic expressions) in multi-level logic circuits. In this paper, we first discuss techniques for two-level and multi-level logic optimization in historical viewpoints.

Techniques for two-level logic optimization had mainly been studied in 1970's and 80's. Starting with Quine-McCluskey method

[16] [13] in 1955-1956 which is designed for manual optimization, various exact and heuristic approaches have been tried. Here exact methods mean the numbers of products are guaranteed to be minimum, whereas heuristic methods may be able to deal with much larger problems than exact methods. Although there have been a good progress in exact methods, such as [14], for industrial designs, in most cases, only the heuristic methods are applicable.

On the other hand, the first issue for multi-level logic optimization is how to obtain the multi-level logic circuits. They may be initially given by designers or should be generated from SOP representations which are originally expressed with truth tables. There are techniques so called "division of circuits". A given SOP or multi-level logic circuits can be divided by a given subcircuit or another SOP either algebraically or logically (with a Boolean way of reasoning). Generally speaking algebraic methods work quickly and well for control dominated circuits. On the other hand, for arithmetic circuits, especially complicated ones such as combinational multipliers, Boolean division must be used to generate a high-quality multi-level logic circuits from SOP. The problem, however, is that Boolean division takes a very long time and cannot be applied to large circuits. This issue is well recognized, but still a big issue in logic synthesis

A simple way to optimize multi-level logic circuits is to represent each node or gate in multi-level logic circuits with SOP representations and apply two-level logic optimization methods to each node. Although this can achieve meaningful reduction, it does not utilize logical relationships among internal gates, and because of that, the amount of reduction in circuits can be highly constrained. Therefore, there are a number of researches on the use of such relationships, which are called "internal don't cares" for logic optimization. They are reviewed in Section 3 briefly.

The target of logic synthesis is to generate sequential circuits from the description in hardware description languages (HDL) such as Verilog and VHDL, and there have been researches on optimization of sequential circuits, which is briefly touched in Section 4.

In industrial design environments, not only normal logic synthesis, but also its related problems, such as logic debugging and Engineering Change Order (ECO) are very important. ECO means some sort of small changes in specification after its implementation has been generated, and instead of re-synthesizing the implementation again from the modified specification, it is often better to modify the original implementation to meet with the modified specification. An generalized approach for logic debugging and ECO problems is introduced in Section 5 as partial logic synthesis. Partial logic synthesis problems can be mathematically formulated as Quantified Boolean Formula problems and can be solved by repeatedly applying SAT solvers.

Finally in Section 6, the application of the partial logic synthesis to automatic synthesis of parallel/distributed computing is presented. Given computations in mathematical equations can be automatically converted into the computations by multiple cores under user-specified communication constraints. The basic idea and its scalability are discussed with applications to deep learning based on multi-layer neural networks in mind.

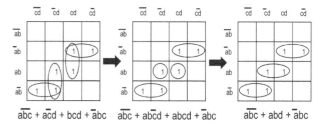

$$\overline{ab}c + a\overline{c}d + bcd + \overline{a}b\overline{c} \quad \overline{ab}c + a\overline{bc}d + abcd + \overline{a}b\overline{c} \quad \overline{ab}c + abd + \overline{a}b\overline{c}$$

Figure 1: An example of SOP minimization

2 TWO-LEVEL LOGIC MINIMIZATION

The exact methods are basically to generate all prime implicants for the target function and to solve the set-covering problem which covers the entire function with a minimum set of prime implicants. The fundamental problem with this approach is the fact that the numbers of prime implicants increase exponentially with respect to the numbers of variables in the function (primary inputs to the circuits). Although there have been developed ways to represent all of prime implicants implicitly [7], it is still very difficult to deal with logic functions having more than 20 variables There is a new formulation on the problem as shown in[14] which gives a new insight into the problem.

It is basically impossible to generate all prime implicants and solve the associated set-covering problem, if the target function has a large number of variables. Therefore, in heuristic methods, only small subsets of prime implicants are generated and manipulated. Most of the heuristic methods perform the minimization as iterative processes, that is, the SOP expressions are iteratively transformed into smaller ones. The basic idea is to change the "shape" of the SOP so that smaller representation may be coming up. The most well developed algorithm for SOP minimization is called "Espresso" algorithm [6]. It is an iterative process consisting of "reduce", "expand", and "irredundant" operations.

Let us discuss with the example shown in Figure 1. Suppose the logic function to be minimized is shown by the Karnaugh map in the left side. There are four product terms for the representation of the function in the left, and there is no redundancy in this SOP, that is, if any one of the product terms is missing, the logic function becomes a different one. There is, however, a SOP representation having only three product terms as shown in the right of the figure. Therefore, the SOP representation in the left, is a local minimal solution which is a typical result of heuristic minimization. The main issue in the heuristic minimization methods is how to escape from the local minimal solutions and approach to the global minimum as much as possible.

As the local minimal solutions have no redundancy, simple redundancy removal does not work. Generally speaking, in order to reach better solutions, the solutions must once become worse. In the context of two level logic minimization, this correspond to "reduce" operation. In the case of the example in Figure 1, after the reduction operation, the SOP representation becomes the one in the center of the figure. The two products terms are reduced or shrunk vertically in the figure. Then "expand" operation which enlarges product terms is applied. If the direction of the expansion is different from the original direction, there are chances of reaching smaller SOP representations as shown in the figure.

The idea of iterative optimization is widely used in many problems, and Espresso algorithm is also based on that. One big difference of Espresso algorithm from the other two level logic optimization methods is the use of "unate recursive paradigm". A logic function $f(x_1, x_2, ..., x_n)$ is positive unate in x_i

if $f(x_1, x_2, .., x_{i-1}, 1, x_{i+1}, .., x_n) \geq f(x_1, x_2, .., x_{i-1}, 0, x_{i+1}, .., x_n)$. A logic function $f(x_1, x_2, ..., x_n)$ is negative unate in x_i

if $f(x_1, x_2, .., x_i = 1, .., x_n) \leq f(x_1, x_2, .., x_i = 0, .., x_n)$.

If none of the above is satisfied, the function is binate with respect to that variable. If a logic function in either positive or negative unate for all variables, it is said to be a unate function. Unate functions take important roles in tautology checking, computation of complements and others. In general if a function is unate, tautology checking and computation of complements can be efficiently processed. Unate recursive paradigm is to case split the function by the binate variables first when analyzing the function. Experimentally unate recursive paradigm works very efficiently for most of the functions used in hardware designs. Boolean reasoning inside Espresso algorithm is based on unate recursive paradigm, and it can quickly minimize very large functions, such as the ones having more than 1,000 variables.

Although it is not mentioned above, the general two level logic optimization problems are defined with on-set, off-set, and don't care-set (DC-set). For the input values corresponding to the DC-set, minimization processes can freely assign 0 or 1 values to don't care values in order to minimize the numbers of product terms. As mentioned above, if we try to optimize the function for a node (gate) in the circuit by two-level logic optimization, there are don't cares which come from the relationships among the gates including the target gate in the circuit. Two-level logic minimization should utilize the don't cares effectively.

3 MULTI-LEVEL LOGIC OPTIMIZATION

Multi-level logic circuits can be represented as Boolean networks [3] where a node represents a gate or cell in the circuits and a edge represents a connection among gates. The functionality of a gate/cell can be expressed with SOP representations. Then a straightforward and simple way to optimize a Boolean network is to apply two-level optimization to each gate in the circuit. As discussed above, when minimizing a gate, it is very important to utilize the don't cares derived from the relationships among gates nearby.

A simple utilization of such don't cares is illustrated in Figure 2. Given an entire circuit to be optimized, first a region which is the current target of optimization is determined. This is often called "windowing". Once the region or window is selected, multi-level optimization is applied only inside the region. This windowing scans the entire circuit for its optimization as a whole.

For the example shown in Figure 2, the circuit shown in the middle is extracted. From the circuit, we get the following equations among the signals:

$$f = a + y, \quad g = b \cdot c + \overline{b} \cdot \overline{c}, \quad y = \overline{a} \cdot x, \quad x = \overline{b} \cdot c + b \cdot \overline{c}.$$

These equations cannot be further optimized by applying Espresso, if we do not consider don't cares which exist inside the region. There are two types of don't cares which are generated based on the relationships among inside the region. The first one is called observability don't cares (ODC) defined for each gate in the region. This is based on the fact that under some input values, the output value of the gate may not influence the output of the region. Let us discuss on ODC for the gate y in the region. If a is 1, regardless of the value of y, the outputs of the region (f, g) keep the same values. So, $a = 1$ is the ODC for y. That is, if $a = 1$, the value of y can be anything, and so the equation for y is simplified as follows:

$$y = \overline{a} \cdot x = x.$$

The second type of don't cares is called satisfiability don't cares (SDC). This is based on the fact that for a gate in the region, the relationships among the output of the gate and the inputs of the gate must follow the functionality of the gate. For example, for the gate, x, as $x = \overline{b} \cdot c + b \cdot \overline{c}$, the values of $(x, b, c) = (0, 1, 0) = (0, 0, 1) = (1, 0, 0) = (1, 1, 1)$ can never be realized. There is also similar SDC for the gate, g. Based on these the circuit in the region can be simplified to the one shown in the bottom of Figure 2.

As can be seen from the example, multi-logic optimization is a very powerful way to minimize multi-level circuits. The main issues in multi-level logic optimization are how to extract useful but as small as possible ODC and SDC when minimizing each gate in the target region. There have been lots of researches on the generation of ODC and SDC, and some of the useful methods for the calculation of don't cares have been implemented in logic synthesis tools, such as MIS [5] and SIS [17]. More recently similar efforts have been incorporated into the data structure for multi-level circuit, call AIG (And Inverter Graph) in the logic synthesis and verification tool, ABC [4].

Multi-level logic synthesis from truth tables works well for control dominated circuits where the numbers of levels in the circuits are not large. On the other hand, it does not work at all for complicated circuits, such as combinational multipliers where the numbers of levels in the circuits are large. For example, if 8-bits by an 8-bits combinational multiplier circuit is synthesized from its truth table (around 32,000 rows in on-set) using the state-of-the-art logic synthesis tools, the number of the gates in the circuit becomes around 40,000 gates. This is 100 times larger than the number of the gates in the array multiplier with ripple carry chains (around 400 gates) which is area minimal manual implementation. Please note that the 40,000 gates implementation synthesized by the logic synthesizers does not have any stuck-at fault redundancy. This is a little bit surprising, but due to the way to generate the multi-level circuits, it is guaranteed for the synthesized circuits to be non-redundant. Theoretically the 40,000 gates circuit can be simplified down to 400 gates, but no multi-level logic optimization techniques can do so as of today. One issue is the size of windows when applying

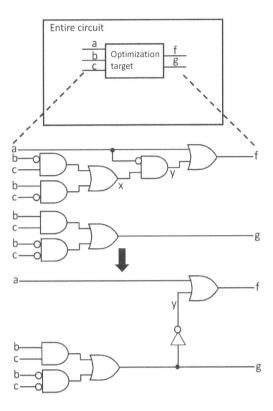

Figure 2: An example of multi-level logic optimization

multi-level logic optimization,. The size of the window which is the optimization target in Figure 2 cannot be so large due to the complexity of computing ODC and SDC.

In the 40,000 gates implementation, there are useful don't cares in the circuit, but they are very largely distributed in the entire circuit. As long as we apply window-based optimization, not much reduction can be expected due to the shortage of don't cares. Therefore, multi-level logic optimization based on Boolean reasoning instead of algebraic methods must be utilized with as large window as possible, or they should be applied to the entire circuit all at once. This is partially confirmed through the following experiment. We used the multi-level logic optimization technique with BDD based representation of logic functions [12] for the entire 6-bits by 6-bits multipliers. The state-of-the-art logic synthesis tools generate 6,262 gates implementation which can be further simplified by the method in [12]. The optimized circuit becomes 1,381 gates. This is still much larger than the array multiplier but shows usefulness of multi-level logic optimization with very large windows.

Generally speaking we may not need to synthesize arithmetic circuits from the truth tables, as there have been already manually designed in many hardware designs. Instead we can just re-use them. But in some situations including approximate computing, new arithmetic circuits may be better to be synthesized from truth tables or similar logic representations if it ever works well. This is definitely still an important research topic.

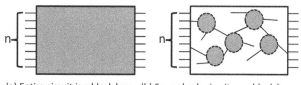

(a) Entire circuit is a block box   (b) Several sub-circuits are block boxes

Figure 3: Basic Idea of Partial Logic Synthesis

4 SEQUENTIAL LOGIC OPTIMIZATION

For sequential circuits, beside the various optimizations for their combinational parts, there are a number of optimization techniques analyzing the sequential behaviors and don't cares, logic optimization with multiple time frames, including state assignments, retiming, and others. We do not have space to be discussed in this paper. Please refer to [17] and [18] for their details.

5 PARTIAL LOGIC SYNTHESIS

In this section we would like to discuss what is called "partial logic synthesis". First we introduce the idea of the partial logic synthesis and its related problems in logic designs processes. Then we show how the partial logic synthesis problem can be solved by utilizing SAT solvers repeatedly, although the partial logic synthesis can be formulated as Quantified Boolean Formula problem which is P-Space complete. Finally application of partial logic synthesis to a number of related problems including ECO (Engineering Change Order) problems as well as automatic test pattern generation of various faults (either single or multiple) is discussed.

5.1 Partial Logic Synthesis Problem

Let us consider combinational circuits having n primary inputs. If its internal structure is totally black box as shown in Figure 3 (a), 2^n number of test patterns are required to completely understand the functionality of the circuit. However, if most of the internal structure is known and a set of small portions of the circuit are black box as shown in (b), still we need exponential numbers of test patterns in order to understand the functionality of the entire circuit? Theoretically there should be such cases, but practically small numbers of test patterns can actually determine the functionality of the entire circuits as shown in the various experimental results on hardware (for example, [9][8]) and on software (for example, [2][1])..

For example, the internal structure of the circuit having two primary inputs shown in Figure 4 is totally unknown and it may realize any of the 16 possible logic functions shown in the figure at the primary output,. Therefore, in order to understand its complete functionality, that is, the truth table for that function ($P1$, $P2$, $P3$, $P4$), we need to check the output value with respect to all possible input values which are in total $2^2 = 4$.

On the other hand, if the internal structure of the circuit is the one shown in Figure 5, i.e., there is a two-input black box and an AND gate as shown in the figure, the entire circuit can implement only four different functions, $g1$, $g2$, $g3$, $g4$, although the internal black box gate may realize all of 16 logic functions. The truth table of the entire circuit (represented as $Q1$, $Q2$, $Q3$, $Q4$) is partially fixed

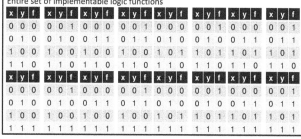

Figure 4: All of 16 functions are implementable

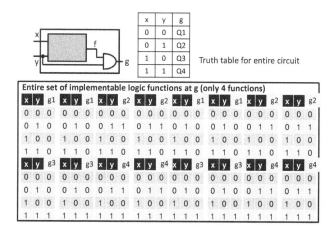

Figure 5: Only four functions are implementable

so that $Q1 = 0$ and $Q3 = 0$. This is because the primary output becomes 0 if the output of the black box gate is 0. Since there are only four logic functions implementable by this circuit, the number of test patterns to completely determine the functionality of the entire circuit becomes just two. As can be seen from this simple example, the required numbers of test patterns for the determination of the functionality of the entire circuit which has a set of small black box circuits are generally very small with respect to the numbers of all possible test patterns.

Now we define the partial logic synthesis problem. It is the problem to automatically fill the vacant subcircuits shown in Figure 6. There are p of vacant subcircuits in the target circuit. We can fill them by any possible logic functions, but the inputs to those logic functions must be the existing sets of inputs to the subcircuits as shown in the figure. We here assume that a circuit or logic formula which is the specification to be realized by the circuit with vacant subcircuits is given separately. Then the partial logic synthesis problem is to fill the vacant subcircuits appropriately in such a way that it become equivalent to the specification. In order to formulate the problem mathematically, each of vacant subcircuits is replaced with a Look Up Table (LUT).

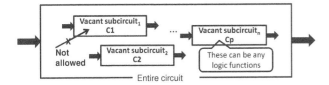

Figure 6: Definition of partial logic synthesis

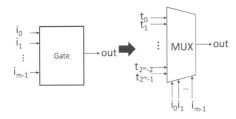

Figure 7: Definition of Loop Up Table (LUT)

A m-LUT is a way to represent any possible logic function with m inputs as shown in Figure 7. Generally speaking, a LUT can be considered as a multiplexer having m control inputs as shown in the figure. By the value combinations of m control inputs, $i_0, i_1, ..., i_{m-1}$, an appropriate value represented by one of t variables is selected and output. All of the vacant subcircuits are replaced with LUTs and let the truth table variables for a kth LUT are $t_0^k, t_1^k, ..., t_{l_m}^k$ where l_m is the number of input to the vacant subcircuit.

Now the partial synthesis problem is defined as follows:
$$\exists t_0^0, t_1^0, ..., t_{l_1}^0, t_1^1, t_1^1, ..., t_{l_2}^1, ..., t_0^p, t_1^p, ..., t_{l_p}^p. \forall in_0, in_1, .., in_n.$$
Circuit with LUT is equivalent to specification.

This is a Quantified Boolean Formula (QBF) and its satisfiability checking belongs to P-Space complete problems. It can be solved by repeatedly applying SAT solvers. Each time a SAT solver is applied, if it is satisfiable, a test pattern is generated which is a partial requirement to be satisfied by the above QBF problem. This process continues until the problem becomes unsatisfiable (UNSAT). At the end of the repeated applications of SAT solvers, the methods shown in [9][8] generate complete sets of test patterns for the conditions of the vacant subcircuits. That is, if the circuits whose vacant subcircuits are filled by some functions behaves equivalent to the specification under all of those test patterns, they are guaranteed to be equivalent for all possible input values which are 2^n different values.

5.2 Example of Partial Logic Synthesis

Let us discuss with an example on partial logic synthesis. The target circuit is a one bit full adder shown in Figure 8 (a). This is a correct implementation, and its buggy circuit example is shown in (b). In (b) an exclusive-OR gate in (a) is replaced with an OR gate which makes the circuit buggy. One way to debug the circuit in (b) is to replace the OR gate with an three input LUT as shown in (c). An LUT is introduced whose inputs are all primary inputs of the circuit. In this case the synthesis problem becomes less complicated as:
$$\forall a, b, c. \exists t.$$
Circuit with LUT is equivalent to specification.

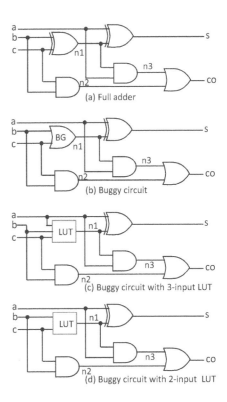

Figure 8: Examples of partial logic synthesis problems

where t denotes the output of the LUT. Although this is easier to solve, the subcircuit may include all or many of primary inputs and the size of the entire circuit may become much larger than the original one. Instead of doing that way, the partial logic synthesis is to use the original inputs to the subcircuit or the LUT as shown in Figure 8 (d).

Now the two circuit to be compared become the ones shown in Figure 9 (a) and (b), and their equivalence is checked by applying SAT solvers to the circuit shown in Figure 10. If the primary output of the circuit is always 0, that is, it can never become 1, the two circuits are equivalent. This is a formal verification as SAT solvers do implicit exhaustive search in entire input value space.

The repeated application of SAT solvers works in the following way for this example. First, the primary output of the circuit shown in Figure 10 can become 1 or not is checked as the following SAT problem:
$$\exists a, b, c, t0, t1, t2, t3.$$
The primary output of the circuit in Figure 10 becomes 1.
Please note that $t0, t1, t2, t3$ are the variable in truth table of the LUT. A SAT solver returns as SAT and generates a solution as shown in Figure 11. Primary input values are $a = 0, b = 1, c = 1$ and there is a constraint in the LUT which is $t3 = 0$. These are the first test pattern generated. In the second application of a SAT solver, the same SAT problem as the first application is solved with the additional constraints that say the primary output must be 0 when $a = 0, b = 1, c = 1$ (or equivalently, the additional constraint is just $t3 = 0$). This process continues until the SAT problem becomes UNSAT, and a complete set of test patterns has been generated.

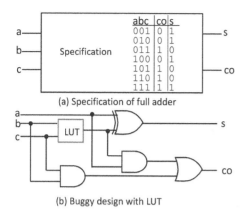

(a) Specification of full adder

(b) Buggy design with LUT

Figure 9: An example of partial logic synthesis: Specification and target circuit

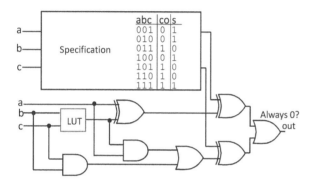

Figure 10: Miter circuit for the partial logic synthesis example

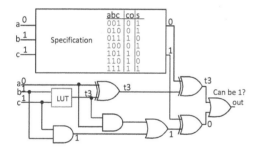

Figure 11: First iteration of the partial logic example process

The experimental results show that if the size of number of LUTs introduced into the circuit is not so large, tens of thousands of gate circuits can be processed by partial logic synthesis methods shown in this paper [9][8].

5.3 Application of Partial Logic Synthesis

Various problems in logic design can be formulated as partial logic synthesis problems. Typical such applications are shown in Figure 12. Partial logic synthesis can be applied straightforwardly to logic

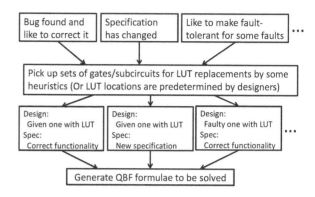

Figure 12: Application of partial logic synthesis

debugging as well as Engineering Change Order (ECO) where the specification is changed slightly after implementations are generated. Also, as LUT can represent any logic function and we can get a complete set of test patterns for the requirements of the functions of the LUTs, partial logic synthesis can also be applied to automatic test patterns of single or multiple various kinds of faults [10][11].

6 AUTOMATIC SYNTHESIS OF PARALLEL/DISTRIBUTED COMPUTING FROM SPECIFICATION

The partial synthesis method introduced in the previous section can be applied to the automatic synthesis of parallel/distributed computing. For example, the matrix-vector products computation shown in the left in Figure 13. Here the target computation is to multiply a 4 by 4 matrix with a length 4 vector. This is a tiny computation and so one core is just enough to compute. But here let us assume that we would like to compute it with 4 cores which are connected trough a ring as shown in the right side of the figure.

There are a number of ways to connect multiple or many cores. Shared bus is a common way, but one data can be sent either to a specific core or broadcast. Also, the bus based connections does not scale well. Another possible way to connect cores is crossbar, but the required hardware resources rapidly increase as the number of cores to be connected increases. Ring connections are something in between them. The required hardware resources are not large, but it can send multiple data to different cores simultaneously. Therefore, we would like to consider the following problem in this section: Given computation such as the matrix-vector products, we would like to come up with a parallel or distributed way to compute it under multiple cores which are connected through a ring. We assume that the ring connection can send data in only one direction.

The matrix-vector products appear in many situations including various neural network based computations including deep learning methods shown in Figure 14. If the two layers in deep learning are completely connected with one another as shown in (a), it is essentially the same computation as matrix-vector products. Also, if the connections between two layers are not sparse as shown in (b), it can still be formulated as matrix-vector products although the shape of the matrix can be very irregular, or it may be better

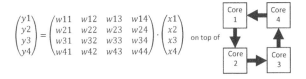

Figure 13: Matrix-vector products computations on top of 4 cores

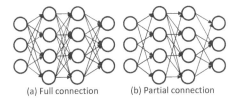

(a) Full connection   (b) Partial connection

Figure 14: Neural networks for deep learning

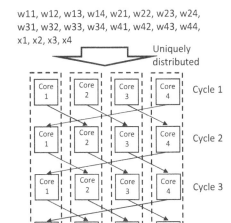

Figure 15: Partial logic synthesis for the matrix-vector products computations

to use one dimensional matrix (which is a vector). From the shape of the neural network such as the one shown in Figure 14 (b), an appropriate vector (one dimensional matrix) by vector multiplication is defined. So the problem of matrix-vector represent a wide varieties of problems including deep learning.

This problem can be considered as a partial logic synthesis problem in the following way. The matrix-vector products computation is the target specification. In the example shown in Figure 13, the target is the multiplication of a 4 by 4 matrix and a vector, and it should be computed on the 4 cores which are connected through the ring. Here we assume that one core can compute one multiplication and one addition (MAC operation) in one cycle and also for each cycle, one data can be sent from a core to the next core throughout the ring. That is, in total four data can be sent in one cycle. As we need to multiply and add by 16 times in this computation and there are in total four cores, the minimum computation cycles are 16/4=4 cycles. Now the problem to solve is to compute 4 by 4 matrix-vector products in 4 cycles on the multiple core systems shown in the right side of Figure 13.

As the optimum computing needs four cycles in computation, the four core implementation shown in the right side of Figure 13 is time-frame expanded by 4 cycles which is shown in Figure 15. Please note that the communications for each cycle follow the ring connection. The inputs are the values of the matrix and the vector. They are distributed into the four cores uniquely, that is, one value goes to only one of the four cores. In a similar way, the outputs from the cores are the values of the computation results. These are the assumptions and also the constraints to be given to the partial synthesis problems. In a core, there can be one computation which corresponds to one multiplication and one addition. Also, one core can send one data to its neighbor for each cycle. Then the partial logic synthesis problem to be solved is to map the matrix-vector products into the four cores shown in Figure 15. It can be formulated as a QBF problem just like other partial logic synthesis problems.

However, this simple approach does not work well especially in terms of scalability. Even 4 by 4 matrix-vector products computation in four cores takes more than one day to synthesize the parallel/distributed computation. The smallest problem, 2 by 2 matrix-vector products computation can be processed in a second or so, but larger ones takes a very long time. In order to resolve this scalability issue, we propose a inductive approach to the synthesis. The idea is to gather useful information or constraints from the synthesis results of small instances of the problems, and use them when synthesizing larger ones. For example, from the synthesis results on 2 by 2 matrix-vector products, we can learn the following two things.

(1) Values of each row on the matrix and the corresponding element in the vector should be allocated to the same core.
(2) The functional units in cores should perform the same functions.

These are illustrated in Figure 16. (a) shows what (1) above means and (b) shows what (2) above means. Although these are the constraints manually learned from the synthesis results, there might a way to generate them automatically, and we are now working for that direction. With appropriate manual learning from the various synthesis results, 32 x 32 matrix-vector products can be computed in four cores in parallel completely. Please refer to [15] for the details. Even the most general case such as N by N matrix-vector products on M cores can be automatically generated.

Now let us discuss an application of the above method to deep learning computations. Deep learning is based on neural network inspired computation where there are multiple layers of neural networks such as the one shown in Figure refnn (a). There are complete connections between two layers. In practice, after the weights have been tuned in training phases, however, there are many connections between neurons whose weights are zero or

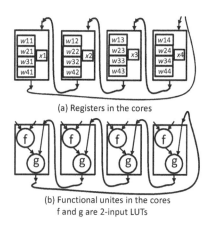

(a) Registers in the cores

(b) Functional unites in the cores
f and g are 2-input LUTs

Figure 16: Structural and communication constraints for 4 core implementation

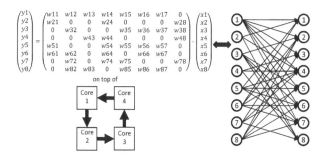

Figure 17: Martix-vector products computations with many 0 elements in the matrix

very close to zero as shown in (b). In such situations, instead of computing many of something multiplied with 0, we would like to completely skip such obvious computations.

Let us examine an example shown in Figure 17. The two layer neural network on the right can be represented with a matrix shown in the left. We see many zeros in the matrix which corresponds to the zero weights. The automatic synthesis method discussed above can also be directly applied to matrix-vector products where there are many zero elements in the matrix. In this example, the size of the matrix is 8 by 8 and so, if we do not skip the computations related to zeros, we need to multiply and add by 64 times which will take 16 cycles on 4 cores which are connected through a ring as shown in the figure. But there are in total 27 zeros in the matrix and so the theoretical minimum number of cycles for the entire computation becomes $(64-27)/4=9.25$. So we need at least 10 cycles for the entire computation even if we skip the multiplications and additions related to zero elements in the matrix. The proposed method above can actually find this 10 cycle computations in a minute or two. At the time when this paper is written, this is only a preliminary result and we are now working on larger examples.

7 CONCLUDING REMARKS

We have discussed basics of logic synthesis algorithms, such as two-level logic optimization, multi-level logic optimization, and sequential optimization. They are the fundamental techniques used today in logic synthesis under industrial environments. Also, partial logic synthesis which can be applied to logic debugging/ECO and automatic test pattern generation (ATPG) for various fault models are introduced and discussed. The issues previously believed to be impossible, such as ATPG for complete multiple stuck-at faults, may become feasible up to some sizes of circuits. We are also working on such direction, i.e., complete ATPG up to triple faults for large circuits which takes only the same order of the time for ATPG of single stuck-at faults [19].

REFERENCES

[1] Rajeev Alur, Dana Fisman, Rishabh Singh, and Armando Solar-Lezama. 2017. SyGuS-Comp17: Results and Analysis. In *Proceedings of 4th Workshop on Synthesis (SYNT@CAV)*.
[2] Rajeev Alur, Rishabh Singh, Dana Fisman, and Armando Solar-Lezama. 2018. Search-Based Program Synthesis. *In Communications of the ACM* 61, 12 (2018).
[3] Karen A. Bartlett, Robert K. Brayton, Gary D. Hachtel, Reily M. Jacoby, Christopher R. Morrison, Richard L. Rudell, Alberto L. Sangiovanni-Vicentelli, and Albert R. Wang. 1988. Multi-level logic minimization using implicit don't cares. *IEEE Transaction on CAD of Integrated Circuits and Systems* 7, 6 (1988), 723–740.
[4] Robert K. Brayton and Alan Mishchenko. 2010. ABC: An Academic Industrial-Strength Verification Tool. In *Proceedings of the 22nd International Conference on Computer Aided Verification*. 24–40.
[5] Robert K. Brayton, Richard L. Rudell, Alberto L. Sangiovanni-Vicentelli, and Albert R. Wang. 1987. MIS: A Multiple-Level Logic Optimization System. *IEEE Transaction on CAD of Integrated Circuits and System* 6, 6 (1987), 1062–1081.
[6] Robert King Brayton, Alberto L. Sangiovanni-Vicentelli, Curtis T. McMullen, and Gary D. Hachtel. 1997. *Logic Minimization Algorithms for VLSI Synthesis*. Kluwer Academic Publishers Norwell, MA, USA.
[7] Olivier Coudert and Jean Christophe Madre. 1992. Implicit and Incremental Computation of Primes and Essential Primes of Boolean Functions. In *Proceedings of the 29th International Design Automation Conference*. 36–39.
[8] Masahiro Fujita. 2015. Toward Unification of Synthesis and Verification in Topologically Constrained Logic Design. *Proc. IEEE* 103, 11 (2015), 2052–2060.
[9] Masahiro Fujita, Satoshi Jo, Shohei Ono, and Takeshi Matsumoto. 2013. Partial synthesis through sampling with and without specification. In *Proceedings of International Conference on Computer Aided Design*. 787–794.
[10] Masahiro Fujita and Alan Mishchenko. 2014. Efficient SAT-based ATPG techniques for all multiple stuck-at faults. In *Proceedings of International Test Conference*. 1–10.
[11] Masahiro Fujita, Naoki Taguchi, Kentaro Iwata, and Alan Mishchenko. 2015. Incremental ATPG methods for multiple faults under multiple fault models. In *Proceedings of International Symposium on Quality Electronic Design*. Santa Clara, USA, 177–180.
[12] Yusuke Matsunaga and Masahiro Fujita. 1989. Multi-level logic optimization using binary decision diagrams. In *Proceedings of International Conference on Computer Aided Design*. 556–559.
[13] Edward J. McCluskey. 1956. Minimization of Boolean Functions. *Bell System Technical Journal* 35, 6 (1956), 1417–1444.
[14] Patrick McGeer, Jagesh Sanghavi, Robert Brayton, and Alberto Sangiovanni Vicentelli. 1993. Espresso-signature: a new exact minimizer for logic functions. In *Proceedings of the 30th international Design Automation Conference*. Dallas, Texas, 618–624.
[15] Yukio Miyasaka, Ashish Mittal, and Masahiro Fujita. 2019. Synthesis of Algorithm Considering Communication Structure of Distributed/Parallel Computing. In *Proceedings of International Symposium on Quality Electronic Design*. Santa Clara, USA.
[16] Willard Van Orman Quine. 1955. A Way to Simplify Truth Functions. *The American Mathematical Monthly* 62, 9 (1955), 627–631.
[17] E.M. Sentovich, K.J. Singh, L. Lavagno, C. Moon, R. Murgai, A. Saldanha, H. Savoj, P.R. Stephan, Robert K. Brayton, and Alberto L. Sangiovanni-Vicentelli. 1992. *SIS: A System for Sequential Circuit Synthesis*. Technical Report UCB/ERL M92/41. EECS Department, University of California, Berkeley. http://www2.eecs.berkeley.edu/Pubs/TechRpts/1992/2010.html
[18] Tiziano Villa, Timothy Kam, Robert King Brayton, and Alberto L. Sangiovanni-Vicentelli. 1984. *Synthesis of Finite State Machines Logic Optimization*. Kluwer Academic Publishers Norwell, MA, USA.
[19] Peikun Wang, Amir Masoud Gharehbaghi, and Masahiro Fujita. 2019. An Incremental Automatic Test Pattern Generation Method for Multiple Stuck-at Faults. In *Proceedings of IEEE VLSI Test Symposium*. Monterey, USA.

From Electronic Design Automation to Cyber-Physical System Design Automation: A Tale of Platforms and Contracts

Pierluigi Nuzzo

Ming Hsieh Department of Electrical and Computer Engineering

Viterbi School of Engineering, University of Southern California

Los Angeles, CA 90089

nuzzo@usc.edu

ABSTRACT

This paper reflects on the design challenges posed by cyber-physical systems, what distinguishes cyber-physical system design from large-scale integrated circuit design, and what could be the opportunities for the design automation community. The paper discusses three challenges that touch upon aspects that are unique to cyber-physical systems, namely, devising novel compositional design methodologies, reasoning about the interaction between discrete and continuous models, and dealing with uncertainty. It then summarizes some of the approaches pursued by the research community to tackle these challenges, with the potential of fostering a new generation of methodologies, algorithms, and tools for system design. Central to the paper is a view of *platforms* and *contracts* as formal notions that can bridge the emerging area of cyber-physical system design automation with paradigms that have been successful in the field of electronic design automation.

ACM Reference Format:

Pierluigi Nuzzo. 2019. From Electronic Design Automation to Cyber-Physical System Design Automation: A Tale of Platforms and Contracts. In *2019 International Symposium on Physical Design (ISPD '19), April 14–17, 2019, San Francisco, CA, USA*. ACM, New York, NY, USA, 5 pages. https://doi.org/10.1145/3299902.3311070

1 INTRODUCTION

Cyber-physical systems (CPSs) result from the integration of "cyber" components (computation and/or communication as well as control) with physical processes of different nature to perform functions that cannot be achieved by the cyber and physical parts in isolation [1, 27, 28, 38, 43, 50, 55]. CPSs are an integral part of our lives; examples range from cars, aircraft, and robots, to energy-efficient buildings, computer-monitored and controlled factory lines, and wearable medical devices. By gathering information from a multitude of sources, processing it, and applying it to affect the physical environment, CPSs are changing the way entire industries operate, and have the potential of radically influencing how we deal with crucial societal problems, including national security and safety,

energy management, civil infrastructure, transportation, manufacturing, and healthcare. However, the complexity and heterogeneity of these systems pose significant design challenges. Current development processes no longer scale to support the rich interactions that are seen in today's products and services or envisioned for tomorrow's Internet-of-Things (IoT), "Industry 5.0," and "smart" autonomous systems scenarios. We refer to the literature for an extensive discussion about CPS design, its foundations, and impact (e.g., see [21, 36, 37, 41, 50, 51, 53, 54, 59]).

This paper reflects on some of the CPS design challenges, what distinguishes CPS design from large-scale integrated circuit design, and what could be the opportunities for the design automation community in this area.[1] The paper expands on a recent note [32] and presents a view of *platforms* and *contracts* in terms of formal notions that can bridge the emerging area of CPS design automation with paradigms that have been successful in the field of electronic design automation (EDA).

2 CYBER-PHYSICAL SYSTEM DESIGN CHALLENGES

CPS designers are expected to manage design spaces that are often too large and heterogeneous to be efficiently explored while providing strong guarantees of correctness, dependability, and compliance with regulations. While model-based engineering tools and virtual prototyping are the *de facto* standard for system development, the *concept design* phase largely remains a manual process, the domain of experienced system architects, often relying on their accrued knowledge and a set of heuristic evaluations to take risky decisions.

At the *system level*, requirement-management tools are still predominantly centered on text-based languages, which creates opportunities for ambiguities and potential conflicts [16, 34]. During *system development*, poorly inter-operable domain-specific languages and tools make it hard to combine the results of different analysis or synthesis methods. The inability to rigorously model and reason about the interactions between different system portions, and specifically between the physical and the cyber parts, increases the risk of unwanted interactions found late in the development process, additional development costs, delays, and serious system vulnerabilities. Design and operation of next-generation intelligent, autonomous CPSs call for new methodologies and algorithms to guide the construction of "systems that people can bet their lives on" [56]. In this respect, the contribution of design automation is

[1] The reflections in this paper originate from my research at the University of California at Berkeley in Alberto Sangiovanni-Vincentelli's group. It is then a pleasure and an honor to dedicate this paper to Alberto, as he receives a Lifetime Achievement Award for his decades-long seminal contributions to the field of electronic design automation.

crucial. It is about distilling the design principles that allow building systems again and again, in a systematic and reproducible way, to achieve what we look for today, and what we dream for tomorrow.

EDA has been successful in taming the complexity of billions of devices on a chip, turning it into elegant designs that can be modified and evolved, and allowing predictably building complex artifacts that have enabled today's CPS applications [49]. How can CPS design automation mirror the success of very large scale integration (VLSI) system design?

3 FROM EDA TO CPS DESIGN AUTOMATION

In this section, we focus on three challenges that touch upon aspects that are unique to CPSs, and are being tackled by the research community, with the potential of fostering a new generation of methodologies, algorithms, and tools for system design. The challenges concern devising novel compositional and hierarchical design methodologies, reasoning about the interaction between discrete and continuous models, and dealing with uncertainty.

3.1 Compositional and Hierarchical Cyber-Physical System Design

Design methodologies – well-defined abstraction layers, hierarchical decomposition mechanisms, regular and reproducible architectures – have been crucial to the success of EDA. These concepts have been formalized within the platform-based design (PBD) methodology, which has been applied to a variety of domains, from automotive [30] to system-on-chip [14], from analog and mixed-signal circuit design [39] to building automation [58] and synthetic biology [15].

3.1.1 Platform-Based Design. *Platform-based design* was introduced in the late 1980s as a rigorous framework to reason about design that could be shared across industrial domain boundaries [37, 48] and support the supply chain as well as multi-layer optimization.

In PBD, at each step, top-down refinements of high-level specifications are mapped into bottom-up abstractions and characterizations of potential implementations. Each abstraction layer is defined by a design *platform*, which is the set of all architectures that can be built out of a *library* (collection) of *components* according to *composition rules*. A pictorial representation of a design step in PBD is shown in Figure 1 and can be seen as a meet-in-the-middle process consisting of two phases.

The *bottom-up phase* consists in building and modeling the component library, which, in a CPS, includes both the system plant and the controller. In the *top-down phase*, the high-level system requirements are formalized and an optimization (refinement) phase called *mapping* is performed, where the requirements are mapped into the available implementation library components and their composition. Mapping is cast as an optimization problem where a set of performance metrics and quality factors are optimized over a space constrained by both system requirements and component feasibility constraints. Mapping is the mechanism that allows moving from a level of abstraction to a lower one using the available components within the library. When some constraint cannot be satisfied using the available library components or the mapping result is not satisfactory for the designer, additional elements can be designed and inserted into the library. For example, when implementing an

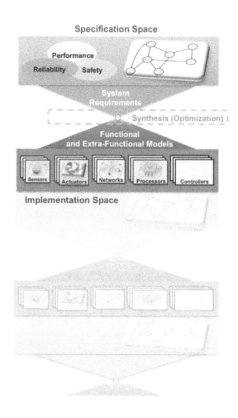

Figure 1: A pictorial view of different abstraction layers in platform-based design.

algorithm with code running on a processor, the functionality of the algorithm is assigned to a processor and the code is the result of mapping the "equations" describing the algorithm into the instruction set of the processor. If the processor is too slow, then real-time constraints may be violated. In this case, a new processor has to be found or designed that executes the code fast enough to satisfy the real-time constraint. After each mapping step, the current representation of the design platform serves as a specification for the next mapping step, until the physical implementation is reached. This recursive process is pictorially represented in Figure 1.

Design paradigms such as PBD are also on the "critical path" to operational CPSs. Moreover, a compositional approach can facilitate reasoning about complex system behaviors and make system integration affordable [6, 41, 42, 53, 55].

3.1.2 Compositional CPS Design and the Role of Contracts. Designers usually decompose a system into different domains, by adopting the most effective mathematical formalisms to represent different portions of the design or different viewpoints (e.g., function, safety, timing, energy) at different abstraction levels. They then leverage the most suitable tools to analyze and synthesize these models and architectures compositionally. CPS design would then benefit from unifying compositional frameworks that can support different analysis techniques, based on formal verification, simulation, and testing, in a consistent way. Further, design methodologies should consider extra-functional viewpoints, including energy and cost, as well as reliability, security, and usability, most of which are difficult to formally quantify today. In fact, aspects that are unique to CPSs tend to challenge the principles of "separation of concerns" and compositionality that have been traditionally successful in hardware or software design [22]. These challenges call for new co-design principles (e.g., co-design for control and computation, for control and communication) as well as a unifying framework providing abstractions, algorithms, and tools that can support them.

Active research efforts in the areas of component-based [13] and contract-based [7, 40] design address these challenges by relying on mathematical models of the interfaces between the components and their environments, termed *contracts*, together with rigorous ways of composing and refining these interfaces. An *assume-guarantee (A/G) contract* captures the assumptions that a component makes on its environment and the behaviors it guarantees in the context of the assumptions. In a contract-based environment, it is then possible to verify system-level properties in a modular and hierarchical fashion, based on the satisfaction of component-level properties [20]. It is possible to support rigorous stepwise refinement to reason about system decompositions, even if the component implementations are not yet available [11, 17]. It is possible to facilitate component reuse, as any components satisfying a contract directly inherit its guarantees and can be used in the design. Contracts can provide a formal foundation and complement the PBD methodology to enable design space exploration and provably-correct concurrent development of system architectures and control algorithms in a modular and scalable way [18, 23, 38, 42].

Different contract theories have been developed over the years, and have shown to be effective for specifying and reasoning about components and their aggregations, especially when component models belong to the same level of abstraction (e.g., algorithm, software, architecture) or adopt the same formalism (e.g., finite automata, dataflow models) [7]. However, there is no universal modeling formalism that can capture every aspect of complex, heterogeneous systems and guarantee, at the same time, tractable analysis. A set of challenges remain when system models are to be formulated and manipulated along the design flow and across different abstraction levels to assess the performance and correctness of the entire system. Recent efforts toward a formalization of *vertical contracts* [40] address these challenges to provide methodological support for multi-view and multi-layer system design with heterogeneous models.

In electronic design, and specifically physical design, the *design rules* have acted as the interface, or the contract, between the circuit designer and the process designers. They allow for a ready translation of a circuit concepts into an actual geometry in silicon, without requiring the designer to understand the intricacies of the fabrication process and the relations between the different masks. In a similar way, and differently from *horizontal contracts*, describing the interactions between components at the same level of abstraction, vertical contracts formalize the relationship between two abstraction levels in the design (e.g., control algorithm and software implementation), which present heterogeneous decomposition architectures as well as behaviors expressed by heterogeneous formalisms. The role of horizontal and vertical contracts is pictorially represented in Figure 2. Vertical contracts

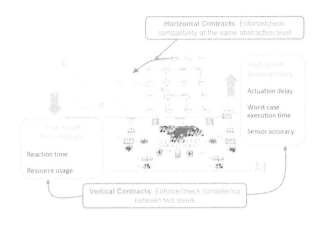

Figure 2: Role of horizontal and vertical contracts in system design.

become a key addition to the existing contact frameworks. For example, they enable reasoning about a richer set of design refinement relations, such as synthesis methods (e.g., hierarchical control synthesis) and optimization-based methods (e.g., optimization-based model-predictive control) to generate correct-by-construction designs from high-level formal specifications.

3.2 Reasoning About the Interaction Between Discrete and Continuous Models

Analysis and design of CPSs also require methods and tools that can efficiently reason about the interaction between discrete models, e.g., used to describe embedded software components, and continuous models used to describe physical processes [35, 52]. In this respect, a central difficulty is the very different nature of the tools used to analyze continuous dynamics (e.g., real analysis) and discrete dynamics (e.g., combinatorics). Advances in formal verification and optimization over the years have led to techniques that can address large-scale problems in either of the two domains. Boolean methods such as satisfiability (SAT) solving have been successful in tackling large combinatorial search problems for the design and verification of hardware and software systems [31]. On the other hand, problems in control, communications, signal processing, data analysis and modeling, and machine learning often rely on mathematical programming (e.g., see [5]), and specifically convex programming [9] as a powerful solution engine. However, despite their strengths, neither SAT solving, nor convex programming would be effective in CPS design, if used in isolation. We need methods and tools that blend concepts from both of them.

An approach to formal reasoning about continuous and discrete dynamics is to model the cyber-physical system as a hybrid automaton [2], including discrete states as well as continuous states governed by differential equations, and use model checking techniques [8, 10, 12, 38] to prove properties about the system or find bugs. Another approach, based on theorem proving, aims at proving properties of hybrid systems by leveraging formulas in appropriate logic languages capturing their behaviors [44]. The scalability of these verification techniques is an active research area, aiming to extend the number of supported state variables, which is currently limited to only a few hundreds [12, 38]. Progress has also been made toward correct-by-construction synthesis approaches that algorithmically generate design artifacts from high-level logic specifications, despite the theoretically higher computational complexity of synthesis versus verification [24, 25, 46, 57]. An active research effort aims to leverage the efficiency and formal guarantees of state-of-the-art constraint solving algorithms in both the Boolean and convex analysis domains toward a novel framework, termed satisfiability modulo convex programming (SMC) [35, 52]. Inspired by the satisfiability modulo theory (SMT) [4] approach, SMC rethinks the connection between logic-based methods and numerical methods for reasoning about the combination of discrete and continuous dynamics that can address the complexity of CPS applications.

3.3 Dealing with Uncertainty

As for integrated circuits, CPSs must operate under the presence of uncertainty that may result from variability (e.g., due to manufacturing tolerances, usage, failures,) noise, or model approximations. However, in CPSs, uncertainty may also result from external conditions that are not under system control: unknown or unpredictable environment conditions, multi-agent dynamics, and even adversarial behaviors. A classic example are CPSs interacting with humans [51]. Researchers are exploring many approaches for modeling and reasoning about uncertainty, including the use of probabilistic models, capable of expressing the likelihood for a certain event to happen. While probabilistic models and probabilistic logics are well-studied for discrete systems, their application to CPSs are active areas of research [19, 26, 29, 33, 45, 47].

4 FAST FORWARD

In the future, it is expected that CPSs will rely less and less on humans, and replace humans, for example, in jobs that require precision, or for tedious or dangerous tasks. The intelligence, situational awareness, and decision-making capabilities of these systems will increasingly rely on machine learning components. Similarly, the design process itself will increasingly use data-driven techniques [51]. Learning-enabled CPSs will, in turn, introduce additional sources of approximation, and require probabilistic and statistical reasoning [3]. Further, they will raise additional concerns about the security implications of their tasks as well as the privacy of the data they process.

Security and privacy will add new dimensions to the design problem and impact all the abstraction layers. In fact, already in the context of hardware platforms, the globalization of the integrated circuit and the associated supply chains poses serious threats to national security, infrastructure, and economy. Modern SoCs are themselves heterogeneous systems combining multiple processor cores and specialized Intellectual Property (IP) blocks that are designed and integrated by different companies. This raises the risk of security threats from untrusted third parties, possibly compromising the root of trust of many IoT systems.

Tackling these fundamental and practical challenges will spur exciting research for design automation at the boundary with formal methods, control theory, real-time systems, machine learning, optimization, and physical platforms, toward advancing the scientific foundations that are necessary to build the planetary-scale, inference-and-decision-making systems we dream of. Design embodies humankind's attempt at creating new artifacts, shaping the surrounding world, and augmenting its capabilities. It is, however, on us to ensure that these artifacts operate safely and enhance our lives.

ACKNOWLEDGMENTS

The author acknowledges the partial support by the Air Force Research Labs (AFRL) and the Defense Advanced Research Projects Agency (DARPA) under agreement number FA8560-18-1-7817.

REFERENCES

[1] Rajeev Alur. 2015. *Principles of cyber-physical systems.* MIT Press.
[2] R. Alur, C. Courcoubetis, T. A. Henzinger, and P. H. Ho. 1993. Hybrid Automata: An Algorithmic Approach to the Specification and Verification of Hybrid Systems. In *Hybrid Systems (LNCS)*, Vol. 736. Springer, 209–229.
[3] Dario Amodei, Chris Olah, Jacob Steinhardt, Paul Christiano, John Schulman, and Dan Mané. 2016. Concrete problems in AI safety. *arXiv preprint arXiv:1606.06565* (2016).
[4] Clark Barrett and Cesare Tinelli. 2018. Satisfiability modulo theories. In *Handbook of Model Checking.* Springer, 305–343.
[5] Alberto Bemporad and Manfred Morari. 1999. Control of systems integrating logic, dynamics, and constraints. *Automatica* 35 (1999).
[6] A. Benveniste, T. Bourke, B. Caillaud, J. Colaço, C. Pasteur, and M. Pouzet. 2018. Building a Hybrid Systems Modeler on Synchronous Languages Principles. *Proc. IEEE* 106, 9 (Sep. 2018), 1568–1592. https://doi.org/10.1109/JPROC.2018.2858016
[7] Albert Benveniste, Benoit Caillaud, Dejan Nickovic, Roberto Passerone, Jean-Baptiste Raclet, Philipp Reinkemeier, Alberto Sangiovanni-Vincentelli, Werner Damm, Thomas A. Henzinger, and Kim G. Larsen. 2018. Contracts for System Design. *Foundations and Trends in Electronic Design Automation* 12, 2-3 (2018), 124–400. https://doi.org/10.1561/1000000053
[8] Luca Benvenuti, Davide Bresolin, Pieter Collins, Alberto Ferrari, Luca Geretti, and Tiziano Villa. 2012. Ariadne: Dominance Checking of Nonlinear Hybrid Automata Using Reachability Analysis. In *Reachability Problems*, Alain Finkel, JÃ¼rÃ¤me Leroux, and Igor Potapov (Eds.). Lecture Notes in Computer Science, Vol. 7550. Springer Berlin Heidelberg, 79–91. https://doi.org/10.1007/978-3-642-33512-9_8
[9] S.P. Boyd and L. Vandenberghe. 2004. *Convex Optimization.* Cambridge University Press.
[10] Xin Chen, Erika Ábrahám, and Sriram Sankaranarayanan. 2013. Flow*: An Analyzer for Non-linear Hybrid Systems. In *Proc. Int. Conf. Comput.-Aided Verification (Lecture Notes in Computer Science)*, Vol. 8044. Springer Berlin Heidelberg, 258–263.
[11] Alessandro Cimatti and Stefano Tonetta. 2015. Contracts-refinement proof system for component-based embedded systems. *Science of Computer Programming* 97, Part 3 (2015), 333 – 348. https://doi.org/10.1016/j.scico.2014.06.011
[12] Edmund M Clarke, Thomas A Henzinger, Helmut Veith, and Roderick P Bloem. 2018. *Handbook of model checking.* Springer.
[13] Luca deAlfaro and Thomas A. Henzinger. 2001. Interface theories for component-based design. In *First International Workshop on Embedded Software (EMSOFT)*, Vol. LNCS 2211. Springer-Verlag, Lake Tahoe, CA, 148–165.
[14] Douglas Densmore, Alena Simalatsar, Abhijit Davare, Roberto Passerone, and Alberto Sangiovanni-Vincentelli. 2009. UMTS MPSoC design evaluation using a system level design framework. In *Design, Automation & Test in Europe Conference & Exhibition, 2009. DATE'09.* IEEE, 478–483.
[15] Douglas Densmore, Anne Van Devender, Matthew Johnson, and Nade Sritanyaratana. 2009. A platform-based design environment for synthetic biological systems. In *The Fifth Richard Tapia Celebration of Diversity in Computing Conference: Intellect, Initiatives, Insight, and Innovations.* ACM, 24–29.
[16] Yishai A. Feldman and Henry Broodney. 2016. A Cognitive Journey for Requirements Engineering. In *Ann. INCOSE Int. Symp.* INCOSE.
[17] Ioannis Filippidis and Richard M Murray. 2018. Layering Assume-Guarantee Contracts for Hierarchical System Design. *Proc. IEEE* 106, 9 (2018), 1616–1654.
[18] J. Finn, P. Nuzzo, and A. Sangiovanni-Vincentelli. 2015. A Mixed Discrete-Continuous Optimization Scheme for Cyber-Physical System Architecture Exploration. In *Proc. IEEE/ACM Int. Conf. Comput.-Aided Design.*

[19] Hans Hansson and Bengt Jonsson. 1994. A logic for reasoning about time and reliability. *Formal aspects of computing* 6, 5 (1994), 512–535.

[20] Antonio Iannopollo, Pierluigi Nuzzo, Stavros Tripakis, and Alberto Sangiovanni-Vincentelli. 2014. Library-Based Scalable Refinement Checking for Contract-Based Design. In *Proc. Design, Automation and Test in Europe*.

[21] Ruoxi Jia, Baihong Jin, Ming Jin, Yuxun Zhou, Ioannis C Konstantakopoulos, Han Zou, Joyce Kim, Dan Li, Weixi Gu, Reza Arghandeh, et al. 2018. Design automation for smart building systems. *Proc. IEEE* 106, 9 (2018), 1680–1699.

[22] K. Keutzer, S. Malik, R. Newton, J. Rabaey, and A. Sangiovanni Vincentelli. 2000. System Level Design: Orthogonalization of Concerns and Platform-Based Design. *IEEE Trans. Comput.-Aided Design Integr. Circuits Syst.* 19, 12 (2000), 1523–1543.

[23] Dmitrii Kirov, Pierluigi Nuzzo, Roberto Passerone, and Alberto Sangiovanni-Vincentelli. 2017. ArchEx: An Extensible Framework for the Exploration of Cyber-Physical System Architectures. In *Proc. IEEE/ACM Design Automation Conf.*

[24] M. Kloetzer and C. Belta. 2008. A Fully Automated Framework for Control of Linear Systems from Temporal Logic Specifications. 53, 1 (Feb. 2008), 287–297.

[25] H. Kress-Gazit, G.E. Fainekos, and G.J. Pappas. 2009. Temporal-Logic-Based Reactive Mission and Motion Planning. 25, 6 (Dec 2009), 1370–1381.

[26] Marta Kwiatkowska, Gethin Norman, and David Parker. 2007. Stochastic model checking. In *International School on Formal Methods for the Design of Computer, Communication and Software Systems*. Springer, 220–270.

[27] E. A. Lee. 2008. Cyber Physical Systems: Design Challenges. In *Proc. IEEE Int. Symposium on Object Oriented Real-Time Distributed Computing*. 363–369. https://doi.org/10.1109/ISORC.2008.25

[28] Edward A. Lee and Sanjit A. Seshia. 2017. *Introduction to Embedded Systems, A Cyber-Physical Systems Approach* (Second ed.). MIT Press.

[29] Jiwei Li, Pierluigi Nuzzo, Alberto Sangiovanni-Vincentelli, Yugeng Xi, and Dewei Li. 2017. Stochastic contracts for cyber-physical system design under probabilistic requirements. In *Int. Conf. Formal Methods and Models for Co-Design*. 5–14.

[30] Chung-Wei Lin, Qi Zhu, and Alberto Sangiovanni-Vincentelli. 2014. Security-aware mapping for TDMA-based real-time distributed systems. In *Proceedings of the 2014 IEEE/ACM International Conference on Computer-Aided Design*. IEEE Press, 24–31.

[31] Sharad Malik and Lintao Zhang. 2009. Boolean satisfiability from theoretical hardness to practical success. *Commun. ACM* 52, 8 (2009), 76–82.

[32] Pierluigi Nuzzo. 2018. Building 'Systems That You Can Bet Your Life On' Again and Again: Challenges and Opportunities for Cyber-Physical System Design Automation. *'What is' Column, ACM SIGDA (Association for Computing Machinery Special Interest Group on Design Automation) E-Newsletter* 48, 10 (Oct. 2018).

[33] Pierluigi Nuzzo, Jiwei Li, Alberto L Sangiovanni-Vincentelli, Yugeng Xi, and Dewei Li. 2019. Stochastic Assume-Guarantee Contracts for Cyber-Physical System Design. *ACM Transactions on Embedded Computing Systems (TECS)* 18, 1 (2019), 2.

[34] Pierluigi Nuzzo, Michele Lora, Yishai Feldman, and A. Sangiovanni-Vincentelli. 2018. CHASE: Contract-Based Requirement Engineering for Cyber-Physical System Design. In *Proc. Design, Automation and Test in Europe*. Dresden, Germany, 839–844.

[35] P. Nuzzo, A Puggelli, S. Seshia, and A. Sangiovanni-Vincentelli. 2010. CalCS: SMT solving for non-linear convex constraints. In *Proc. Formal Methods in Computer-Aided Design*. 71–79.

[36] Pierluigi Nuzzo and Alberto Sangiovanni-Vincentelli. 2014. Let's Get Physical: Computer Science Meets Systems. In *From Programs to Systems. The Systems perspective in Computing*, Saddek Bensalem, Yassine Lakhneck, and Axel Legay (Eds.). Lecture Notes in Computer Science, Vol. 8415. Springer Berlin Heidelberg, 193–208. http://dx.doi.org/10.1007/978-3-642-54848-2_13

[37] Pierluigi Nuzzo and Alberto Sangiovanni-Vincentelli. 2017. System Design in the Cyber-Physical Era. In *Nanoelectronics: Materials, Devices, Applications,*, Vol. 2. 363–396.

[38] Pierluigi Nuzzo, Alberto Sangiovanni-Vincentelli, Davide Bresolin, Luca Geretti, and Tiziano Villa. 2015. A Platform-Based Design Methodology with Contracts and Related Tools for the Design of Cyber-Physical Systems. *Proc. IEEE* 103, 11 (Nov. 2015).

[39] P. Nuzzo, A. Sangiovanni-Vincentelli, X. Sun, and A. Puggelli. 2012. Methodology for the Design of Analog Integrated Interfaces Using Contracts. *IEEE Sensors J.* 12, 12 (Dec. 2012), 3329–3345.

[40] Pierluigi Nuzzo and Alberto L Sangiovanni-Vincentelli. 2018. Hierarchical System Design with Vertical Contracts. In *Principles of Modeling*. Vol. 10760. 360–382.

[41] P. Nuzzo, A. L. Sangiovanni-Vincentelli, and R. M. Murray. 2015. Methodology and Tools for Next Generation Cyber-Physical Systems: The iCyPhy Approach. In *Proc. INCOSE Int. Symp.*

[42] Pierluigi Nuzzo, Huan Xu, Necmiye Ozay, John B. Finn, Alberto L. Sangiovanni-Vincentelli, Richard M. Murray, Alexandre Donzé, and Sanjit A. Seshia. 2014. A Contract-Based Methodology for Aircraft Electric Power System Design. *IEEE Access* 2 (2014), 1–25. https://doi.org/10.1109/ACCESS.2013.2295764

[43] National Institute of Standards and Technology (NIST). 2013. Strategic Vision and Business Drivers for 21st Century Cyber-Physical Systems.

[44] André Platzer. [n. d.]. *Logical Analysis of Hybrid Systems: Proving Theorems for Complex Dynamics*. Springer, Heidelberg. https://doi.org/10.1007/978-3-642-14509-4

[45] André Platzer. 2011. Stochastic differential dynamic logic for stochastic hybrid programs. In *Int. Conf. Automated Deduction*. 446–460.

[46] Vasumathi Raman, Alexandre Donzé, Dorsa Sadigh, Richard M Murray, and Sanjit A Seshia. 2015. Reactive synthesis from signal temporal logic specifications. In *Proc. Int. Conf. Hybrid Systems: Computation and Control*. ACM, 239–248.

[47] Dorsa Sadigh and Ashish Kapoor. 2016. Safe Control under Uncertainty with Probabilistic Signal Temporal Logic. In *Proceedings of Robotics: Science and Systems (RSS '16)*.

[48] A. Sangiovanni-Vincentelli. 2007. Quo Vadis, SLD? Reasoning About the Trends and Challenges of System Level Design. *Proc. IEEE* 3 (2007), 467–506.

[49] Alberto Sangiovanni-Vincentelli. 2010. Corsi e ricorsi: The EDA story. *IEEE Solid-State Circuits Magazine* 2, 3 (2010), 6–25.

[50] Alberto Sangiovanni-Vincentelli, Werner Damm, and Roberto Passerone. 2012. Taming Dr. Frankenstein: Contract-Based Design for Cyber-Physical Systems. *European Journal of Control* 18, 3 (2012), 217–238.

[51] Sanjit A Seshia, Shiyan Hu, Wenchao Li, and Qi Zhu. 2017. Design automation of cyber-physical systems: challenges, advances, and opportunities. *IEEE Transactions on Computer-Aided Design of Integrated Circuits and Systems* 36, 9 (2017), 1421–1434.

[52] Y. Shoukry, P. Nuzzo, A. L. Sangiovanni-Vincentelli, S. A. Seshia, G. J. Pappas, and P. Tabuada. 2018. SMC: Satisfiability Modulo Convex Programming. *Proc. IEEE* 106, 9 (Sep. 2018), 1655–1679. https://doi.org/10.1109/JPROC.2018.2849003

[53] Joseph Sifakis. 2015. System design automation: Challenges and limitations. *Proc. IEEE* 103, 11 (2015), 2093–2103.

[54] J. Sztipanovits, T. Bapty, X. Koutsoukos, Z. Lattmann, S. Neema, and E. Jackson. 2018. Model and Tool Integration Platforms for Cyber-Physical System Design. *Proc. IEEE* 106, 9 (Sep. 2018), 1501–1526. https://doi.org/10.1109/JPROC.2018.2838530

[55] Janos Sztipanovits, Xenofon Koutsoukos, Gabor Karsai, Nicholas Kottenstette, Panos Antsaklis, Vijay Gupta, Bill Goodwine, John Baras, and Shige Wang. 2012. Toward a science of cyber–physical system integration. *Proc. IEEE* 100, 1 (2012), 29–44.

[56] J. Wing. 2008. Cyber-Physical Systems. In *Computing Research News*, Vol. 20.

[57] T. Wongpiromsarn, U. Topcu, N. Ozay, H. Xu, and R. M. Murray. 2011. TuLiP: a software toolbox for receding horizon temporal logic planning. In *Intl. Conf. Hybrid Systems: Computation and Control*.

[58] Yang Yang, Alessandro Pinto, Alberto Sangiovanni-Vincentelli, and Qi Zhu. 2010. A design flow for building automation and control systems. In *Real-Time Systems Symposium (RTSS), 2010 IEEE 31st*. IEEE, 105–116.

[59] Qi Zhu and Alberto Sangiovanni-Vincentelli. 2018. Codesign Methodologies and Tools for Cyber–Physical Systems. *Proc. IEEE* 106, 9 (2018), 1484–1500.

My 50-Year Journey from Punched Cards to Swarm Systems

Alberto Sangiovanni Vincentelli

Department of EECS, University of California
Berkeley, California, USA
alberto@berkeley.edu

EXTENDED ABSTRACT

The article is a reflection on my journey during the development of the EDA field, from its early days to its explosive growth and present maturity. The two special issues of the Solid State Circuit Society Magazine "Corsi e Ricorsi: Alberto Sangiovanni Vincentelli and the Evolution of EDA", published in 2010 [1, 2], contain a set of papers that pinpoint some of the stages of this journey.

When I graduated from College in 1971, integrated circuits were in their infancy: few tens of transistors were the norm. Masks were prepared by hand on rubylith with pain and fear to make mistakes. Computers were large mainframes but paling with respect to the computing power that we have available today. There were no graphic terminals and the common ways to provide inputs to a computer were paper tapes and punched cards. Not really an exciting field to invest my future in (or at least so it seemed!). I have always been attracted by algorithms and mathematical formalism, thus I began my research work on system theory with particular attention to large-scale systems. When I went to Berkeley in 1975, I began my work in EDA with numerical analysis methods for solving large scale systems of ODEs. At that time, I joined the Berkeley integrated circuit simulation effort by developing some of the numerical algorithms embedded in the most used academic program in the world, SPICE. My students (E. Lelarasmee and J. White) developed a new set of relaxation-based algorithms (waveform relaxation) for ODEs that not only influenced generations of fast circuit solvers still in use today but also created a new numerical analysis area called dynamic iteration.

In the early 1980s, spurred by my collaboration with IBM, I expanded my research interests to automatic IC layout and logic synthesis. While spending a sabbatical at the IBM Yorktown Research Center, I saw the power of the simulated annealing approach to optimization as proposed by Kirkpatrick. My students and I studied a mathematical analysis of the convergence properties of the algorithm. Based on these findings, we developed automatic layout algorithms embodied in Timber Wolf, authored by C. Sechen, YACR (Yet Another Channel Router) and Mosaico

ISPD '19, April 14–17, 2019, San Francisco, CA, USA.

© 2019 Copyright is held by the owner/author(s).

ACM ISBN 978-1-4503-6253-5/19/04.

DOI: https://doi.org/10.1145/3299902.3311071

that were extensively used in industry (Intel, DEC, TI, National Instruments, Motorola, AMD, and ST Microelectronics, all used the layout tools we developed). Contemporary to this work, my collaborators, my students and I developed a suite of algorithms and programs for two-level (ESPRESSO) and multi-level (MIS) logic synthesis. Logic synthesis was a breakthrough technology as it allowed transforming a Register-Transfer Level description into a set of optimized logic gates by using mathematical techniques. These techniques are still the ones in use today.

Figure 1: Robert Bryton and Alberto Sangiovanni Vincentelli at the Darlington Award ceremony (1988).

By 1982, it was clear that the body of knowledge assembled by the Berkeley group was having a very strong impact in industry worldwide. Pressure mounted to form a new EDA company that could bring this technology to market in a robust and sustainable way. Together with colleagues Newton and Solomon, I founded SDA, which later became Cadence. IC design was largely carried out with few expensive tools running on large mainframes or specialized graphic processors. The design process was slow, often manual and error prone for the lack of verification and analysis tools. The electronic industry was confronted with serious productivity problems. We changed the situation: the introduction of layout editing and simulation on inexpensive general-purpose workstations as well as the introduction of algorithms for the automatic layout of gate-array and standard-cell chips yielded at least one order of magnitude productivity improvements. It made it possible to develop semiconductor chips that were working correctly the first time as opposed to the several manufacturing runs needed earlier. SDA was the first software-only company: other EDA companies in existence at that time were offering a mix of hardware and software solutions. The focus on software only solutions helped providing margins that propelled the company to be one of the 10 largest software companies in the world today.

Parallel to the foundation of SDA, I was interacting closely with most of the leading semiconductor operations in the world: IBM, Intel, Bell Labs, Texas Instruments, HP, ST Microelectronics, Hitachi, Fujitsu, Philips as advisor for design methods and tools. In 1984, the Intel 386 design team headed by Gelsinger decided to rely upon the entire suite of tools we had developed so far. The success of the design and of the tools was a landmark in University-Industry collaboration. The DEC Alpha processor was developed using our design tools in an unprecedented effort to reduce power consumption without losing performance.

After the Berkeley logic synthesis tools became widely used, Aart de Geus and a group of North Carolina GE developers teamed with Richard Newton and me to form Synopsys. At that time, I was instrumental in evangelizing the shift from a channels-and-rows based semi-custom architecture to the sea-of-gates/sea-of-cells architecture. My PhD students (R. Rudell and A. Wang) formed a core part of the product team for Design Compiler, the most successful single product in the history of the EDA industry to date, which was heavily influenced by our results and, in particular, by the contributions of Robert Brayton.

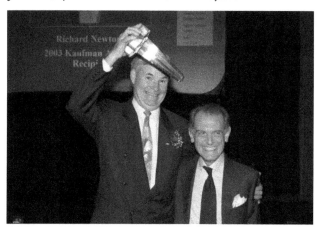

Figure 2: Richard Newton and Alberto Sangiovanni Vincentelli celebrating Richard's Kaufman Award (2003).

By 1992, Cadence and Synopsys were the two leading companies in EDA. Both were public companies and started expanding into each other's markets. Because of conflict of interest, I had to make a hard choice between the two companies. Since 1992, I played a fundamental role in Cadence as a Board Member, Chief Consultant first and then Chief Technology Advisor by helping to guide the technology development process in the company and helping to form its strategy. In 2001, Cadence CEO Bingham and I received in the name of Cadence the IEEE Corporate Innovation Recognition Award.

In the 1990s, I focused my attention to system design and, in particular, to the automotive field. During that period, I started my collaboration with Magneti Marelli and Daniele Pecchini who allowed me to test the ideas and to develop them further in an industrial environment. During this period, I also worked with Mercedes and BMW to help with the development of methodologies and tools for automotive design. The result of this collaboration is the development, in collaboration with Alberto Ferrari, of the foundations of Platform-based Design (PBD), a novel approach to system design. In 1998, the Gigascale System Research Center (GSRC) was established in Berkeley. PBD was a major result of that research program where I led the system-level design group. Because of my interest in the foundations of the design process, PBD was developed to cover the design process for complete systems as large as an automobile or an airplane as well as for subsystems such as a chip or an Electronic Control Unit. The method leverages mathematical concepts that allow assembling designs with heterogeneous components and verifying their properties. Magneti Marelli, a European Tier-1 supplier of automotive electronics, deployed broadly the methodology during the period 1995-1998, obtaining major results in productivity and quality. UTC has recently mounted a major program to introduce a version of the methodology across its various businesses with the efforts of Alberto Ferrari. These efforts continued with Musyc and then with Terra Swarm, two MARCO programs supported by DARPA and the Semiconductor Industry Association, where Cyber-Physical Systems (CPS) and Swarm Systems where the main focus.

In 2006, following the development of work on hybrid and embedded systems with Marika Di Benedetto, Edward Lee and Shankar Sastry, a group was formed to push for a major research effort on systems where interactions between interconnected computing systems and the physical world are of primary importance. This push yielded the manifesto for cyber-physical systems that started a major research and development effort worldwide. Industry 4.0, as articulated by a 2011 acatech (the German Academy of Science and Technology) report, is based on CPS. The manifesto was the basis for an NSF program that started in 2011 and it is still going today.

In parallel, given my European interests and interactions, I contributed to the formation of the European Community Artemis Joint Technology Initiative, a Public Private Partnership that involves most of the European system and electronics companies. Several EU projects in collaboration with A. Benveniste, P. Caspi, W. Damm and J. Sifakis investigated theory and implementation issues in CPS. With M. Di Natale and students, and in particular, with L. Carloni, A. Pinto, C. Pinello, Q. Zhu and A. Davare, we aimed at defining new architectures for chips and systems where guarantees on timing and functionality could be rigorously assessed.

With the strong interest on synthetic biology brewing at Berkeley, D. Densmore developed a set of tools based on PBD, to design new form of life from bio-bricks, an effort that Densmore is still pursuing in his academic career and start-up efforts. An additional application of PBD is in energy efficient buildings. The Singapore Berkeley SinBerBEST effort has been the home of this research that started in collaboration with UTC, students Q. Zhu, Y. Yang and M. Maasoumy, and C. Spanos.

PBD took an interesting turn when it was married with Contract-based Design developed once more in collaboration with A. Benveniste, W. Damm, R. Passerone and others. In particular, the application of PBD to the design of aircraft power distribution systems married with contracts yielded an interesting set of tools and methodologies in collaboration with R. Murray and with the substantial contribution of P. Nuzzo. Contract-based design is now an important effort that is pursued in several academic and industrial circles. Given the growing interests in security, we are presently pursuing with S. Seshia the application of contracts to secure hardware and software systems including swarm systems such as autonomous vehicles.

Figure 3: Alberto's group picture in the Donald O. Pederson Center for Electronic Systems Design at Berkeley (2014).

In summary, my journey has been a continuous search for new avenues where theory can be married to applications and yield provable improvements in all aspects of design.

CCS CONCEPTS

• Design • Verification • Design reuse and communication-based design • Platform-based design • Electronic design automation (EDA) • Logic synthesis • Physical design • Methodologies for EDA • Embedded software

KEYWORDS

Electronic Design Automation; System Level Design

BIOGRAPHY

Alberto Sangiovanni Vincentelli has served on the faculty of the University of California, Berkeley since 1976 and currently holds the Edgar L. and Harold H. Buttner Chair of Electrical Engineering and Computer Sciences at the University of California at Berkeley. As both an academic and entrepreneur, Alberto Sangiovanni Vincentelli propelled electronic design automation (EDA) into an indispensable engineering discipline with his scientific contributions, collaborations with industry and by co-founding the two largest EDA companies (Cadence and Synopsys) in the world. During the 1990s, Sangiovanni Vincentelli developed the foundations of "platform-based design," a comprehensive

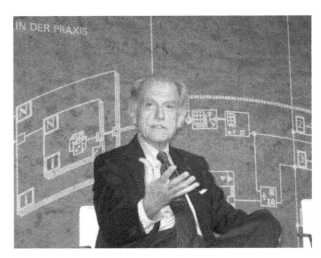

design and analysis methodology for electronic systems. In 2001, he received the Kaufman Award for his pioneering contributions to EDA from the Electronic Design Automation Consortium. In 2011, he was awarded the IEEE/RSE Maxwell Medal *"for groundbreaking contributions that have had an exceptional impact on the development of electronics and electrical engineering or related fields"*. He received an honorary Doctorate from Aalborg University (Denmark) and one from KTH (Sweden). Dr. Sangiovanni Vincentelli presently serves on the Board of Directors of Cadence Design Systems Inc., KPIT Technologies, Sonics, Cogisen, Expert System, UltraSoC (Chairman of the Board), and on the Advisory Board of Atlante Ventures, XSeed, and Walden International. An advisor to leading companies such as Elettronica, Camozzi Group, LendLease, Intel, HP, TI, ST Microelectronics, Mercedes, BMW, Magneti Marelli, Telecom Italia, United Technologies, General Motors and Pirelli, he served as the President of the "Comitato Garanti per la Ricerca" of the Italian Government, the Chairman of the Strategy Committee of Fondo Strategico Italiano and is serving as member of the Advisory Board of the Politecnico di Milano, and as Chairman of the Advisory Board of the MIND (Milano Innovation District) Program. He is a member of the National Academy of Engineering, an IEEE and ACM Fellow. He has published more than 950 papers and 17 books in the areas of EDA, design methodologies, control, hybrid systems and system-level design.

ACKNOWLEDGMENTS

My contributions would not have been possible without the support and collaboration of my dearest colleagues and friends, Bob Brayton and Richard Newton, as well as my graduate students and co-workers. I want to acknowledge the support I received over the years from DARPA, the National Science Foundation, the European Community and industry.

REFERENCES

[1]   Corsi e Ricorsi: Alberto Sangiovanni Vincentelli and the Evolution of EDA, *IEEE Solid State Circuit Society Magazine*, vol. 2, n. 3, Summer 2010
[2]   Corsi e Ricorsi: Alberto Sangiovanni Vincentelli and the Evolution of EDA, *IEEE Solid State Circuit Society Magazine*, vol. 2, n. 4, Winter 2010.

Analog Layout Synthesis

Are We There Yet?

Prasanth Mangalagiri
Intel Corporation
Santa Clara CA USA
prasanth.mangalagiri@intel.com

ABSTRACT

Over the past decade, spurred by advances in mobile computing, there has been a fundamental shift in computing needs of consumer applications. There has been an industry-wide transition from highly CPU-centric to a peripheral-centric, connectivity and data-driven computing. This has paved way to the resurgence of Analog Mixed Signal Designs in both system-on-chip, and core computing architectures. However, the design automation capabilities used in production analog design flows have remained primarily manual with assisted-automation. Analog layout design and layout parasitic dependent circuit convergence remain a key bottleneck in industrial analog IP design.

In this talk, we analyze the current state of analog design automation. We present a continuum of design scenarios, ranging from leading-edge design, to design migration across incremental process derivatives, and define the context of analog layout synthesis in each of these scenarios. We present an overview of recent advances in EDA research specific to analog layout automation [1] [2] and discuss their strengths and weaknesses when adapted to industrial analog IP design flows. Motivated by the confluence of emerging trends in EDA [3], and machine learning research [4], we discuss opportunities to bridge the "last-mile" gaps in automation, by combining constraint-driven, generator-based automation approaches, with statistical data-driven predictive methods.

CCS CONCEPTS

• Physical synthesis • Placement • Reliability • Inductive inference

KEYWORDS

Analog Layout Synthesis; Machine Learning; Layout Migration; Physical Design Automation; Design Convergence; EDA.

ACM Reference format:
Prasanth Mangalagiri. 2018.
Analog Layout Synthesis: Are We There Yet? In *Proceedings of International Symposium on Physical Design (ISPD'19), April 14–17, 2019, San Francisco, CA, USA*. ACM NY, NY, USA. 1 page.
https://doi.org/10.1145/3299902.3311065

BIOGRAPHY

Prasanth Mangalagiri is a Senior Staff Software Engineer at Intel Corporation. He also serves as the Analog Mixed Signal (AMS) Strategic Planner for Product Development Solutions (PDS) group within Intel. He received his Ph.D. in computer science and engineering from The Pennsylvania State University, and his bachelor's from Indian Institute of Technology, Madras. Dr.Mangalagiri's research interests span across a variety of topics in the area of analog physical design automation, design migration, analog layout re-synthesis, placement and routing algorithms, machine learning applications to analog layout automation, and novel approaches towards accelerating analog design convergence.

REFERENCES

[1] Helmut E. Graeb. 2010. Analog Layout Synthesis: A Survey of Topological Approaches (1st ed.). Springer Publishing Company, Incorporated.
[2] Juergen Scheible and Jens Lienig. 2015. Automation of Analog IC Layout: Challenges and Solutions. In Proceedings of the 2015 Symposium on International Symposium on Physical Design (ISPD '15). ACM, New York, NY, USA, 33-40. DOI: https://doi.org/10.1145/2717764.2717781
[3] Andrew B. Kahng. 2018. Reducing time and effort in IC implementation: a roadmap of challenges and solutions. In Proceedings of the 55th Annual Design Automation Conference (DAC '18). ACM, New York, NY, USA, Article 36, 6 pages.DOI: https://doi.org/10.1145/3195970.3199854
[4] William L Hamilton, Rex Ying, and Jure Leskovec. Inductive representation learning on large graphs. Neural Information Processing Systems (NIPS), 2017.

Lagrangian Relaxation Based Gate Sizing With Clock Skew Scheduling - A Fast and Effective Approach

Ankur Sharma
ankur_sharma2@mentor.com
Mentor Graphics, Fremont, USA

David Chinnery
david_chinnery@mentor.com
Mentor Graphics, Fremont, USA

Chris Chu
cnchu@iastate.edu
Iowa State University, Ames, USA

ABSTRACT

Recent work has established Lagrangian relaxation (LR) based gate sizing as state-of-the-art providing the best power reduction with low run time. Gate sizing has limited potential to reduce the power when the timing constraints are tight. By adjusting the arrival times of clock signals (clock skew scheduling), the timing constraints can be relaxed facilitating more power reduction.

Previous LR attempts at simultaneous gate sizing and skew scheduling solved a minimum-cost network flow problem for updating the Lagrange multipliers in each LR iteration, and for optimality assumed continuous sizes with convex delay models. We propose an alternative approach, modifying a LR discrete gate sizing formulation with table lookup non-convex delay models, which are more accurate for modern process technologies. For the Lagrange multiplier update, we use a projection heuristic that is much faster than solving the minimum cost network flow problem.

On the ISPD 2012 gate sizing contest benchmark suite, our proposed approach outperforms the previous min-cost flow based approach by saving 5.3% more power and is 70x faster. Compared to sizing alone with the state-of-the-art LR gate sizer, skew scheduling with sizing saves 19.7% more power with a small runtime penalty.

CCS CONCEPTS

• **Hardware** → **Combinational synthesis**; **Circuit optimization**.

KEYWORDS

Lagrangian relaxation; discrete gate sizing; Vt assignment; clock skew; multi-threading; gate sizing contest

ACM Reference Format:
Ankur Sharma, David Chinnery, and Chris Chu. 2019. Lagrangian Relaxation Based Gate Sizing With Clock Skew Scheduling - A Fast and Effective Approach. In *2019 International Symposium on Physical Design (ISPD '19), April 14–17, 2019, San Francisco, CA, USA*. ACM, New York, NY, USA, 9 pages. https://doi.org/10.1145/3299902.3309746

1 INTRODUCTION

In modern designs, power consumption has increased substantially as larger circuits are being integrated on a single chip while the

ISPD '19, April 14–17, 2019, San Francisco, CA, USA
© 2019 Association for Computing Machinery
ACM ISBN 978-1-4503-6253-5/19/04...$15.00
https://doi.org/10.1145/3299902.3309746

technology continues to shrink. That results in high power density causing reliability challenges, large cooling cost in data centers, and quicker discharge of the batteries in mobile devices. Circuit performance is also limited by power due to higher power densities. Thus, reducing the power has become a major concern.

In physical design, gate sizing is one of the most frequently used circuit optimizations. Each gate can be implemented by several possible cell options, with different sizes and threshold voltages (Vth). Different cell options trade off area or power for delay. A gate-sizer has to choose a suitable cell for every gate to minimize the objective cost while meeting the design timing constraints.

Synchronous circuits have combinational gates forming *data paths* and sequential gates that receive the clock signal. The setup timing constraint requires the data path signal to reach the sequential gate before the arrival of the clock signal. If a data path violates such a constraint, a gate sizing tool would resize gates on the path to speed it up. An alternative is to delay (*skew*) the arrival of the clock at the sequential gate.

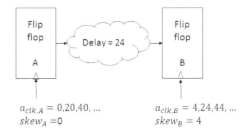

Figure 1: Example of clock skew to meet the timing constraint.

An example is shown in Figure 1. There are two flip-flops, A and B. They receive the same clock edge every 20 time units. There is a combinational block between them with a worst path delay of 24. The data signal is required to arrive at flip-flop B in ≤20. By delaying the arrival at the clock pin of B by 4 units, the timing constraint can be satisfied. Assigning clock skews to improve performance of the design is *clock skew optimization* [1]. A gate sizer with only cell sizes to vary is limited in how much power/area it can recover. Varying the clock skew provides an additional degree of freedom that gate sizers can utilize to improve the results as demonstrated previously [2–4]. These previous works make simplifying assumptions like continuity in sizes and convexity of delay models, and their approaches are very slow on larger designs.

In this paper, we propose a new flow for effective simultaneous gate sizing and clock skew scheduling that seamlessly integrates with the state-of-the-art gate sizing tool. For comparison, we also extend the previous approach from Wang et al. [3]. Wang et al. transformed the original timing graph to eliminate the skew variables and in the process introduced loops in the graph. The Lagrangian dual problem on the transformed graph was modeled as a min-cost network flow problem. Assuming continuity in the cell sizes and convexity of the delay models, their algorithm maximized the dual cost to realize primal optimality, if the primal problem was feasible. We detail how to apply their algorithm with more realistic constraints, i.e., discrete cell sizes and non-convex delay models, and discuss several limitations of this approach in the presence of these realistic constraints. We refer to this approach as *NetFlow*.

Our proposed approach for simultaneous gate sizing and skew scheduling is built upon a state-of-the-art LR gate sizing algorithm. We add skews variables to the LR formulation while keeping the timing graph directed acyclic. The timing graph must be acyclic to apply the projection based Lagrange multiplier update heuristic which is crucial to the performance of state-of-the-art gate sizing tools. We propose a new flow to simultaneously update skew along with the cell sizes and the Lagrange multipliers. We discuss our skew update strategy and propose modifications to the Lagrange multiplier update strategy in order to reflect the modified timing constraints caused by skewed clocks. We refer to this approach as *EGSS* which stands for *Effective Gate* sizing with *Skew Scheduling*. For benchmarking, we use the ISPD 2012 gate sizing contest benchmark suite [5]. Compared to NetFlow, EGSS achieves an average of 5.3% additional power savings, and is 70x faster in total run time.

Our main contributions are as follows:

- We derive an LR formulation for the simultaneous gate sizing and clock skew scheduling problem while preserving the directed acyclic structure of the underlying timing graph.
- We propose a modified Lagrange multiplier update heuristic accounting for the skew.
- We present a simultaneous gate sizing and clock skew scheduling approach that seamlessly integrates with the state-of-the-art gate sizing tool. We empirically verify it's efficiency.
- In the context of discrete gate sizing with non-convex delays, we identify and empirically demonstrate several limitations of achieving primal optimality via dual maximization.

The rest of the paper is organized as follows. Section 2 summarizes previous work on LR gate sizing and sizing with skew scheduling. Section 3 formulates the problem. Sections 4 and 5 present NetFlow then EGSS. Section 6 discusses limitations of achieving primal optimality via dual optimality. Section 7 briefly describes the greedy refinement strategies that we use in this work. We present the experimental results in Section 8 and conclude in Section 9.

2 PREVIOUS WORK

The gate sizing problem has been researched for several decades. Earlier, most of the approaches assumed continuity in the gate sizes, convex delay models and experimented on relatively smaller designs. The gate sizing contests organized by Intel in ISPD 2012 [5] and ISPD 2013 [6] gave a fresh momentum to research in this area. The objective in the contests was to minimize the leakage power under the delay constraints. Contests were based on realistic constraints, discrete cell options and table lookup based non-linear delay models, and provided a suite of small to large designs having up to a million gates for benchmarking. Most of the post-contest

publications in gate sizing utilized the contest framework for benchmarking and thus, greatly pushed ahead the state-of-the-art.

Some of the post-contest publications like [7] used sensitivity guided greedy metaheuristics to reduce timing violations and then reduce the power. Daboul et al. [8] modeled the gate sizing problem as a resource sharing problem. However, most of the gate sizers that were published used LR formulation [9–13]. Li et al. [9] first achieved minimum clock period and then recovered power using the min-cost network flow formulation. Ren et al. [14] also used network flow for discrete cell sizing, but neither of their formulations considered skew. Flach et al. [11] improvised on the projection based Lagrange multiplier update heuristic that was originally proposed in [15]. They demonstrated the least power results on the ISPD 2012 gate sizing contest designs. Sharma et al. [12] proposed a multi-threaded LR gate sizer and reported the least runtime, which they further improved in [13]. They proposed a simple and tunable framework for projection based Lagrange multiplier update which significantly improved the convergence. LR gate sizing using the projection heuristic has been demonstrated to yield designs with lower power and much smaller runtime compared to the other approaches. The original LR gate sizing idea is credited to [16].

Some of the previous works on simultaneous gate sizing and skew scheduling include [2–4, 17, 18]. Chuang et al. [2] directly solved the primal problem by formulating it as a linear programming problem using the piecewise-linear (PWL) approximations of the convex delays. Roy et al. [18] assumed continuous sizes and convex delays, and thus were able to minimize the Lagrangian subproblem simultaneously over size and skew variables using a bound constrained optimization solver. Without giving much details they claim to use the projection heuristic of [15] for updating Lagrange multipliers. Wang et al. [3] eliminated the skew variables from the primal problem in order for the Hessian of the primal objective to be positive definite so that optimality of their algorithm can be guaranteed. As a result, the timing graph could no longer be acyclic. Wang et al. maximized the dual cost by solving the min-cost network flow formulation of the Lagrangian dual problem. While they prove primal optimality under the assumptions that sizes are continuous and delay models are convex, these assumptions are not valid in modern design methodologies which would limit the effectiveness of their approach. Shklover et al. [4] accounted for the cost of implementing the clock skew via clock tree. Although they formulate a simultaneous discrete gate sizing and skew scheduling problem using LR, they mainly focus on clock tree optimization via dynamic programming. For sizing of the datapath gates and Lagrange multiplier update, they simply refer to the previous works [3, 16, 18]. The multiplier update strategies used in these previous works [3, 16, 18] are either too slow, especially on large designs, or have problem converging to a good solution [15].

3 PROBLEM FORMULATION

In order to formally define the problem, we use the notation tabulated in Table 1. The objective is to minimize the leakage power subject to the delay constraints, maximum load constraints, and maximum slew (transition time) constraints. Skew variables are bounded. Only combinational gates can change size, sequential gates are a fixed size. The primal problem is formally defined as:

Table 1: Commonly used notations.

Notation	Meaning
T	Target clock period
$\mathcal{G}$	Set of gates in the design
$\mathcal{X}_g$	Discrete set of cells for gate g
$x_g \in \mathcal{X}_g$	Current cell for gate g
$\mathcal{FF}$	Set of flip-flops in the design
$\mathcal{PO}$	Set of primary outputs in the design
w_k	Skew at flip-flop $k \in \mathcal{FF}$
$\mathcal{N}$	Set of nodes in the timing graph
$\mathcal{E}$	Set of timing arcs in the timing graph
$d_{ij}(\boldsymbol{x})$	Delay function of the timing arc (i, j)
λ_{ij}	Lagrange multiplier for the timing arc (i, j)
a_i	Arrival time at node i
a_{d_k}, a_{q_k}	Arrival times at D and Q pins of flip-flop k
$setup_k, d_{clk2q_k}(\boldsymbol{x})$	Setup and clock to Q delay of flip-flop k
$\lambda_{d_k}, \lambda_{q_k}$	Lagrange multipliers associated with the setup and the clock to Q delay timing arcs of flip-flop k
$gate\_power(x)$	Power of cell x
$p(\boldsymbol{x})$	Total power of the design
$max\_load(x)$	Maximum load capacity of cell x
$\boldsymbol{x}, \boldsymbol{w}, \boldsymbol{a}, \boldsymbol{\lambda}$	Respective set of variables x, w, a and λ
$load_g(\boldsymbol{x})$	Capacitive load at the output of gate g
$slew_i(\boldsymbol{x})$	Slew at node i
max_slew	Maximum slew defined in the cell library

$$\underset{\boldsymbol{x},\boldsymbol{a},\boldsymbol{w}}{\text{minimize}} \quad p(\boldsymbol{x})$$

$$
\begin{aligned}
\text{subject to} \quad & a_i + d_{ij}(\boldsymbol{x}) \le a_j && \forall (i,j) \in \mathcal{E} \\
& a_{po} \le T && \forall po \in \mathcal{PO} \\
& a_{d_k} \le T + w_k - setup_k && \forall k \in \mathcal{FF} \\
& w_k + d_{clk2q_k}(\boldsymbol{x}) \le a_{q_k} && \forall k \in \mathcal{FF} \quad (1) \\
& load_g(\boldsymbol{x}) \le max\_load(x_g) && \forall g \in \mathcal{G} \\
& slew_g(\boldsymbol{x}) \le max\_slew && \forall g \in \mathcal{G} \\
& x_g \in \mathcal{X}_g && \forall g \in \mathcal{G} \\
& w_{min} \le w_k \le w_{max} && \forall k \in \mathcal{FF}
\end{aligned}
$$

where minimization is over the set of discrete cell variables $\boldsymbol{x}$, continuous arrival time variables $\boldsymbol{a}$, and continuous skew variables $\boldsymbol{w}$. $p(\boldsymbol{x})$ is the sum of the power over all the gates, $p(\boldsymbol{x}) = \sum_{g \in \mathcal{G}} gate\_power(x_g)$. Since Wang et al. [3] did not consider the power cost of skew implementation, for a fair comparison against their NetFlow approach, we also do not account for the clock tree power in our formulation (1). For an example of how to incorporate clock power, refer [4]. Although our EGSS approach complements the work of Shklover et al. [4], we cannot compare against them because they used proprietary designs which are not available.

We use table lookup based non-linear, non-convex delay models for modeling cell arcs. Per ISPD 2012 contest framework, interconnect is modeled by a lumped capacitance without any resistance, so the net timing arcs have zero delay. Even if interconnects are modeled by distributed RC trees as in the ISPD 2013 contest, the

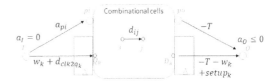

Figure 2: Timing graph for EGSS approach. Graph is directed acyclic with skew variables.

problem formulation and our approach would not change. With RC interconnects, the main challenge is the interconnect and the cell delay modeling which is beyond the scope of this work.

Timing constraints in the primal problem (1) are usually modeled by a timing graph. The underlying timing graph used by our proposed EGSS approach is shown in Figure 2. It was presented by Wang et al. in [3]. The graph has two dummy nodes and several dummy edges. Two dummy nodes are the global input I, and the global output O. There are dummy edges from I to output pins on flip-flops (Q_k); from I to primary inputs (pi); from input pins on flip-flops (D_k) to O; and, from primary outputs (po) to O. Although Wang et al. transformed it to eliminate skew variables and in the process introduced loops (directed cycles) in the timing graph, we instead propose to retain skews as variables and preserve the graph's directed acyclic structure. Further, Wang et al. had a backward edge from O to I with a weight of $-T$ which created more loops. Unlike that, to avoid loops in the timing graph, we adjust weights on the dummy edges so that the arrival times at I and O satisfy the following properties: $a_I = 0$ and $a_O \le 0$, as shown in Figure 2. In the presence of a clock tree, our timing graph can be extended to include timing arcs from the clock tree without creating loops. But it is not clear how skew variables can be eliminated in the presence of timing constraints along the clock tree.

Following the methodology of Chen et al. for gate sizing [16], we also relax the timing constraints. To penalize violations in the timing constraints, each constraint is associated with a non-negative Lagrange multiplier. These multipliers indicate the timing criticality of the corresponding arc. For a given set of Lagrange multipliers $\boldsymbol{\lambda} \ge 0$, the Lagrange function can be defined as:

$$
\begin{aligned}
L_{\boldsymbol{\lambda}}(\boldsymbol{x}, \boldsymbol{a}, \boldsymbol{w}): \quad & p(\boldsymbol{x}) + \sum_{(i,j) \in \mathcal{E}} \lambda_{ij} \times \left(a_i + d_{ij}(\boldsymbol{x}) - a_j\right) \\
& + \sum_{po \in \mathcal{PO}} \lambda_{po} \times \left(a_{po} - T\right) \\
& + \sum_{k \in \mathcal{FF}} \lambda_{d_k} \times \left(a_{d_k} - T - w_k + setup_k\right) \\
& + \sum_{k \in \mathcal{FF}} \lambda_{q_k} \times \left(w_k + d_{clk2q_k}(\boldsymbol{x}) - a_{q_k}\right)
\end{aligned}
\quad (2)
$$

LR gate sizing formulations typically do not relax the maximum load and maximum slew constraints. We also propose not to relax the skew bounds (last constraint of (1)), since such violations are easy to compute. The Lagrangian dual function is the minimum value of the Lagrangian function over $\boldsymbol{x}$, $\boldsymbol{a}$ and $\boldsymbol{w}$, for given $\boldsymbol{\lambda}$,

$$g(\lambda) = \underset{\boldsymbol{x}, \boldsymbol{a}, \boldsymbol{w}}{\text{minimize}} \quad L_\lambda(\boldsymbol{x}, \boldsymbol{a}, \boldsymbol{w})$$

$$
\begin{aligned}
\text{subject to} \quad & load_g(\boldsymbol{x}) \le max\_load(x_g) && \forall g \in \mathcal{G} \\
& slew_g(\boldsymbol{x}) \le max\_slew && \forall g \in \mathcal{G} \quad (3)\\
& x_g \in \mathcal{X}_g && \forall g \in \mathcal{G} \\
& w_{min} \le w_k \le w_{max} && \forall k \in \mathcal{FF}
\end{aligned}
$$

The Lagrangian function is affine in arrival times, so for the dual function to be finite, the multipliers must satisfy the *flow constraints* shown in (4). This argument is due to Wang et al. [3].

$$\sum_{\{v|(i,v)\in\mathcal{E}\}} \lambda_{iv} = \sum_{\{u|(u,i)\in\mathcal{E}\}} \lambda_{ui} \quad \forall i \in \mathcal{N}\backslash\{I, O\} \quad (4)$$

Denote by Ω the Lagrange multipliers satisfying (4):

$$\Omega = \{\boldsymbol{\lambda} | \boldsymbol{\lambda} \text{ satisfies (4) and } \boldsymbol{\lambda} \ge 0\}$$

Applying the flow constraints (4) to (2), arrival time variables can be eliminated, and by ignoring the constant terms involving T and $setup_k$, the Lagrangian function can be simplified as

$$
\begin{aligned}
P_{\lambda \in \Omega}(\boldsymbol{x}, \boldsymbol{w}) : \quad & p(\boldsymbol{x}) + \sum_{(i,j)\in\mathcal{E}} (\lambda_{ij} \times d_{ij}(\boldsymbol{x})) + \\
& \sum_{k\in\mathcal{FF}} \lambda_{q_k} \times d_{clk2q_k} + \sum_{k\in\mathcal{FF}} \left(\lambda_{q_k} - \lambda_{d_k}\right) \times w_k
\end{aligned}
$$
$$(5)$$

For $\lambda \in \Omega$, the dual function can be re-written as the following minimization problem, the *Lagrangian relaxation subproblem* or LRS_λ,

$$
\begin{aligned}
g(\boldsymbol{\lambda} \in \Omega) = \underset{\boldsymbol{x}, \boldsymbol{w}}{\text{minimize}} \quad & P_\lambda(\boldsymbol{x}, \boldsymbol{w}) \\
\text{subject to} \quad & \text{constraints in (3)}
\end{aligned}
$$
$$(6)$$

The Lagrange dual problem (*LDP*) maximizes the dual function (6),

$$
\begin{aligned}
\underset{\boldsymbol{\lambda} \in \Omega}{\text{maximize}} \quad & g(\boldsymbol{\lambda}) - \sum_{po\in\mathcal{PO}} \lambda_{po} \times T + \\
& \sum_{k\in\mathcal{FF}} \lambda_{d_k} \times (setup_k - T)
\end{aligned}
$$
$$(7)$$

The LDP is solved iteratively. In each iteration, for given $\boldsymbol{\lambda}$, LRS_λ (6) is solved to update $\boldsymbol{x}, \boldsymbol{w}$; and for given $\boldsymbol{x}, \boldsymbol{w}$, LDP objective is maximized in the neighborhood of current $\boldsymbol{\lambda}$. Thus, $\boldsymbol{\lambda}$ are incrementally updated. With updated $\boldsymbol{\lambda}$, LRS_λ is solved again in the next LDP iteration (also referred to as LR iteration).

4 NETFLOW

Before describing our proposed EGSS approach in Section 5, we first discuss the NetFlow approach. The core idea of NetFlow (but not the name) is due to Wang et al. [3]. We make two changes. To optimally solve LRS_λ, Wang et al. assumed continuous sizes and convex delay models. We extend their LRS_λ solver to apply it to discrete sizes and table lookup based delay models. Also we fill in the missing details for setting bounds on the Lagrange multipliers.

Wang et al. transformed the timing graph to eliminate skew variables from the set of primal variables. This transformation resulted in directed cycles in the timing graph, as shown in Figure 3. Therefore, their Lagrangian function $L_\lambda^{NF}(\boldsymbol{x})$ is different than ours

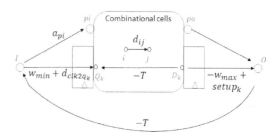

Figure 3: The timing graph for NetFlow which has directed cycles due to additional edges from D_k to Q_k from eliminating skews.

(2). See [3] for the complete expression of $L_\lambda^{NF}(\boldsymbol{x})$. The Lagrangian relaxation subproblem for NetFlow (LRS_λ^{NF}) is defined as:

$$
\begin{aligned}
g^{NF}(\boldsymbol{\lambda} \in \Omega) : \underset{\boldsymbol{x}}{\text{minimize}} \quad & L_\lambda^{NF}(\boldsymbol{x}) \\
\text{subject to} \quad & \text{constraints in (3)} \quad (8)\\
& \text{except } w \text{ bounds}
\end{aligned}
$$

g^{NF} is the dual function. Then, LDP^{NF} is defined as,

$$\underset{\boldsymbol{\lambda} \in \Omega}{\text{maximize}} \quad g^{NF}(\boldsymbol{\lambda}) \quad (9)$$

Wang et al. proposed a minimum cost network flow formulation, $MCNF_\lambda$, to solve LDP^{NF} in the neighborhood of current $\boldsymbol{\lambda}$,

$$
\begin{aligned}
\underset{\Delta\boldsymbol{\lambda}}{\text{minimize}} \quad & \left\langle -\nabla g^{NF}(\boldsymbol{\lambda}), \Delta\boldsymbol{\lambda} \right\rangle \\
\text{subject to} \quad & \Delta\boldsymbol{\lambda}_{lb} \le \Delta\boldsymbol{\lambda} \le \Delta\boldsymbol{\lambda}_{ub} \quad (10)\\
& \Delta\boldsymbol{\lambda} + \boldsymbol{\lambda} \in \Omega
\end{aligned}
$$

where, $\nabla g^{NF}(\boldsymbol{\lambda})$ is the gradient of the dual function g^{NF} at $\boldsymbol{\lambda}$; and $\langle . \rangle$ denotes the dot product. To solve the gate sizing problem, the dual function is maximized over $\Delta\boldsymbol{\lambda} \in \Omega$. The intuition behind the algorithm is to iteratively improve the dual $g^{NF}(\boldsymbol{\lambda})$ by maximizing its first-order approximation in neighborhood of the current $\boldsymbol{\lambda}$.

Pseudo-code is shown in Algorithm 1. All Lagrange multipliers are initialized to 0 as that is a trivial dual feasible solution. LRS_λ^{NF} is solved to initialize the sizes. Since the multipliers are all zeros, the optimal solution to LRS_λ^{NF} is the minimum power subject to maximum load and slew constraints. Then, we initialize the skews to 0 and update the timing. The timing is needed to compute the bounds on $\Delta\boldsymbol{\lambda}$. Our bound computation strategy is discussed later in this section, and our skew update strategy is discussed in Section 5. After the initialization, LDP^{NF} is iteratively solved. In each iteration, firstly the lower and the upper bounds are computed. Then, $MCNF_\lambda$ (10) is solved using the computed bounds. Optimal solution $\Delta\boldsymbol{\lambda}^*$ gives the steepest ascent direction of $g^{NF}(\boldsymbol{\lambda})$. Then, a line search is performed along $\Delta\boldsymbol{\lambda}^*$ in order to improve g^{NF} in 5 equispaced steps. At each step, LRS_λ^{NF} is solved. Based on the step-size that yielded the maximum g^{NF}, the multipliers are updated. Then, skews and timing are updated, only for the purpose of computing the bounds. Iterations continue until the change in g^{NF} is below a threshold, or a maximum number of iterations are reached. Since the problem is discrete and non-convex, this approach has several limitations which are discussed in Section 6. Consequently, even though the dual function converges, often there are some timing violations and scope for further power reduction. Therefore, we add a greedy refinement step at the end to try to recover any remaining timing violations and reduce power.

Algorithm 1 Pseudo code for NetFlow

1: $\boldsymbol{\lambda} = 0$. Solve $LRS_{\boldsymbol{\lambda}}^{NF}$ (8) for $\boldsymbol{x}$
2: Initialize skew to w_{min}. Update timing.
3: **while** $g^{NF}(\boldsymbol{\lambda})$ has not converged and iterations $< N$ **do**
4:     $(\triangle\boldsymbol{\lambda}_{lb}, \triangle\boldsymbol{\lambda}_{ub}) \leftarrow$ compute bounds on $\triangle\boldsymbol{\lambda}$
5:     Solve $MCNF_{\boldsymbol{\lambda}}$ (10) for optimal $\triangle\boldsymbol{\lambda}^*$
6:     Perform line search on $g^{NF}(\boldsymbol{\lambda} + step \times \triangle\boldsymbol{\lambda}^*) \rhd 0 < step \le 1$ for an increase in g^{NF}.
7:     Update $\boldsymbol{\lambda}$
8:     Update skew. Update timing (for bound computation)
9: Greedy refinements

Solving $LRS_{\boldsymbol{\lambda}}^{NF}$. The strategy in [3] to solve the subproblem (8) assumes continuity in sizes and convexity of delay models. With discrete sizes and non-convex delay models, it becomes a difficult combinatorial problem. We adapt the LRS solver routine from the discrete LR gate sizing tool [9]. Although it does not guarantee optimality, its variants are the basis of state-of-the-art gate sizers [11, 13]. In this routine, all gates are traversed in the forward topological order. For each gate, assuming other gates are fixed, all the cell sizes are evaluated and the cell is chosen which minimizes the objective. To compute the objective quickly, timing is propagated only among the fanin and the fanout gates. To topologically order the cyclic timing graph, we cut it at the flip-flops. We also apply multi-threading techniques from [12] to parallelize the LRS solver.

Bound Computation. Wang et al. [3] did not give details on how to set the bounds. Based on the insights from the state-of-the-art LR gate sizing works, we propose to set the upper and lower bounds on $\triangle\lambda_{ij}$ for each combinational cell timing arc (i, j), as follows:

$$\triangle\lambda_{ij,ub} = \max \left\{ \frac{\lambda_{ij} \times |(q_j - a_i - d_{ij})|}{T}, \bar{\lambda} \times M \right\}$$

$$\triangle\lambda_{ij,lb} = \max \{-\lambda_{ij}, -\triangle\lambda_{ij,ub}\} \qquad (11)$$

where, q_j is the required time at node j; $\bar{\lambda}$ is the average value of multipliers over all the arcs; and M is a tuning parameter. We make the upper bound proportional to the current value of the Lagrange multiplier and the slack along the arc. If either of them is large, that indicates the need for large changes in the multiplier. For near-critical arcs, the upper bound can be very small which slows convergence. Hence, we ensure that the upper bounds are at least of the order of the average multiplier value across the design. Lower bounds are set to guarantee non-negative multipliers. For some arcs, including the arc from O to I, it is not necessary to set explicit bounds as their multiplier values are determined by other incident arcs, being constrained by the Ω space.

5 EGSS: EFFECTIVE GATE SIZING WITH SKEW SCHEDULING

In this section we describe our approach for simultaneous gate sizing and skew scheduling. We call it *EGSS*. We modify portions

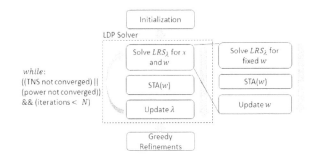

Figure 4: Flow of our proposed EGSS. STA is static timing analysis.

of a state-of-the-art LR gate sizer. In particular, we re-use the LRS solver from the existing gate sizer, propose a new skew update strategy, and extend the projection based heuristic for the Lagrange multiplier update which is much faster than solving the minimum cost network flow problem as done in NetFlow.

Figure 4 shows the overall flow of EGSS. It has three stages: initialization, solving LDP, and greedy refinements. Initially, gates are sized to minimum power cell sizes subject to the maximum load and slew constraints; skews are initialized to the minimum values; timing is updated; and Lagrange multipliers are initialized to one and projected onto the Ω space. Unlike NetFlow, because of the multiplication in the Lagrange multiplier update which is discussed later in this section, the multipliers cannot be initialized to zero.

The LDP solver fixes most timing violations and reduces the power. In each iteration, it solves the $LRS_{\boldsymbol{\lambda}}$ (6) over size and skew variables, updates timing, and updates the multipliers. During the first few iterations, multipliers are updated to reduce total negative slack (TNS). The TNS is the total of all the timing violations in the second and third constraint of (1). Once the timing violations are reduced, multipliers are updated to focus on reducing power. There are extra checks in the LRS solver to avoid timing violations. Like NetFlow, greedy refinements are performed in the last stage.

5.1 Solving $LRS_{\boldsymbol{\lambda}}$

In LR gate sizing, sizes are the only variables in the Lagrangian relaxation subproblem (LRS). The LRS is a tough combinatorial problem, and adding skew variables for skew scheduling makes it even more difficult. Heuristically, we solve $LRS_{\boldsymbol{\lambda}}$ (6) separately for sizes and skews. The objective of $LRS_{\boldsymbol{\lambda}}$ from (5) can be split into two functions: a function of sizes, and a function of skews, $P_{\boldsymbol{\lambda}\in\Omega}(\boldsymbol{x}, \boldsymbol{w}) = H_{\boldsymbol{\lambda}\in\Omega}(\boldsymbol{x}) + Q_{\boldsymbol{\lambda}\in\Omega}(\boldsymbol{w})$ where,

$$H_{\boldsymbol{\lambda}\in\Omega}(\boldsymbol{x}) = p(\boldsymbol{x}) + \sum_{(i,j)\in\mathcal{E}} \lambda_{ij} \times d_{ij}(\boldsymbol{x}) + \sum_{k\in\mathcal{FF}} \lambda_{q_k} \times d_{clk2q_k}(\boldsymbol{x})$$

$$Q_{\boldsymbol{\lambda}\in\Omega}(\boldsymbol{w}) = \sum_{k\in\mathcal{FF}} \left(\lambda_{q_k} - \lambda_{d_k} \right) \times w_k$$

$$(12)$$

In our scheme to solve $LRS_{\boldsymbol{\lambda}}$, we first minimize $H_{\boldsymbol{\lambda}\in\Omega}(\boldsymbol{x})$ assuming skews are fixed, then update timing, and lastly update skews based on the $Q_{\boldsymbol{\lambda}\in\Omega}(\boldsymbol{w})$ function - see Figure 4. Note that skews do not affect $H_{\boldsymbol{\lambda}\in\Omega}(\boldsymbol{x})$, and sizes do not affect $Q_{\boldsymbol{\lambda}\in\Omega}(\boldsymbol{w})$, so they can be optimized separately. Shklover et al. [4] had a similar framework to solve LRS_λ, but used different algorithms to minimize $H_{\lambda \in \Omega}(\boldsymbol{x})$ and update skew.

To minimize $H_{\lambda \in \Omega}(\boldsymbol{x})$, we use the LRS solver from [12]. This LRS solver is similar to that for the NetFlow approach in Section 4, but it performs a *local slack check* during every cell size evaluation. Each new candidate cell size is checked for local timing degradation. Only a cell size that either does not or minimally degrades the local timing can be assigned to a gate. This check is necessary to keep the timing violations under control while reducing power. This check is not applied while solving LRS_λ^{NF} (8) because the NetFlow objective is dual maximization, and reduction in TNS and power (primal objective) is expected as a consequence.

5.2 Skew Update

Consider minimizing $Q_{\lambda \in \Omega}(\boldsymbol{w})$ (12) to determine skews subject to the bounds. Since the objective is linear in skews, minimization is trivial. For each flip-flop k, if $\lambda_{q_k} > \lambda_{d_k}$, then $w_k = w_{min}$, else $w_k = w_{max}$. Intuitively, if the Q pin is more timing critical than the D pin, then reduce the skew to reduce timing violations at the Q pin. If the D pin is more timing critical, then increase the skew to increase the slack at the D pin. Note that always setting skew to either of the extreme values can cause oscillations. Hence, we propose the following skew update strategy,

$$\triangle w_k = \frac{slack_q - slack_d}{2}$$
$$w_k = \max\{w_{min}, \min\{w_{max}, w_k + \triangle w_k\}\} \tag{13}$$

5.3 Modified Lagrange Multiplier Update

The projection based Lagrange multiplier update strategy is crucial for fast convergence and final solution quality. A simple framework for this multiplier update was proposed in [13]. We extend it to account for the skew impact. If skew at a flip-flop is positive, then the timing paths ending at its D pin have a larger required time which reduces the rate at which multipliers increase. Pseudo code for the Lagrange multiplier update is shown in Algorithm 2.

Algorithm 2 Lagrange multiplier update algorithm

---

for each flip-flop k **do**

$\quad \lambda_{d_k} = \lambda_{d_k} \times \left(1 + \frac{a_{d_k} + setup_k - T - w_k}{T}\right)^K$

for each primary output po **do**

$\quad \lambda_{po} = \lambda_{po} \times \left(1 + \frac{a_{po} - T}{T}\right)^K$

for each timing arc (i, j) **do**

$\quad \lambda_{ij} = \lambda_{ij} \times \left(1 + \frac{a_i + d_{ij} - q_j}{T}\right)^K \quad \triangleright q_j$: required time at j

Projection to satisfy flow constraints. Refer [15]

---

6 NETFLOW VS EGSS: LIMITATIONS OF OPTIMIZING THE PRIMAL PROBLEM VIA DUAL MAXIMIZATION

The NetFlow approach is based on results from Lagrangian duality theory [19], that under certain conditions which generally hold

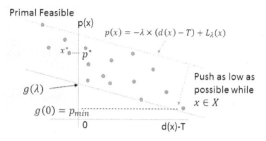

Figure 5: Minimization of Lagrangian function $L_\lambda(x)$ for a single gate circuit is shown in the power-delay space parameterized by the discrete cell size x. X-axis is delay shifted to the right by T. Y-axis is the power. Each dot corresponds to a unique cell size x. Left of the power axis ($d(x) - T \leq 0$) is primal feasible. Minimum feasible power p^* and minimum possible power p_{min} are indicated above.

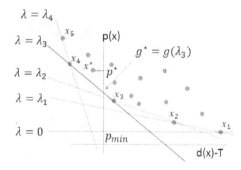

Figure 6: Maximization of dual function $g(\lambda)$ is shown for a single gate circuit in (a) primal space and, (b) dual space. g^* is the dual optimal attained at $\lambda = \lambda_3$. Due to non-convexity and discreteness there is a non-zero duality gap, $p^* - g^*$. For the same reasons, $L_{\lambda_3}(x)$ is minimized at x_4 and x_3. While x_4 is primal feasible, x_3 is not.

for the convex and continuous primal problems, primal optimality can be attained by maximizing the dual function. However, for non-convex discrete gate sizing which is NP-hard [20], NetFlow has limitations:

- A non-zero duality gap
- Minimizer $\boldsymbol{x}^*$ of the Lagrangian while solving LRS for the optimal set of dual variables $\boldsymbol{\lambda}^*$ may not be primal feasible
- Discreteness tends to cause oscillations

We explain these limitations with the help of a simple illustration of the process of dual maximization in the primal space.

Consider a single inverter circuit with cell size x as the only variable. Let power of the circuit be $p(x)$ and delay be $d(x)$. Figure 5 shows these values for different sizes of the inverter. Each point corresponds to a distinct size. Let $\lambda \geq 0$ be the Lagrange multiplier associated with the timing arc of the inverter. Then, the Lagrange function can be written as $L_\lambda(x) = p(x) + \lambda \times (d(x) - T)$. In the power-delay space, this is a line with slope $-\lambda$ and the intercept on the $p(x)$ axis is the value of the Lagrangian function. Solving LRS, or computing the dual function, is equivalent to minimizing $L_\lambda(x)$, i.e., pushing the line as low as possible as long as it passes through at least one design point. This process is illustrated in Figure 5.

Table 2: A summary of the results for ISPD 2012 benchmarks suite [5] is shown for three flows: Sharma et al. [13] which is the baseline for comparison - it assumes a fixed skew; NF (NetFlow); and EGSS. For NetFlow and EGSS minimum and maximum skew bounds are 0 and 165ps. The final optimized netlist for each design from all three flows has zero timing violations.

Benchmark	Comb. Gates	Clock T, (ps)	Leakage Power (W)			Power saved (%)		Total Runtime (min)			Speedup (X)	
			[13]	NF	EGSS	Vs [13]	Vs NF	[13]	NF	EGSS	Vs [13]	Vs NF
DMA_slow	23109	900	0.135	0.111	0.104	23.1	6.6	0.07	7.90	0.08	0.9	94.0
pci_bridge32_slow	29844	720	0.098	0.073	0.072	26.9	2.2	0.09	8.70	0.10	0.9	88.0
des_perf_slow	102427	900	0.583	0.420	0.404	30.6	3.7	0.32	21.09	0.30	1.1	69.2
vga_lcd_slow	147812	700	0.329	0.310	0.310	5.9	0.2	0.44	28.35	0.44	1.0	64.0
b19_slow	212674	2500	0.569	0.577	0.556	2.2	3.7	0.83	45.75	1.24	0.7	37.0
leon3mp_slow	540352	1800	1.335	1.326	1.321	1.0	0.4	2.52	194.90	2.91	0.9	67.0
netcard_slow	860949	1900	1.763	1.762	1.762	0.1	0.0	2.35	343.90	2.82	0.8	122.0
DMA_fast	23109	770	0.245	0.173	0.137	44.3	20.8	0.08	9.20	0.10	0.8	92.0
pci_bridge32_fast	29844	660	0.141	0.083	0.078	44.7	6.2	0.10	9.20	0.11	0.9	84.0
des_perf_fast	102427	735	1.436	0.686	0.615	57.2	10.3	0.40	23.39	0.34	1.2	69.1
vga_lcd_fast	147812	610	0.417	0.318	0.316	24.3	0.8	0.56	27.90	0.50	1.1	55.3
b19_fast	212674	2100	0.729	0.823	0.682	6.5	17.1	1.13	19.58	1.61	0.7	12.2
leon3mp_fast	540352	1500	1.449	1.393	1.360	6.1	2.4	3.13	233.10	3.56	0.9	65.5
netcard_fast	860949	1200	1.846	1.804	1.800	2.5	0.2	3.33	237.05	3.98	0.8	59.5
Overall average			0.791	0.704	0.680	19.7	5.3	1.10	86.43	1.29	0.9	69.9

Now we explain dual maximization using Figure 6. Initially, when $\lambda = 0$, we know that $g(0) = p_{min}$, where p_{min} is the lowest possible power. $\lambda = 0$ corresponds to the horizontal line and $L_0(x)$ is minimized at x_1 as shown in the Figure 6. As λ increases, the slope of the line increases and the dual cost also increases. For $\lambda < \lambda_1$, x_1 minimizes $L_\lambda(x)$. At $\lambda = \lambda_1$, both x_1 and x_2 minimize the Lagrangian function. The dual function continues to increase with λ as long as $\lambda \leq \lambda_3$, and attains a maximum of g^* at $\lambda = \lambda_3$. At $\lambda = \lambda_3$, the Lagrangian function is minimized at x_3 and x_4, but only x_4 is primal feasible. So even if the dual optimum is attained, there is no guarantee that the primal feasible solution can be achieved. Observe also that the primal optimal value $p^* = p(x^*)$ is more than the dual optimal g^*. The gap $p^* - g^*$ is the duality gap.

These limitations are due to both non-convexity and discreteness. While NetFlow tries to maximize the dual cost and has the above-mentioned limitations, EGSS uses Lagrange multipliers to help attain primal feasibility and then reduce the power. EGSS rapidly increases the Lagrange multipliers initially to attain feasibility. That causes very low dual cost and high power. Then, using the local slack check while solving LRS, the design is forced to stay in the feasible region while Lagrange multipliers are reduced to recover power. NetFlow requires an optimal LRS solver, which it is not, to maximize the dual cost; but EGSS deliberately sacrifices the optimality of the LRS solver to maintain primal feasibility.

7   GREEDY TIMING AND POWER RECOVERY

Optimized designs obtained from the LDP solver have some timing violations and additional power that can be recovered. In the case of NetFlow, due to the limitations discussed in Section 6, there are large timing violations and a lot of power to be recovered. Hence, greedy refinements are more important for NetFlow. In either case, it is a common practice to apply a timing recovery followed by a power recovery algorithm - both are greedy and local in nature. The timing recovery and power recovery algorithms that we implemented have

been adapted from [11] and [12]. Below we have summarized only the main steps for both the algorithms. For details refer to [11, 12].

For timing recovery, we sort all gates in the decreasing order of the number of timing critical end-points that are in the fan-out cone of each gate. Each gate is upsized in this order. In order to compute the change in TNS, timing is updated in an incremental fashion. If the TNS improves (reduces) then the new size is committed and the gates are re-sorted, otherwise the upsizing is undone and the next gate in the order is upsized. This process continues as long as the TNS is non-zero and it is reducing. During timing recovery we avoid reducing Vth because that significantly worsens the power.

To reduce power, we first try to increase Vth for each gate. If Vth cannot be increased without worsening TNS, then downsizing is considered. Gates are traversed in forward topological order.

8   EXPERIMENTS AND RESULTS

We used the ISPD 2012 gate sizing contest benchmark suite. We performed experiments on two quad-core Intel(R) Xeon(R) 3.50GHz CPUs. To solve the min-cost flow problem we used Gurobi [21]. For line search, we used a step size of 0.2 and evaluated 5 steps at uniform spacing. We used $M = 10$ for computing bounds. Our C++ code is multi-threaded using OpenMP [22], and we use 8 threads to solve LRS. We used PrimeTime [23] version E-2010.12, to verify the timing after NetFlow and EGSS. Each final design has zero TNS, and all constraints are satisfied.

We use the sizing results from [13], which also used 8 threads, as the baseline as it is the fastest and has competitive power results. This baseline only sizes the gates, with fixed zero skew at all clock pins. We use a minimum skew w_{min} of 0 and a maximum skew bound of 165ps for NetFlow and EGSS. Table 2 summarizes the results from all three flows. Compared to the baseline, EGSS saves on average 19.7% more power, because EGSS schedules skew simultaneously with gate sizing. The benefit of skew scheduling is more on designs with tighter timing constraints ('fast'), where

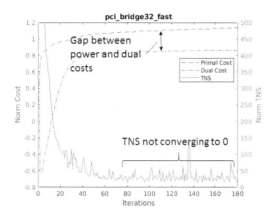

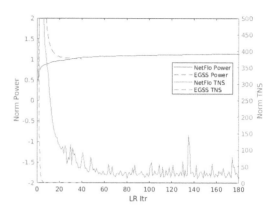

Figure 7: Primal cost (power), dual cost, and TNS profiles for Net-Flow for pci_bridge32_fast. The left Y-axis is the normalized dual or primal cost, and the right Y-axis is the TNS normalized with respect to the target clock period of 660ps. Here, the maximum skew bound is zero to highlight the limitations of the NetFlow approach.

Figure 8: Power and TNS profiles for pci_bridge32_fast for NetFlow and EGSS. The maximum skew bound is set to zero for both.

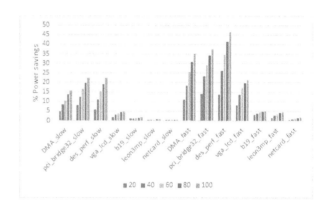

the average power saved is 26.5%. By carefully scheduling the skew, timing constraints can be satisfied without having to upsize the gates or decrease their Vth, both of which increase leakage power. EGSS has only 17% slowdown in the total runtime.

Compared to NetFlow, EGSS saves 5.3% more power and is 70X faster. In NetFlow, the greedy refinement stage accounts for an average of 5.4% power reduction (not shown in Table 2), whereas it accounts for only 0.4% power reduction in EGSS. This shows that the core idea behind EGSS is more effective than that of NetFlow.

The main reasons for larger runtime of NetFlow are: 1) Solving the min-cost flow problem is orders of magnitude more runtime expensive compared to the projection based Lagrange multiplier update shown in Algorithm 2. The latter has a linear time complexity in the number of gates. Using a network flow solver instead of Gurobi may be faster. 2) NetFlow has a slower convergence than EGSS, so it takes more iterations. 3) Each NetFlow iteration is more expensive due to solving LRS several times during the line search.

Figure 7 shows dual cost, power, and TNS profiles for NetFlow on pci_bridge32_fast. Although the dual cost converges to a maximum value, TNS does not converge down to 0. Also, there is a distinct gap between the dual cost and the primal cost (total gate power of the design), possibly due to a non-zero duality gap.

Figure 8 compares the TNS and power profiles from EGSS and NetFlow. Early on, EGSS has high power as TNS rapidly reduces. But then it recovers the power. It converges in less than 40 iterations with near-zero TNS and lower power than NetFlow. Across all the benchmarks, EGSS takes on average only 2 iterations to converge the TNS and an additional 18 iterations to reduce the power.

In another experiment with EGSS, we varied the maximum skew bound through 20, 40, 60, 80 and 100ps. Correspondingly, the average power savings compared to the baseline are 5.3%, 9.0%, 11.7%, 14.0% and 15.7%. Larger skew bounds allow larger adjustments in the clock arrival times at different clock pins which can be potentially used to save more power. Figure 9 shows the improvement in power with increasing skew bounds for each design. b19, leon3mp

Figure 9: The percentage reduction in power for EGSS for different maximum skew bounds: 20ps, 40ps, 60ps, 80ps, and 100ps. The minimum skew bound is 0.

and netcard designs are already closer to minimum power, hence we do not observe as significant power savings as other designs.

9 CONCLUSION

Gate sizing is a crucial circuit optimization technique. The power reduction from gate sizing can be enhanced by allowing variable skew. We investigated two approaches for simultaneous gate sizing and skew scheduling. The network flow approach derives a Lagrangian dual problem from the primal problem and tries to maximize the dual objective. We detailed limitations arising from the non-convexity and the discreteness of the primal space, due to which dual maximization cannot guarantee primal feasibility and thus is sub-optimal, as shown by our experimental results. In the second approach, we extend the state-of-the-art high performance Lagrangian relaxation based gate sizing. We first make use of the variable skew to recover the bulk of the timing violations in just two iterations, on average. Then, we iteratively reduce power. In each iteration, skew is updated to redistribute the slack between each side of the flip-flop. Compared to the state-of-the-art gate sizer which treats skew as fixed, our proposed flow for simultaneous gate sizing and clock skew scheduling reduces power by an average of

19.7% on the ISPD 2012 gate sizing contest designs with only 17% higher run time.

10 ACKNOWLEDGMENTS

This work is partially supported by a grant from Mentor Graphics.

REFERENCES

[1] J. P. Fishburn. Clock skew optimization. *IEEE Transactions on Computers*, 39(7):945–951, July 1990.

[2] W. Chuang *et al.* Timing and area optimization for standard-cell vlsi circuit design. *IEEE Transactions on Computer-Aided Design of Integrated Circuits and Systems*, 14(3):308–320, 1995.

[3] J. Wang *et al.* Gate sizing by Lagrangian relaxation revisited. *IEEE Transactions on Computer-Aided Design of Integrated Circuits and Systems*, 28(7):1071–1084, 2009.

[4] G. Shklover *et al.* Simultaneous clock and data gate sizing algorithm with common global objective. In *International Symposium on Physical Design*, pages 145–152, 2012.

[5] M.M. Ozdal *et al.* The ISPD-2012 discrete cell sizing contest and benchmark suite. In *International Symposium on Physical Design*, pages 161–164, 2012.

[6] M.M. Ozdal *et al.* An improved benchmark suite for the ISPD-2013 discrete cell sizing contest. In *International Symposium on Physical Design*, pages 168–170, 2013.

[7] J. Hu *et al.* Sensitivity-guided metaheuristics for accurate discrete gate sizing. In *International Conference on Computer-Aided Design*, pages 233–239, 2012.

[8] S. Daboul *et al.* Provably fast and near-optimum gate sizing. *IEEE Transactions on Computer-Aided Design of Integrated Circuits and Systems*, 37(12):3163–3176, 2018.

[9] L. Li *et al.* An efficient algorithm for library-based cell-type selection in high-performance low-power designs. In *International Conference on Computer-Aided Design*, pages 226–232, 2012.

[10] V. S. Livramento *et al.* A hybrid technique for discrete gate sizing based on lagrangian relaxation. *ACM Transactions on Design Automation of Electronic Systems*, 19(4):40, 2014.

[11] G. Flach *et. al.* Effective Method for Simultaneous Gate Sizing and V-th Assignment Using Lagrangian Relaxation. *IEEE Transactions on Computer-Aided Design of Integrated Circuits and Systems*, 33(4):546–557, 2014.

[12] A. Sharma *et al.* Fast Lagrangian relaxation based gate sizing using multi-threading. In *International Conference on Computer-Aided Design*, pages 426–433, 2015.

[13] A. Sharma *et al.* Rapid gate sizing with fewer iterations of lagrangian relaxation. In *International Conference on Computer-Aided Design*, pages 337–343, 2017.

[14] H. Ren *et al.* A Network-Flow Based Cell Sizing Algorithm. In *The International Workshop on Logic Synthesis*, 2008.

[15] H. Tennakoon *et al.* Gate sizing using Lagrangian relaxation combined with a fast gradient-based pre-processing step. In *International Conference on Computer-Aided Design*, pages 395–402, 2002.

[16] C.-P. Chen *et. al.* Fast and exact simultaneous gate and wire sizing by Lagrangian relaxation. *IEEE Transactions on Computer-Aided Design of Integrated Circuits and Systems*, 18(7):1014–1025, 1999.

[17] H. Sathyamurthy *et al.* Speeding up pipelined circuits through a combination of gate sizing and clock skew optimization. *IEEE Transactions on Computer-Aided Design of Integrated Circuits and Systems*, 17(2):173–182, 1998.

[18] S. Roy *et al.* An optimal algorithm for sizing sequential circuits for industrial library based designs. In *Asia and South Pacific Design Automation Conference*, pages 148–151, 2008.

[19] S. Boyd *et al.* *Convex optimization.* Cambridge university press, 2004.

[20] W. Ning. Strongly NP-hard discrete gate-sizing problems. *IEEE Transactions on Computer-Aided Design of Integrated Circuits and Systems*, 13(8):1045–1051, 1994.

[21] Gurobi. http://www.gurobi.com/.

[22] L. Dagum *et al.* OpenMP: an industry standard API for shared-memory programming. *IEEE Computational Science & Engineering*, 5(1):46–55, 1998.

[23] Synopsys PrimeTime user guide. http://http://www.synopsys.com.

Adaptive Clustering and Sampling for High-Dimensional and Multi-Failure-Region SRAM Yield Analysis

[1,2]Xiao Shi, [3]Hao Yan, [3]Jinxin Wang, [3]Xiaofen Xu, [3]Fengyuan Liu, [3]Longxing Shi, [1,2]Lei He

[1]State Key Lab of ASIC & System, Microelectronics Dept., Fudan University, China
[2]Electrical and Computer Engineering Dept., University of California, Los Angeles, CA, USA
[3]Electrical Engineering Dept., Southeast University, China

pokemoon2009@g.ucla.edu,yanhao@seu.edu.cn,jxwang1995@gmail.com,xxf_deborah@seu.edu.cn,liu_lfy@seu.edu.
cn,lxshi@seu.edu.cn,lhe@ee.ucla.edu

ABSTRACT

Statistical circuit simulation is exhibiting increasing importance for memory circuits under process variation. It is challenging to accurately estimate the extremely low failure probability as it becomes a high-dimensional and multi-failure-region problem. In this paper, we develop an Adaptive Clustering and Sampling (ACS) method. ACS proceeds iteratively to cluster samples and adjust sampling distribution, while most existing approaches pre-decide a static sampling distribution. By adaptively searching in multiple cone-shaped subspaces, ACS obtains better accuracy and efficiency. This result is validated by our experiments. For SRAM bit cell with single failure region, ACS requires 3-5X fewer samples and achieves better accuracy compared with existing approaches. For 576-dimensional SRAM column circuit with multiple failure regions, ACS is 2050X faster than MC without compromising accuracy, while other methods fail to converge to correct failure probability in our experiment.

CCS CONCEPTS

• **Hardware → Yield and cost modeling**;

KEYWORDS

Process Variation; Failure Probability; SRAM; High Dimension; Failure Regions

ACM Reference Format:
Xiao Shi, Hao Yan, Jinxin Wang, Xiaofen Xu, Fengyuan Liu, Longxing Shi, Lei He. 2019. Adaptive Clustering and Sampling for High-Dimensional and Multi-Failure-Region SRAM Yield Analysis. In 2019 International Symposium on Physical Design (ISPD'19), April 14–17, 2019, San Francisco, CA, USA. ACM, New York, NY, USA, 8 pages. https://doi.org/10.1145/3299902.3309748

1 INTRODUCTION

As microelectronic devices shrink to deep submicrometer scale, circuit reliability has become an area of growing concern for efficient circuit sizing and design. Among various integrated circuits (ICs),

SRAM circuits are highly duplicated with minimum size devices that require extremely small failure probability [1]. This failure probability is a rare event that deterministic analysis is infeasible.

In general, modern statistical circuit simulation methods are applied to model the stochastic behavior under process variation. Standard Monte Carlo (MC) method remains the gold standard, which repeatedly collects samples and evaluates circuit performance with transistor-level simulation. Although circuit simulation has been remarkably accelerated through the years [2], MC is extremely time-consuming under the "rare-event" scenario because millions of simulations are required to capture one single failure event.

Instead of sampling randomly with standard MC, more efficient approaches have been proposed to sample from the likely-to-fail region, which can be grouped into two major categories:

(1) **Classification:** Statistical Blockade (SB) [3] constructs a classifier to filter out the samples that unlikely to fail and only simulate the remaining samples. A safety margin is applied in [3] to decrease classification error. More recently, recursive SB [4] and REscope [5] improve the classifier to conditional classifier and SVM non-linear classifier. However, training such classifiers is expensive in high dimension and the effectiveness deteriorates very quickly with extremely small failure probability.

(2) **Importance Sampling:** As a classic modification of MC method, Importance Sampling (IS) tries to build a distorted sampling distribution to assemble the failure region. For example, Mixture Importance Sampling (MixIS) [6] uses the mixture of a uniform distribution, the original distribution and a shifted distribution centered at the failure region as target distribution. Norm Minimization (MNIS) [7] and Spherical Sampling (SS) [8] methods spherically search the parametric space and then shift the sampling distribution toward the minimum L_2-norm point of a set of failure samples. In order to tackle multi-failure-region circuit cases, methods in [9, 10] attempt to construct multiple shift vectors and perform mixture importance sampling. The drawbacks of these approaches is that IS is inefficient to collect samples and evaluate yield rate, and the effectiveness is highly dependent on the quality of distorted sampling distribution.

Among others, Particle Filter [11] utilizes a resampling step followed by an IS step to accelerate failure region exploration and failure rate evaluation. Adaptive Impotance Sampling (AIS) [12] method takes one step forward. AIS develops an unbiased estimator along with the resampling iterations, which can eliminate the time consuming static IS step. However, these modified IS methods suffer from sample diversity degeneracy. In the multi-failure-region circuit case, the resampling scheme is more prone to converge to the region with higher importance, at the expense of neglecting less important regions. This property leads to biased sampling distribution, and it comes with smaller failure probability estimation.

In this paper, we present an accurate and efficient algorithm based on Adaptive Clustering and Sampling (ACS) method to estimate the failure rate of high-dimensional and multi-failure-region circuit cases. The basic idea of the algorithm is to cluster failure samples and build global sampling distribution at each iteration. Specifically, in clustering step, we propose a multi-cone clustering method, which partitions the parametric space and clusters failure samples. Then global sampling distribution is constructed from a set of weighted Gaussian distributions. Next, we calculate importance weight for each sample based on the discrepancy between sampling distribution and target distribution. Failure probability is updated at the end of each iteration. This clustering and sampling procedure proceeds iteratively until all the failure regions are covered.

Our main contribution is summarized in three aspects: first, we initialize our ACS algorithm with hyperspherical presampling method, which reduces dimension by sampling from a set of hyperspherical surfaces. Second, we propose an adaptive scheme to explore high-dimensional space and search for failure regions. As iteration continues, each partial IS estimator provides a better estimation, and global sampling distribution will tilt toward failure region. Moreover, our estimator is adapted parallelly in different directions, which can effectively improve sample diversity.

2 BACKGROUND

2.1 Rare Event Analysis

Let $f(x)$ denote multivariate probability density function (PDF) of circuit process variation x. Let Y be the observed performance metric, such as memory read/write time, amplifier gain, etc. This metric Y usually requires expensive transistor-level circuit simulation to evaluate.

In statistical circuit simulation, it is of great interest to estimate the probability of Y belonging to a subset S of the entire parametric space. For example, under circuit failure probability estimation scenario, we generally assume the performance specification is $Y \notin S$. On the contrary, a failure occurs when $Y \in S$. Thereby, we introduce indicator function $I(x)$ to identify pass/fail of Y:

$$I(x) = \begin{cases} 0, & if \quad Y \notin S \\ 1, & if \quad Y \in S \end{cases} \tag{1}$$

Therefore, the probability P_{fail} can be calculated as

$$P_{fail} = P(Y \in S) = \int I(x) \cdot f(x) dx \tag{2}$$

Note that the integral in equation (2) is intractable because $I(x)$ is unavailable in analytical form. Conventionally, Monte Carlo (MC) method enumerates a sample set $\{X_i\}_{i=1}^{N}$ according to $f(x)$ and evaluates their indicator values $\{I(X_i)\}_{i=1}^{N}$ to generate an unbiased estimation of $\hat{P}_{fail}$:

$$\hat{P}_{fail} = \hat{P}(Y \in S) = \frac{1}{N} \sum_{i=1}^{N} I(X_i) \xrightarrow{N \to +\infty} P(Y \in S) \tag{3}$$

2.2 Importance Sampling

When P_{fail} is an extremely small value, standard MC becomes inefficient because it requires millions of simulations to collect one single failure event. To avoid massive simulations, an intuitive idea is to sample from a "distorted" sampling distribution $g(x)$ that tilts toward the failure region S.

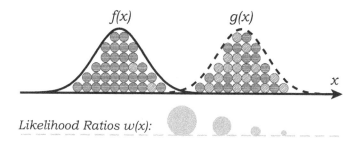

Figure 1: Scale illustration of likelihood ratios in mean-shift importance sampling

Figure 1 illustrates a one-dimensional example of IS method. It samples from a shifted distribution $g(x)$ which contains more failure samples. Failure probability can thus be calculated as:

$$P_{fail} = P(Y \in S) = \int I(x) \cdot \frac{f(x)}{g(x)} \cdot g(x) dx \tag{4}$$

$$= \int I(x) \cdot w(x) \cdot g(x) dx \tag{5}$$

If shifted PDF $g(x)$ is properly chosen, $\hat{P}_{IS,fail}$ can converge to failure probability P_{fail} with much smaller sample size because failure in $g(x)$ is not rare. Theoretically, the optimal sampling distribution $g^{opt}(x)$ is the failure event distribution, which can be expressed as:

$$g^{opt}(x) = \frac{I(x) \cdot f(x)}{P_{fail}} \tag{6}$$

However, $g^{opt}(x)$ cannot be calculated with (7) deterministically because the analytical form of $I(x)$ is unavailable and P_{fail} is unknown. In practice, people propose various approaches to build $g^{opt}(x)$ with optimal shift vector. For example, MNIS [7] shifts $f(x)$ to pass/fail boundary, HDIS [13] shifts to centroid of a cluster of failure samples, and HSCS [9] shifts to multiple centroids by clustering failure samples. However, static IS with predefined $g(x)$ suffers from two major drawbacks:

First, existing IS approaches consist of two stages: a presampling stage to calculate mean shift vector and importance sampling stage to evaluate P_{fail}. However, the complexity of constructing optimal shift vector increases exponentially with circuit dimension. A classic modification of static IS is applying adaptive scheme to search for failure regions.

Moreover, the likelihood ratio $w(x)$ is substantially biased when the discrepancy between $f(x)$ and $g(x)$ is huge. In this case, only a few samples with larger weight contribute to estimation, which results in higher variance and unstable performance.

3 ADAPTIVE CLUSTERING AND SAMPLING ALGORITHM

3.1 Algorithm Description

Algorithm 1 summarizes the main steps of proposed ACS method. The objective of this algorithm is to iteratively explore multiple failure regions in different directions and update failure rate at the end of each iteration. In the initialization step, we collect M samples $\{X_i^{(0)}\}_{i=1}^M$ by hyperspherical presampling, and group these samples into k clusters $\{C_j^{(0)}\}_{j=1}^k$ using our multi-cone clustering algorithm. At each iteration t, we construct a local sampling distribution $g_j^{(t-1)}(x)$ in each cluster $C_j^{(t-1)}$ based on the samples that assigned to it. Our global sampling distribution $g^{(t-1)}(x)$ is built from a weighted mixture of all the local sampling distributions $\{g_j^{(t-1)}(x)\}_{j=1}^k$. Next we generate M new samples $\{X_i^{(t)}\}_{i=1}^M$ from $g^{(t-1)}(x)$, and calibrate the cluster sets $\{C_j^{(t)}\}_{j=1}^k$. At the end of each iteration, we update failure probability estimation by averaging all the partial IS estimators $\hat{P}_{fail,t} = \frac{1}{tM} \sum_{l=1}^t \sum_{i=1}^M w_{i,l}$ up to present. This iteration proceeds iteratively until our estimation converge to certain confidence interval.

3.2 Hyperspherical Presampling

One major challenge in implementing our ACS algorithm is to generate some initial samples that can locate multiple failure regions. In practice, an effective initialization method can help improve sample diversity, convergence speed, and capability to explore parametric space. It is quite difficult to recover from a set of poor starting samples, and the adaptation may converge to a local optimum in the parametric space.

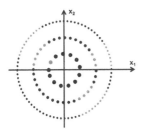

Figure 2: Incremental hyperspherical presampling (for finding initial samples to enable local exploration)

In order to develop a good initialization, as demonstrated in Figure 2, we implement a hyperspherical presampling procedure. This procedure starts with circuit nominal distribution, which indicates a unit hypersphere in parametric space. The radius of this unit hypersphere denotes the variance of circuit parameters. To cover multiple failure regions, we gradually increase the radius of hypersphere until M failure samples are captured. Our presampling method is a dimension reduction process by restricting the samples on a union of hyperspherical surfaces. This method can accelerate the exploration in the high dimensional space while maintaining sample diversity.

Algorithm 1: ACS Algorithm

Initialization:

1. Set iteration index $t = 0$, generate initial failure sample set $\{X_i^{(0)}\}_{i=1}^M$.

2. Assign failure samples $\{X_i^{(0)}\}_{i=1}^M$ to cluster set $\{C_j^{(0)}\}_{j=1}^k$. Define $N_j^{(0)}$ the number of failure samples in the cluster $C_j^{(0)}$, we note that $\sum_{j=1}^k N_j^{(0)} = M$.

Repeat

Update iteration index $t = t + 1$.

   1. Cluster sampling distribution:

   In each cluster:

   (a) Construct Gaussian distribution as sample proposal:

$$q_i^{(t-1)}(x) = N(X_i^{(t-1)}, \Sigma)$$

   where Σ is predefined covariance matrix.

   (b) Calculate probability density for $N_j^{(t)}$ failure samples:

$$\beta_{i,t-1} = f(X_i^{(t-1)})I(X_i^{(t-1)}) \qquad i = 1, ..., N_j^{(t)}.$$

   (c) Construct local distribution $g_j^{(t-1)}(x)$:

$$g_j^{(t-1)}(x) = \frac{1}{\sum_{i=1}^{N_j} \beta_{i,t-1}} \sum_{i=1}^{N_j} \beta_{i,t-1} \cdot q_i^{(t-1)}(x)$$

   2. Sample propagation:

   Generate M samples from global distribution $g^{(t-1)}(x)$:

$$X_i^{(t)} \sim g^{(t-1)}(x) = \frac{1}{\sum_{i=1}^M \beta_{i,t-1}} \sum_{j=1}^k \sum_{X_i \in C_j^{(t)}} \beta_{i,t-1} \cdot g_j^{(t-1)}(x)$$

   3. Cluster calibration:

   Re-cluster current failure samples $\{X_i^{(t)}\}_{i=1}^M$ into new set $\{C_j^{(t)}\}_{j=1}^k$ and update $\{N_j^{(t)}\}_{j=1}^k$.

   4. Failure probability calculation:

   (a) Compute incremental importance weight:

$$w_{i,t} = \frac{\pi(x)}{g^{(t-1)}(x)} = \frac{f(x)I(x)}{g^{(t-1)}(x)} \qquad i = 1, ..., M.$$

   (b) Update unbiased estimator using all samples up to present iteration:

$$\hat{P}_{fail,t} = \frac{1}{tM} \sum_{l=1}^t \sum_{i=1}^M w_{i,l}$$

Until

Relative standard deviation (FOM): $\rho = \frac{\sqrt{\sigma_{\hat{P}_{fail}}^2}}{\hat{P}_{fail}} \leq 0.1$

In Algorithm 1, the number of initial failure samples, M, can be arbitrarily user specified. We note that there exists a trade-off between estimation accuracy and algorithm complexity: the larger M is, the higher estimation accuracy we can achieve while sacrificing simulation runtime. In our experiments, we collect 100 samples on each hypersphere until 10% or more samples fail.

3.3 Multi-Cone Clustering

After we collect a set of failure samples located on several discrete hyperspherical surfaces with different radius, we need to cluster these samples with the boundary of multiple disjoint failure regions. Conventional clustering algorithms apply techniques such as graph-based methods, density-based methods and boundary-based methods. They group sample points into optimal clusters by evaluating the Euclidean distance between sample pairs, as defined in (8).

$$EuclideanDistance(X^{(1)}, X^{(2)}) = \|X^{(1)} - X^{(2)}\| \qquad (7)$$

However, clustering samples that are randomly distributed in high dimensional open space is challenging. As the dimension of parametric space increases, the ratio of Euclidean distance between nearest and farthest neighbors is closer to 1. In such cases, the nearest neighbor problem becomes ill-defined and qualitative clustering methods are unapproachable.

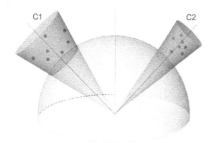

Figure 3: Partition the space into non-overlapping cones along radial directions.

Alternatively, at each iteration, we cluster the sample points based on their directions rather than Euclidean distance. We partition the high-dimensional space into a union of disjoint cones, while maintaining whole space coverage. For each cone-shaped subspace, we build a nonlinear mapping from sample space to feature space. As illustrated in Figure 3, all distinct sample points in each cone are projected to the unit hypersphere surface in the radial direction. We note that the location of images projected on the unit hypersphere describes the direction of sample points. The distance metric of each sample pair is evaluated by the cosine distance of direction vectors, as defined in (9).

$$CosineDistance(X^{(1)}, X^{(2)}) = 1 - \frac{X^{(1)} \cdot X^{(2)}}{\|X^{(1)}\| \|X^{(2)}\|} \qquad (8)$$

As shown in Algorithm 2, a k-means based algorithm is implemented to cluster the failure samples $\{X_i\}_{i=1}^{M}$ according to their direction. The algorithm proceeds as follows. We first generate k unit length vectors $\{V_j\}_{j=1}^{k}$ as initial direction vectors arbitrarily, where k is a user specified parameter. Each sample X_i is then assigned to the closest cluster C_{λ_i} according to the cosine distance. Next, the direction vector of each cluster is updated to the average of associated sample vectors. This assignment and update procedure is repeated until cluster membership stabilizes.

Although k-means algorithm has advantages of its simplicity to implement and efficiency, it searches for clusters in a greedy fashion,

---

Algorithm 2: Multi-cone Clustering Algorithm

Input:
　　Failure sample set: $\{X_i\}_{i=1}^{M}$
　　Initial cluster number: k

Output:
　　Cluster label for samples: $\{\lambda_i\}_{i=1}^{M}$

Initialization:
　　Randomly initialize k unit length direction vectors $\{V_j\}_{j=1}^{k}$ and corresponding empty clusters $\{C_j\}_{j=1}^{k}$.

Repeat
　　(1) For each sample X_i, calculate cosine distance with all the direction vectors $\{V_j\}_{j=1}^{k}$:
$$CosineDistance(X_i, V_j) = 1 - \frac{X_i \cdot V_j}{\|X_i\| \|V_j\|}.$$
　　　　Update $\lambda_i = \underset{j}{\arg\min}\, CosineDistance(X_i, V_j)$ and assign X_i to cluster C_{λ_i}.
　　(2) For each cluster C_j, update its direction vector:
$$V_j = \frac{1}{|C_j|} \sum_{X \in C_j} X.$$
　　　　where $|C_j|$ denotes the number of samples in cluster C_j.

Until
　　Sample labels $\{\lambda_i\}_{i=1}^{M}$ remain unchanged.

---

which makes it sensitive to bad initialization and outliers. In our experiment, we start from multiple set of initial direction vectors, and minimize sum of cosine distance as error function. Thus, our clustering result is more robust and more prone to converge to global optimum rather than local optimum.

We also note that the number of clusters, k, can be tuned to improve the effectiveness of our k-means algorithm. Larger k always improves the cluster cohesiveness by decreasing squared error, but this comes at the expense of higher computational cost. We explore this trade-off by utilizing different k values. In practice, k is fixed as $\sqrt{M}$, where M is the number of failure samples to be clustered.

3.4 ACS Estimator Analysis

3.4.1 ***Unbiasedness of ACS Estimator.*** In this section, we prove that our ACS estimator $\hat{P}_{fail}$ is unbiased between iterations. The unbiasedness of estimator is evaluated by its expected value. It guarantees the estimation built from random measure $\{X_i^{(t)}, w_{i,t}\}_{i=1}^{M}$ is consistent, and it converges to failure probability P_{fail}.

$$E[\hat{P}_{fail}] = E[\frac{1}{tM} \sum_{l=1}^{t} \sum_{i=1}^{M} w_{i,l}] \qquad (9)$$

$$= \frac{1}{tM} \sum_{l=1}^{t} \sum_{i=1}^{M} E[\frac{f(x)I(x)}{g^{(l-1)}(x)}] \qquad (10)$$

$$= \frac{1}{tM} \sum_{l=1}^{t} \sum_{i=1}^{M} \int \frac{f(x)I(x)}{g^{(l-1)}(x)} g^{(l-1)}(x) dx \qquad (11)$$

$$= \frac{1}{tM} \sum_{l=1}^{t} \sum_{i=1}^{M} \int f(x)I(x) dx = P_{fail} \qquad (12)$$

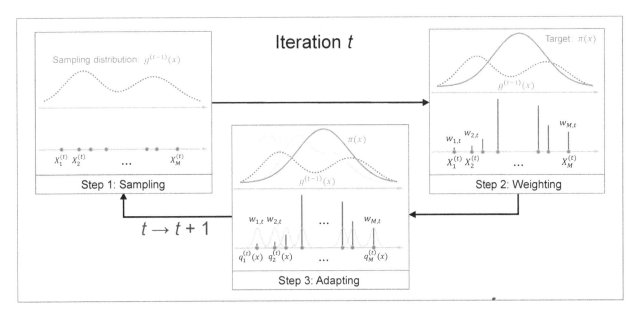

Figure 4: Flow diagram that shows the adaptation of ACS estimator. The target distribution are shown by solid lines, while the sampling distributions are plotted with dashed lines. The initial sampling distribution gradually tilts toward target distribution by reweighting sample proposals.

3.4.2 Adaptation of ACS Estimator. The ACS methodology is based on an iterative process which proceeds parallelly in multiple disjoint clusters. With the adaptation of ACS estimator, our sampling distribution $g^{(t)}(x)$ gradually evolves to accurately approximate the target probability density $\pi(x)$. As demonstrated in Algorithm 1, this procedure consists of three main stages: generating samples from sampling distribution (sampling), calculation of the incremental importance weight for each of the samples (weighting) and updating the parameters to define the new sampling distribution for next iteration (adapting). Figure 4 shows the flow diagram of the stages in ACS.

The adaptive mechanism of ACS is driven by the uncertainty in the partial IS estimators, which can be quantified by their variance. To be specific, each sample forms a sample proposal $q_i^{(t)}(x)$ that can describe local features of the target distribution $\pi(x)$. In order to obtain a discrete probability distribution that approximates target distribution, we introduce incremental importance weight $w_{i,t} = \frac{\pi(x)}{g^{(t-1)}(x)}$, which quantifies the discrepancy between target distribution $\pi(x)$ and current sampling distribution $g^{(t-1)}(x)$. Then we average out all the sample proposals $q_i^{(t)}(x)$ based on their $w_{i,t}$ and generate new sampling distribution $g^{(t)}(x)$ for next iteration. This concept is very similar to the methodology in Kernel Density Estimation (KDE) method, where each $q_i^{(t)}(x)$ represents a kernel. As iteration continues, more observations will be added to target distribution $\pi(x)$ to make it closer to real failure region distribution. And our sampling distribution approximates the target distribution $\pi(x)$ through a random walk, as shown in Figure 4. With this ACS adaptation scheme, our sampling distribution can search to achieve full failure region coverage, and focus on the most important failure boundaries.

3.4.3 Comparison with other IS estimators. In comparison with conventional static IS with deterministic mixture, our ACS algorithm has two primary advantages. First of all, our ACS estimator can spread out throughout the parametric space while maintaining sample diversity. To be specific, a major challenge for other AIS methodologies in statistics community is the diversity of samples is prone to degenerate as iteration proceeds. These approaches utilize a resampling scheme to sample with replication from a series of sample proposals. Resampling method tilts to approximate failure event distribution. However, this random walk is generated globally in a greedy fashion, which may focus on the major failure regions and neglect the minor ones. And it also yields higher computational complexity. Our ACS estimator, on the contrary, is completely parallelized in different directions, and the evaluation of failure probability is also performed in parallel. It accelerates the convergence of our estimation and all the failure regions on different directions are separately protected between iterations.

Moreover, ACS estimator outperforms other IS based estimator in terms of Effective Sample Size (ESS). ESS is defined as:

$$ESS = \frac{1}{\sum_{i=1}^{M} (\bar{w}_{i,t})^2} \tag{13}$$

where $\bar{w}_{i,t}$ is the normalized incremental importance weight for each sample in all iterations. It reflects the number of samples that contribute to corresponding estimator. Our ACS estimator bias the sampling distribution to the samples with larger $\bar{w}_{i,t}$. In the next iteration, more samples with larger weight will be generated. Thus $\bar{w}_{i,t}$ is naturally balanced and it is more likely to converge to optimal $w^* = \frac{1}{M}$, which maximizes ESS to M. In this case, each sample uniformly contributes to the estimator and the estimator is stabilized.

Table 1: Accuracy and efficiency comparison on 18-dimensional SRAM bit cell

	MC	HSCS	AIS	Proposed
Failure prob.(error)	1.24e-5(0%)	1.18e-5(4.6%)	1.32e-5(6.1%)	1.22e-5(1.5%)
Presampling # sim.	0	7000	3000	1100
Importance Sampling # sim.	1e7	8688	5111	1736
Total # sim. (speedup)	1e7(1X)	15688(637X)	8111(1233X)	2836(3526X)

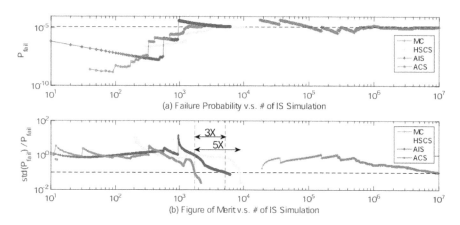

(a) Failure Probability v.s. # of IS Simulation

(b) Figure of Merit v.s. # of IS Simulation

Figure 5: Evolution comparison of failure prob. and FOM on SRAM bit cell

4 EXPERIMENT RESULT

In this section, we first evaluate our proposed ACS method on a typical SRAM bit cell with 18 variables. More realistically, we verify ACS on high-dimensional SRAM column with 576 variables. We also implement different methods, including MC, HSCS [9] and AIS [12], and compare from both accuracy and efficiency perspective. The experiment environment is HSPICE with SMIC 40nm model.

4.1 Experiments on 6T SRAM Bit Cell

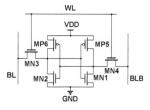

Figure 6: The schematic of typical 6T SRAM cell

Figure 6 shows the schematic of a typical 6-transistors SRAM bit cell. Four transistors $MN1$, $MP5$, $MN2$ and $MP6$ form two cross-coupled inverters and utilize two steady states '0' and '1' to store data in the memory cell. The other two access transistors MN3 and MN4 work as switches for read and write operation. In this experiment, we consider various failure mechanisms, including reading failure, writing failure and data retention failure. We will compare different methods (MC, HSCS, AIS, proposed) in terms of accuracy and efficiency.

4.1.1 Accuracy Comparison. To verify the accuracy of proposed ACS algorithm, Figure of Merit (FOM), ρ, is applied to represent the accuracy convergence and confidence of estimation. The definition of FOM is:

$$\rho = \frac{\sqrt{\sigma^2_{\hat{P}_{fail}}}}{\hat{P}_{fail}} \quad (14)$$

where $\hat{P}_{fail}$ indicates failure probability and $\sigma_{\hat{P}_{fail}}$ indicates the standard deviation of $\hat{P}_{fail}$. We define one estimation has $(1 - \epsilon)100\%$ accuracy with $(1-\delta)100\%$ confidence when $\rho < \epsilon\sqrt{log(1/\delta)}$. In our experiment, we draw a dashed line when ρ reaches 0.1 to indicate the 90% accuracy with 90% confidence, which is an extensively used ρ value in the literature [9, 12].

We compare the convergence of failure probability estimation and FOM calculation in Figure 5. We observe that the estimation of MC, HSCS, AIS and proposed ACS all converge when sufficient simulations are allowed. As illustrated in Table 1, the ground truth MC estimation is 1.24e-5 (4.37σ). Among these methods, the proposed ACS algorithm is most accurate with only 1.5% relative error, while the results of HSCS and AIS have 4.6% and 6.1% relative error, respectively.

4.1.2 Efficiency Comparison. The efficiency of MC, HSCS, AIS and ACS is shown in Figure 5. We notice that ACS has the fastest convergence among these algorithms. It is attributed to our unbiased estimator, which is updated parallelly in disjoint clusters. It is far more efficient than static sampling distribution in HSCS and global resampling scheme in AIS. To be specific, as shown in Table 1, our ACS method converge to 90% confidence with only 1736 IS simulations, while HSCS and AIS need 8688 and 5111 IS simulations to obtain the same FOM value. In addition, the proposed ACS algorithm requires 1100 presampling simulations. In comparison, HSCS and AIS need 7000 and 3000 times, respectively. This result demonstrates that proposed method is less sensitive to initial states. In total, ACS algorithm can achieve 3526X speedup over MC, 5X over HSCS and 3X over AIS.

4.2 Experiments on SRAM Column Circuit

A simplified schematic of SRAM column consisted of 32 bit cells is shown in Figure 7. Compared with a single bit cell in the previous low-dimensional experiment, we consider the impact of peripheral circuit and generate a more accurate estimation of failure probability. The configuration in Figure 7 demonstrates the worst-case scenario of read operation, in which accessed bit $CELL<0>$ stores "0" and other idle bits store "1". In this case, the leakage current through idle bits (storing complementary value to the accessed bit) increases read access time and impedes a successful read. In our experiment, we simulate various SRAM failures in reading, writing and standby mode. There are in total 576 variation parameters in this test case, which is a high-dimensional problem.

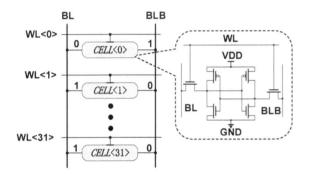

Figure 7: The schematic of 576-dimensional SRAM column circuit

4.2.1 Comparison of Visualized Failure Regions. In order to investigate the different performance in high-dimensional circuit case, we project the sample points on two most important dimensions, $Vth0$ of $MN1$ and $Vth0$ of $MN3$. Figure 8 shows the visualized multiple failure regions in 2D parametric space for different methods. Based on MC sampling in Figure 8(a), three disjoint failure regions are clearly displayed. We notice that it contains two major failure regions and a minor one in the lower right corner. Here green dot denotes the mean value for original distribution on these two dimensions.

As shown in Figure 8(b), HSCS groups failure samples into clusters, and utilizes min-norm points to generate shifted Gaussian distributions that cover multiple failure regions. The location of min-norm points are depicted as black triangles in Figure 8(b). It is, however, less effective on high-dimensional circuit, as it is challenging to locate the min-norm points on the failure boundary. With biased min-norm points, we note that majority of captured samples are not generated in failure regions. Thus it requires more simulations in both presampling and IS steps. In Figure 8(c), AIS

converges to wrong P_{fail} value because only two failure regions are notified. The minor failure region in the lower right corner disappears during iterations. It is due to the unbalanced weights for each sample. Samples with smaller weights are more prone to be eliminated in the global resampling procedure. The proposed ACS algorithm successfully searches for all three failure regions after a few iterations. And we notice that the whole sample set is focused on the most important failure boundary, which dominates the failure probability estimation. Therefore, ACS method outperforms other methods in terms of failure region exploration and convergence speed.

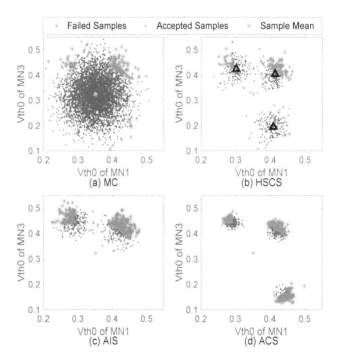

Figure 8: Multiple failure region coverage test (failed samples/ accepted samples/ sample mean are colored)

4.2.2 Accuracy and Efficiency Comparison. In this section, we compare the evolution of the failure probability and FOM in Figure 9. The ground truth failure probability is estimated by brute-force MC. Among HSCS, AIS and ACS algorithms, only our ACS method is capable of converging to gold failure probability. HSCS converges to wrong failure rate with much slower speed because static deterministic mixture IS estimator cannot work in high-dimensional case. AIS also cannot generate correct failure rate estimation. For multi-failure-region SRAM column circuit, some less important failure regions are neglected by AIS global resampling process, which leads to smaller failure probability.

To be specific, as shown in Table 2, the gold failure probability estimated by MC is 1.6e-5 (4.3σ) with 10 million simulations. Only ACS algorithm succeeds in giving accurate estimation with 3.1% relative error. The number of simulations in presampling and IS steps are 2000 and 2878, respectively. Therefore, the proposed ACS algorithm can obtain 2050X speedup w.r.t MC.

Table 2: Accuracy and efficiency comparison on 576-dimensional SRAM column

	Monte Carlo	HSCS	AIS	Proposed
Failure prob.(error)	1.60e-5(0%)	9.82e-6(error)	2.23e-6(error)	1.55e-5(3.1%)
Presampling # sim.	0	18000	5000	2000
Importance Sampling # sim.	1e7	28699	11253	2878
Total # sim. (speedup)	1e7(1X)	46699	16253	4878(2050X)

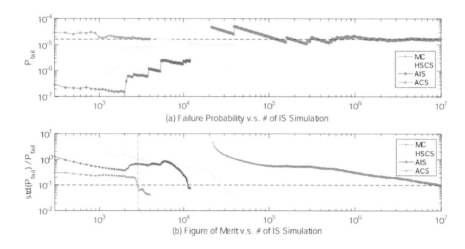

(a) Failure Probability v.s. # of IS Simulation

(b) Figure of Merit v.s. # of IS Simulation

Figure 9: Evolution comparison of failure prob. and FOM on SRAM Column

5 CONCLUSION

In this paper, we present an Adaptive Clustering and Sampling method to efficiently estimate the rare-event failure probability of SRAM circuits. This method first applies hyperspherical presampling to generate a set of initial samples in high dimension. Next, an iterative clustering and sampling scheme is performed to search for failure regions and update estimation. The experiments demonstrate that proposed algorithm can provide extremely high accuracy and efficiency. Experiments on SRAM bit cell indicate that ACS achieves 3526X speedup over MC and 3-5X over other state-of-the-art methods. On SRAM column circuit in high dimension and with multiple failure regions, ACS is 2050X faster than MC method, while other IS based approaches fail to provide reasonable accuracy.

6 ACKNOWLEDGMENT

This work was supported in part by the National Natural Science Foundation of China under Grant NSFC 61874152.

REFERENCES

[1] Dennis Sylvester, Kanak Agarwal, and Saumil Shah. Variability in nanometer cmos: Impact, analysis, and minimization. *Integration, the VLSI Journal*, 41(3):319–339, 2008.

[2] L He, Fang Gong, Rahul Krishnan, and Hao Yu. Exploiting parallelism by data dependency elimination: A case study of circuit simulation algorithms. *IEEE Design & Test of Computers*, page 1, 2012.

[3] Amith Singhee and Rob A Rutenbar. Statistical blockade: a novel method for very fast monte carlo simulation of rare circuit events, and its application. In *Design, Automation, and Test in Europe*, pages 235–251. Springer, 2008.

[4] Amith Singhee, Jiajing Wang, Benton H Calhoun, and Rob A Rutenbar. Recursive statistical blockade: An enhanced technique for rare event simulation with application to sram circuit design. In *VLSI Design, 2008. VLSID 2008. 21st International Conference on*, pages 131–136. IEEE, 2008.

[5] Wei Wu, Wenyao Xu, Rahul Krishnan, Yen-Lung Chen, and Lei He. Rescope: High-dimensional statistical circuit simulation towards full failure region coverage. In *Proceedings of the 51st Annual Design Automation Conference*, pages 1–6. ACM, 2014.

[6] Rouwaida Kanj, Rajiv Joshi, and Sani Nassif. Mixture importance sampling and its application to the analysis of sram designs in the presence of rare failure events. In *Design Automation Conference, 2006 43rd ACM/IEEE*, pages 69–72. IEEE, 2006.

[7] Lara Dolecek, Masood Qazi, Devavrat Shah, and Anantha Chandrakasan. Breaking the simulation barrier: Sram evaluation through norm minimization. In *Proceedings of the 2008 IEEE/ACM International Conference on Computer-Aided Design*, pages 322–329. IEEE Press, 2008.

[8] Masood Qazi, Mehul Tikekar, Lara Dolecek, Devavrat Shah, and Anantha Chandrakasan. Loop flattening & spherical sampling: Highly efficient model reduction techniques for sram yield analysis. In *Proceedings of the Conference on Design, Automation and Test in Europe*, pages 801–806. European Design and Automation Association, 2010.

[9] Wei Wu, Srinivas Bodapati, and Lei He. Hyperspherical clustering and sampling for rare event analysis with multiple failure region coverage. In *on International Symposium on Physical Design*, pages 153–160, 2016.

[10] Mengshuo Wang, Changhao Yan, Xin Li, Dian Zhou, and Xuan Zeng. High-dimensional and multiple-failure-region importance sampling for sram yield analysis. *IEEE Transactions on Very Large Scale Integration (VLSI) Systems*, 25(3):806–819, 2017.

[11] Hiromitsu Awano, Masayuki Hiromoto, and Takashi Sato. Efficient aging-aware sram failure probability calculation via particle filter-based importance sampling. *IEICE Transactions on Fundamentals of Electronics, Communications and Computer Sciences*, 99(7):1390–1399, 2016.

[12] Xiao Shi, Jun Yang, Fengyuan Liu, and Lei He. A fast and robust failure analysis of memory circuits using adaptive importance sampling method. In *2018 55th ACM/ESDA/IEEE Design Automation Conference (DAC)*, pages 1–6. IEEE, 2018.

[13] Wei Wu, Fang Gong, Gengsheng Chen, and Lei He. A fast and provably bounded failure analysis of memory circuits in high dimensions. In *Design Automation Conference (ASP-DAC), 2014 19th Asia and South Pacific*, pages 424–429. IEEE, 2014.

ISPD 2019 Initial Detailed Routing Contest and Benchmark with Advanced Routing Rules

Wen-Hao Liu, Stefanus Mantik, Wing-Kai Chow, Yixiao Ding,
Amin Farshidi, Gracieli Posser

Cadence Design Systems, USA

{ whliu, smantik, wkchow, yxding, afarshid, gposser }@cadence.com

ABSTRACT

Detailed routing becomes the most complicated and runtime consuming stage in the physical design flow as technology nodes advance. Due to the inaccessibility of advanced routing rules and industrial designs, it is hard to conduct detailed routing academic researches using the modern real-world designs. ISPD18 hosts the first detailed routing contest [1] and releases a set of benchmarks synthesized by industrial tools with practical routing rules. ISPD18 contest spurs detailed routing researches and provides students the opportunity to become familiar with the industrial designs and rules. On top of ISPD18 detailed routing contest, we host another detailed routing contest in ISPD19 [2] to consider several advanced routing rules and make the contest problem one step closer to the real-world routing challenges in advanced technology nodes. ISPD19 detailed routing contest encourages participants to use double-cut vias to improve yield and result quality. In addition, in order to drive the development of efficient routing frameworks, the deterministic multithreading feature is encouraged but optional in this contest.

ACM Reference Format:

Wen-Hao Liu, Stefanus Mantik, Wing-Kai Chow, Yixiao Ding, Amin Farshidi, Gracieli Posser. 2019. ISPD 2019 Initial Detailed Routing Contest and Benchmarks with Advanced Routing Rules. In ISPD '19: 2019 International Symposium on Physical Design, April 14–17, 2019, San Francisco, CA, USA. ACM, New York, NY, USA, 5 pages.
https://doi.org/10.1145/3299902.3311067

1 INTRODUCTION

When technology node advances with more complex design rules, routing problem becomes more and more challenging. Particularly, detailed routing plays a very important role for new node enablement. If detailed routing is not able to find solutions satisfying all design rules, new node enablement will be delayed. Therefore,

industry invests a lot of resources on improving detailed routing engines to pursue the routing solutions with better timing, lower power and lower design-rule-checking violations (DRVs). However, due the lack of real-world testcases and the design rule information, it is hard to conduct the up-to-date academic research to tackle the modern detailed routing challenges.

To spur detailed routing research from academia, Cadence hosts the first ISPD contest on detailed routing problem in 2018 [1]. In this contest, the benchmarks synthesized by industrial tools are released, which consider the practical routing rules like spacing table, cut spacing, end-of-line spacing, and min-area rules. In addition, the global routing guide associated with each benchmark is provided, and detailed routers are required to honor the routing guides as much as possible while minimizing DRVs.

ISPD18 contest leads to development of several academic detailed routers [3-5]. The work in [3] proposes a negotiation-based rip-up-and-rerouting scheme with via-aware track assignment; TritonRoute [4] presents a mixed integer-linear programing based routing framework; and the router presented in [5] adopts a minimum-area-captured path search algorithm to find the routing paths obeying routing rules. The routers presented in [3-5] all have multithreading features and are able to obtain deterministic routing results. They have also discussed how to efficiently use memory to handle large-scale designs. With these innovations, the academic detailed routers become more practical to handle real-world designs. Accordingly, the DATC Robust Design Flow (RDF) project [6] can integrate these routers to enable an academic flow from logic synthesis to detailed routing, which builds a foundation for future EDA researches.

On top of ISPD18 initial detailed routing contest, we host another detailed routing contest in ISPD19 to consider several advanced routing rules and objectives to make the contest problem one step closer to the real-world routing challenges faced in advanced nodes. The extensions of this year's contest are listed below:

(1) This contest considers the advanced routing rules including parallel run spacing, adjacent cut spacing, and corner-to-corner spacing, which are common to see in sub-16nm designs.

(2) To improve yield, reality, and timing, double-cut vias are widely used in industrial designs. In this contest, we provide double-cut via library and encourage contest participants to use double-cut vias.

(3) The benchmarks used in this contest have power and ground (PG) structures. The PG structure may occupy a lot of routing resources and make the routing problem more difficult. Detailed routers need to efficiently handle the required spacing between routing wires and PGs; otherwise they may easily trigger spacing violations.

(4) This contest generates diverse benchmarks from either commercial place-and-route tool Innovus [7] or academic DATC RDF flow [6].

(5) During contest evaluation process, we set tighter runtime limit for each benchmark based on its design size. We try to encourage the development of more efficient and scalable routing framework.

The remaining sections are organized as follows. Section 2 gives the overview of ISPD18 contest problem. Section 3 introduces the new rules and extensions considered in ISPD19 contest. In Section 4, the evaluation metrics used in this contest are detailed. Section 5 describes how the benchmarks are generated. Finally, acknowledgement is presented in Section 6.

2 OVERVIEW OF ISPD18 CONTEST

ISPD18 initial detailed routing contest assumes that a given global routing result is already well optimized for certain metrics (e.g., congestion and timing). Then, a detailed router needs to honor the global routing result in order to keep the optimized metrics and meanwhile avoid DRVs. In addition, the following connectivity constraints, routing rules, and detailed routing metrics are considered in ISPD18 contest:

- Open
- Short
- Spacing Table
- End-of-line spacing
- Cut spacing
- Min area rule
- Global routing guide honoring
- Wrong-way routing minimization
- Off-track routing minimization
- Wirelength and via minimization
- Multithreading determinism

For more details of these rules and metrics, please refer to the ISPD18 contest paper [1]. Also, the details of rule representation can be found in the LEF/DEF document [8]. Note that different technology nodes, different foundries, or different designs may have different routing rules. ISPD18 contest only consider the most common and major routing rules.

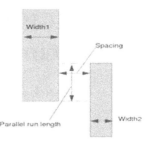

Fig. 1. Example of parallel run spacing

3 NEW RULES AND OBJECTIVES CONSIDERED IN ISPD19 CONTEST

A detailed router is subject to various design rules to satisfy manufacturing requirements from the foundries. In various technology nodes, the design rules are usually different. In ISPD19 contest, we further consider several advanced spacing rules which are very common and critical to handle during the initial detailed routing. In addition, we consider double-cut via insertion as one of our objectives. We believe the contest will be more practical and challenging by applying the rules and objective described in this section.

3.1 Advanced Spacing Rules

The new routing rules considered in this year's contest include parallel run spacing, adjacent cut spacing, and corner-to-corner spacing rules. The violations triggered by these rules cannot be easily detected just based on the distances between two objects. The required spacing values from these rules are *dynamic*, which may be affected by the routing length, other objects, or the routing directions. Accordingly, the difficulty of detailed routing increases dramatically after those advanced spacing rules emerge.

3.1.1 Parallel Run Spacing

Spacing table in LEF file specifies the required spacing between two objects according to the parallel-run length between two objects and the widths of the objects. Parallel-run length is the projection length between two objects. Figure 1 illustrates how the width, parallel-run length, and the required spacing are defined in the spacing table. In general, the spacing table contains multiple length thresholds. Once the parallel-run length is over a bigger length threshold, larger required spacing will be triggered.

3.1.2 Adjacent Cut Spacing

The adjacent cut rule specifies the minimum spacing allowed between via cuts on the same net or different nets when the cut has two, three, or four via cuts that are

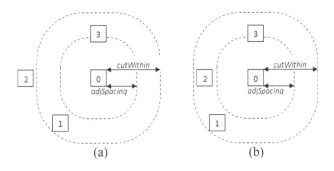

Fig. 2. **Example of adjacent cut spacing rule**

less than *cutWithin* distance, in microns, from each other as illustrated in Figure 2. A cut is considered adjacent if it is within *cutWithin* distance of another cut in any direction (including a 45-degree angle). Figure 2(a) shows cut #0 has only two neighboring cuts, which satisfy adjacent-cut-3 rule, while Figure 2(b) shows the same cut but with three neighboring cuts, which will violate the adjacent-cut-3 rule.

3.1.3 Corner-to-corner Spacing

The rule specifies the required spacing between a convex corner and any edge. The spacing value is calculated in MAXXY method. Specifically, given two rectangular objects R1(lx, ly, ux, uy) and R2(lx, ly, ux, uy). Let dX be the corner-to-corner distance between two objects in X direction. Then, dX = max((R1.lx - R2.ux), (R2.lx - R1.ux)). Similarly, let dY be the corner-to-corner distance between two objects in Y direction. Then, dY = max((R1.ly - R2.uy), (R2.ly - R1.uy)) Then, the MAXXY distance between the two objects is: max(dX, dY). The rule is only triggered when the parallel run length between two objects is less than or equal to 0. In addition, if the width of the object containing the corner is greater than width value specified in the table, then the corresponding spacing is applied. The optional keyword EXCEPTEOL specifies that the corner-to-corner spacing rule does not apply to a corner which is an end-of-line (EOL) edge with width less than a predefined width *eolWidth*.

Figure 3 shows three different routing configurations. Figure 3(a) shows the routing configuration that needs to meet the corner-to-corner spacing rule where the spacing required is governed by the width of the wide metal (width = 0.15) and the spacing is measured in MAXXY fashion. Configuration in Figure 3(b) will not have corner spacing violation if the rule has the EXCEPTEOL 0.080 keyword where the rule is exempted due to end-of-line edge less than 0.080 that is adjacent to the corner (which applies to both the lower metal and the upper metal). Figure 3(c) shows a routing configuration that does not have any corner spacing violation. In this case, the parallel run length between the convex corner of the wide

metal and the nearby wire is greater than 0, thus the corner spacing rule does not apply.

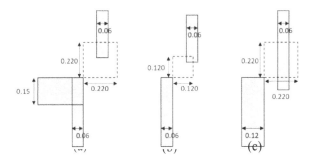

Fig. 3. **Example of corner-to-corner spacing rule**

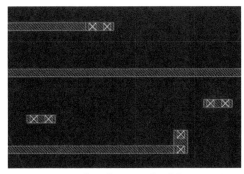

Fig. 4. **Example of using double-cut vias**

3.2 Double-Cut Via Insertion

For reality and performance concerns, detailed routers prefer to use double-cut/multi-cut vias rather than single-cut vias [9, 10]. This contest will provide both double-cut and single-cut vias in the via library. During solution evaluation, single-cut vias will be more expensive than double-cut vias in order to encourage the usage of double-cut vias. In addition, for some situations, min-area rule can be satisfied by using double-cut vias carefully. Figure 4 shows an example of using double-cut vias.

4   EVALUATION METRICS

In this contest, we have set a 64GB restriction on memory usage for the routers. Each benchmark has a specific runtime limit ranging between 1 hour and 12 hours, depending on the routing difficulty. A routing solution is considered as valid if the solution output is in the correct DEF format and there is no open net.

The solution quality is measured with Eq. (1). A router which produces a routing solution with lower *scaled_score* is considered as better in this contest.

$$scaled\_score = original\_score * (1 + np + rf) \quad (1)$$

TABLE 1 EVALUATION METRICS

Metric	Weight
Shorted metal / cut area	500
Number of shorted metal / cut	500
Number of min-area violations	500
Number of parallel run length violations	500
Number of EOL spacing violations	500
Number of cut spacing violations	500
Number of corner spacing violations	500
Total length of out-of-guide wires	1
Total number of out-of-guide vias	1
Total length of off-track wires	0.5
Total number of off-track vias	1
Total length of wrong-way wires	1
Total number of multi-cut vias	2
Total number of single-cut vias	4
Total length of wires	0.5

TABLE 2 BENCHAMRK INFORMATION

	#std	#blk	#net	#pin	#layer
ispd19_sample	22	0	11	0	9
ispd19_sample2	22	1	16	0	9
ispd19_sample3	5	1	7	5	16
Ispd19_sample4	67	0	22	0	9
ispd19_test1	8879	0	3153	0	9
ispd19_test2	72094	4	72410	1211	9
ispd19_test3	8283	4	8953	57	9
ispd19_test4	146442	7	151612	4802	5
ispd19_test5	28914	6	29416	360	5
ispd19_test6	179881	16	179863	1211	9
ispd19_test7	359746	16	358720	2216	9
ispd19_test8	539611	16	537577	3221	9
ispd19_test9	899341	16	895253	3221	9
ispd19_test10	899404	0	895253	3221	9

where *original_score* represents the result quality of a given detailed routing solution, *np* denotes the non-deterministic penalty, and *rf* denotes a runtime factor.

- The *original_score* is measured by the weighted sum of the metrics shown in Table 1, which is computed by the released evaluator [2], and Cadence P&R tool Innovus [7] is used to verify DRC violations. Note that the lengths in Table 1 use one M2 pitch size as one unit.

- The non-deterministic penalty score reflects the debugging and maintenance difficulty for a non-deterministic router. We run a router multiple times for each benchmark. If we observe different results among different runs, the median *scaled_score* will be chosen and 3% of non-deterministic penalty score will be added to the final score for the benchmark. Otherwise, if the results are consistent among different runs, no non-deterministic penalty will apply. Namely, *np* in Eq. (1) will be zero.

- The runtime factor *rf* is defined in Eqs. (2) and (3), where *rwt(b)* represents the wall time of a detailed router for benchmark *b*, and *mwt(b)* represents the median wall time of all submitted detailed routers from contestants for the benchmark *b*. The runtime factor is limited between -0.1 and +0.1.

$$rf = \min(0.1, \max(-0.1, f)) \quad (2),$$
$$f = 0.02 * \log_2(rwt(b) / mwt(b)) \quad (3).$$

5 BENCHMARKS

The testcases used for the contest benchmarks are derived from three real-world designs, a single-core 32-bit processor with four memory cores, a quad-core 32-bit processor with 16 on-chip memory blocks, and a dual-tone multi-frequency encoder/decoder. The original sizes for the designs are 37k nets, 147k nets, and 9k nets,

respectively. The designs are synthesized using generic 28nm cell libraries. Cadence Genus [11] and Innovus [7] are used to perform logic synthesis, floorplanning, and placement on the designs. In addition, two designs are adapted from the 2015 ISPD Blockage-Aware Detailed Routing-Driven Placement Contest Benchmarks [12] with 65nm cell libraries. These two designs are placed using the placement engine from DATC RDF [6]. In order to be used as benchmarks for the contest, we simplify the designs, so they pertain to the core essence of the contest while still maintaining the accuracy of the initial design intent. The followings are the simplification steps done on the designs:

- Non-default rules are removed to reduce the additional complexity introduced by wide wires.
- Since the primary goal for this contest is DRC cleanliness and wirelength, timing related information is removed.
- Only design rules listed in previous section are kept and the remaining is removed.

Table 2 shows the benchmark information, where #std, #blk, #net, #pin, and #layer denote the number of standard cells, macro blockages, nets, IO pins, and metal layers, respectively. The sample benchmarks (ispd19_sample*) are derived from the original single-core design. The nets are selected randomly. A placement run is called for the selected instances that are connected to those selected nets to produce a compact floorplan. These testcases will be used as a sample for the contestants to make sure their binary is able to read the design data correctly and perform the initial detailed routing process. These sample tests will not be used for evaluation purpose. On the other hand, "ispd19_test*" are the official benchmarks used to evaluate and rank the detailed routers developed by the contestants.

6 ACKNOWLEDGEMENT

We would like to thank the following people: Patrick Haspel, Cheryl Mendenhall, Anton Klotz, Sai Durga Dasu, Tracy Zhu, Shraddha Susarla and Kira Jones from Cadence Academic Network for the great support on the Innovus licenses and also on the contest and ISPD promotion; Neal Chang from Chip Implement Center (CIC) in Taiwan for helping universities to setup Cadence licenses; Yufeng Luo, Mehmet C. Yildiz, Zhuo Li, Chuck Alpert, Jing Chen, and Ismail S. Bustany for their insight and help on this contest; Jinwook Jung and Iris Hui-Ru Jiang for helping creating two benchmarks using DATC RDF; Guilherme A. Flach, Jucemar Monteiro and Mateus Fogaça for the adjustments on Rsyn academic tool to support the requirements for this contest and help students get the setup easily.

REFERENCES

[1] Stefanus Mantik, Gracieli Posser, Wing-Kai Chow, Yixiao Ding, Wen-Hao Liu, ISPD 2018 Initial Detailed Routing Contest and Benchmarks, In Proc. of the International Symposium on Physical Design (ISPD), p.140-143, March 25-28, 2018, Monterey, California, USA.

[2] ISPD19 Contest website: http://www.ispd.cc/contests/19/index.htm

[3] Fan-Keng Sun, Hao Chen, Ching-Yu Chen, Chen-Hao Hsu, Yao-Wen Chang, A multithreaded initial detailed routing algorithm considering global routing guides, In Proc. of the International Conference on Computer-Aided Design (ICCAD), p.1-7, November 05-08, 2018, San Diego, California, USA.

[4] Andrew B. Kahng, Lutong Wang, Bangqi Xu, TritonRoute: an initial detailed router for advanced VLSI technologies, In Proc. of the International Conference on Computer-Aided Design (ICCAD), p.1-8, November 05-08, 2018, San Diego, California, USA.

[5] Gengjie Chen, Chak-Wa Pui, Haocheng Li, Jingsong Chen, Bentian Jiang, Evangeline F. Y. Young. Detailed Routing by Sparse Grid Graph and Minimum-Area-Captured Path Search, In Proc. of the Asia and South Pacific Design Automation Conference (ASPDAC), p.754-760, January 21-24, 2019, Tokyo, Japan.

[6] Jinwook Jung, Iris Hui-Ru Jiang, Jianli Chen, Shih-Ting Lin, Yih-Lang Li, Victor N. Kravets, Gi-Joon Nam, DATC RDF: an academic flow from logic synthesis to detailed routing, In Proc. of the International Conference on Computer-Aided Design (ICCAD), p.1-4, November 05-08, 2018, San Diego, California, USA.

[7] Cadence P&R Tool Innovus: https://www.cadence.com/content/cadence-www/global/en_US/home/tools/digital-design-and-signoff/hierarchical-design-and-floorplanning/innovus-implementation-system.h

[8] Cadence, Inc. LEF/DEF 5.3 to 5.8 exchange format: www.si2.org/openeda.si2.org/projects/lefdef

[9] Yixiao Ding, Chris Chu and Wai-Kei Mak, Self-Aligned Double Patterning-Aware Detailed Routing With Double Via Insertion and Via Manufacturability Consideration, In IEEE Trans. on Computer-Aided Design of Integrated Circuits and Systems (TCAD), vol. 37, no. 3, p.657-668, March 2018.

[10] Youngsoo Song, Jinwook Jung, Daijoon Hyun, and Youngsoo Shin, Timing optimization in SADP process through wire widening and double via insertion, In Proc. of Design-Process-Technology Co-optimization for Manufacturability XII (SPIE 10588), 105880R, March 20, 2018, San Jose, California, US.

[11] Cadence logic synthesis tool: https://www.cadence.com/content/cadence-www/global/en_US/home/tools/digital-design-and-signoff/synthesis/genus-synthesis-solution.html

[12] Ismail S. Bustany, David Chinnery, Joseph R. Shinnerl, Vladimir Yutsis, ISPD 2015 Benchmarks with Fence Regions and Routing Blockages for Detailed-Routing-Driven Placement, In Proc. of the International Symposium on Physical Design (ISPD), p.157-164, March 29 – April 01, 2015, Monterey, California, USA.

Freedom From Choice and the Power of Models: in Honor of Alberto Sangiovanni-Vincentelli

Edward A. Lee
eal@eecs.berkeley.edu
UC Berkeley

ABSTRACT

Discovery, invention, and design are all about models. When we say "Joseph Priestly discovered oxygen in 1774," we do not mean that Priestly dug up a canister of oxygen, recognized it as something new, and released it, for the first time, into the air. We mean instead that Priestly came up with a model for the composition of air and the role of one of its components. The model was the discovery, not the O_2 molecule. Models in engineering and science are strongly affected by the modeling paradigm within which a model is constructed. Priestly's paradigm was firmly rooted in a theory of phlogiston, a fire-like element released in combustion, and his inability to break out of this rut made his work more like idiosyncratic philosophy than like science. The constraints of a modeling paradigm can be debilitating, but at the same time, they are essential. The constraints define the "platform" in "platform-based design" [2]. No effective modeling paradigm lacks constraints, and those constraints do not just limit our thinking, they also enable our thinking. In engineering, constraints are even more important because models that cannot be turned into real, working systems are not useful models. Whereas in science the value of a model lies in how well it matches a pre-existing physical system, in engineering, the value of a manufactured physical system lies in how well it matches a model [1]. Sangiovanni-Vincetelli has pointed out that modeling constraints provide a "freedom from choice" that makes it easier to build models for which we can create matching physical realizations. Because of this, engineers strive to grow the number of relevant modeling paradigms, those for which we can build effective physical realizations, whereas scientists strive to shrink the number of relevant paradigms, those needed to explain the physical world.

CCS CONCEPTS

• General and reference → General literature;

KEYWORDS

modeling, platform-based design

ACM Reference Format:
Edward A. Lee. 2019. Freedom From Choice and the Power of Models: in Honor of Alberto Sangiovanni-Vincentelli. In *2019 International Symposium on Physical Design (ISPD '19), April 14–17, 2019, San Francisco, CA, USA.* ACM, New York, NY, USA, 1 page. https://doi.org/10.1145/3299902.3320432

1 BIOGRAPHY

Edward A. Lee is Professor of the Graduate School in EECS at UC Berkeley. He is the author of several books and more than 300 papers and has delivered more than 180 keynote and other invited talks at venues worldwide. Lee's research focuses on cyber-physical systems, which integrate physical dynamics with software and networks. His focus is on the use of deterministic models as a central part of the engineering toolkit for such systems. He is the director of iCyPhy, the Berkeley Industrial Cyber-Physical Systems Research Center. From 2005-2008, he served as chair of the EE Division and then chair of the EECS Department at UC Berkeley. He led the development of several influential open-source software packages, notably Ptolemy and its spinoffs. His degrees are from Yale (BS), MIT (SM), and Berkeley (PhD). From 1979 to 1982 he was a member of technical staff at Bell Labs in Holmdel, New Jersey. He is a co-founder of BDTI, Inc. and has consulted for a number of other companies. He is a Fellow of the IEEE, was an NSF Presidential Young Investigator, won the 1997 Frederick Emmons Terman Award for Engineering Education, received the 2016 Outstanding Technical Achievement and Leadership Award from the IEEE Technical Committee on Real-Time Systems (TCRTS) and The Berkeley Citation in 2018.

Photo by Rusi Mchedlishvili

REFERENCES

[1] LEE, E. A. *Plato and the Nerd — The Creative Partnership of Humans and Technology.* MIT Press, 2017.
[2] SANGIOVANNI-VINCENTELLI, A. Defining platform-based design. *EEDesign of EETimes* (Feburary, 2002 2002).
Permission to make digital or hard copies of part or all of this work for personal or classroom use is granted without fee provided that copies are not made or distributed for profit or commercial advantage and that copies bear this notice and the full citation on the first page. Copyrights for third-party components of this work must be honored. For all other uses, contact the owner/author(s).
ISPD '19, April 14–17, 2019, San Francisco, CA, USA
© 2019 Copyright held by the owner/author(s).
ACM ISBN 978-1-4503-6253-5/19/04.
https://doi.org/10.1145/3299902.3320432

Author Index

NOTES

www.ingramcontent.com/pod-product-compliance
Lightning Source LLC
LaVergne TN
LVHW060142070326
832902LV00018B/2907